3-16

17-44

family structure
and
interaction

family structure

and

interaction:

a comparative analysis

Gary R. Lee

Washington State University

J. B. Lippincott Company
Philadelphia
New York / San Jose / Toronto

Copyright © 1977 by J.B. Lippincott Company

ISBN 0-397-47364-8

Library of Congress Catalog Card Number 76-32091

Printed in the United States of America

9 8 7 6 5 4 3 2 1

Library of Congress Cataloging in Publication Data

Lee, Gary R
  Family structure and interaction.
  Bibliography: p. 297
  Includes index.
  1. Family. I. Title.
HQ728.L48   301.42'1   76-32091
ISBN 0-397-47364-8

To
Naomi
and
Laura

contents

acknowledgments

The author of a textbook typically makes few truly original contributions to the state of knowledge in a field. His or her task, rather, is to synthesize and communicate the work of others. I am therefore indebted, first and foremost, to the many fine scholars in the area of comparative family organization and behavior whose work I have tried to represent. I hope that this book can serve as a reference work for some of them as well as a text for their students, and thus help further the progress of the discipline; I will be moderately satisfied if, at least, it does no harm.

Thanks are due to my mentors at the University of Minnesota, especially Ira Reiss, Reuben Hill, and Joan Aldous, who instructed me in the ways of sociology and whose work has been a continual source of inspiration. My colleagues and friends at Washington State University, including Ivan Nye, Viktor Gecas, Marilyn Ihinger, John Finney, Lee Freese, Louis Gray, Steven Burkett, and particularly Charles Bowerman, have been helpful beyond the call of duty and understanding about the time I have had to take from other tasks to complete this project. Their scholarly advice and criticism have improved this volume immensely. My graduate students have been alternately helpful and pesky, as they should be. They have made many valuable contributions to my thinking, and at the same time have made sure that I did not forget my other responsibilities. Mr. A. Richard Heffron of J.B. Lippincott Company has provided many insights into the process of writing a textbook which have been invaluable to a beginner such as myself, and has been supremely patient with my many delays in completing the manuscript. Whatever merit this book may contain is due primarily to the instruction, advice, and support of these people.

Finally, as any author soon discovers, writing a book takes a great deal of time away from one's family. It also makes one ornery. My wife Naomi and daughter Laura have put up with my frequent absences and continual preoccupation for the better part of three years without complaint, and have been supportive and understanding far beyond any reasonable expectations. This book is dedicated to them.

For those errors and inadequacies which this book inevitably contains, there is no one to blame but my wife.

preface

In recent years there has been a considerable increase in the quantity and quality of comparative family research. But, for some reason which I have been unable to ascertain, this has been accompanied by a decline in the number of textbooks available in the field. This is unfortunate, since comparative research is capable of contributing insights into the theoretical explanation of human behavior which are beyond the capacities of intrasystemic research. It is my intention, in writing this book, to collect, organize, and synthesize some of the extant material in comparative family sociology and related disciplines and to provide the student ready access to this material.

I make no claim for comprehensiveness in this book, in terms of either the topics covered or the intensiveness of the coverage. There is a vast and rapidly expanding literature in comparative family sociology, and this literature is more than tangentially related to research and theory in a number of other academic areas, including, of course, noncomparative family sociology. My intention is to show how comparative research has made unique contributions to theory development in the sociology of the family, and to demonstrate the likelihood that these contributions will increase in the future. Throughout the book, the focus is on knowledge about family structure and behavior which has been generated, refined, or extended by comparative family research, and on the ways in which comparative inquiry has contributed to family theory.

In line with this objective, the organization of the book is topical rather than systemic. That is, rather than sequentially describing a series of family systems and then summarizing the descriptions, we will deal with topics in the sociology of the family where comparative research has augmented understanding and explanatory capabilities. There are other excellent works available (for example, *The Family in Various Cultures*, by Queen and Habenstein [fourth edition; Lippincott, 1974]) which describe a number and variety of family systems. Our objective here is explanation, and our specific goal a synthesis of the explanatory contributions and potential contributions of comparative family sociology.

To this end, the first part of the book discusses the theoretical and empirical methodology of comparative sociology. These two chapters are not intended as a field guide for the researcher, but rather as a statement to the student as to what he or she can expect, and cannot expect, from comparative study. The second part of the book deals with theories about the structure of the various components of family systems: marriage, the family "proper," and kinship. Finally, the third part investigates intrafamily relationships, including premarital, marital, and parental relations.

This is, of course, not the "definitive" work in comparative family sociology. It is intended merely to introduce the advanced undergraduate or beginning graduate student to the discipline, and hopefully to whet his or her appetite for further inquiry. My entire motivation for writing this book is the firm conviction that, if a greater proportion of the next generation of family scholars is alerted to the potential of comparative research for the explanation of human behavior, our explanatory capacities will increase more rapidly.

part one

Comparative sociology

The objective of this volume is to document and explain the contributions which comparative social research has made to our understanding of family behaviors. In other words, we shall apply the method of comparative sociology to the subject of family behavior.

Our task in these first two chapters is to explain the nature of comparative sociology: how it differs from related disciplines, how it is done, and perhaps most importantly, why it is done. We will cover strategies of research and theory construction in comparative social inquiry, problems which are likely to arise when one attempts to implement these strategies, and the status of proposed solutions to these problems. An adequate understanding of what we know is dependent upon at least a rudimentary grasp of how we know it.

It is not the purpose of these chapters to prepare students or others to actually do comparative social research. This is far beyond the capacities of a small part of a small book, and there have been several very worthy volumes and countless articles written on various aspects of this subject. The first part of the book simply prepares the reader to understand the rest of it.

Comprehension of the latter chapters will, I believe, be considerably increased if the material in Part One is carefully scrutinized and internalized. This is true even for students who are fairly extensively trained in sociological methodology. The problems encountered in comparative research are of the same kind as those which plague all systematic social inquiry, but they are generally different in terms of locus, degree of severity, and available solutions. The prospects for the construction of explanatory theory are also of a different order.

In Chapter One we outline the basic parameters of comparative sociology, paying particular attention to its differences from other disciplines and the distinct advantages it offers relative to noncomparative social research. Chapter Two tackles some of the more pressing methodological issues facing comparative sociology. Then, in Part Two, we will begin to apply the comparative method to the study of the family.

chapter one

Comparative sociology: the nature of the discipline

Introduction

In its earliest stages, sociology was almost by definition a comparative science. Family sociology, in particular, was based upon data from a variety of societies and cultures. The purpose in the initial endeavors was to discover characteristics of family behavior which were common to all mankind, transcending geographic and cultural boundaries. But while the objectives of the early family scholars were ambitious, their methods left a great deal to be desired according to modern standards.

These early reports were macroscopic in scope, covering great sweeps of social space and social time, comparing marriage, kinship, and socialization patterns in several societies with a view to establishing phases of evolutionary development of family forms. The methods of data collection were poor, resting upon historical and anecdotal records of doubtful validity built up from reports of travellers and missionaries with

3

minimal training in ethnography. Methods of analysis were descriptive and impressionistic, producing few firm propositions that could be left unchallenged. (Hill 1962:425)

But the continued development of scientific methodology, and its gradual incorporation into the social and behavioral sciences, produced demands for data of greater reliability and validity than the early comparativists could generate. One consequence of this was a swing away from macroscopic analyses, in the direction of empirical inquiries of lesser scope which permitted greater control over the quality of the data. The period between the two world wars was virtually devoid of significant comparative family research in the sociological vein.

More recently, however, there has been a trend back to comparative study by family sociologists. Hill, in fact, argues that the discipline has come "full circle," and is again concerned with " ... propositions about marriage and the family which transcend the boundaries of nation and culture" (1962:426). Recent comparative family research, though, differs greatly from the earlier attempts in terms of both objectives and the methods by which these objectives are pursued. Sociologists, recognizing that comparative study has the potential to contribute invaluable and otherwise unobtainable information of crucial relevance to the explanation of human behavior, have oriented themselves toward the solution of problems in data collection and analysis which comparative research presents. In the process, important methodological innovations as well as meaningful substantive findings have been generated.

The avowed purpose of this book is to approach the sociology of the family from a comparative point of view. The contents of the book represent, then, the intersection of two subareas of sociology: the sociology of the family and comparative sociology. The former area constitutes the substance of our study; the latter, the method. It behooves us to state clearly exactly *how* we are going to study our subject matter before we commence studying it. This first chapter therefore presents a brief outline of the nature of comparative sociology, its prospects, and some of its problems. In the second chapter, we will deal with the special methodological intricacies of comparative research.

The distinctiveness of comparative sociology

It is only logical that an author should begin a textbook with a definition of the field of study. Unfortunately, in the case of most social sciences at least, this is much easier said than done. The authors of most texts find it necessary to first describe what their fields of study are *not*. This one is no exception.

Aside from the problems inherent in the definition of sociology, which I will happily leave to those writing introductory texts, the field of *comparative* sociology is exceedingly difficult to define. There are at least two reasons for this. First, by "comparative" we intend to convey that this particular branch of sociology studies or compares societies or social systems. What, then, distinguishes comparative sociology from anthropology, which is often referred to as the study of "other societies"? Second, all sociological research involves some kind of comparison—indeed, this is true of virtually all scientific research, whatever the subject matter. How do we then differentiate comparative sociology from any other variety of sociological investigation?

Sociology and anthropology

Anthropology is traditionally one of the most difficult of the social sciences to distinguish from sociology. These two academic fields, along with psychology, study virtually all facets of human behavior rather than specific dimensions such as political or economic activity. A rather haphazard survey of a dozen introductory sociology and anthropology texts (those which happen to appear on my shelves) showed that, in spite of the difficulty of making this distinction, they all felt constrained to try it.

By far the majority of these attempts were based upon a distinction in what (or perhaps who) is studied: anthropology studies "them," sociology studies "us."[1] More precisely, anthropology is often held to be the study of small, preliterate, sometimes "primitive" societies, whereas sociology purports to study large, complex, "modern" civilizations. Contemporary authors seem to be following the lead of Homans (1950:192-193), who argued that all social scientists study human organization, and therefore that " . . . (A) social anthropologist is a sociologist of primitive peoples, a sociologist, an anthropologist of civilizations."

While in practice this distinction often serves rather well to differentiate the work of anthropologists from that of sociologists, it doesn't do a very good job of defining the disciplines. There are, in fact, urban anthropologists, and there are sociologists who study preliterate societies, both without violating the basic canons of their fields. Gouldner and Gouldner (1963: 17-19) claimed over a decade ago that this basis for differentiating the two disciplines was outdated.

Some authors have also made this distinction in terms of the method, rather than the subject, of study. For example, Hoebel (1966:

12-13) notes that anthropologists have emphasized participant observation, while sociologists depend more upon large samples and the requisite statistical procedures for dealing with them. But this may be an artifact of the type of society studied. It is difficult to participate in and observe a demonstrably representative sample of a society as diverse and heterogeneous as the United States, and it is more than a little foolish to bother with a representative sample of a society of a few hundred rather homogeneous souls. It is true that in practice sociology and anthropology differ in terms of the kinds of societies they typically study, and therefore in terms of the procedures they employ, but these differences do not get to the heart of the matter either singly or collectively.

A workable and theoretically significant distinction was constructed nearly a generation ago by Goldschmidt, who argued that the " ... sociologist is concerned with social explanation, rather than cultural ... " (1953:287; see Rose 1971:11-15, for a similar distinction). The anthropologist, then, is more likely to construct his explanations of human behavior in terms of cultural factors. What is the difference?

Anthropology, or rather that branch known as cultural anthropology,[2] studies the manners in which different aspects of the way of life of a people "hang together in patterns" (Tumin 1973:9). In other words, what are the uniformities of belief, ritual, value structures, and ideational representations of social structure which distinguish and uniquely identify the members of a singular social system? Cultural anthropology is largely concerned with the description of such uniformities and consistencies with reference to particular peoples. Behavior is explained by reference to some cultural pattern which pertains to the members of a society and directs their behavior. The unit of analysis, then, is the *culture,* "the integrated sum total of learned behavior traits characteristic of the members of a society" (Hoebel 1966:561).

Sociologists also employ the concept of culture, of course; however, they do so in a notably different manner. Rather than regarding culture as the unit of analysis, they tend to employ cultural factors as *conditions* under which other factors may operate.[3] These other factors, for the sociologist, consist primarily of aspects of social structure: the patterns of social relationships among and between the incumbents of differentiated social positions, and the differences in behaviors, attitudes, and characteristics of individuals which correspond to these variations in their structural locations.

Both sociologists and anthropologists are in the business of explaining human behavior. The difference between them lies in the ways in which they prefer to construct these explanations. The anthropologist relies more heavily upon culture as a direct explanation of behavior (Eisenstadt 1961: 201-202), whereas the sociologist looks more toward patterns of social interaction between those persons who are subject to the influence of a culture. This position is articulated well by Leonard Pearlin, who notes that anthropology

> ... focuses on culture, which is mirrored in the uniformities among people within a society, in the beliefs and modes of action they share. Sociological analyses depend more on the location of differences between collectivities, for it is only by delineating patterned variations among groups that we can identify the structural arrangements contributing to these variations.(Pearlin 1971:14)

Scheuch (1967:20–23) argues that the concept of "culture" is best employed to designate conditions under which specific relationships between social variables occur. To invoke culture as a direct explanation of behavior patterns or other individual data is " ... an aggravated version of the ecological fallacy" (1967:23; see also Scheuch 1968). A group of people may indeed exhibit certain behavior patterns because their culture directs them to do so, but in what sense does culture *explain* these behaviors? To pursue this issue we must inquire into the antecedents of the cultural directives, so in a very real sense the level of the question has simply been shifted.[4]

In a study of the antecedents of variation in socialization practices (to be reviewed in Chapter Nine), Olsen distinguishes clearly between cultural and structural modes of explanation:

> The crucial causal agents in (cultural explanations) are ideas, and the most important intervening variable is the extent to which a group is in contact with new ideas. ... In contrast, the structural approach sees ideas as derivative, with some aspect of experience as the first link in the causal chain. Structural arrangements are seen as creating sets of experience that shape perceptions of reality. (Olsen 1974:1414; see also Olsen 1973)

It is not true that anthropology relies for its explanations of behavior solely upon culture and that sociology picks exclusively upon social structure. The difference lies, rather, in different approaches to and uses of the concept of culture. Furthermore, the distinction is one of degree rather than of kind. But it is nonetheless a useful distinction. From this perspective it makes sense for the anthropologist, who is looking for uniformities, to study smaller, less complex societies with homogeneous cultures, which the well-trained participant observer can more readily grasp. Conversely, the sociologist requires a substantial amount of variation in the structural variables with which he or she is concerned in order to chart their interrelations, since factors which are constant rather than variable cannot be related to other phenomena. He or she is therefore well advised to study the more heterogeneous social systems which exhibit the necessary variability in the objects of study. The differences between sociology and anthropology in the subjects and methods of study are thus artifacts of the different kinds of explanations of human behavior which the adherents of the respective disciplines attempt to construct.

We are not pretending here to differentiate the professional behaviors and explanatory preferences of all anthropologists from those of all sociologists in a categorical sense. Many anthropologists construct theories with characteristics which are clearly sociological according to our distinction, and the reverse is also true. The lines between academic departments do not always correspond to the theoretical distinctions between disciplines, and in any case the latter are not always unambiguously demarcated, as we have seen. The difference in explanatory preferences between these two disciplines to which we have pointed is, though, inferred from the behavior of members of the respective disciplines and is consistent with most of the existing theory which they have produced.

We shall have several other points to make about the use of the concept of culture in comparative sociology in subsequent sections of these chapters. Our next task, though, is to locate comparative sociology within the context of general sociological inquiry.

The role of comparison in sociology

Sociological inquiry is inherently comparative. Any empirical or theoretical statement in sociology is the product or representation of some kind of comparison. When we compute a measure of association or correlation between two variables, we generate a comparative statement: units which differ among themselves on one variable also show corresponding differences on a second variable. A correlation coefficient, or any measure of association, represents the degree of correspondence, and is thus a statement of comparison. For example, when we say that there is a negative relationship between age at marriage and rate of marital disruption (Bumpass and Sweet 1972:755), we are saying that people who marry at relatively young ages have been *compared* with people who marry later, and those who marry young are more likely to experience marital disruption.

If all sociology is built upon comparisons, what is the peculiar significance of the term "comparative sociology"? Is the comparative component of the phrase wholly redundant? In a logical sense, yes. But according to traditional usage, the designation "comparative sociology" has taken on a somewhat unique and specific meaning. It is the task of this section to isolate and define the particular types of sociological experience which are indicated by this term.

There is fairly widespread agreement among sociologists that comparative sociology implicates more than one social system as the arena of study. This means that studies of some single society other than one's own are *not* comparative studies, in spite of the tendency of some sociologists to refer to them as such (Marsh 1967:17). These studies provide data which may be used for comparative analyses (Straus 1968), but they are not themselves comparative.[5]

Some definitions of comparative sociology stipulate only that, to qualify as comparative, a study must involve "... the systematic and explicit comparison of data from two or more societies" (Marsh 1967:11). This is the simplest and most general type of definition, but others argue that comparative research may be considered to involve comparisons across time as well as across societies:

> (We) use the term *comparative method* to refer to social scientific analysis involving observations in more than one social system, or in the same social system at more than one point in time. (Warwick and Osherson 1973:8)

If comparative inquiry includes comparisons across time as well as those across systems or societies, how does this form of comparative sociology differ from historical analyses? In brief, temporal comparative analyses are not primarily historical because they involve comparisons of data collected at two or more points in time. Thus, a study of the "The Two-Parent Household: Black Family Structure in Late Nineteenth-Century Boston" (Pleck 1972) is in this classification a historical work,[6] whereas "A Century of Declining Paternal Authority" (Mogey 1957) implies that processes of change will be documented by examining and comparing several points in time, and is therefore comparative.

A crucial distinctive feature of comparative social inquiry is that two or more social systems, the characteristics of which differ to some degree, are compared so that the effects of the different systemic characteristics may be apprehended and explained. Comparative sociologists are interested in temporal comparisons, then, not because they wish to chart historical processes, but because a society may manifest different systemic properties over time. The variables of interest in such comparisons involve these systemic properties, not the historical periods within which they take on specific values. Thus temporal comparisons do involve two or more social *systems,* although the data come from only one society.

For the moment, then, we will adopt Warwick and Osherson's definition of comparative research as appropriate for our purposes. This does not mean, however, that in this book we will examine only those particular studies which conform to this definition. As others (Straus 1968) have pointed out, comparative inquiry may be furthered by "secondary" analyses of studies done in one society or at one point in time. By comparing the results of two or more such studies, we may be able to formulate useful and valid generalizations on a comparative level. Much of the work we will do in this book involves such secondary comparisons.

Types of comparative research

We have argued thus far that comparative research involves the study of more than one social system. Observations in multiple social systems may be made in several different ways. The problems and potentials of any given piece of research depend upon the kinds and levels of observations which are made in the systems under study. To facilitate communication, we shall distinguish and label three varieties of comparative research: cross-cultural, cross-societal, and cross-national.[7]

In this terminology, a *cross-cultural* study is one in which the data concerning each society under study consist of characterizations of typical behavior patterns, institutions, structures, etc., of that society. These data are usually garnered from ethnographic reports. The ethnologist or social anthropologist who examines a sample of ethnographies, or who employs one of the "data banks" such as the Human Relations Area Files, the World Ethnographic Sample (Murdock 1957), or its successor the Ethnographic Atlas (Murdock 1967), is looking for correlations between traits of societies or cultures. One might, for example, investigate the relationship between the type of family system which characterizes various societies and the economic systems of these societies (Nimkoff and Middleton 1960; Osmond 1969; Blumberg and Winch 1972). In so doing, one would make one observation for each variable on each society: the United States, for example, is characterized by a nuclear or conjugal family system and an industrial economy. The unit of analysis in this case is the society, because observations are made *only* on the societal (or cultural) level. The objective of this type of research is to formulate theoretical statements about similarities or differences *between* societies or cultures (Zelditch 1971: 271-272).

In *cross-societal* research also, observations are made only at the societal level. The difference between cross-societal and cross-cultural research is that in the former the observations consist at least in part of aggregated statistical measures of characteristics of the societies. Rather than relying on ethnographers' judgments of whether a society is characterized by nuclear or extended families, the cross-societal researcher would find census data on average household size in each society under study. (These two variables are not quite identical; see Chapter Five.) Lieberson and Hanson (1974), for example, constructed indices of language diversity and national development for several societies, based on information supplied by the governments of these societies, and examined the correlation between these variables. The advantage of this method is that available statistics are probably (although not necessarily) more reliable, as descriptions of large populations, than are ethnographic reports. The major disadvantage is that many societies have no or very few such statistics, and the range of variables for which adequate information is available is highly limited.

A *cross-national* study, finally, is one in which observations are made both on societies and on units (usually, but not always, individuals) *within* societies. The cross-national researcher draws a sample from each society to be studied and measures relevant variables in each sample. Thus, to vary an earlier example slightly, we might investigate the cross-national correlation of family structure and economic status by collecting a sample of observations on family composition and family income in a number of societies. We would then examine the degree to which the correlations between these variables are similar or different across the societies from which our samples were drawn (Zelditch 1971:271–272).

Of the three types of comparative research, cross-national is clearly the most powerful analytic tool. We will discuss the reasons for its superiority in more detail in the next chapter, but essentially they involve the ability to examine cross-systemic patterns in relationships between variables measured at the intrasystemic level. This advantage is of such importance that some scholars have opted to define the entirety of comparative research exclusively as

> ... inquiry in which more than one level of analysis is possible and the units of observation are identifiable by name at each of these levels. (Przeworski and Teune 1970:36-37)[8]

While the ability to operate at more than one level of analysis is extremely advantageous, cross-cultural and cross-societal research also have their strong points. Principally, they lend themselves to the examination of larger numbers of societies than does cross-national research, and the investigator is usually able to employ existing data.

We have made this distinction not to point out the superiority of one or another type of comparative research, but rather to facilitate later discussion of the different problems which they pose and the different types of analytic questions for which they are appropriate. We will return often to the differences between cross-cultural, cross-societal, and cross-national research as we proceed to discuss the theoretical and methodological bases of comparative sociology.

Comparative sociology and sociological theory

Comparative research in social science is exceedingly difficult to do responsibly. It is also expensive, in terms of time, money, and other scarce resources. Why, then, do we bother? Why not content ourselves with intrasystemic research and save the expense and aggravation?

The answer, of course, is that we can accumulate knowledge by comparative research which is not available by other means. This gain in knowledge is both descriptive and explanatory. Comparative research provides us with information about the cultures, life styles, and social patterns of people in other societies (the descriptive component), and also lends certain unique advantages to the process of *explaining* human behavior.

The explanatory advantages of comparative research are of greatest interest to us here. This does not mean that descriptive information is unimportant: without description, there is no explanation. A knowledge of the family practices of other societies is valuable to the student for such purposes as increasing appreciation of intercultural variability and uniformity in family practices, augmenting the student's objectivity, and heightening awareness of the unique and not-so-unique features of family behavior in one's own society (Kenkel 1973:5-8). However, a great number of scholars have provided a plethora of descriptive information. Our task here is to organize this information in such a way as to construct meaningful explanations of human social behavior, particularly such behaviors as relate to family phenomena.

The primary purpose of this book is not to describe the mating practices of Italian peasants, or to report what the Trobriand Islanders do on Saturday nights. We are interested, rather, in *why* they do it. We will attempt to understand and explain the great variety of behaviors, attitudes, and social structures that are relevant to family systems. This means that we will be organizing, synthesizing, and constructing social *theory* concerning the family, taking advantage of the opportunities for theory construction provided by comparative research.

What are these opportunities? In a very general sense, comparative research offers three advantages for theory construction or explanation over and above the capacities of intrasystemic research. These include increasing generality, maximizing variance, and introducing system-level variables into empirical analyses. We shall deal briefly with each.

Increasing generality

The objectives of any science are basically twofold: "...to describe particular phenomena in the world of our experience and to establish general principles by means of which they can be explained and predicted" (Hempel 1952:1). Comparative research in the social and behavioral sciences furthers both of these objectives, by broadening the range of our experience and by insuring that our explanatory principles are indeed general.

As many researchers have noted (see particularly Marsh 1967:5-6), most social scientific research has been carried out in a relatively small corner of the world. Many aspects of the behavioral patterns of North Americans, and to a lesser extent Western Europeans, have been studied quite intensively, and at least rudimentary explanations of some of these behaviors have been formulated. But will the same explanations be appropriate and valid in other societies, under different cultural and ecological conditions? If we do a study of marital power relationships in Detroit (Blood and Wolfe 1960), it is not because we have no interest in the causes and consequences of the balance of marital power in Greece, but because Detroit happens to be more convenient and accessible than Athens. In order to determine whether our findings are in fact general, in the sense that they enable us to explain and predict the behavior of *human beings* rather than just the residents of our hometown, we must examine and test them under conditions which vary as widely as possible. This means, optimally, cross-systemic research.

This particular advantage of comparative research is quite obvious, and is thus usually accorded rather cursory attention by advocates of comparative study (Straus 1968:569; Warwick and Osherson 1973:9). However, answers to questions of the generality of findings or explanations are usually not of the simple yes-or-no variety, but are rather exceedingly complex. Simple explanations which are universally valid are very rare; we often find that different explanations of a particular phenomenon are appropriate under different conditions.[9] Sociology is a "nomothetic" rather than an "idiographic" science; that is, the sociologist seeks the general principles which explain human behavior rather than the simple representation of reality in microcosm. Since different explanations may be appropriate under different conditions, it is necessary for complete explanation to incorporate varying conditions and their consequences into the theories we construct. The advantage of comparative research, in this regard, is that it maximizes the probabilities of being able to sort out the explanations which are accurate and useful under varying conditions and allows for the possibility of explaining these variations themselves. This leads us to the second major advantage of comparative study: maximizing variance.

Maximizing variance

Probably the single greatest advantage of comparative research, according to many of its practitioners (Marsh 1967:7-9; Frey 1970: 181) is that it provides us with the ability to expand the range of the variables under consideration in a research project. Many objects of study exhibit greater variability in samples of several societies than they do in samples of only one society. This is helpful to the researcher in two related ways (Sears 1916:445-446). First, a cross-systemic sample will often yield greater extremes on relevant variables than an intrasystemic sample. If we wish to study the determinants of family structure or composition, for instance, we would have great difficulty collecting a sufficient number of observations on "extended" families (families including positions in addition to those of parents and dependent children) in the United States. However, such families are more common, and more readily located, in other kinds of societies. Or if we were interested in the consequences of marital authority patterns, we could probably find more cases of extreme husband-dominance if we considered a variety of societies than if we take our observations only from our own. The consequences of extreme husband-dominance may well be different, both in kind and in degree, from those of moderate husband-dominance.

The second advantage of the maximization of variance offered by comparative research is that, by making observations on many societies, we can often observe variation in factors which do not vary in any given society. This second advantage is clearly a special case of the first (Frey 1970: 279). The variance in a given phenomenon may be increased from none at all (in which case it is a constant, not a variable), to some level which permits an analysis of the causes or consequences of variation in that phenomenon. One example which comes readily to mind is the study of the consequences of marital structure or composition for marital adjustment. In the broadest meaning of the term, there is only one type of marital structure extant in the United States: monogamy, the marriage of one husband to one wife. Obviously the researcher cannot examine the consequences of plural (polygamous) marriage for marital adjustment if one confines one's research to this society, because there will be no examples of polygamy. But by adding even one society which permits polygamous marriage to the study, differences in marital adjustment among monogamous marriages in exclusively monogamous societies, monogamous marriages in societies which permit polygamy, and polygamous marriages can be examined.

Scientific explanations of social phenomena are constructed, at the most basic level, from correlations: measures of the extent to which two or more phenomena are associated with one another. A measure of correlation, expressed in slightly different terms, is a measure of the degree to which two phenomena covary, or vary together. As we said earlier, the statement that age at marriage and probability of marital disruption covary is equivalent to the statement that certain marital ages and certain probabilities of disruption coincide. But in order for two phenomena to covary, each one must first *vary*. The social scientist cannot study a constant.

In the above example of the relationship between marital structure and marital adjustment, the sociologist employing strictly American data cannot even study the influence of *monogamy* on marital adjustment, much less polygamy. Simply put, there is nothing to compare with monogamy. A constant, by definition, does not covary with anything else, because it does not vary. Comparative research, then offers us the opportunity to transform phenomena which are constants in one social system into variables which can be studied in terms of their relationships to other variables, and which thus become appropriate objects of scientific inquiry. By extension, the greater the amount of variance exhibited by any given variable, the greater the opportunity to examine the intricacies of its interrelationships with other variables, and the better the chances of detecting its correlations with those other variables in the first place. This is why it is important to maximize the variance in the objects of scientific study, and a major reason why comparative research is an integral part of the development of explanatory theory in the social sciences.

System-level variables

The third advantage of comparative research emanates directly from the second. According to Robert Marsh,

> The main reason . . . for the comparative analysis of societies is simply that in many of our assertions the *units* being talked about *are* societies, and one should therefore examine more than one such unit—hopefully several or many. (Marsh 1967:8-9)

In other words, if we are to study societies, we require a number of them. We cannot legitimately formulate generalizations about the effects of some special characteristic of American society upon the inhabitants of the United States without in some way comparing this society to at least one other, which differs in some specifiable manner on the crucial characteristic. Otherwise our generalizations will be, at best, implicit and intuitive.

The logic here follows from that of the previous section. Some of the variables on which variance is maximized, or rather produced, by comparative research are variables pertaining to social systems: *system-level variables.* It is impossible to examine the effects of a democratic political system on political participation by studying only democratic systems, just as it is impossible to estimate the influence of monogamy upon marital adjustment without observing some marriages which are not monogamous. If one studies only one social system, all systemic characteristics are necessarily constants, and are thus not susceptible to scientific analysis.

The production of variance in societal and cultural characteristics is of such obvious and fundamental importance that Straus has defined comparative research as

> . . . those investigations which study the same or equivalent variables in two or more socieites, *for the purpose of using "society" or "culture" as one of the variables in the analysis*—usually as independent or as control variable. (Straus 1968:565; see also Straus 1970)

In one important sense, Straus is quite right: one cannot study systemic factors without studying two or more systems. But his phraseology may be somewhat misleading. Let us return for a moment to the definition of comparative research proffered by Przeworski and Teune (1970:6-7), which we now recognize as pertaining to cross-national research:

> Comparative research is inquiry in which more than one level of analysis is possible and the units of observation are identifiable by name at each of these levels.

Why must the untis of observation be identifiable by name? Przeworski and Teune go on to say that ". . . the goal of comparative research is *to substitute the names of variables for the names of social systems*" (1970:8; italics added). Consider, for example, the following two statements drawn from research by Rodman (1967, 1972) and his associates:

1. The correlation between husband's socioeconomic status and husband's marital power is positive in the United States and France, but negative in Greece and Yugoslavia.
2. The correlation between husband's socioeconomic status and husband's marital power is positive where cultural norms are relatively equalitarian, but negative where the norms are more patriarchal.

According to the data synthesized by Rodman, both of these statements are empirically true.[10] However, the first is descriptive while the second is explanatory. Rodman has hypothesized that one factor which distinguishes the United States and France, on the one hand, from Greece and Yugoslavia, on the other, is the cultural specification of the "appropriate" locus of marital decision-making authority. This cultural variable has been substituted for the names of the societies involved in the comparison. Statement 1 above simply states that the four societies differ on a certain correlation; statement 2 attempts to explain *why* they differ as they do. Statements of the second type—that is, general explanatory statements—constitute the objectives of comparative research.

> Again, Przeworski and Teune phrase this point well:
> . . . to say that systems differ is to say that some characteristic that distinguishes these systems influences the observed relationship. Whenever identification of a particular system contributes to explanation one must ask what it is about these systems that influences the phenomenon being explained. (Przeworski and Teune 1970:48)

The comparative researcher who must identify a society or social system in which a particular process or relationship occurs by name in an explanatory statement is admitting that his theory cannot account for the events observed in this system. In other words, in our theoretical statements we invoke the proper names of social systems only to indicate residual or unexplained variance: we have not been able to incorporate these cases into our explanatory logic or statements.

Thus, to say that comparative researchers employ "society" or "culture" as a variable in analysis is not quite complete.[11] The researcher rather attempts to implement *variables at the societal or cultural level* by comparing two or more societies which differ along specifiable dimensions. It is only in this way that systemic factors may be incorporated into scientific explanations of social events and processes.

Summary

Comparative social research offers three general kinds of advantages for the construction of explanatory theory. By means of comparative study, we increase the generality of our theories, maximize variance in the phenomena under study, and introduce systemic (societal or cultural) factors into explanations. If these advantages are pursued to the fullest possible extent, comparative research can expand the potential for explanation and understanding of human behavior considerably beyond that possible by intrasystemic research. But there are many attendant problems with which the comparative researcher must deal. These problems differ from those encountered in noncomparative social research in terms of degree rather than kind; these differences of degree, however, are often substantial, and they have very real effects on procedures and results. The next chapter introduces some of the methodological and theoretical issues which must be faced by anyone wishing to do, or to understand and evaluate, comparative research.

Notes

1. The specific authors who rely on this distinction are, in my admittedly biased sample, Bierstedt (1957:9–10), Herskovits (1965:8), Hoebel (1966: 12–13), Wilson (1966:19–20), DeFleur *et al.* (1971:13), Popenoe (1971:6), Dressler and Carns (1972:428), and Leslie *et al.* (1973:4).

2. We are admittedly glossing over the very important differences between various subfields of anthropology, for the sake of simplicity. This discussion should be taken to refer specifically to cultural anthropology, which is the branch most in need of distinction from comparative sociology. I agree with Faris (1964:31), Wilson (1966:19–20), and others who note that according to the British usage of the terms, comparative sociology and social anthropology are virtually indistinguishable.

3. Scheuch (1968:200) distinguishes between the use of culture as "an entity and a unit in analysis" and as "a set of conditions for units in analysis." If the concept is used in the first manner, the outcome of investigations will be either to identify cultural universals or to distinguish between societies, depending on the purpose of the comparison. If the second usage is employed, the comparative research attempts either to demonstrate the generality of propositions relating noncultural factors across cultures or to specify the time-space coordinates of such propositions. Although Scheuch had a different purpose in mind, it would appear that the typical anthropological usage of culture corresponds to his first method of treatment, and the sociological to the second.

4. This is not to say that cultural explanations are invariably insufficient; I am simply expressing my particular preference, which is an operating premise throughout this book.

5. As Kluckhohn (1953) and Naroll (1968) have noted, ethnographers studying another culture tend implicitly, and perhaps unavoidably, to compare it with their own. But this is a source of error, and does not make their studies comparative in any meaningful sense.

6. Such studies, however, may provide data for cross-temporal comparative research in the same manner that studies of single societies may provide data for subsequent cross-systemic comparisons.

7. I am not sure if the distinction I am about to make is relatively original with me, or if I have inadvertently co-opted it from an existing source which has since escaped me. If anyone recognizes (and wishes to acknowledge) his or her own work or that of a colleague in what follows, please advise me. I will most eagerly apologize and set the record straight. For the sake of completeness, Frey (1970:178–179) distinguishes cross-cultural from cross-national research. His distinction, though, hangs more on the types of systems being studied than on the kinds of data collected from the systems, but in practice his method and mine would yield similar results.

8. Hopkins and Wallerstein (1967) also argue that the type of research we are terming cross-national differs so greatly from other forms of comparative research it ought to be considered an independent and separate field of endeavor. I agree that the differences between cross-national and cross-societal research are numerous and important, but many of the guiding principles are the same. Consequently we will proceed to consider all three types as valid sources of sociological information, making the necessary distinctions among them where required.

9. Straus (1968:569) notes quite correctly that the most valuable findings in

comparative research are usually the *inconsistencies* between societies in the applicability of explanations. We shall recur to this point later.

10. For an in-depth discussion of this issue, see Chapter Eight.

11. This is not to say that Straus is wrong; I suspect his meaning is similar to that of Przeworski and Teune. My preference for their statement is due to the greater clarity and explicitness of their terminology. Societies are not actually *employed as* variables in comparative research; they are rather *replaced by* variables in the process of data analysis and theory construction.

chapter two

Methodological issues in comparative research

Introduction

There are no fundamental differences in principles or logic between cross-system and within-system research (Frey 1970:183). There are, however, numerous differences in the ease with which basic research strategies may be implemented. The methods of comparative research are the same as those of any form of systematic social inquiry, but the problems encountered in the process of doing it differ in degree if not in kind.

The discussion of problems and pitfalls in comparative research which follows is certainly not sufficient to prepare the reader to handle these difficulties in his or her own research. There are currently many excellent compilations on comparative research methods available, virtually all of which are much more complete and extensive than this chapter pretends to be.[1] However, the student of social phenomena of any sort should be sensitized to the problems, as well as the advantages, of the means by which knowledge is and has been acquired. Only through at least rudimentary familiarity with the problems of comparative research and the status of proposed solutions will the student be able to fairly evaluate the utility of the material presented in the remainder of this volume.

There are three methodological issues in comparative research which deserve special attention: sampling, measurement, and causal analysis (explanation). We will deal with each sequentially.

Sampling

Virtually all sociological research is accomplished by means of studying a sample of the population in which the investigator is interested. A good sample is selected in such a way that it adequately represents the population from which it is drawn, in order that the researcher may generalize his or her findings from the sample to the population. In the usual type of intra-systemic research, this means that units (most often individuals) are selected by some random procedure. This insures that each member of the population has an equal chance of appearing in the sample. If random methods of sample selection are followed, and if the sample is of adequate size, the laws of probability make it likely that each element of the population is represented in the sample in the same proportion that it constitutes of the population as a whole. We can then estimate the likelihood that distributions and relationships found in the sample also exist in the population.

The basic principles of sampling are the same in any kind of social research. However, comparative studies present unique problems in the application of these principles. These problems stem primarily from the fact that, in cross-societal or cross-cultural research, one must sample social systems rather than individuals. Cross-national research requires the sampling of both social systems and units within those systems. The actual procedures employed for these two tasks obviously differ to a certain extent, and the analytic penalties for failure to approximate ideal methods are also somewhat different. We will therefore discuss them separately.

Sampling societies

Cross-cultural and cross-societal sampling. In cross-societal or, particularly, cross-cultural research, it is possible to deal with a fairly large sample of societies. This is because one is dealing with data which have already been compiled (either population statistics or ethnographic reports), and is thus spared the time and expense of collecting new data. Also, the population from which the researcher is sampling is, by survey research standards, quite small. Murdock (cited in Marsh 1967:14) has estimated that no more than five thousand distinct societies have existed in the history of the world.

If it is possible to draw large samples of a small population, why is the sampling of societies problematic for cross-cultural research? There are several reasons. First, data are available for only a fraction of the number of societies which have existed or currently exist. The most comprehensive and extensive coded compilation of cross-cultural data currently available is Murdock's (1967) Ethnographic Atlas, which contains information on 1170 societies.[2] It would seem perfectly logical and defensible to simply employ these data, or to sample from the total list, and this is in fact what cross-cultural researchers have often done. But we cannot assume that the societies on which we have data are representative of those societies on which we do not (Naroll 1968). Furthermore, the original reports from which the Ethnographic Atlas was compiled vary widely in quality and in extent of coverage. Original errors or inadequacies in the recording and classification of data by ethnographers may be compounded by coding errors in the Atlas itself (see Kobben 1968; Naroll 1970).[3] No method of sampling from the Atlas can eliminate the biases inherent in the Atlas itself (see Swanson 1960; McEwan 1963; Murdock and White 1969).

There is also the problem, in studying societies, of determining exactly what a society is. If we are to draw a sample of societies, we need to know which entities are eligible for inclusion in the sample. This is a surprisingly perplexing problem. Marsh (1967:12) draws upon the previous work of H. Johnson (1960) and Parsons (1951) in developing four criteria which social systems must fulfill in order to be classified as societies. These are (1) a definite territory; (2) recruitment of new members primarily by sexual reproduction; (3) a comprehensive culture; and (4) political independence. These criteria are obviously difficult to operationalize in a concrete way. What constitutes a comprehensive culture, or for that matter political independence?

Even though societies are often difficult to define, some form of definition in both theory and practice is absolutely necessary. In many cases, equating a politically defined nation-state with a society can confound analyses. Veronica Stolte-Heiskanen observes that

> Insofar as administrative boundaries are unquestioningly substituted for socio-cultural ones, it often becomes impossible to account for the role of *national* differences in the findings. (Stolte-Heiskanen 1972:35).

In terms of Marsh's four criteria, what she is saying is that the unit which is politically independent and the unit which has a comprehensive culture do not always overlap perfectly. Differences between peoples which are attributable to elements of culture or social organization may be obscured because several distinct cultural factions coexist within one political unit, or because a distinction between sovereign polities bifurcates a relatively homogeneous culture.[4]

In cross-cultural research, the mistake of treating one social system as two or more analytic units is likely to spuriously inflate the correlations we derive, since the multiple observations we make on the single unit are likely to produce the same values of the variables being measured.

> If a unit is not independent, no new information . . . is obtained by studying it twice, and no additional confirmation of (a hypothesis) is obtained by counting it twice. (Zelditch 1971:282-283)[5]

The comparative researcher must therefore take steps to insure that each case in his or her sample is in fact an independent observation. This has, in part, been done in the compilation of ethnographic data banks. There are also further checks that can be made for independence of cases in cross-cultural studies, which we will discuss below under the heading "diffusion."

Cross-national sampling. We have discussed, up to this point, the sampling of societies in cross-cultural and cross-societal research. Cross-national investigations also require a sampling or selection of societies. The sampling problems we have already covered also pertain, to a greater or lesser degree, to cross-national research. However, difficulties of a somewhat different nature present themselves to the cross-national researcher, largely for two reasons: (1) the investigator must deal with a much more restricted number of societies, and (2) in general, data must be collected independently within each society under investigation.[6]

The second difficulty here obviously accounts for the first. Cross-national research is extremely expensive and time-consuming, and often involves a great deal of administrative effort in securing the cooperation of researchers, agencies, and governments in the societies under study.[7] Cross-national studies therefore usually involve only a handful of societies (rarely more than half a dozen), and often employ samples from only two countries. Since the researcher is able to select only a very small sample of societies, sampling in cross-national research is particularly crucial.

Before we proceed to the principles involved in the selection of societies for cross-national study, we should point out that a problem of cross-cultural research is also very relevant here: that of defining the units of analysis at the systemic level. Stolte-Heiskanen's warning on the dangers of substituting administrative boundaries for sociocultural delimiters is very important in cross-national research as well as in the other types (Stolte-Heiskanen 1972:35). If we wish to determine the effects of systemic characteristics upon behavior, we must be able first to distinguish one system from another. Basic to this kind of distinction is the recognition that people who fall under one administrative or governmental jurisdiction may in fact be extremely diverse, and should not be treated as a homogeneous entity simply because they salute the same flag (or are supposed to). Pearlin introduces his study of family relations in Turin, Italy, by explicitly noting that his Turinese respondents are not necessarily "typical" of Italians in general,

> . . . for there are no typical Italians. In fact, it is quite certain that if this study had been conducted in the South (of Italy) or in any rural area our results would not have been the same. (Pearlin 1971:4-5)

Pearlin carries through on this point by noting, in conjunction with later comparisons of data collected in Italy with data from the United States, that he is not comparing Italians with Americans, but rather residents of Turin, Italy with those of Washington, D.C., or specific other American samples. He knows that Italy is a very heterogeneous society and treats it as such in his analyses, avoiding undue claims of comprehensiveness. And just as national borders do not automatically contain homogeneous peoples, they do not necessarily separate diverse and distinct cultural groups. The general point here is that, if one wishes to make generalizations concerning the effects of systemic characteristics by employing data from two or more social systems, one had best be sure that the members of each sample are uniformly exposed to the specified systemic factors.

Ideally, the cross-national researcher should select societies on a random or probability basis. But for the reasons mentioned above, this is a literal impossibility given the current state of the art. Also, when samples are very small as in cross-national research, the advantages of probability sampling are obviously very much reduced. Naroll (1968:253) claimed that all cross-national studies up to 1968 involved purposive samples of societies; this is still the case, and is likely to continue to hold true in the forseeable future. But it is nonetheless possible to select societies in such a way that the analytic possibilities are maximized.

There are essentially two operative strategies of selecting social systems for cross-national research (Frey 1970:199-202; Przeworski and Teune 1970:32-39), which should be conceived of as poles of a continuum rather than as dichotomous opposites. The first is termed by Frey the method of *maximizing similarity*. Przeworski and Teune (1970:32-34) call it the "most similar systems" design, and Naroll (1968:240-248) labels it the method of "concomitant variation." The researcher following this logic intentionally selects systems such that they are as similar to one another as possible *on all dimensions except those of particular interest to the study*. Ideally these social systems would have a small number of known differences between them. In explaining differences between systems in a dependent variable, or in a relationship between variables, the factors which are common to all systems are irrelevant. Only those dimensions along which the societies differ can constitute causes of the variation between them in the objects of explanation, and the number of such differentiating dimensions is minimized by the method of system selection.[8]

This procedure is extremely valuable in concrete research situations. There are, however, the inevitable problems. First, the range of phenomena one can study is severely restricted by the necessity of finding societies which differ *only* on the variable(s) of interest. Second, it is probably quite obvious that there is no pair of social systems in existence between which there are a finite number of differences. There are, though, degrees of similarity or difference: the investigator following the "most similar systems" design would be well advised to compare the United States with Canada rather than with India. The fact that even very similar countries vary on a great number of dimensions does create problems in analysis, however.[9]

The second method of selecting societies is called the strategy of *maximizing diversity* (Frey 1970). Przeworski and Teune (1970:34-39) term it the "most different systems" design.

> The aim in this case is to get countries that differ from each other as fundamentally and as extensively as possible. Then if one finds, across countries of such great diversity, regularities in the within-country relationships between variables, the generality of such relationships can be presumed. (Frey 1970:200)

This method is used principally to determine the generality of propositions and empirical generalizations and the precise point in a system of relations at which systemic factors become relevant to explanation.

> The initial assumption (when using the "most different systems" design) is that individuals were drawn from the same population; in other words, that systemic factors do not play any role in explaining the observed behavior. Further investigation consists of testing, step by step, this assumption in the course of cross-systemic research. As long as this assumption is not rejected, the analysis remains at the *intra-systemic* level; whenever the assumption is rejected, systemic factors must be considered. (Przeworski and Teune 1970:34-35)

In studies where societies are selected for their diversity, the differences between systems, however great, are ignored as long as the samples from the various societies do not differ in terms of patterns of intercorrelation between variables. The analyst attempts to explain as much of the variation in the dependent variable as possible without taking systemic differences into account. The level of analysis is shifted to the systemic when all relevant generalizations which are valid for all societies in the sample have been formulated (Przeworski and Teune 1970:34-39).

There are two primary advantages of the strategy of maximizing diversity. First, since it revolves around the elimination of irrelevant systemic factors, it does not require prior identification of important societal characteristics, except in the sense that they must be measured at some point in the study. In the "most similar systems" method, one selects societies which are similar on all except the important characteristics one wishes to study; this implies that one knows what these important characteristics are before one studies them. The "most different systems" approach to sampling societies does not presume this advance knowledge. Second, those intrasystemic relationships which we observe to exist under a wide diversity of systemic conditions may be invested with a great deal of confidence; this is the most stringent test of their generality.[10]

But Frey (1970:200) points out that the latter advantage may turn out to be a disadvantage, depending on the results of the analysis of intrasocietal relationships. Specifically, if one fails to find patterns of interrelationships which hold for all the societies under investigation, one is up the proverbial creek. The "most different systems" approach, then, entails a greater number of risks than other methods of selecting societies. Furthermore, some (such as Smelser 1973:74–75) point out that problems of comparability are magnified in comparisons of vastly different social systems, and thus advocate restricting comparative analyses to societies which are similar to one another until our methods are better developed. The most reasonable answer to this objection, obviously, is that our methods are already quite well developed, and will experience further development much more rapidly if we apply them to challenging research problems and situations. A diversity of societies is indeed more difficult to handle in comparative research in a number of ways, but successful resolution of the problems it poses can produce considerable progress in both method and theory.[11]

Whether social systems are selected according to the criterion of maximizing similarity or that of maximizing diversity has many important implications for data analysis, particularly in terms of estimating the effects of system-level variables. However, it is still the case that in most crossnational research, systems are selected according to the criteria of "administrative convenience" (Frey 1970:199), accessibility, or the particular interests (recreational as well as professional) of the researcher. Because of the difficulties in implementing other strategies, this will probably be the case for some time to come. We have been, thus far, talking about adjusting the selection of social systems to accommodate the logical requirements of the theories to be tested. In those cases where this is not possible or efficient, it is reasonable to tailor the theories to the differential availability of social systems. In other words, certain samples of societies will be appropriate for the testing of certain hypotheses, but not others. We must simply be wary of conclusions drawn from crossnational research which are not warranted by the nature of the societies studied. For example, a generalization to the effect that urbanization is universally associated with high rates of delinquency would not be warranted if based on a comparison of the United States and Canada, nor would an assertion that urbanization is *the* cause of greater delinquency rates in the United States than in Uruguay be defensible. Researchers must often take the set of social systems available to them as a "given," and operate within the constraints imposed by this set. There is no harm in that, provided that these constraints are recognized.

The comparative researcher simply cannot ignore such influences on the sampling of societies as administrative convenience and accessibility, at least not given the current state of international relations and of funding for social research. However, the results of comparative studies can be made much more meaningful by the careful selection of societies with regard to the objectives of the research. Basic sampling procedures must of necessity be compromised, particularly in cross-national research where only a few societies can be studied. But this does not mean that one simply gives them up. Different sets of societies are appropriate for different kinds of comparisons. If the researcher has no choice in the selection of societies, it behooves him or her to adjust the type of comparison accordingly. Where even a small degree of latitude exists, choices should be exercised in the most rational manner possible. In the case of cross-national research, this usually means either maximizing the similarity of the systems to be studied, or maximizing their diversity. The choice between these principles depends on the nature of the theoretical issues being pursued.[12]

Sampling within societies

Once societies have been selected for comparative study, the researcher must assemble information on or about the societies which will be used in the comparisons. The cross-national investigator must select units for study from within each of the social systems in the sample. These units are most often, but not always, individuals. All of the usual rules and procedures for sampling apply. However, additional problems are encountered in cross-national studies because the samples derived from each system should not only represent that system in some meaningful way, but must also be comparable to one another (Zelditch 1971:286).

Elmo Wilson (1958:230-231) has pointed out the unique difficulties the researcher encounters in drawing samples from societies whose record-keeping systems are not as efficient or extensive as is the case in the United States. Random sampling, of course, requires a reasonably exhaustive list of the population from which the sample is to be drawn, in order that each member of the population will have an equal probability of appearing in the sample. Lists which even approximate exhaustiveness are literally unavailable in most societies. However, there are two factors which prevent the absence of such lists from making cross-national research impossible.

First, as Wilson (1958), Frey (1970), and others have noted, is areal probability sampling, in which the researcher randomly selects particular places or dwellings, and then selects the respondent from within the dwelling. This method is also fraught with difficulties, but if properly executed will yield a representative sample. Its greatest advantage is that it does not require a complete population list.

The second factor which allows us to conduct cross-national studies in spite of sampling difficulties is that the researcher may neither want nor need completely representative samples of each society in the study (Scheuch 1968). Some categories of populations may be irrelevant for certain research questions. Insistence on identical sampling procedures and outcomes in each society may generate more heat than light; the guiding principles of cross-national sampling should be the theoretical premises of the individual study, rather than a set of unbending procedures.

Scheuch's point is well taken. However, it does not obviate the necessity for *comparable* samples across societies. The point is rather that, while comparability is usually achieved by following identical sampling procedures in each sampling arena, it is a mistake to emphasize the means to the goal at the expense of the goal. Because conditions may differ considerably across societies, sampling procedures must be adjusted to achieve comparability in spite of the varying conditions. Different procedures may yield similar results in various societies, and identical procedures may produce quite different results if applied without consideration of societal differences. What is important is that the samples be *equivalent*: representative of each society or of an equivalent segment of each society, with the appropriate segment dictated by the concerns of the research, and clearly identified by the researcher. If samples are not comparable in this sense, it is easy for differences between *samples* to be mistaken for differences between *societies* (Blood and Hill 1970; Stolte-Heiskanen 1972).

If one knows exactly the sources and types of nonequivalence between samples in cross-national research, one can adjust accordingly and still derive meaningful comparisons. For example, if one sample is biased according to sexual composition, comparisons can be made separately for each sex.[13]

Warwick and Osherson (1973:36-39) note four crucial problems in within-society sampling which continually plague cross-national research. These include the use of noncomparable sampling frames, differing selection procedures, misrepresentation of population elements, and differential response rates. The first two problems are important partly because they culminate in the third: samples which over- or underrepresent various population elements. If the samples in each society are biased in the same direction, comparisons are still possible. If, however, samples are biased in different or unknown directions, differences observed between societies may be due instead to differences in the characteristics of the samples. Unless the biases are known, and unless the researcher takes specific account of them, the validity of comparative generalizations is impossible to establish.

But even if the sampling frames, selection procedures, and proportional representation of population elements in each sample are comparable, differential response rates between societies seriously reduce the comparative potential of samples. Nonresponse is a critical problem in any survey research. The nonrespondent, by definition, cannot be studied. As soon as he succumbs to the scientist's pressure and agrees to participate in the study, he ceases to be a nonrespondent. The crucial point is that people who will not or cannot participate in a social survey may differ in systematic ways from those who do agree to participate.

The problem of nonresponse in cross-national research is greatly compounded if the researcher achieves widely differing response rates in different societies. A common example of this point is a study of political participation in five societies by Almond and Verba (1963), in which data were collected from the United States, Italy, Germany, Mexico, and the United Kingdom. Response rates varied widely across societies, from 83 percent in the United States to 59 percent in Britain. Scheuch (1968:194), in evaluating this study, points out that if

> ... the chance of inclusion in the sample is associated with participation in public affairs—which appears to be a reasonable assumption—then the highly different completion rates may account for some of the observed differences (between societies).

The point here is not that cross-national studies are useless unless it can be demonstrated that the samples derived from each society have precisely identical characteristics. No such samples have ever been achieved, nor is it likely that the ideal will be reached in the near future. It is very important, though, that the researcher be cognizant of the limitations produced by sampling inadequacies, and that the reader be informed of these limitations. In any given piece of cross-national research the ideal will be approximated to a greater or lesser degree. Judgments regarding the value and utility of a research project will be made on the basis of the closeness of the approximation. Both the researcher and the reader must be aware of the hazards of cross-national sampling, and adjust their conclusions according to the degree to which obstacles have been recognized and dealt with effectively.

Measurement

Once the comparative researcher has selected the societies to be studied and has determined an appropriate method of sampling units from within these societies (whether these units be individuals or ethnographies), some means of obtaining information from the units must then be devised. This is the problem of measurement, of making the observations which will constitute the data for the study.

Many lengthy books have been devoted to the subject of measurement, without even considering the problems which arise when observations need to be made in two or more social systems. This is not a book on measurement, however, but a book on one branch of comparative sociology. Consequently, our immediate concern is not with measurement as such, but with the *comparability* of the results of measurement procedures. Thus, although many data employed by ethnologists and cross-cultural researchers are collected by means of participant observation, we will forego a discussion of this methodology since in practice the participant observer is interested in maximizing his descriptive account of the single culture he is observing, not in the comparability of his results with ethnographic studies of other cultures.[14] We will also avoid unnecessary excursions into measurement methodologies except as they directly affect the issue of comparability.

Morris Zelditch (1971:273) formulates the general problem of comparable measurement well by breaking it into two components. He argues that two or more social systems are comparable if and only if they collectively satisfy two criteria: (1) there is some variable common to each unit; and (2) the meaning of this variable is common across all units. Satisfying the first criterion is relatively simple, but the issue of common meaning is not.

This is why comparative measurement is so important. Two or more phenomena must have something in common in order to be meaningfully compared: we must compare the same things. But the issue is more complex than it first appears. The first-grader may be told that three apples and two apples make five apples, but three apples and two oranges make three apples and two oranges—apples and oranges can't be added because they are different things. From one perspective this is true; but from another, three apples and two oranges make five fruits. These two seemingly diverse phenomena do have something in common, and if that common thing happens to be the thing we are counting, they can be routinely combined. The problem in comparative measurement comes down, in large part, to exactly this problem: what are we comparing?

Although the measurement issue has achieved its greatest visibility in the literature on cross-national research, similar problems arise in the other two types as well. We will discuss each briefly before proceeding to measurement in cross-national research.

Measurement in cross-cultural and cross-societal research

Why should the researcher employing secondary data (ethnographies, census statistics, or other types of data which have been previously collected or compiled) need to worry about measurement? Presumably measurement has already been accomplished by the person or organization that originally collected the information. However, often the information was collected for different purposes than the researcher has in mind, and there may be considerable variation in the definition and operationalization of the variables in the study.

In the case of cross-cultural studies based on ethnographic reports, we must deal with the problem of the selection of data sources. Even the user of a comprehensive body of data such as the Human Relations Area Files or the Ethnographic Atlas must be cognizant of the fact that the information contained in the files has been selected from the field of available information, and that the data have been through several coding processes in which errors and inadequacies are virtually bound to arise. Marsh (1967:262–267) points out that the sheer amount of ethnographic coverage varies widely across societies, with smaller societies being more adequately covered relative to their size. There is also great variability in the relative coverage of societal subsystems (kinship, religion, economy, etc.). The cross-cultural researcher can't be sure whether this variation represents actual societal variation or simply variation in the interests of ethnographers and the operation of selective perception. Naroll (1960, 1962) has elucidated a procedure for "data quality control" based upon the qualifications of ethnographers who supply the original data. A form of content analysis for estimating the effects of selective perception in the construction of ethnographic reports has been proposed by J.W.M. Whiting (1954). While these procedures are undeniably helpful to the researcher in selecting the best available sources of information, they cannot guarantee that each ethnographer whose material is employed has measured or observed relevant variables in a manner consistent with the purposes of the cross-cultural researcher, or with those of the other ethnographers whose reports constitute the basic data for cross-cultural studies. The researcher dependent on secondary data cannot escape the fact that he or she had no control over the collection of the data, and inevitably possesses less information about them than does the original ethnographer.

Thus one central problem faced by the cross-cultural researcher is the relatively unknown validity of his or her basic data. (This does not mean, of course, that the data are *ipso facto* invalid, but rather that it is difficult to estimate the *degree* of their validity.) There is also some inevitable slippage involved in the coding of ethnographic data into forms suitable for use in cross-cultural surveys. Kobben (1968) lists "defective classification by ethnologists" as a major source of difficulty in comparative research: data from ethnographers' reports may be improperly classified or coded in "data banks" such as the Ethnographic Atlas. This is not surprising in view of Goodenough's warning about the differences between the tasks of ethnographers and ethnologists:

> . . . what we do as ethnographers is, and must be kept, independent of what we do as comparative ethnologists. An ethnographer is constructing a theory that will make intelligible what goes on in a particular social universe. A comparativist is trying to find principles common to many different universes. His data are not the direct observations of an ethnographer, but the laws governing the particular universe as the ethnographer formulates them. (Goodenough 1956:37)

As in the case of the original ethnographic data, ethnological coding error is not a problem in the sense that it renders cross-cultural data useless, but rather in that it limits the confidence we can place in our conclusions since we can't entirely estimate its extent. However, this problem is not insurmountable provided that coding error is *random* rather than systematic. Kobben (1968) notes that "right" and "wrong" classifications won't simply cancel one another out, but will rather operate to obscure or reduce the size of potentially significant correlations. If two variables are correlated with one another in reality, but one or both have been improperly coded and the source of the error is random, the effect will be a reduction in the observed correlation; the estimated correlations will be low (see also Naroll 1968). Most social scientists agree that it is better to overlook a significant relationship than to artificially construct one which does not in fact exist.

But this is the case only if the coding error is truly random. Any kind of *systematic* bias could serve to inflate correlations. Naroll (1968:264–247) proposes a method of searching for systematic bias in both ethnographic and ethnologic coding which he calls the "control factor method." He suggests that the researcher look for correlations between the variables implicated in the study and factors believed to affect the quality of the data. In the case of ethnographic data, such factors might be training of the ethnographer, time spent in the field, knowledge of the native language, etc. If no correlations appear, then the researcher may proceed with some degree of confidence in the data; if they do, the data are suspect. Unfortunately, few researchers have bothered with this kind of check.

Another device that may be employed to check the coding of ethnologists is to have the same ethnographic data coded by two or more coders and measure reliability by the relative proportions of agreements and disagreements. Rose and Willoughby (1958:400) achieved 85 percent agreement working with subject classifications in the Human Relations Area Files, which is within limits of toleration. These kinds of tests caused Marsh (1967: 270) to conclude that there is no evidence of any systematic coding bias in the HRAF, the World Ethnographic Sample, or subsequent compilations of cross-cultural data which now include Murdock's Ethnographic Atlas.

In cross-societal research similar problems arise in connection with the quality of statistical data provided by governmental or other sources. In using census figures on income, or on household size and composition, or on virtually any other variable, one must be sure that the data were collected in the same way in each society. Otherwise their comparability is greatly reduced. Some nations, of course, provide grossly inadequate data on their populations, either because of limitations on their funding or data-collection technology, or because they are constructing an image for political purposes. But even in the absence of such obvious distortions, the methods by which governments collect and assemble population statistics vary considerably. This variability influences the kinds of comparisons one may make. Zelditch (1971:286), for example, points out that one would be ill-advised to make comparisons between France and the United States, based on governmental statistics, involving personal income. Most of us are well aware that the U.S. government spares no effort in determining and verifying exact personal incomes of its citizenry. The French, on the other hand, regard income as an intensely private and personal matter, and never ask directly about a citizen's exact income. Even for taxation purposes incomes are estimated indirectly.

Obviously comparisons between France and the United States involving personal income should not be made from such data. While each method of data collection may serve the purposes of the sponsoring government equally well, the comparative researcher cannot justifiably consider the results to be equivalent measures of the same variable. The researcher's solution, in cases such as this, is generally to recognize that the data are not comparable and to forego the comparison. One major disadvantage of both cross-cultural and cross-societal research is that the investigator is dependent not only upon existing data, but upon existing data which are comparable. Comparability is not only difficult to achieve, it is often very difficult to estimate, especially when someone else has collected the data.

Measurement in cross-national research

The cross-national researcher must elicit responses to his or her questionnaire or interview schedule from a sample of respondents in each of several societies. The problems in this regard are essentially those of any survey research: constructing reliable and valid indicators of the variables to be measured. However, the comparative researcher's task is somewhat more difficult and complex because, if two or more societies are to be compared, care must be taken to insure that measures are equally reliable and valid for each society.

We noted above that if the cross-national researcher draws samples from various societies in different ways or achieves differential response rates across societies, then any differences observed among societies may be due to differences among the samples rather than among the societies. The results of the study may be artifacts of the methods employed, rather than representations or consequences of actual societal variability. The same is true for differences in measurement. If we wish to test a hypothesis regarding the relationship between two or more variables in several societies, we must be confident that the meaning of each variable is relatively constant across societies.[15]

Part of the problem arises from the fact that the cross-national researcher must often deal with societies in which different languages are spoken. One must obviously have versions of the questionnaire or interview schedule available in each relevant language. This creates major problems in terms of comparability, particularly in light of the now-famous "Sapir-Whorf hypothesis," which, in its most radical form, asserts that language determines thought. As Marsh (1967:275) notes, this extreme form of the hypothesis, ". . . if correct, would make it difficult, if not impossible, to attain meaning equivalence and would virtually eliminate the possibility of analyzing social structure comparatively." However, the less radical version of this hypothesis (Whorf 1952), rather than asserting that language determines thought, argues that different linguistic communities perceive reality in different ways depending upon the structure and content of the languages.[16] One must, therefore, take account of these differences in perception in the construction of measurement instruments.

The problem of meaning equivalence has traditionally been defined as a problem of translating the questionnaire or interview schedule into each required language without altering the meaning of items or response categories in the translation process. To this end, many sophisticated techniques have been developed, most of which involve the procedure of "back-translation." In this method, a questionnaire is translated from its original language into the language of another society by a translator skilled in both languages. This second version is then given to another bilingual, who translates it back into the first language without seeing the original form. The two versions of the questionnaire in the first language are then compared to isolate inconsistencies and differences in meaning between them. Sometimes the differences are resolved by consultation and compromise among the translators; other, more rigorous versions of the method call for the translation process to be repeated until the back-translated version is a virtual duplicate of the first form.[17]

However, as many comparative scholars have pointed out, an effective translator must be bicultural as well as bilingual (see, for example, Frey 1970:277). Simple duplication of a questionnaire in multiple languages does not guarantee that responses to the items will be comparable in terms of equivalent meaning. R. Anderson (1967:126) and Straus (1969:233) note that the problem of measurement equivalence in comparative research is a special case of the general problem of the validity of measurement. An item or scale is valid to the extent that it actually measures the variable which it is purported to measure. An index which is a valid measure of a variable in one culture may be invalid in another, even if the wording is duplicated in the translation process. Conversely, one might construct different measures of the same variable in several cultures which are equally valid for each.[18] Marsh (1967:271-272) has differentiated between two types of equivalence, "formal" and "functional." Formal equivalence involves the application of identical measurement procedures in various cultures (subject, of course, to the limitations of translation error). Functional equivalence refers to equivalence in the meanings of the results obtained from measurement procedures. Straus (1969:234) makes a similar distinction between "phenomenal identity" (identical procedures) and "conceptual equivalence," which he defines as "... the extent to which the indicators—whatever their manifest content—index the concept under investigation" (1969:234-235). Both Marsh and Straus contend that, while functional equivalence is of course the objective of comparative measurement, employing phenomenally identical procedures may result in a *loss* of functional equivalence.

Straus gives, as a hypothetical example, the administration of a standard intelligence test for children developed in the United States. Used on American youngsters, we may assume that the test measures some dimension or dimensions of factors related to intelligence (note how cleverly I am sidestepping this issue). However,

> (T)he items used in most standard intelligence tests contain many references to objects and events which would be outside the range of experience of a village child in Africa or India. ... Thus, children getting the highest scores will not necessarily be the brightest children, but rather the more "Westernized." (Straus 1969:235)

A test which measures intelligence in America and "Westernization" in India is of no comparative use. This is true regardless of the quality of its translation.

Blood and Hill (1970) provide another useful illustration of the point that one must often measure the same variable by different items in different societies. They discuss the problems encountered in adapting a measure of marital power developed in the United States (Blood and Wolfe 1960) for use in other societies, particularly Japan (Blood and Takeshita 1964). The original scale of conjugal power consisted of eight items, asking whether the husband or wife has final decision-making authority in such matters as what car to buy, whether or not the wife should work, and what house or apartment to take. There are numerous problems in the application and interpretation of this scale in the United States (see, for example, Safilios-Rothschild 1970; Turk and Bell 1972; Olson and Rabunsky 1972), but its use in other societies is much more problematic because the decision-making areas tapped by the items in the scale are differentially relevant. In urban Japan, housing is often provided by one's employer; the same is true of life insurance, which is another area covered in the scale. Asking the same questions in both societies would produce meaningless results. Nonetheless, marital power is a relevant concept in all societies. The problem is to adapt one's questions to the variability in social and cultural structure inherent in comparative research, but at the same time to retain sufficient conceptual equivalence to enable comparison.[19]

Numerous methods have been suggested for maximizing conceptual equivalence in comparative measurement. Among the most obvious is the use of expert judges, who evaluate potential indicators of concepts on the basis of their appropriateness for the cultures under study (Straus 1969:237). This technique, though, depends ultimately on the subjective judgments of people who may be differentially familiar with the various cultures and the concepts of interest. The use of cultural experts is a very advisable (indeed, perhaps necessary) first step, but in addition more empirically rigorous methods should be employed wherever possible.

There are several methods in existence for the construction of comparable measures across cultures which do not depend solely upon judges' ratings. Two of the most promising have been developed by Thomas and Weigert (1972) and Przeworski and Teune (1970).

The method proposed by Thomas and Weigert involves pretesting a questionnaire which has been carefully subjected to the back-translation process on a sample of bilinguals. The bilingual subjects are randomly selected and assigned the different language versions of the questionnaire. Response distributions are then analyzed for significant differences. The appearance of such differences indicates one of two things: (1) inadequate translation; or (2) language relativity, along the lines of the Sapir-Whorf hypothesis. The first problem is soluble by adjustments in translation; the second is not. One cannot distinguish between these two interpretations of empirical differences between the two language versions except by altering translations and repeating the process. However, this procedure does allow the researcher to identify nonequivalent measures.

While this method has considerable merit, several problems in its utilization are apparent. Among the most important is the expense in both time and money that it requires. One must employ a substantial number of bilinguals in the sample in order to perform meaningful statistical analyses of response distributions. Thomas and Weigert used schoolchildren in Puerto Rico who were fluent in both English and Spanish. But samples of bilinguals are not always so readily available to the researcher. Furthermore, an investigator doing research in more than two different cultures with different languages must do a similar comparison between each pair of languages involved in the study, and then adjust translated versions of the questionnaire in all languages to maximize equivalence. For a study involving six cultures, for instance, the first stage of the process (administering the questionnaire to samples of people who are bilingual in each pair of relevant languages) would require fifteen comparisons. The complexities of *checking* for points of nonequivalence in such a case are more than a little awesome, to say nothing of rectifying them once they have been discovered.

The Thomas and Weigert method may therefore be useful when one is comparing samples from two societies, but the difficulties in its application increase geometrically as the number of societies in the sample increases. There is also a very real possibility that bilinguals in a pretest sample may respond differently than monolinguals in the study itself, because of the very fact that they are bilingual. In addition, not many researchers have the resources to conduct such elaborate pretests of their measuring instruments.

The procedure advocated by Przeworski and Teune (1966-67, 1970), while somewhat more complex, offers the possibility of broader applicability. They explicitly recognize that one may have to ask completely different questions across societies in order to produce equivalent results. In the earlier (1966-67) paper, a procedure called the "identity-equivalence method" is proposed. First, the researcher establishes a set of items which will initially be employed as a measure of a given variable in all societies under investigation. Added to these items are questions designed only for specific societies, which are believed on an *a priori* basis to be valid for those societies. After the data are collected, the set of formally identical items is analyzed for unidimensionality without regard to societal differences, by means of a test for homogeneity. Those items which "scale" according to such a statistical test are retained as identical measures of the variable in question for all societies; those which do not are dropped. The retained items are defined as equivalent across systems. The remaining "system-specific" items are then analyzed in terms of their correlations with the formally identical items in each system. "Those indicators which are specific to each country and which are correlated with the identical indicators are maintained to have equivalent cross-national validity" (Przeworski and Teune 1966-67:558).[20] This is an improvement over the use of the identical items alone because resultant scales will contain a greater number of items; this increases the reliability of the scale.

Frey (1970:284-286), while recognizing the value of this procedure for analyzing equivalence (which he calls the "approach through unidimensionality") also points out that it has its limitations. First, the investigator's subjective judgment is involved in the construction of the master list of potentially scalable items. Therefore it is possible that one might miss very valuable indicators. However, as Frey notes, this is helpful in that irrelevant correlations do not affect scale construction. Second, and most importantly, the requirement that there be some set of formally identical items severely restricts the applicability of the method. We know already that formal equivalence is by no means a guarantee of conceptual equivalence. Adding the requirement of scalability is an important safeguard against nonequivalence, but what happens if one cannot derive a scalable set of identical items from the initial pool? If one employs only the "identity-equivalence" method, one is up the proverbial creek again.

Frey suggests (1970:286-288) a second method of analyzing equivalence, the "approach through validation," which he says is more often employed, but implicitly so. This method evaluates the cross-national equivalence of a scale not on the basis of correlations among the items it contains, but rather according to correlations between the set of items and measures of other variables with which it is *expected* to correlate. Frey differentiates these two approaches as follows:

> In the unidimensional approach, a core equivalence is asserted on the basis of showing that the *same set of items* (formally identical) hang together across systems, i.e., that the items exhibit similar, nonrandom patterns of relationship *among each other* without regard to system. In the validational approach, equivalence is asserted on the basis of demonstrating that *different system-specific sets of items* all measure a variable which is similarly and predictably related to *designated other variables* in each system. (Frey 1970:286)

The validational approach is clearly an extension of the logic of construct validity: that is, does the variable as measured behave, in relation to other variables, in ways that are predictable and understandable based upon theoretical knowledge of the underlying concept? This method of assessing equivalence is also advocated by Straus (1969:238). The problem for the researcher employing any kind of construct validity is the availability of some theory which would enable the prediction of correlations between the variable whose validity is being assessed and some "designated other variables" measurable in each system.[21] If there is no basis for such predictions, construct validity cannot be assessed. However, one can usually come up with defensible predictions—the question is *how* defensible they will be.

Frey also correctly points out that the validational approach is complementary to the identity-equivalence method of Przeworski and

Teune. The two procedures are in no way contradictory, and may be employed simultaneously in the development and demonstration of equivalence in measurement. In fact, in their later volume, Przeworski and Teune (1970) incorporate construct validity into their method as an approach which is applicable when the researcher has only system-specific indicators at his or her disposal. In this situation, they argue that the strongest possible assessment of equivalence consists of two criteria: (1) the similarity of relationships among multiple indicators of the same variable, even though the specific indicators are different; and (2) the similarity of the behavior of the set of indicators to other variables.[22]

Of course, one must remember that societies or social systems should not be directly compared to one another on univariate distributions involving only system-specific indicators. Indeed, any univariate comparison is hazardous. But in cross-national research the objective is to assess the similarity of processes or relationships across social systems, not simply to assert that two or more systems are similar to or different from one another with respect to some single variable.

When our purposes are explanatory rather than descriptive, we require measures which are valid within systems and reliable across systems (Przeworski and Teune 1970:114). Neither of these purposes is well served by employing formally equivalent measures in all systems. The conceptual equivalence of indices may be assessed by examining the similarity of intercorrelations between multiple measures of the same variable, and of the correlations between this set of measures and other criterion variables, across all systems. If these patterns are sufficiently similar across all systems in the investigation, then one may argue that one's indicators are conceptually equivalent even though they contain no identical items.[23]

Explanation

In the first chapter of this book, we argued that the advantages of comparative research hinge upon the opportunities it provides for the development of theoretical explanations of human behavior. However, in order to actualize these opportunities, certain methodological obstacles must be overcome—or at least the distortion which they cause must be minimized. We have dealt with recognized problems and with attempts at solving these problems, which involve the selection of social systems and of observations on or within those systems and the methods of deriving observations which are demonstrably comparable.

But, once comparable observations on several social systems have been assembled, the comparative investigator is faced with the most crucial part of the task: to transform the set of observations into meaningful explanatory theory. This is the ultimate objective of any research. Unless it is accomplished effectively, the efforts and resources expended in the collection of observations are wasted. The comparative researcher must know what kinds of questions to ask and of whom to ask them, or the answers will be of very limited value. But he or she must also know what to do with the answers. This is the problem of explanatory analysis.

Zelditch (1971), in his paper on "intelligible comparisons," argues that there is no set of rules or procedures one may follow, in comparative research, which will automatically and necessarily produce meaningful explanatory theory. He concludes that

> . . . there is no royal road to intelligible comparisons that, if only the map is obediently read, can be followed by the foolish or ignorant investigator to certain and valuable results. Not only a sound knowledge of the foundations of the rules, but also trained judgment and knowledge of the subject are required to design and interpret intelligible comparisons. (Zelditch 1971:307)

Up to this point, the methods we have discussed pertain to the generation of information regarding relationships between two or more variables. If our information is properly collected, we may organize it into statements of association between multiple phenomena, with reasonable assurance that these associations actually exist. But it is at this point that the task of the scientific theorist begins. The objective of any science is not merely to discover and catalog correlations between variables, but rather to explain them. If the problems involved in the collection of comparative data are dealt with successfully, the comparative researcher has opportunities to pursue explanations of greater generality, abstraction, and thus theoretical significance than does the social scientist who has data from only one social system.

The construction of social theory, or any other variety of scientific explanation, is hardly a simple matter. Popper (1968:27-34) explains in a convincing and comprehensible manner that theoretical statements (or, for that matter, general descriptive statements) may never be proven. This is true whether the statement is derived inductively by inference from previous observation or deductively from theoretical premises before it is subjected to empirical test. However, general explanatory statements may be *disproven.* The task of the scientist who wishes to explain some facet of behavior is, therefore, to eliminate alternative or competing explanations until he or she arrives at one for which all attempts at disproof have been unsuccessful.[24]

In attempting to eliminate alternative explanations for specific correlations, the comparative researcher faces certain difficulties which differ from those encountered by noncomparative investigators, in degree if not in kind. In order, from the most specific to the most general, they are the problems of overidentification, diffusion, and the historicist or holistic objection to comparative generalizations. The difficulties to which each of these problems pertains center around the construction of causal, explanatory theory with data from multiple social systems.[25] We turn first to the problem of overidentification.

Overidentification

The problem of overidentification (or overdetermination) is endemic to comparative research, and particularly to cross-national studies. It is virtually certain to arise when the contribution of system-level variables to explanation is being evaluated. In general, a variable is overidentified when its variance can be accounted for in more than one way. Because different combinations of independent variables are equally effective in "explaining" the variance in the dependent variable, one cannot make an empirically based choice between the competing explanations.

In a statistical sense, overidentification means that we have more estimating equations than we have unknowns—in effect, an embarrassment of riches (Wonnacott and Wonnacott 1970:185-188). In a practical sense, for the comparative researcher, overidentification results from a situation where the number of observed differences between social systems exceeds the number of social systems in the analysis. The smaller the size of the sample in terms of systems, the greater the risk of overidentification. In cross-national research, one may have a very large sample of individuals, but one will almost invariably have a small sample of societies or social systems. It is therefore at the systemic level of analysis that the problem of overidentification is particularly acute. For this reason, Smelser (1973:47-55) differentiates comparative research from "statistical" research: the number of cases (systems) is usually too small to permit the statistical manipulations necessary to precisely identify sources of variance in dependent variables. "Because of the restricted number of cases," he says, "the investigator relies on systematic comparative illustration" (1973:51).

Examples of overidentification are abundant in the comparative research literature, but one should suffice. Thomas et al. (1974:63-85) discuss, among several other topics, determinants of adolescent conformity, with data drawn from four samples in New York City, St. Paul, Minnesota, San Juan, Puerto Rico, and Merida, Yucatan, Mexico.[26] They hypothesized that conformity would vary inversely with extent of urbanization-industrialization, with the samples ranked in the above order from most to least urbanized-industrialized. They found that the rank order of samples according to mean conformity scores did indeed correspond quite closely to their ranking on the urbanization-industrialization continuum (1974:68); thus their hypothesis was supported.

The question then becomes, is the cross-national variation in adolescent conformity *due to* urbanization-industrialization? Are adolescents in Merida more conforming than those in New York *because* Merida is less urbanized and industrialized? The answer, of course, is "maybe." Other variables might also reproduce this same rank-ordering of these societies. The authors themselves point out (1974:64) that the Latin cultures in their study contain stronger normative prescriptions for intrafamily conformity than does the culture of the United States, and that therefore the effects of urban-industrial social structure cannot be disentangled from the effects of specific cultural components. This is also true of any other variable or combination of variables which would order the samples in the same way.

> Any set of variables that differentiates . . . systems in a manner corresponding to the observed differences of behavior (or any interaction among these differences) can be considered as explaining these patterns of behavior. . . . Although the number of differences among similar countries is limited, it will almost invariably be sufficiently large to "overdetermine" the dependent phenomenon. (Przeworski and Teune 1970:34)

How, then, can one distinguish causal from noncausal relationships in a situation of overidentification? In a strictly empirical sense, one can't. Multivariate statistical analysis of the variety used in sample surveys is out, since the number of societies is too small to permit it.[27] Smelser (1973:77–80) suggests that the researcher may attempt to replicate the correlation believed to represent the correct causal interpretation at a different level of analysis. For example, one might deduce from a hypothesis regarding differences between societies one which pertains to differences between individuals. If Thomas *et al.* are correct in their argument that urbanization-industrialization leads to a decrease in adolescent conformity on the cross-national level, then within societies we might expect to observe inverse associations between conformity and such variables as community size and nonagricultural occupations. Of course, the original hypothesis would not be "confirmed" by the observation of such correlations, but it would become more credible by virtue of the additional support which the observations would indirectly provide. If the secondary hypotheses were not supported, one would have reason to suspect the original theory.[28]

We might state this point in somewhat more general terms: the researcher needs a good theory by means of which to interpret his or her data. Thomas *et al.* (1974:63–67) present an argument which makes an inverse correlation between conformity and urbanization-industrialization understandable in a causal sense. Their four samples might be ranked in the same order by an infinite number of variables—proportion of the population with red hair, for example—but we have no reason to suspect that having red hair should influence conformity. Their theoretical logic provides one framework within which their data are interpretable, and it is capable of generating additional hypotheses the testing of which would shed further light on the theory. Thus, while they do not eliminate all alternative explanations of conformity by their research, their contribution is nonetheless considerable.

The problem of overidentification in cross-national research makes causal analysis much more difficult, but not impossible. The key to minimizing its effects is to begin with a good theory, on the basis of which the correlations one expects to observe are understandable and predictable. The same might be said for the problem of diffusion, to which we now turn.

Diffusion

Earlier, in the section on sampling societies in cross-cultural research, we pointed out that observations must be independent of one another in order to yield true estimates of cross-cultural correlations and to permit the laws of probability to operate in inference. This problem was discussed in connection with the definition of societies. Actually, the implications of the independence-of-observations issue are more general than that. A given culture may possess a particular trait because of one of two general kinds of processes. Either (1) the trait is causally or functionally related to other traits in the social, cultural, or ecological system pertaining to the culture, or (2) the trait was learned or "borrowed" from some other culture.[29] This is known as the problem of *diffusion*, also termed "Galton's problem" after the anthropologist who raised this objection to Tylor's (1889) introduction of the cross-cultural survey methodology.[30]

Diffusion creates problems not in the observations of correlations, but in their explanation. Diffusion becomes problematic when we attempt to explain *why* cross-cultural correlations exist. The "cause" of a diffusional correlation is to be found in the realm of historical patterns of contact between cultures. Diffusional relationships are thus grist for the historian's mill; they will not aid the social scientist's search for the general explanatory principles of human behavior.

How are diffusional correlations distinguished from those which may have theoretical implications? There are several extant methods of doing this, all of which are premised upon the assumption that cultures are more likely to borrow traits from neighboring rather than distant cultures. The techniques of checking for diffusion therefore involve modifications of standard sampling procedures to allow for geographic stratification, either in the selection of a cross-cultural sample or in the analysis of correlations observed on a non-stratified sample.

Murdock's (1957) World Ethnographic Sample consisted originally of 565 societies, divided into six "culture regions." Each of these culture regions was then subdivided into ten "culture areas," containing between five and fifteen (hopefully distinct) societies. One may then compute correlations on a sample of one society from each culture area (B. Whiting 1950), or compute correlations separately for each culture area or region (Whiting and Child 1953; Aberle 1961). If correlations remain between the variables of interest after these procedures have been followed, the argument that they are due to some process other than diffusion is strengthened.[31]

Naroll (1961), however, argued that diffusion does not necessarily stop at the boundaries of culture areas, although geography obviously has an important effect. He proposed that researchers take account of "diffusion arcs," or pathways along which migration, trade, and other carriers of culture did move or could have moved. The simplest method of employing the concept of diffusion arcs to test for the influence of diffusion is to array the societies in one's sample along some geographic axis, together with the values each society takes on each variable in the analysis. The distributions of the variables and the correlations along the arc may then be inspected statistically to determine whether they tend to cluster. If they do, then a diffusional explanation is indicated. If not, one proceeds under the assumption that the relationship is "functional."[32]

Murdock and White (1969) have constructed a sample of 186 societies garnered from the Ethnographic Atlas (Murdock 1967), selected in such a way as to minimize the possible influence of diffusion. The societies in this sample are widely dispersed, according to the culture regions and culture areas developed earlier by Murdock. This sample, called the Standard Cross-Cultural Sample, may be employed for the investigation of research questions in which a large sample is of less importance to the analysis than is the diffusion problem.

In theory, however, it is impossible to eliminate diffusion as an explanation of any correlation between cultural traits. The methods developed by Murdock, Naroll, and others are extremely valuable as checks on cross-cultural correlations, but they are all based in one way or another upon dispersion of cultural traits along geographic lines. In these days of mass communication and cultural contact through many media, geography would not seem to be the barrier to diffusion that it once was. (Of course, we must recognize that many ethnographic data were collected from peoples who had little or no access to modern media.) Thus, one or more of the above-mentioned checks for diffusion should be utilized, insofar as possible, in any cross-cultural research. But if these checks come out negative, the possibility of diffusion as an explanation of cross-cultural correlations has been minimized, not eliminated.

There are, however, a couple of theoretical arguments against the power of diffusionist explanations which we must take into account. First, Naroll and D'Andrade (1963) have argued that the dichotomy between diffusional and functional relationships is perhaps somewhat overdrawn. They define three types of explanations rather than two. The first is "hyperdiffusional" or historical: the variables of interest have spread by cultural borrowing or migration, but are as likely to diffuse separately as together. Their correlation, then, is purely diffusional and has no significance for the formulation of explanatory theory. The third type of explanation is "undiffusional" or functional: here there is no evidence of diffusion of the relevant variables, and their relationship is thus solely a result of causal processes. The intermediate form of explanation, termed "semidiffusional," is appropriate in cases where the variables have in fact diffused, but have done so *together*. Their correlation is therefore a representation of both a diffusional and a functional relationship.[33] If conceptually distinct cultural traits or characteristics are adopted by societies concurrently, it seems reasonable to suspect that there is more to their intercorrelation than historical accident. If one assumes that cultures are functional systems, the simultaneous adoption of unrelated cultural traits seems rather unlikely. A semidiffusional relationship between two or more phenomena should therefore indicate to the researcher that some form of causal or functional relationship does obtain between these phenomena, particularly if the traits in question become enduring components of the cultures which import them. It is therefore the truly hyperdiffusional correlation which the social scientist must eliminate from his explanatory scheme.

A second warning against overestimating the importance of diffusion comes from Zelditch (1971:283-285). He points out that the more abstract are one's concepts, the less likely it is that any association between indicators of these concepts will be attributable to diffusion.

> History transmits only concrete similarities; abstract concepts should and do imply traits that are concretely dissimilar; therefore, no common history explains their properties. (Zelditch 1971:284)

Thus, while the problem of diffusion is important and has justifiably occupied the attentions of many students of comparative research, the obstacle to explanatory theory which it presents is not insurmountable. It becomes relevant in cases where we are investigating relatively concrete phenomena in a sample of societies which may have some historical connection with each other. And in these situations, Naroll and others have provided us with methods to check for its influence which are at least partially effective. However, the general point raised by "Galton's problem" is extremely important: not all correlations among cultural traits represent causal or functional relationships.

The historicist objection

One of the arguments against which the comparative researcher must contend states, in effect, that obtaining valid information from comparisons of a number of cultures or societies which can be used in the construction of general explanatory theory is simply impossible on logical grounds. This position is sometimes called "historicism." It stems in large part from the influence of anthropologists in the early part of the twentieth century, including most notably Bronislaw Malinowski, Franz Boas, Robert Lowie, and Ruth Benedict. The seminal early statement of this position was probably that of Boas (1896). In simplest form, the historicist objection follows from the contention that all cultures are unique.

Warwick and Osherson summarize the argument as follows:

> Reacting against the comparative excesses of the evolutionists, these writers moved away from a cross-cultural methodology. Specifically, Boas and his followers in the "historical" school of anthropology contended that there were *no* general laws of culture and that the task of the profession was to seek the unique patterning of culture within single societies. Malinowski's functionalism, in turn, emphasized the tendency of culture traits to form a unique, coherent whole. His approach also led to the intensive study of single societies, and a suspicion of multicultural comparisons. (Warwick and Osherson 1973:5)

Zelditch (1971:276) summarizes the logical foundations of the argument succinctly. First, in order for two or more units or systems to be comparable, the meaning of the variables to be compared must be the same in each system. Therefore, in the comparisons of specific traits, one must incorporate the various contexts within which these traits occur into the comparisons, since the trait derives its meaning from the context. But the context of the trait is the total configuration of all traits contained in the culture of which it is a part. Therefore, one must compare entire cultures to generate meaningful comparisons.

But this also is impossible, because of the initial point of the argument that cultures are unique. Unique phenomena are not comparable. The historicist argument therefore leads to a direct contradiction: only whole cultures may be compared,[34] but whole cultures are incomparable; therefore, meaningful cultural or societal comparisons are impossible. The upshot of this is that understanding and explanation may be achieved only by intensive studies of single, unitary cultures. If each unique culture is fully understood, the events which occur within it will be explicable in terms of that cultural context.[35]

Zelditch (1971:276-280) considers the argument between historicists and comparativists to be a manifestation of a "paradigm clash," and thus not susceptible to resolution by logical or empirical means. If one accepts the historicist premise that cultures are unique and that each trait in a cultural configuration affects the meaning of each other trait, then the conclusion that neither whole cultures nor specific components of cultures may be compared does indeed follow logically. Furthermore, the premise is not subject to empirical verification or disconfirmation. Therefore, researchers who *believe* in the value of comparative inquiry reject the historicist argument because it contradicts their values and preferences, and proceed with their task.

However, others are of the opinion that the dispute is susceptible of resolution. Nagel (1961:462) says that the historicist position stems from a logical confusion between two distinct questions: first, whether it is possible to formulate theories across systems, and second, whether the conditions under which the theories so formulated may be applied are the same in all systems. A negative answer to the latter question does not in any way necessitate a negative answer to the former. He goes on to say that

> ... the recognized differences in the ways different societies are organized and in the modes of behavior occurring in them may be the consequences, not of incommensurably dissimilar patterns of social relations in those societies, but simply of differences in the specific values of some set of variables that constitute the elementary components in a structure of connections common to all societies. (Nagel 1961:462)

In other words, we ought not mistake differences in the values of relevant variables, even though these differences may be extreme, for differences in the variables themselves. If there are no variables common to all societies in a study, then these societies cannot be compared. But if the values which a set of common variables takes are different, then we have accomplished one of the primary purposes of comparative research (maximizing variance; see Chapter One), and comparison may proceed.

Przeworski and Teune (1970:5-11), in their discussion of nomothetic and idiographic approaches to comparative inquiry, deal extensively with the historicist objection. According to Theodorson and Theodorson (1969: 369-370), a nomothetic science is one which "... is primarily concerned with studying the general rather than the particular, and is concerned less with description than with the development of scientific laws." An idiographic discipline, on the other hand,

> ... is primarily descriptive and concerned with individual, unique facts.

> History is regarded as an idiographic discipline because it is more concerned with studying particular events and configurations of events in specific settings than with deriving general principles and scientific laws. (Theodorson and Theodorson 1969:369)

It is obvious that the historicist position advocates an idiographic approach to comparative study; the formulation of general "laws" or propositions is held to be impossible.

According to Przeworski and Teune (1970:5-11), those who opt for the idiographic approach claim that nomothetic methods in comparative inquiry are inappropriate for two primary reasons. First, the scientist seeking general explanations must necessarily ignore unique or particular (that is, historical) events, since these are not generalizable. However, such events may have important effects on the objects of investigation. Second, the configuration of the features or traits of particular social systems creates patterns of determination, or causal processes, which are unique to each system. "Therefore the identification of the social system in which a given phenomenon occurs is a part of its explanation" (Przeworski and Teune 1970:7).

It is undeniably true that specific historical events and unique interactions among the features of particular systems may affect just about any object of investigation. But these may still be subsumed under general laws to the extent that the unique events in question constitute specific instances of abstractly defined variables. This is a matter of the language of measurement, or the way in which we define the phenomena of interest. Furthermore,

> (T)he fact that behavior takes place within a relatively isolated context may mean that a certain proportion of the explanation of this behavior may be found among factors extrinsic to all systems—universal factors— and a certain proportion may be found among factors that are intrinsic to particular systems and not generalizable across systems. (Przeworski and Teune 1970:12-13)

These authors go on to say that whenever the researcher uncovers a system-specific factor which appears to be essential to the explanation of a behavior, the appropriate conclusion is not that all systems are unique and thus incomparable, but rather that it is necessary to identify some general factor which has not yet been considered, and which would subsume the system-specific factor in question as a special case or instance. The goal of comparative research is, thus, to effect the replacement of the proper names of social systems, in explanations of behavior, with the names of general, abstract variables. To the extent that this can be accomplished, idiographic or descriptive statements may be replaced with nomothetic or explanatory statements, and a scientific explanation of the behaviors in question has been achieved.[36]

Przeworski and Teune go on to point out that there

will generally be some "residual variance" in the behavior under investigation, which cannot be accounted for by general laws and which, therefore, must be attributed to system-specific factors. But this attribution need not be permanent. As the theory is advanced and extended through research, it will hopefully come to account for progressively greater proportions of the variance. The central question is the *extent* to which we can explain behavior by general laws, not whether behavior can or cannot be so explained. The unique value of comparative research in this regard is that it permits the investigator to introduce systemic variables into explanations (Przeworski and Teune 1970:43–46), by inquiring as to whether relationships between variables within systems are the same in all systems. If they are, then systemic factors are irrelevent to the explanation of the dependent variable. If not, then by comparing the characteristics of systems we may be able to determine *why* the relationships are different, and incorporate this knowledge into our theory.

Conclusion

From this rather cursory review of the methodology of comparative sociological research, it is obvious that there are many obstacles to successful execution of even the most carefully planned research design. The difficulties which the comparative researcher is bound to encounter in sampling, measurement, and data analysis are indeed considerable. And these problems are never really "solved" in any final sense.

But we are beginning to develop at least partial, standardized methods of minimizing the difficulties encountered in comparative research. It is worth pointing out again that problems in comparative social inquiry are not generically different from those which occur in any kind of empirical research. The differences are those of degree. And because comparative research is not generically different from other kinds of research, when the challenges of comparison cause investigators to develop new solutions or refine old ones, their innovations are generally applicable to noncomparative sociological inquiries as well.[37] Because of the difficulty of the problems they face, it is likely that in the future comparative researchers will make a disproportionately high contribution to the development of sociological methodology.

In spite of the difficulties inherent in selecting and collecting comparative data and the frequency with which these data manage to elude simple analysis, sociologists and other behavioral scientists continue to pursue comparative investigations. The reason is that the benefits to be derived are considerable, particularly along the lines we suggested in Chapter One of increasing generality, maximizing variance, and taking account of system-level variables. Furthermore, comparative research is a challenge of considerable magnitude to even the most highly skilled investigator. Provided that problems of international relations and administrative recalcitrance can be solved or forestalled, comparative research will likely become much more common in the future.

One final word of caution is necessary here. This chapter, like most other treatises on methodology, expresses the problems encountered in comparative research in their most extreme forms, for purposes of clarity. Proposed solutions to these problems have been stated in terms of ideal, and sometimes quite abstract, procedures. After taking stock of all the complexities and intricacies of the method of comparative sociology mentioned here, attainment of good comparative research may seem a virtually impossible ideal.

It's not. The perfect piece of research, comparative or otherwise, has yet to be done, and it's not likely to happen in our lifetimes. But individual research projects are not done in "right or wrong" fashion. The ideal, which has yet to be perfectly defined, is more or less closely approximated in all research. Where it is missed by a wide margin, the correct procedure is not to give up, but to append the appropriate qualifications and evaluate the results accordingly.

In the chapters which follow, we shall begin the task of reporting and synthesizing existing research and theory relevant to the domain of comparative family sociology, commencing with cross-cultural analyses of various aspects of family structure. None of the studies to be discussed are perfect. Some of them, in fact, border on the indefensible in terms of one or more of the benchmarks of quality research we have elucidated here. But there is something to be learned from each one, even if it's only how to do a better job next time. We will, of course, insert methodological evaluations and critiques where appropriate, and explain the important studies in sufficient depth so that the careful reader can insert his or her own evaluations of their utility. The points discussed in this chapter should be of some help to the student who wishes to understand the substantive findings and theories in comparative family study more fully.

Notes

1. These works include, in part, Moore (1961), Andreski (1964), Merrit and Rokkan (1966), Rokkan (1968), Holt and Turner (1970), Przeworski and Teune (1970), Vallier (1971), and Warwick and Osherson (1973). There are also valuable methodological chapters contained in Marsh (1967) and in the volumes edited by Hill and Konig (1970) and Etzioni and DuBow (1970).

2. The number of societies represented in the Ethnographic Atlas is currently increasing as more ethnographies are being coded.

3. Actually these are problems of measurement, not sampling. They are relevant at this point, however, because they indicate that in cross-cultural and cross-societal studies our sampling processes are restricted by the availability of usable data. We will discuss the quality of data in ethnographic sources in the section on measurement below.

4. This point is equally important in cross-national research, to which we will turn shortly.

5. Zelditch (1971:280-282) also enjoins the comparative researcher to be certain that all units being compared in any given instance are of the same level. If one society is sufficiently large and diverse to cause the analyst to mistakenly treat it as if it were four or five independent units, it may actually be a manifestation of a different level of organization than others in the sample, and should be treated with extra caution.

6. Straus (1968) points out that secondary analyses of the cross-national variety are perfectly possible and may be quite useful. However, this does not obviate the basic point here, since at some point someone has to collect the data which are subjected to the secondary analysis.

7. Frey (1970:202-229) discusses many of the problems involved in the organization and administration of cross-national investigations. Adams (1974) gives vivid illustrations of the problems the researcher may encounter in relating to governmental agencies. See also Hill (1962) for a discussion of the value of, and problems in, obtaining and maintaining collaboration in cross-national investigations.

8. Straus (1968:569) seems to be advocating the use of this method by saying that societies should be selected to represent variation in "some latent variable whose effect is to be studied." By implication, then, the researcher would attempt to minimize variation in theoretically extraneous factors. See the discussion of "overidentification" later in this chapter.

9. Smelser (1973:77-78) contends that, when faced with this problem, the researcher may establish ". . . the salience or importance of a particular association . . . (by) the replication of the suspected association at a different analytic level." The reader is referred to Smelser for a detailed explanation and illustration of this method. We will also discuss it briefly below. However, while replication at a different (usually smaller) analytic level may potentially make one's hypothesis more credible and help to distinguish between alternative explanations, there may be different causal processes operating

at the different levels. Furthermore, such a replication is not always possible in practice.

10. This is so because multiple tests of a proposition under a diversity of conditions eliminate a greater number of alternative propositions. See Stinchcombe (1968:18-22).

11. Marsh (1967:288-291) argues that stratified random samples of societies are likely to be the most productive of useful generalizations. As bases for stratification, he suggests some form of geographic criterion to minimize the effects of diffusion, together with levels of societal complexity or differentiation to maximize the diversity of societies in the sample and insure a broad representation of societies of different types. If employed in cross-national research, this method would approximate the "most different systems" strategy. See also the discussion by Frey (1970) of the "factorial matrix" method, which is relevant in that it defines an ideal type of system selection.

12. The different analytic methods and theoretical objectives appropriate for samples of social systems selected by each of these methods is a fascinating subject which is worthy of much more extensive analysis, but due to considerations of space we must leave it to others. See Przeworski and Teune (1970:31-73) for a particularly enlightening treatment of the issue.

13. An excellent treatment of sampling is contained in Frey (1970:229-239).

14. However, Kluckhohn (1953) and Naroll (1968:239-240) correctly observe that the investigator of a single society or culture is always and inevitably comparing it with his or her own. This type of comparison is very weak theoretically, however, since the comparison is not explicit or systematic and since there is no way of determining the typicality or representativeness of the investigator's own culture or the one being studied.

15. Part of the measurement problem in comparative research is that interview situations may be defined and responded to differently by interviewees in different cultures. Problems of "clinical witnesses," "courtesy bias," and culturally sensitive topics are often encountered; the nature of these problems and appropriate solutions to them vary greatly across cultures. For interesting discussions and examples of these difficulties, see Keesing and Keesing (1958), Mitchell (1965), Naroll (1968), and Adams (1974).

16. The moderate version of the Sapir-Whorf hypothesis is much more defensible than the extreme form from an empirical point of view. For an excellent review and synthesis of relevant research, see Marsh (1967:275-278).

17. For variations and elaborations of back-translation methods, see Barioux

(1948), Schachter (1954), Casagrande (1954), and Anderson (1967). There is also a large and important body of literature on the relative merits of different kinds of bilinguals for translation purposes; for summaries of this material, see Lambert *et al.* (1958, 1959), Marsh (1967:273-275), and Frey (1970:277-278).

18. Przeworski and Teune (1970:96-100) argue quite correctly that the question of comparative validity does not arise in the evaluation of operational definitions or direct measures, where the underlying concept is completely defined by the index of that concept (for instance, "IQ is what the IQ test measures"). The question of validity arises only when one must make measurement *inferences* from direct observations to measurement statements, and questions of comparative validity are relevant only when the rules of inference vary across systems. The advocate of operational definitions might then argue that the problem of the validity of measurement in comparative research can be avoided entirely by employing only operational definitions. However, for a variety of reasons, the theoretical significance of a concept whose sole definition and meaning are operational is highly limited. "Direct measurement is immediately dependent upon specific observations and hence is highly sensitive to the differences of social contexts" (Przeworski and Teune 1970:100).

19. Frey (1970:241) argues that the debate over formal versus functional equivalence is a waste of time: all researchers aim for functional equivalence. This point is undoubtedly correct. However, there is considerable value in the debate, since it points out that equivalent meanings are not necessarily attained by identical procedures. Frey is right in that no one is really arguing in favor of formally equivalent measures as an appropriate objective of comparative measurement; in that sense there is no debate. The issue, though, involves how to attain conceptual equivalence. For a more detailed discussion of the sources of nonequivalence, see Scheuch (1968).

20. This refers, of course, only to those system-specific items which were designed for measurement of the concept in question, not to any and all items which happen to correlate with the set of identical indicators.

21. Note that the "criterion variables" do not need to be the same in all systems. The objective is to estimate validity *within* systems.

22. Unfortunately we have neither the time nor the space to recapitulate their entire logic here. For their detailed treatment of establishing equivalence with system-specific indicators only, see Przeworski and Teune (1970:126-130). For the serious student of comparative theory and method, the entire volume is strongly recommended.

23. There are also techniques for the measurement of certain kinds of variables across social systems which are held to be "culture free." These include projective techniques such as the Rorschach Test and the Thematic Apperception Test (Barnouw 1963:239-298; Frey 1970:261-266), and "self-anchoring scales" (Kilpatrick and Cantril 1960; Cantril and Free 1962; Cantril 1963, 1965; Frey 1970:272-275). Since these are designed as measures of specific kinds of variables rather than as general measurement techniques, we will forego discussion of them here.

24. For a more complete introduction to and explication of this logic, see Stinchcombe (1968:15-28).

25. The reader should note that in this section on theory construction, we are *not* talking about the applicability of various "conceptual frameworks" to comparative research. Although the development of an appropriate conceptual system is crucial in any scientific task, the logic of theory construction proceeds independently of the concepts which give substance to the theory. We are currently interested in the construction of causal theories; at several subsequent points in the book we will inquire into the utility of specific conceptual frameworks for the investigation of particular theoretical problems. For the reader who is more interested in the comparative value or merit of existing conceptual structures, Sheldon Stryker (1972) derives tenable comparative propositions on family variables from symbolic interaction theory, and Robert Winch (1972) points to an integration of functionalism and exchange theory in comparative research. See also William Goode (1973:64-94), who argues that functionalism is actually a particular perversion of causal terminology.

26. See also Thomas and Weigert (1971).

27. These methods can, however, be used in cross-cultural research, since it is possible to sample a much larger number of societies.

28. A good example of the derivation of hypotheses pertinent to intrasystem research from theory based on cross-systemic analyses is contained in Winch's work on the determinants of extended familism. See Winch *et al.* (1967), Winch and Greer (1968), and Winch (1974).

29. This dichotomous statement of the problem is admittedly an oversimplification; we will rectify it shortly. See the discussion of "semidiffusion" below.

30. For a more complete history of Galton's problem, see Naroll (1968:258).

31. More detailed explanations and criticisms of this method are contained in McEwen (1963:162) and Marsh (1967:288-291).

32. There are numerous techniques available for making such a check, most of

which have been developed by Naroll. See, for example, Naroll (1961, 1964), Naroll and D'Andrade (1963), and summaries by Naroll (1968:258-262) and Marsh (1967:297-303).

33. For an excellent summary of this position, upon which my own is based, see Marsh (1967:299-300).

34. For this reason, Zelditch and others use the term "holist" to designate this position.

35. An example of one application of this logic to a criticism of the cross-cultural survey methodology may be found in Holy and Blacking's (1974) critique of a study of the antecedents of marriage ceremonies by Rosenblatt and Unangst (1974).

36. See also Suchman (1964:129). The reader will recognize that this point was stated in Chapter One as a basic objective of comparative research. To the extent that this objective can be accomplished, it constitutes empirical evidence in favor of the comparativist position and against historicism.

37. Warwick and Osherson (1973:10-11), in fact, mention an idea very similar to this as one of the principle advantages and contributions of comparative research.

part two

Cross-cultural family organization

Up to this point in the text, we have discussed some of the theoretical and methodological principles which form the basis of comparative sociology. But comparative sociology is itself a method of inquiry, which may be applied to the analysis of virtually any substantive area in the sociological domain. Our particular substantive interest is, of course, the family, to which we now turn.

The next four chapters deal with several related aspects of family organization. In Chapter Three we inquire into cross-cultural uniformities in family organization: what features, if any, do the family systems of all societies share? This is part of the question of whether all social systems indeed possess a subsystem which may be termed "the family." We also investigate, in this chapter, possible original causes of the emergence of the family as a feature of human social organization. In Chapter Four we begin our study of variation in family phenomena with an inquiry into varieties of marital organization; each extant type of marriage is described, its frequency and distribution estimated, and its possible causes examined. Chapter Five initiates our consideration of the "family proper"; here again we concern ourselves primarily with variation in family structures and with the sources or antecedents of such variation. Finally, Chapter Six deals with the structural parameters of kinship systems, those broader collectivities of people who are biologically and socially related to one another, which include related families.

chapter three

The family: origins and universality

Introduction

The task of this chapter is to investigate cross-cultural uniformities in the structure of the family. There are two theoretically relevant questions we will ask about family structures. First, how did they originate? Second, do all societies have some institution or structure we may reasonably call "the family," and if so, what do these structures have in common?

The first question, that of origins, has attracted relatively less attention of late than it did in the earlier years of the development of anthropology. It is almost inherently a question that can never be fully answered because of a data base which is severely limited, for obvious reasons. However, there has recently been some revival of interest in the topic because of a possible theoretical connection between how the family originated and the definition and source of sex roles in modern society. The issue of the universality of the family is important less for its substantive content than for the points which this debate highlights about the nature and use of concepts and definitions in scientific research and theory. But there are several important implications of either a positive or a negative answer to the question of whether or not the family is universal, and in the pursuit of the empirical issue of universality we shall have the opportunity to investigate several rather unusual family systems and to highlight the extent of variation in family structures.

Origins of the family

The question of how and why the family originated is conceptually distinct from the question of an "evolutionary sequence" in the development of family forms, which was pursued by some early social scientists (for example, Morgan 1878; Maine 1885; McLennan 1896; Bachofen 1897; Lang 1903; Westermarck 1921; Briffault 1931; Engels 1962). For quite some time, it was intellectually fashionable for social observers to speculate as to how the family must have evolved to its present form, as manifest in Western society. The product of these speculations generally took the form of a sequence of evolutionary stages through which, according to the various arguments, the family must have passed in its course toward the "highest" form attained in "civilized" societies. The starting point was usually assumed to be some state of "original promiscuity" or random and temporary mating, which gave way to other forms (the sequence of which varied markedly from author to author) as "progress" ensued. The common thread underlying these arguments, although they differed in their particulars, was that the family was progressing from "lower" to "higher" forms in conjunction with mankind's progress toward "civilization."

To us today these speculations may seem a bit naive and somewhat less than useful. But within the intellectual climate of the times the issues were highly relevant (see Hadden and Borgatta 1969:17). The "unilinear evolutionist" perspective employed in these works, however, was the source of considerable controversy among the anthropological profession even before the turn of the century. The data base for evolutionary speculations was very poor, the available data were definitely open to multiple interpretations, and the logic of the arguments lent itself readily to ethnocentric value judgments and related biases (see Kenkel 1973:11-13). In fact, Franz Boas' (1896) early argument against the comparative method in general (see the discussion of "historicism" in Chapter Two) was actually a reaction against the excesses of unilinear evolutionism.

A precise chronological account of how the family has developed over time is now recognized to be beyond the current capacities of science. This is partly because the data required for precision are now largely inaccessible, and partly because the chronology would be different for different social systems. Arguments that changes in family structure have historically followed some single developmental sequence are scientifically untenable in light of current evidence, regardless of the particular sequence postulated. In any case, scientific theory construction methods indicate that, if one wishes to explain or predict changes in family phenomena, one should look for general explanatory variables which influence the object of inquiry independently of time and space. Some of these explanatory variables may be discovered by comparing family systems at different points in time and/or under varying ecological and cultural conditions, a task which we shall attempt throughout the remainder of this book. But the question of how, why, and under what conditions the family originated as a social institution is logically independent of questions regarding developmental or sequential changes in the family.

The issue of the origins of the family has been shown in some recent arguments (Gough 1971; Sprey 1971-72) to be related to certain characteristics of modern sex-role definitions and performance. The family, whatever the structure it takes in particular societies, is virtually always an association between adults of both sexes and dependent children. The question of how and why the family originated pertains, then, to patterns of interdependence between the sexes. Since nonhuman primates do not have families in the sense that we normally employ the term (see van den Berghe 1973), it is reasonable to suppose that there is something peculiar to the human condition which led, at some indeterminate point in the past, to the emergence of family structures.

The most important recent work on the origins of the family has been done by Hockett and Ascher (1964) and Gough (1971). Since Gough's argument was informed by the earlier work of Hockett and Ascher, and since their positions do not differ substantially, we shall rely primarily upon Gough for a statement of current thought on the topic.[1] She points to two basic changes, one physiological and one ecological, which she feels were important in the genesis of family structures.

There was a period of prehistory, the Miocene period, during which rather extensive climatic changes occurred. The climate in many regions gradually became drier, and subtropical forests slowly gave way to open grasslands or savannahs. Some primates, largely tree dwellers up to this point, "...had to come down from the trees and adapt to terrestrial life" (Gough 1971:763). This caused changes in the economic subsistence patterns of these primates which, according to the reasoning, eventuated in certain physiological changes:

> The spread of indigestible grasses on the open savannahs may have encouraged, if it did not compel, the early ground dwellers to become active hunters rather than to forage for small, sick, or dead animals that came their way. Collective hunting and tool use involved group cooperation and helped foster the growth of language out of the call-systems of apes. Language meant the use of symbols to refer to events not present. It allowed greatly increased foresight, memory, planning, and

division of tasks—in short, the capacity for human thought. (Gough 1971:763)

This produced an increase in the complexity of the brain, which led, for humans, to a larger cranial size. But along with this, the upright stance prompted by living on the ground rather than in trees reduced the size of the pelvis. The human female, consequently, could not carry her child for so long a time and still survive the process of giving birth. A third and crucial physiological change then took place as a result of the first two:

> To compensate, humans are born at an earlier stage of growth than apes. They are helpless longer and require longer and more total care. This in turn caused early women to concentrate more on child care and less on defense than do female apes. (Gough 1971:764)

Some (such as R. Adams 1960) argue that the inordinately long period of human infant dependency on the mother implies that the basic family unit is the mother-child dyad. But the fact that such a great proportion of the adult woman's time and energy is spent caring for dependent children means that she will be much better off, and increase the chances of survival for both herself and her offspring, if she associates with a male or males who are not encumbered with child-care responsibilities. This is particularly true in terms of defense and the provision of food, especially where hunting plays an important role in the subsistence base. As Adams (1960) argues, there may be no *necessary* reason for the mother-child dyad to form an alliance with the child's father, but Hockett and Ascher (1964) point out that, for a variety of reasons, it was probably efficient to do so. This would provide advantages at least in terms of stability of the family unit. In any case, for our purposes the role of *sociological* father ("pater") is much more important than the role of *biological* father ("genitor"). These two roles, in any given case, may or may not coincide in the same person. The point, though, is that a stable alliance between mother and child was probably necessitated by the child's long period of virtually complete dependency. This, in turn, makes the mother dependent upon others, probably males, for protection and certain subsistence functions. The unit that arose from this network of interdependencies would thus be a small group based upon kinship, and could be labeled a "family" without stretching the meaning of the term too much.[2] (See also Reynolds 1968.)

According to this logic, then, the family originated among human beings because a certain division of labor between the sexes was found to be convenient or efficient and maximized the probability of survival for individuals and groups in the kind of environment we have described. The logic here implies that the origin of sex roles, or the differentiation between the sexes in terms of socially defined behavioral expectations, coincided with the origin of the family. If the argument is correct, then men have been assigned protective and productive tasks, and women domestic and child-care responsibilities, since the earliest periods of the existence of mankind. The question then arises as to whether this sort of distinction between the sexes is somehow "right" or "natural."

Gough (1971) has argued that the convenience of sex-role differentiation early in human history does not have any implications for current practices, particularly in terms of power differentials between men and women. Many of the original causes of differences between male and female social roles have been obviated by advances in technology and changes in social organization. It is no longer *necessary*, in the sense of promoting or insuring survival, that the female spend her full time caring for offspring. On the other hand, Sprey points out that the issue is unresolved at the moment, and is now independent of data on family origins:

> Much of the debate on this issue (of sex-role performance) still centers around the question of whether or not sex roles are in essence purely "man-made" or do reflect genuine psycho-biological differences between men and women. . . . (T)he answer to this question is an empirical one, and must be settled scientifically. At this writing all that can be said is that despite the strong ideological views in support of complete male-female biological equivalence as social beings, the hypothesis that selectively evolved, categorical, innate differences in "interests and capacities for social bonding" (Tiger 1970; also Tiger and Fox 1971) between the sexes do exist has not been disproven. (Sprey 1971-72: 8-9)[3]

If the family did in fact originate in the manner specified in this argument, the implications for early sex-role patterning are quite clear.[4] The implications for current differences in behavior between the sexes are much less so. D'Andrade (1966) theorizes that existing behavioral differences between the sexes are attributable to the human propensity to generalize stimuli. That is, human beings have generalized from the few sex differences that are directly related to physiological differences (sexual dimorphism) to the great number of differences that are only indirectly connected to physiology, if at all. We will examine this contention in greater detail in subsequent chapters.

According to this line of reasoning, the factors which culminated in the origin of the family consist of biological and ecological parameters which pertain to human beings everywhere. Members of all societies share virtually identical biological characteristics (at least those relevant for this argument), and, although the particulars vary, share certain common orientations to the natural environment. Since the factors identified as causing the origin of the family are relatively constant across societies, the family itself should be a structural feature of all societies. That is, the conclusion reached by Hockett and Ascher (1964), Gough (1971) and others regarding how the family originated implies that the family should be universal. This question forms the topic of our next section.

Universality of the family[5]

When we ask whether or not the family is universal, we are not inquiring as to whether everyone lives in a family. The answer to that question, at any given point in time, would clearly be negative. We are, rather, asking two distinct questions about the distribution of the family *as a social institution,* with the inquiry at the societal level of analysis. The first question is entirely empirical, the second strictly theoretical. Neither question is answerable at the moment in a definitive sense, but we can come close on at least the first of them.

On the empirical level, we are asking whether or not each and every society, past and present, has or has had a social institution which we may designate "the family." Given proper conceptualization of relevant terms and adequate data, both of which are rather serious problems, this question is susceptible to a "yes or no" type of answer. Several recent authors (for example, Adams 1971:39-40) conclude that the issue is actually a matter of semantics not susceptible to empirical resolution, while others (Smelser 1973: 80-86; Winch 1971:25-27; Stolte-Heiskanen 1972) consider the question to be atheoretical and advise us to be content with the generalization that the family is "virtually universal" and to forego further analysis in this area in favor of more productive endeavors.

However, if the question is properly conceived, there is a very important theoretical side to it which should not be overlooked. This involves an understanding and explanation of social order in terms of the minimal requirements for the existence and maintenance of human society. If it is the case that all societies do have some form of family structure as a central feature of their social organization, then the family may be *necessary* for the persistence of society. The theoretical relevance of the question of family universality, in this sense, may be emphasized by turning the question around and asking, "Is it possible for a society to survive *without* the family?"

Phrased in this way, the question might be answered in the affirmative, but never in the negative. If we find a single society which does not manifest some form of family structure, then we may conclude that it *is* possible for a society to get along without the family. But if we do not, this does not prove that the famly is necessary, but only that it is empirically universal according to available evidence. Just because all societies *do* have a family, we need not infer that they *must* have a family. However, an empirical finding that the family is in fact universal, while it would in no sense prove the hypothesis that it is necessary, required, or indispensable for human social organization, would make that hypothesis more credible.[6] Scientific hypotheses are, in fact, never "proven," but the more we are unsuccessful in our attempts to disprove them the more credible they become (see Popper 1968; Stinchcombe 1968). In this light, there is no such thing as "virtual universality" when considering this issue; the family is either universal or it is not. An explanation of why the family is universal, and thus *perhaps* necessary or required in human society, would be very different from an explanation of why it is almost universal. It would be based on different premises and have a very different set of implications. It is theoretically important, then, to determine which of these circumstances obtains.

Any empirical examination of the prevalence of the family cross-culturally must of necessity begin with a definition of the term. Whether or not the family exists in any given society depends largely upon what we consider the family to be. Thus, a great deal of the debate over this issue has involved the appropriateness of various definitions of the family. On the one hand, we need a definition that is sufficiently broad to include within its domain family systems which are different from our own, in order to avoid ethnocentrism and to take account of the obvious plasticity of human behavior. On the other hand, we must avoid a definition which is so all-inclusive that virtually any social structure could be identified as a family; this would render the concept useless for empirical examination. In the review which follows, the arguments and data presented by each researcher are accompanied by the definition of the family employed. Each definition must be carefully evaluated as a central component of the theory presented.

George Murdock

One of the earliest and still most widely known points of view on the universality of the family was expressed by Murdock in his seminal anthropological work *Social Structure* (1949:1-12). Based on a survey of ethnographic reports on 250 societies (the forerunner of the Human Relations Area Files), Murdock concluded that the family is in fact universal. He also concluded, somewhat surprisingly, that the form taken by the family in all societies consists of "... a married man and woman with their offspring" (Murdock 1949:1), which is the type of family most characteristic of the United States and other industrialized societies. Murdock noted that this particular family unit may be embedded within a network of other related individuals, such that it is not the *entire* family structure typical of some societies, but it is the "building block" or nucleus from which all other family forms are constructed. Hence, Murdock applied the term "nuclear family" to this social group. In his words,

> The nuclear family is a universal human social grouping. Either as the
> sole prevailing form of the family or as the basic unit from which more

complex family forms are compounded, it exists as a distinct and strongly functional group in every known society. (Murdock 1949:2)

Thus, according to Murdock, the *minimal* family structure present in all societies is the nuclear family. Furthermore, even where this unit is only part of a more extensive or complex family system, it "stands out" in some way; it is distinct from the rest of the family system and constitutes a unit which is at least semi-independent.

Murdock says that this distinctiveness stems not only from the (presumed) fact that the members of the nuclear family constitute a social group, but also from the social consequences or functions which are attributable to the nuclear family. There are, in his argument, four universal functions of the nuclear family: sexual, reproductive, educational, and economic. In any given society the nuclear family may, and in all probability will, have more than these four functions, but the additional functions are variable. These four are held to be constant across all societies.

By stating that a universal function of the family is the regulation of sexual relationships, Murdock is not denying the existence of pre-marital, extramarital, or nonmarital sex. He is saying, rather, that the primary sexual outlet for most adults in all societies is one component relationship of the nuclear family, the marriage. One consequence or function of the nuclear family is therefore the provision of a socially legitimate sexual outlet for adults, which is, in Murdock's logic, an essential or necessary feature of any society:

> The relationship between father and mother in the nuclear family is solidified by the sexual privilege which all societies accord to married spouses. As a powerful impulse, often pressing individuals to behavior disruptive of the cooperative relationships upon which human social life rests, sex cannot safely be left without restraints. All known societies, consequently, have sought to bring its expression under control by surrounding it with restrictions of various kinds. On the other hand, regulation must not be carried to excess or the society will suffer through resultant personality maladjustments or through insufficient reproduction to maintain its population. (Murdock 1949:4)

The necessary balance between regulation and freedom in sexual relations is accomplished in all societies, in Murdock's view, by the institution of marriage, which is a part of the nuclear family.

A relationship between a man and a woman which includes a provision for sexual relations will, more likely than not, result in children. (This is admittedly common knowledge, but it bears mentioning in this context.) If marriage is the primary heterosexual relationship in all societies, it therefore follows that it will also be the primary agent of reproduction. This is the second of Murdock's four universal functions of the family. Once children are added to (produced by) the marital union, we are speaking of the nuclear family in its entirety rather than one of its component relationships. Murdock points out (1949:9-10) that the reproductive function, like the sexual function, is necessary to insure the survival of any society. It is also necessary for a society to do more than simply produce children; they must be cared for in a physical sense and they must be trained to perform the adult roles deemed appropriate for them by their culture. This involves, obviously, more than the teaching of occupational skills. It revolves around the basic processes of language development and the transmission of culture:

> The young human animal must acquire an immense amount of traditional knowledge and skill, and must learn to subject his inborn impulses to the many disciplines prescribed by his culture, before he can assume his place as an adult member of his society. The burden of education and socialization everywhere falls primarily upon the nuclear family. (Murdock 1949:10)

And finally, this nuclear family unit which provides for sexual relations, reproduction, and socialization also contains within it at least one important basis for the division of labor in any society: sex. Murdock points to the greater physical strength of men and the capacities of women for certain kinds of lighter labor as a critical differentiation in the division of economic tasks and responsibilities:

> By virtue of their primary sex differences, a man and a woman make an exceptionally efficient cooperating unit. . . . All known human societies have developed specialization and cooperation between the sexes roughly along this biologically determined line of cleavage. It is unnecessary to invoke innate psychological differences to account for the division of labor by sex; the indisputable differences in reproductive function suffice to lay out the broad lines of cleavage. (Murdock 1949:7)

The basis for the division of labor between adults of opposite sex is thus found within the structure of the family. Murdock regards the differentiation of tasks between husband and wife as a crucial part of the definition of marriage and the family; he points out that sexual unions occur without economic cooperation, and there are many economic relationships which do not involve sex, but these two kinds of relations are united only in marriage (1949:8). And marriage is always at least in part an economic relationship, in the sense that labor is divided between spouses.

The general theoretical position taken by Murdock is what Wallace (1969:36-44) identifies as "functional imperativism." The logic is essentially to identify certain functions which must be performed, or consequences which must occur, in any society, in order to permit the continuation and stability of the society. The researcher then identifies the structural arrangements by which the various functions are accomplished. While the functions are assumed to be constants (i.e., necessary in any stable society), the structures with which they are associated are generally treated as variables. But what Murdock is asserting is that there is a limit to the plasticity or flexibility of human behavior: the functions of sexual gratification, reproduction, education (or at least rudimentary socialization), and economic cooperation are *invariably* associated, on the societal level, with the nuclear family structure. This invariant empirical association between structure and function led Murdock to conclude that the nuclear family is universal because it is "inevitable" or necessary for the performance of the basic functional requirements noted. One more brief quotation from Murdock should suffice to make the point:

> In the nuclear family or its constituent relationships we see assembled four functions essential to human social life—the sexual, the economic, the reproductive, and the educational. Without provision for the first and third, society would become extinct; for the second, life itself would cease; for the fourth, culture would come to an end. The immense social utility of the nuclear family and the basic reason for its universality thus begin to emerge in strong relief. . . . No society, in short, has succeeded in finding an adequate substitute for the nuclear family, to which it might transfer these functions. It is highly doubtful whether any society ever will succeed in such an attempt, utopian proposals for the abolition of the family to the contrary notwithstanding. (Murdock 1949:10-11).

While Murdock's argument is fairly complex in its entirety, it may conveniently be summarized by means of two empirical hypotheses. The first, which is really an "existential" statement rather than a general explanatory hypothesis (Zelditch 1971:270), is that the nuclear family is universal as a structural feature of social systems. The second is that the nuclear family is *invariably* associated with the four functions of sexual gratification, reproduction, education or socialization, and economic cooperation. Each of these hypotheses is subject to empirical test. The discovery of *one society* which does not conform to *both* of these hypotheses is sufficient to permit the rejection of Murdock's thesis. That is, two kinds of evidence would lead to this rejection: (1) evidence of a society in which the positions composing the nuclear family (those of husband-father, wife-mother, and offspring-sibling) do not go together in such a way as to constitute a distinct social group; and/or (2) evidence of a society in which the nuclear family is structurally present, but where one or more of the four functions posited by Murdock are fulfilled by some other social structure.

While many authors today still treat Murdock's hypotheses as confirmed facts (see, for example, Leslie 1973:13-18), evidence has been accumulating since shortly after the appearance of his thesis to the effect that there are several concrete exceptions to his generalizations. One such exception may be the Nayar of South India, whose rather unusual marital practices will be discussed in the next chapter (see Gough 1959; Mencher 1965). Nayar adults of both sexes continued to reside in their mother's household for their entire lives. The residential family unit, therefore, consisted primarily of brothers and sisters and the children of the sisters; it did not contain a married couple. The reciprocal economic obligations between husbands and wives were very minimal indeed. The women were obliged to mourn for their "ritual husbands" upon their deaths, "visiting husbands" gave the women with whom they consorted small gifts of toiletry articles symbolic of their relationship, and the socially designated father of a child was responsible for compensating the midwife for her services at the birth. But this was about the extent of it. To argue that husband, wife, and children constituted a viable economic unit in any significant sense of the term is stretching the meaning quite a bit. Children were cared for and raised by the family unit consisting of their mother and her brothers and other "matrilineal" kin;[7] this unit did not include a father, either social or biological. Thus education and economic cooperation were clearly not functions of the nuclear family, and if we accept the argument that the nuclear family was not a discrete social group among the Nayar, then sexual gratification and reproduction were also non-nuclear-family functions, since "husband" and "wife" were not members of the same family.

Some social scientists have had considerable difficulty in getting others to take the Nayar family system seriously. There is some debate as to whether the Nayar are (or were) actually a society; we will return to this problem shortly. There is also considerable disagreement over the interpretations of various ethnographic reports. Some of the disagreements, though, may have been produced by an indoctrination to Murdock's position and a resultant limiting of flexibility in considering alternative possibilities.

A valuable illustration of multiple interpretations of the same material is given by Bell and Vogel (1968) in an edited collection of works in which they reprint Gough's (1959) treatise on the pertinence of the Nayar example for the issue of the universality of the family. Bell and Vogel introduce Gough's article with the following remarks:

> On the basis of extensive field and historical research, Dr. Gough concludes that there is some differentiation between the ritual and the de facto husband, but nevertheless the nuclear family unit, broadly defined, is distinct. Thus, Gough's evidence suggests that the Nayar "exception" (to Murdock's hypothesis) was not a real exception. (Bell and Vogel 1968:80)

But this does not appear to be Gough's conclusion. In the article which Bell and Vogel reproduce, she writes:

> The Nayars of this area were thus highly unusual. For they had a kinship system in which the elementary (i.e., nuclear) family of father, mother, and children *was not institutionalized as a legal, productive,*

distributive, residential, socializing or consumption unit. Until recent years, some writers have thought that at least as a unit for some degree of co-operation in economic production and distribution, the elementary family was universal. This view has been put forward most forcibly by Murdock (1949). Radcliffe-Brown (Radcliffe-Brown and Forde 1950:73ff.), however, was one of the earliest anthropologists to observe that if the written accounts of the Nayar were accurate, the elementary family was not institutionalized among them. (Gough 1959; in Bell and Vogel 1968:88; italics added)

In light of reports such as Gough's, it seems difficult indeed to continue to treat Murdock's generalizations as unchallenged by the Nayar case.[8]

Another possible exception to the universality of the nuclear family is given by the experience of the Israeli kibbutz, reported most completely and notably by Melford Spiro (1954, 1956, 1958). Kibbutzim (the plural form of kibbutz) are small, self-contained, experimental societies within the state of Israel, founded on a collectivistic ideology which stresses the primacy of the community over the individual and favors the implementation of procedures to eliminate socially structured inequality. One structure which produces inequality, or at least inequity, according to this ideology, is the traditional family, particularly because the performance of the roles of wife and mother tends to remove women from career positions, or at least to place them at a competitive disadvantage relative to men. The kibbutz community was designed, therefore, to minimize or obliterate sex differences in social positions and social roles.

For our purposes, the relevant features of kibbutz social organization involve the experimental structures devised to replace traditional marital and family forms.[9] When a couple wished to become married, they would simply request to the people in charge of housing that they be allocated a double-occupancy apartment. When one became available they would move in and would henceforth be considered a "couple" by the community unless or until they decided the arrangement was no longer mutually rewarding, at which point they would put in a request for different residential arrangements. No cooking, laundering, or other domestic maintenance tasks were accomplished at the household level; these were community functions. Another community function was the care and raising of children. At the age of approximately four days, children were removed from their parents and placed in a "children's house" where they were fed, clothed, housed, and ultimately educated by adult kibbutz members whose career responsibilities involved child-rearing and teaching. Children and parents would visit one another after work and on Saturdays. The parent-child relationships did involve considerable identification and affection, but the nuclear family clearly did not constitute a residential or an educational unit.

Furthermore, neither the married couple nor the parent-child group constituted an economic unit. Each adult in the kibbutz was an independent worker who contributed to the community economy by his or her labor and whose consumer needs were provided for by the kibbutz as a whole. The children, also, were in no way dependent upon their parents for their livelihood. Their sustenance was assured by the community's collective support of the children's houses.

Spiro feels that the kibbutz he studied was a clear exception to Murdock's generalization that the nuclear family is universal, primarily because economic cooperation and education/socialization were nonfamily functions. In his words,

> Since the kibbutz couple does not constitute a marriage because it does not satisfy the economic criterion of marriage, it follows that the couple and their children do not constitute a family, economic cooperation being part of the definition of the family. . . . More important, however, in determining whether or not the family exists in the kibbutz is the fact that the physical care and the social rearing of the children are not the responsibilities of their own parents. But these responsibilities, according to Murdock's findings, are the most important functions that the adults in the family have with respect to the children. (Spiro 1968:72)[10]

Spiro's point, essentially, is that parents and children in the kibbutz do not constitute an economic, a residential, or an educational unit, and that most of the functions which Murdock claims are invariably family functions are accomplished in the kibbutz by the community as a whole. In fact, he argues that kibbutz members perceive and psychologically define one another as kin, and behave toward one another as kin, regardless of biological connections. This is demonstrated in community solidarity, the collective raising of children, and perhaps most strikingly in the practice of kibbutz exogamy: members of one kibbutz rarely, if ever, marry other members of the same kibbutz, in spite of the absence of any formal or informal sanctions against such unions (Spiro 1968:75-76). Spiro considers this to be a behavioral manifestation of the feeling of kinship that pervades the community: age-mates behave toward one another as if they were siblings. It buttresses his argument that the family in the kibbutz has been replaced as a functioning social structure by the community as a whole, contrary to Murdock's statement that no society has ever found, or is every likely to find, an effective substitute for the nuclear family.

In an addendum written four years after his original paper, Spiro (1968:76-79) reconsiders his position that the kibbutz has no family structure. He notes that the "couple" relationship in the kibbutz does have certain distinctive features, involving particularly such aspects as common residence, high levels of interaction and intimacy, and sexual exclusivity. The relationship between parents and children also evinces certain family-like characteristics, which do serve to identify this unit as distinctive. His point here, though, is that the family may in fact exist in kibbutz society, but not in the form that Murdock defines it. He still considers the kibbutz to be a counter-instance with respect to Murdock's definition, and suggests that the definition of the family which Murdock proposed requires modification in light of the kibbutz case. Since it is Murdock's definition which we are evaluating, the relevant conclusion is that Spiro's kibbutz does appear to be exception to it.

There are also several other societies in which the characterization of the family system as nuclear, in Murdock's sense of the term, is marginal at best. Richard Adams (1960) reported very high rates of female-headed households for certain Latin American countries and ethnic groups. He argues that the basic unit of kinship analysis should be the dyad, particularly the mother-child dyad. Other family forms, including the nuclear as well as extended varieties, emerge from alliances between the mother-child dyad and other individuals or groups, including most frequently, but not necessarily, the husband-father.

The major problem with this argument is that Adams is operating on a somewhat different level of analysis than Murdock and others. In a strictly factual sense and on the level of individual families, it is obviously the case that many people live in families which do not contain all three nuclear positions. The frequency of "incomplete" nuclear families varies widely across societies, as well as within societies. Apparently, though, nuclear (or perhaps more extended) families were still in the majority for all societies on which Adams had information.[11] Furthermore, it is not at all clear that we should use statistical breakdowns of the frequency of various family forms as the basis for categorizing a society's family system. The character of a family system and the statistically most frequent family type are, in our mode of analysis, two different variables.

This kind of point has somewhat more relevance, though, when it can be demonstrated that some form of family which does not contain all three nuclear positions is in the clear *majority* for a society. For example, Blake (1961) reported that about two thirds of all children born to lower-class, black Jamaicans were illegitimate; thus the families into which they were born contained no incumbent of the husband-father position. According to Rodman (1965a, 1966, 1971), however, it is common among the lower classes in the Caribbean to "cohabit" with an opposite-sex adult, in more or less stable and permanent relationships, until past the child-bearing period (see Chapter Seven below). Children, during this time, generally reside with the mother and the man she is living with, who may or may not be the biological father. Thus, even though legal marriage is relatively uncommon for young and middle-aged adults, most people eventually do marry, and most households contain an adult couple of opposite sexes together with children. There is also a pattern, probably in the minority, of adult women and their officially illegitimate children living in the households of their own mothers, thus creating a residential unit similar to that found among the Nayar. The difference between the Nayar and Caribbean systems is primarily at the normative level: in Jamaica and Trinidad, at least, preferences are for legal marriage and nuclear households, but these preferences are rarely realized.[12] In a normative sense, then, one might argue that the nuclear family is in fact typical of Caribbean societies, even in areas where the official illegitimacy rate is high. The point, however, is quite controversial, and several authors (see particularly Reiss 1965, 1971:11-13) favor the point of view that there are Caribbean societies which do not conform to Murdock's generalization.

A study of North American Indian tribes also points out that the nuclear family is at best a very minor feature of social organization in several of them (Driver 1961:291-292). This is because the husband-father position and its associated social roles are sometimes quite indistinct; adult males identified and interacted more with their own kin group than with their wives and children. This situation occurred only among those Indian societies in which descent was reckoned along female lines (matrilineally) and where postmarital residence was with the family of the wife (matrilocal).[13] This descent pattern, interestingly enough, is the same as that practiced by the Nayar, who clearly did not have the nuclear family. In such situations, it is apparently possible for the families and kin groups of adult females to take over many of the functions which, according to Murdock, are invariably functions of the nuclear family.

Other examples of societies which appear to lack the nuclear family structure, or in which the nuclear family does not function as Murdock hypothesizes, could be elucidated. We have, however, covered the most prominent and frequently cited examples. Although there is *some* basis for disagreement about the merits of each example, taken collectively they provide fairly substantial evidence against the universality of the nuclear family. The wisest move, from a scientific point of view, in cases where there are some reservations about the accuracy of an hypothesis, is the conservative one: reject it. There is, at least, sufficient doubt about the universality of the nuclear family such that alternatives ought to be explored. The nuclear family is indeed exceedingly common; those societies in which it does not exist, either as the independent and predominant family structure or as the basis or "nucleus" of more extended forms, are clearly exceptions to the general rule. Murdock's statement of general characteristics of family systems is highly adequate from a descriptive point of view, in both its structural and functional aspects. However, since the nuclear family as he defines it does not appear to be *universal,* it is not a *necessary* component of human social organization.

The conclusion that the *nuclear* family is not an empirical universal, while valuable in itself, does not imply that the *family* is not universal. It means, rather, as Spiro (1968:76-79) and others have suggested, that we ought to search for an alternative definition of what constitutes a family. Murdock's definition of the nuclear family is quite detailed, and the more components attached to such a definition the less likely that the definition is universally applicable. We need, perhaps, a definition of broader scope. There have been several attempts along these lines, of which two are perhaps most interesting and instructive. They are those of Reiss (1965) and Weigert and Thomas (1971).[14]

Ira Reiss

Reiss' (1965) analysis of the universal components of family systems contains within it what is probably the most comprehensive original critique of Murdock's position to date. He concluded, on the basis of the information we covered above, that Murdock's definition is empirically inadequate as a statement of universal family components, and that a less specific definition is necessary to attain the objective of universality.

The definition Reiss offers is in fact much less specific in terms of structure, and less ambitious on the functional side, than was Murdock's. The cross-cultural evidence convinces Reiss that there is at least one society in the world in which sexual gratification, reproduction, and/or economic cooperation are not attached to any kind of family relationship. Furthermore, examples such as the kibbutz point out that many aspects of socialization may be, and in fact are, the province of nonfamily social structures. Reiss proposes, though, that a particular kind of socialization, which he calls "nurturant socialization," is always one consequence of family relationships. By nurturant socialization he means specifically the provision of emotional care and response, love and affection, particularly to infants.

Reiss (1965:449-450) cites evidence from studies of primate development (see especially Harlow 1958, 1962; Harlow and Harlow 1962) and studies of maternal separation (Yarrow 1964) as evidence in favor of his position that human infants must receive emotional support (nurturant socialization) in the early years of life if they are to develop into normal, functioning adults. Nurturant socialization is thus posited to be a functional prerequisite or requirement of human society. The question then becomes: how do various societies make structural provisions for nurturant socialization of the newborn? And what do these structures have in common?

Societies such as the Nayar, and perhaps the Caribbean and North American Indian societies we noted earlier, indicate that the nuclear family is not an inevitable feature of social organization, particularly with respect to the socialization function. (We'll discuss the case of the kibbutz in a moment.) Reiss hypothesizes that the element common to all social structures which provide nurturant socialization is simply that they are structured according to kinship.[15] Furthermore, he argues that the socializing agent must be a "primary group," permitting intimate and continued interaction among members, and must therefore be a relatively small group. What Reiss is actually positing here is not simply a definition which may be universally applied, but rather, like Murdock, an hypothesis subject to empirical test. He phrases the hypothesis as follows:

> The family institution is a small kinship structured group with the key function of nurturant socialization of the newborn. (Reiss 1965:449)

It is important to note that the empirical hypothesis contained in this definition does not involve the term "family." The hypothesis says, rather, that in all societies the social unit which is primarily responsible for the function of nurturant socialization is structured according to kinship. Reiss also stipulates that, when this coincidence of structure and function is observed, we may appropriately apply the label "family" to the small kinship-structured group. However, this stipulation has no empirical content, and is quite incidental to the hypothesis proposed.

Since Reiss' definition is actually an empirical hypothesis or proposition, it may be rejected if it does not conform to the evidence. What kinds of evidence might result in its rejection? This definition, like Murdock's, is subject to rejection if we find *one* society which does not conform to its specifications. Obviously, a society in which kinship-structured groups do not exist, or in which nurturant socialization of the newborn does not occur, would be a counter-instance to this definition.[16] This, however, does not seem likely. But a society in which the function of nurturant socialization is accomplished by some group which is not structured according to kinship would also cause the definition to be rejected. Some debate is possible on this point, primarily involving the Israeli kibbutz.

It will be recalled that, in the kibbutz, infants are separated from their parents at a very early age and entrusted to the care of "nurse-teachers" in a "children's house." From this time on, the responsibility for the physical care and education of the child lies with those who work in the children's houses. But Reiss (1965) argues that the child's parents are still very directly involved in the provision of emotional response, or, specifically, *nurturant* socialization. In this contention Reiss has strong support from Spiro, who describes the parent-child relationship in the kibbutz in these terms:

> Although the parents do not play an outstanding role in the socialization of their children, or in providing for their physical needs, it would be erroneous to conclude that they are unimportant figures in their children's lives. Parents are of crucial importance in the *psychological*

development of the child. They serve as the objects of his most important identifications, and they provide him with a certain security and
love that he obtains from no one else. If anything, the attachment of
the young children to their parents is greater than it is in our own society. (Spiro 1968:74)

Reiss' definition, then, is sufficiently broad in its structural component and specific in its functional component to include even the
experimental kibbutz. Because of these characteristics, this definition is not
nearly as descriptive of typical family systems as those proposed by Murdock
and others. But as far as our empirical knowledge of variability in family systems
extends at the moment, the definition seems to capture the minimal structural
and functional elements of all past or present family systems. This does not
prove in any way that the family as defined by Reiss is necessary or essential for
the survival of human societies, but at least we have not been able to *disprove*
such an argument empirically.

At the moment, it does not appear that Reiss' defini-
tion has been rejected by evidence of any society in which the function of
nurturant socialization is primarily accomplished by some structure other than a
small kinship-structured group. The Nayar and other societies mentioned as
counter-instances to Murdock's definition are not problematic for this one. This
does not mean, of course, that such evidence may not come to light at any time,
either in the form of new information about an existing society or in the form of
a new, large-scale, experimental society or community designed in such a manner
that it contradicts the definition. But the point is that Reiss' definition is in fact
an hypothesis, which may be, but has not yet been, rejected by the data. Until
such time as it is rejected, it is reasonable to operate on the premise that it is
empirically accurate.

An interesting argument has recently been proposed,
however, to the effect that Reiss' definition is incorrect on *logical* rather than
empirical grounds. The authors of this argument, Weigert and Thomas (1971),
propose an alternative definition, the relative merits of which we will now
examine.

Weigert and Thomas

Weigert and Thomas (1971:188–192) believe that Reiss'
definition of the family is incorrect, not because of existing counter-instances to
it, but because of certain inconsistencies in the method of its formulation, and
because it does not seem to them to allow for the *possibility* of counter-instances.
We will deal with these objections one at a time.

The first point, that Reiss' definition is improperly
formulated, revolves largely around a contention that the definition is tautologi-

cal or circular: in other words, not subject to empirical disproof. They interpret Reiss as starting with the premise that nurturant socialization is a universal family function and then looking at the variety of structures which have accomplished this function.

> Now that he has enunciated the universal function of the family (nurturant socialization), Reiss can label all institutions which perform this function as "family institutions." . . . (N)urturant socialization carries the label "family" such that whatever structure may be built around it is also called a family structure. Tautologically, therefore, whatever structure performs the function of nurturant socialization is a family structure. (Weigert and Thomas 1971:189)

If this assertion is correct, Reiss' hypothesis is true "by definition." He would simply be saying that we should call any social structure which performs the nurturant socialization function a family. Such arguments involve only the meanings we assign to terms, and cannot possibly be "wrong" in any empirical sense.

A brief perusal of the form of Reiss' definition, however, indicates that this is not the case. He does not say that any structure which functions for nurturant socialization should be called "the family," but rather that any structure which performs this function will be organized according to kinship. The label "family" may be applied to this *association* between structure and function, and this stipulation is of course tautological. But the association proposed by the definition is an empirical hypothesis and is *not* tautological, since each of its terms has an independent meaning.

The second major objection raised by Weigert and Thomas (1971:189) is that Reiss' definition violates the "postulate of indispensability," which is a basic error in the application of functionalist logic expressed by Robert Merton (1968:86–90). Merton points out that, for a variety of very good reasons, it is a mistake to assume that any particular social structure is necessary or indispensable for the fulfillment of any given function. Such assumptions operate to restrict the investigator's ability to perceive alternative ways in which a function might be fulfilled, or, in Merton's terminology, "functional alternatives" (1968:88).[17] Weigert and Thomas present their argument this way:

> Unless we are to be caught by the erroneous "postulate of indispensability," we cannot insist on the necessary universality of the "small kinship structured group" . . . as a "family" structure. Likewise, we cannot insist that nurturant socialization is a "family" function unless we limit ourselves to the observation that societies in the present and past had their "families" perform this function. (Weigert and Thomas 1971:189)

This point is worth considering carefully; as a general

guideline for the formulation of social theory, the postulate of indispensability is very important. However, I doubt that it applies in this specific case. It is one thing to assume or "insist" that a specific structure is indispensable for the accomplishment of some function, and quite another to *hypothesize* that a structure is invariably associated with a function. Weigert and Thomas argue quite persuasively against the former procedure; Reiss, however, did the latter. Hypotheses hypothesize, they do not insist. The key here, once again, is that Reiss' definition is perfectly susceptible to empirical rejection given adequate data.

Because of the problems they perceive with Reiss' definition, Weigert and Thomas suggest an alternative of their own. They contend that it is necessary for culture to be transmitted to each succeeding generation in order to mold infants into functioning human beings, and they term the relevant component of cultural transmission "symbolic patternvalue."[18] They contend, furthermore, that all that is required by way of social structure for the transmission of symbolic patternvalue is at least one developed social self (a socialized individual) in association with the infant. This is equivalent to an assertion that no particular structure is necessary. From this logic emanates their definition of the family:

> (F)amily is the primary order of the communication of symbolic patternvalue to the newborn. (Weigert and Thomas 1971:193)

In other words, the functional requisite specified is the "communication of symbolic patternvalue," and the social unit which accomplishes this communication, in any given society, is to be labeled "the family."

This definition, quite obviously, is not subject to falsification. It contains no hypothesis. It is, in short, a definition of a different order than Reiss' or Murdock's. The juxtaposition of these several definitions gives us an opportunity to make a rather important point about the nature and use of definitions in social science.

Quite a few years ago, Robert Bierstedt (1959) pointed out to sociologists a distinction between two very different kinds of statements which are both indicated by the term "definition." The first kind, a "nominal" definition, is by far the most common. The author of a nominal definition simply conveys, by the use of that definition, an intention to employ one word or phrase, the meaning of which is given, for another word or phrase which is lengthier, more cumbersome, or less clear. Nominal definitions are neither right nor wrong, and it is in fact meaningless to inquire as to whether or not they are correct, because they are tautologies. The meaning of one part of the definition is given by the other part. Such definitions may be more or less conventional according to accepted usage, but they cannot be right or wrong in any empirical sense because they have no empirical content, no "truth value." Weigert and

Thomas' definition of the family is a nominal definition: they convey by it their intention to apply the label "family" to any social structure which communicates "symbolic patternvalue" to the newborn. There is no evidence that could be marshaled for or against such a definition. The term "family" means, *by definition,* what they define it to mean.

Reiss' definition, however, is of a different kind. Bierstedt applies the term "real definition" to statements of this sort; they may also be called "universal affirmative propositions" (Bierstedt 1959:132). These statements are more than nominal definitions, since they contain propositions which have "truth value"—that is, they can be empirically evaluated. But they are also something more than ordinary propositions, which state simply that two or more phenomena are related in a particular way: they assert that two or more conceptually distinct phenomena are *empirically equivalent,* or that the empirical association between the components of the definition is invariant. To restate Reiss' definition, he is hypothesizing that, at the societal level, the primary agent of nurturant socialization is *always* a small kinship-structured group. (This is why one counter-instance would be sufficient for the rejection of this definition.) This is very different from saying that we should call small kinship-structured groups families. It is an empirical proposition subject to refutation by observational evidence.

Real definitions are not "better" than nominal definitions, they are simply different. They serve entirely different purposes and are evaluated by completely different criteria: real definitions according to whether or not they are true, nominal definitions according to whether or not they are useful for communication. The definition of the family offered by Weigert and Thomas is not an alternative to that of Reiss, because they are two very different kinds of statements. One is a particular and rigorous kind of empirical proposition; the other is a "dictionary definition" which cannot be empirically tested. It makes no sense, and serves no purpose, to substitute one of these kinds of definitions for the other.[19]

Conclusion

We may find, eventually, that Reiss' definition of the family is incorrect on empirical grounds: that is, we may find one or more societies in which nurturant socialization of the newborn is accomplished by some social structure which is not organized according to kinship. It is also possible that we may be able to expand or elaborate on either the structural or functional component of Reiss' definition if we find that the family systems of all societies actually have more in common than Reiss says they do. But for the moment, Reiss' proposition has not been empirically rejected. If and when it is, it will either be replaced by another real definition, or we will conclude that it cannot be replaced and that there are no two family-related characteristics which coincide in all societies. The latter finding would be conclusive evidence that the family is not a necessary component of human social organization. But so far we have found no evidence sufficient to reject Reiss' proposition.

If Reiss' definition of the family is "wrong," which it may well be, it is wrong on empirical rather than logical grounds. For the moment, though, since we have no evidence to contradict it, it is reasonable to proceed under the premise that all societies have groups which are structured according to kinship, and which function for (at least) nurturant socialization of the newborn. But while these are the two minimal defining characteristics of family systems, all such systems are much more complex and diverse than this. Reiss' definition may be taken as a statement of the uniformity of family systems, but what of their variability? The variation in family systems cross-culturally is indeed considerable, and the process which determines the family structure in any given society is quite complex. The range of variation in family structure, and the causes or sources of this variation, are the topics of the next two chapters.

Notes

1. See also Washburn and DeVore (1961). Their argument differs from the others in certain particulars, but agrees on the general explanatory factors.

2. See the following discussion of the universality of the family for an inquiry into the nature of definitions of the family.

3. The issue of sex-role differentiation will be analyzed in more detail in Chapter Eight. For the moment, we are concerned only with the correspondence between the origins of the family and early sex-role distinctions.

4. In this connection, it is interesting to note that Gough's (1971) article on the origins of the family was written specifically for a special issue of *Journal of Marriage and the Family* on "Sexism in Family Studies."

5. This section draws heavily on my previous article on this topic (Lee 1975a).

6. For the reader familiar with functional theory and its terminology, it may appear that our phrasing of the question violates Merton's (1968:86-90) "postulate of indispensability." However, this error is committed when one *assumes* the indispensability of a particular social structure for the accomplishment of some specified function, not when such indispensability is employed as an hypothesis. For a more detailed treatment of this issue, see Lee (1975a) and the discussion below. See also Wallace (1969:36-44) for a

concise explanation of the method of theory construction known as "functional imperativism," which forms the basis for this type of argument.

7. Persons to whom they are related through their mothers. See Chapter Six.

8. It is interesting to note that Marion Levy (1965), in a chapter written for another book, takes Bell and Vogel to task in a footnote for the seeming inconsistency between their introduction to Gough's article and the content of the article itself. The Gough article and its introduction orginally appeared in the 1960 edition of the Bell and Vogel compilation. Even more interesting is the fact that Levy's paper, together with the footnote in question, is reprinted in the second (1968) edition of Bell and Vogel; their introduction to Gough's paper, however, remained unchanged. See also Reiss (1965) for a similar observation on this introduction.

9. For a much more complete, yet concise, account of this topic, see Spiro (1954). It should also be noted, as Spiro does, that he studied only one kibbutz. There are and have been a great many kibbutzim in Israel, which exhibit a great deal of heterogeneity. Thus we are not attempting a general description of all kibbutzim, but simply reporting and assessing a case study of one of them. (It will be recalled that disproof of Murdock's hypothesis requires only one negative case.)

10. Citations are to Spiro's 1954 paper, which is reprinted, together with an addendum written in 1958, in Bell and Vogel (1968:68–79).

11. The highest frequency of female-headed households at the societal level observed by Adams was 26 percent for Nicaragua. He reports percentages of up to nearly 40 for certain regions and ethnic groups from his own research and that of Raymond Smith (1956) on British Guiana. For a more intensive treatment of the conceptual differences between the nature of systems and the statistical frequency of types comprising the systems, see our discussion of marital structure in Chapter Four.

12. We will discuss reasons for this particular difference between ideal and actual behavior in some detail in Chapter Seven.

13. See Chapter Six for definitions and detailed discussion of these terms.

14. For other definitions which are highly descriptive but are not empirically universal, see Stephens (1963:8) and Gough (1971:760).

15. In constructing the structural component of this definition, Reiss is following the lead of Levy and Fallers (1959).

16. However, a society which evinced neither kinship-structured groups nor nurturant socialization would *conform* to the hypothesis. See Lee (1975a).

17. Wallace (1969:27) suggests that the term "structural alternatives" would be more appropriate for this concept, since it refers to alternative structures for the fulfillment of specific functions.

18. This interpretation of the meaning of the term "symbolic patternvalue" is too abbreviated to communicate the full meaning of the concept as Weigert and Thomas intend it. However, it will suffice for our purposes. For a complete discussion of its meaning, see Weigert and Thomas (1971:192-194).

19. Again, for a much more intensive treatment of the subject of nominal and real definitions, see Lee (1975a) on the issue of universals.

chapter four

Structural variety in marriage

Introduction

Marital systems are almost always components of family systems. Analyses of marital and familial structures cannot proceed entirely independently of one another, because they have important reciprocal effects. The question of the sources of variation in marital structure, however, is to an extent theoretically independent of the issue of sources of variation in family structure. The attempts to explain cross-cultural variability in these two phenomena are, in other words, somewhat different, and thus the questions merit separate attention. We will deal, in this chapter, with the structure of marriage, after a few remarks about the relationship between marital and familial institutions.

For our purposes it is important to define the variables "marital structure" and "family structure" at an early point in the analysis. Family structure is given by the number of social positions (*not* the number of individuals) contained in a family, or in other words the number of different kinds or categories of individuals of which the family is comprised. Marriage, in contrast, has by definition only two social positions, that of husband and that of wife. The structure of the marriage, in our terminology, depends upon the number of different individuals who fill each position, or are "incumbents" of those positions, at any given time.[1]

George Murdock (1949), as we noted in Chapter Three, has argued that the nuclear family is the "building block" or nucleus around which all other family types are formed.[2] The nuclear family consists of, and is defined by, three and only three social positions: husband-father, wife-mother, and offsping-sibling (Winch 1971:11). According to Murdock, this unit can be "extended" in two basic ways. First, it can be elaborated by virtue of multiple marriage, and becomes a *polygamous* extended family. Second, it can be elaborated by means of generational expansion, to become a *consanguineally* extended family. We will discuss the permutations which may result from each type of extension. However, it now appears that it may be more useful theoretically to consider families which contain plural marriages, but no generational extension, as nuclear families. This is in conformity with my statement above that family structure is defined by number of positions rather than number of individuals; *any* of the three nuclear-family positions may have more than one incumbent without altering the basically nuclear structure of the family itself. A multiple marriage, therefore, makes a multiple marriage, which is something different from an extended family. The major reason for this conceptual distinction is that the theoretical explanations advanced to account for variation in marital structure differ in certain strategic respects from those attempting to account for variation in family structure, as we shall discover in this chapter and the next. It is therefore advisable to avoid conceptual confounding between these two types of structures insofar as possible.

Variation in marital structure

In contrast to his very specific definition of the family, Murdock gives a broad and inclusive definition of marriage: ". . . a complex of customs centering upon the relationship between a sexually associating pair of adults within the family" (1949:1). He does not list what these customs might be, presumably because no one set of customs would apply to marriage in all societies.

Probably all societies have some such set of customs, and a type (or types) of relationship to which they are applied, which we might call "marriage" without too much confusion. However, the great variety of marital systems in the world has caused many researchers to despair of ever constructing a definition of marriage which would incorporate all the varieties, but exclude relationships which are clearly not instances of marriage. The question is, how arbitrary can the researcher be in specifying what is and what is not a marriage? The consensus, in general, is that any relationship which is deemed by the members of a society to be a marriage is, by that fact, a marriage. On this basis, several scholars have attempted definitions, purported to be universally applicable or nearly so, which enumerate the minimal characteristics of marital relationships. An example of such a definition is that of William Stephens:

> Marriage is a socially legitimate sexual union, begun with a public announcement and undertaken with some idea of permanence; it is assumed with a more or less explicit marriage contract, which spells out reciprocal obligations between spouses, and between spouses and their future children. (Stephens 1963:5)

There are several difficulties with this definintion, including such matters as the ambiguity of some of the key terms (socially legitimate," "permanence") as well as the fact that the definition is almost certainly not universally applicable: there are several societies whose marital practices do not conform to one or more stipulations of the definition. Stephens clearly and explicitly recognizes these limitations (1963:5-7). But for the moment, as a statement which is broadly descriptive of the marital practices of *most* societies, this definition will suit our purposes.

The question in which we are currently interested, and which falls under the heading of marital structure, involves the number and kinds of people who are identified by the term "spouse" in Stephens' definition. One should not assume that this term invariably refers to *two* people, one male and one female, who are married to each other. There are, in fact, four different kinds of marital structure, which are distinguished from one another according to the number of people of each sex who are simultaneously involved in a marriage.[3]

Any marriage consists of two and only two social positions: that of husband and that of wife. But this does not mean that the marriage consists of only two individuals, although there must be at least two. If we distinguish between singular and plural incumbency of each position, as is customary, there are four theoretically possible types of marriage: monogamy, polygyny, polyandry, and group marriage (also known as cenogamy).

Monogamy is the type with which members of Western societies are most familiar: the marriage of one husband to one wife. In the United States and most other industrialized societies, it is now the only legal form of marriage. Americans, when they think of a marriage or of anything having to do with a marriage, tend to think of monogamy. It is easy to assume, on the basis of our informal observations, that this is the "normal" type of marriage and that any other form is, if not actually deviant, at least unusual. Not so.

In George Murdock's (1949) sample of 250 societies, he had sufficient information on 238 of them to allow him to determine the "normal" type of marriage for each society. By "normal," in this case, he does not mean the most prevalent form of marriage in a statistical sense, but rather the type of marriage permitted, preferred, and "encouraged by public opinion" (1949:28).[4] Monogamy was described as the preferred or ideal type of marriage for only 43 societies, or 18 percent (1949:28). Societies whose members regard monogamy as the ideal form are clearly in the minority.

If monogamy is not the most preferred form of marriage in the world at the societal level, what is? There are only three possibilities left, all of which are specific types of the more general category of plural marriages, or "polygamy." The first is *polygyny*, the marriage of one husband to two or more wives. The second is *polyandry*, where one wife is married to two or more husbands. Finally, there is *group marriage* or *cenogamy*, which involves two or more representatives of each sex. These three subtypes of polygamy, in combination with monogamy, exhaust the set of logically possible marital forms.

In a cross-cultural sense, and in terms of cultural ideals or preferences, polygamous marriages are far more common than monogamous ones. But the three subtypes of polygamy are far from equally preferred. Murdock found that, of the three varieties of polygamy, in his sample of 238 societies, two favored polyandry, none preferred group marriage, and polygyny was the ideal in 193, or more than 81 percent.

The 238 societies on which Murdock based these estimates are, of course, a very select set of all societies, and it is possible that these estimates may be somewhat extreme. However, on a later and larger sample of 565 societies (Murdock's World Ethnographic Sample), he found (1957:686) polygyny to be favored in almost 75 percent, and monogamy in less than 25 percent. It is clear, then, that polygyny is the ideal in the vast majority of the world's societies. What could possibly cause this pattern?

Polygyny

Several authors have suggested that the widespread popularity of polygyny has its roots in the comparative strength of the male sex drive. For example, Adams notes:

> A thesis proposed to account for the prevalence of polygyny is that men are generally governed by internal sex drives and disposed toward sexual variety to a much greater extent than are women. If this is so, then men are subjected to a greater strain in monogamous marriages than women are. (Adams 1971:17; see Nimkoff 1965:17 for a similar statement)[5]

Since men typically occupy the principle positions of authority, they are able to impose their wishes upon women, and thus to structure the marital institution in such a way as to allow themselves to gratify their drives for sexual variety. Women, who have no such drive and no power to actualize it if they did, are often forced to share their husbands with other women, but almost never allowed the privilege of multiple husbands.

This explanation obviously has a number of major shortcomings, in addition to its clear conflict with current sex-role ideologies. Upon closer inspection, it appears to conform rather poorly to the facts, and to be very culture-bound in certain important respects. Let's look at the evidence. There are at least four strikes against this explanation.

First, it hinges on an assumption about the relative strength of the male and female sex drives. It is not at all clear that the male sex drive is any stronger, in any respect, than the female, contrary to the assumption. In fact, what evidence we have points in the other direction (see Masters and Johnson 1966; Reiss 1971:135). Men are not following any biological imperative by accumulating multiple wives. Their apparently more voracious sexual appetites are, in all probability, outcomes of cultural conditioning. Since this particular social difference between the sexes is common to our culture as well as most others, we have a tendency to attribute the frequency of polygyny to it. But the explanation is culture-bound or ethnocentric. Biology is not irrelevant to the issue, but polygyny is not a direct product of an innately stronger male sex drive, since the male sex drive is not innately stronger.

Second, it sometimes comes as a shock to Westerners that, in societies which prefer polygyny, it is favored by women as well as men. This, too, might be blamed on cultural conditioning, and this is no doubt at least partially correct. People can be taught to respond favorably to just about anything, no matter how inherently objectionable it may "really" be. But, as we will see shortly, polygyny offers women many concrete advantages in those societies where it is practiced, particularly of an economic nature. It appears that women are rarely coerced into accepting polygynous marriages against their wills; in fact, "senior" wives are often instrumental in convincing their (sometimes reluctant) husbands to acquire second and third wives (see Leslie 1973: 27-28). Of course, not all wives are pleased about expanding their marriages (Stephens 163:49-63), but neither are all husbands.

Third, it has often been remarked that polygyny, or any form of multiple marriage, seems to be inconsistent with the natural tendency of populations toward roughly equal sex ratios. A society in which each man is enjoined to take, say, four wives will soon run out of maritally eligible women. This is a primary reason why, even in societies where polygyny is the ideal, most marriages are in fact monogamous. Nature limits the extent to which the ideal can be realized. But there are cultural customs in polygynous societies which do permit polygyny to exist as a going concern and which, not incidentally, make the argument that polygyny is caused by the supposedly stronger male sex drive seem most unlikely. The problem of the generally equal sex ratio is usually handled, according to Murdock and Whiting, by cultural customs concerning sex differences in age at marriage.

> With the proportion of the sexes approximately equal, extensive polygyny means that a good many men have no wives or only one. While some women get married almost immediately after puberty, the men usually do not get their first wife until sometime in their twenties; it is not until they get relatively old that they obtain more than one wife. The result is that a typical polygamous society will have a number of young women married to one old man. (Murdock and Whiting 1951:25)

If polygynous marriage is an institution which functions to satisfy the male sex drive, one would think that multiple wives would be allocated primarily to younger men, whose sexual urges are generally believed to be more intense. But this is definitely not the case; the older men get the wives. Not that they have forgotten what to do with them—on the contrary, there are clearly important sexual aspects of polygynous marriages involving older men. Masters and Johnson (1966) have found that men who are sexually active in their earlier years are quite capable, in the absence of specific sexually debilitating diseases, of continuing to be sexually active at least into the eighties, far beyond the life expectancies of men in most polygynous societies. The point, though, is that polygynous marital systems make it *less* likely than monogamous systems that young adult males, who are actually or supposedly at the peak of their sexual prowess, will get even one wife as an object for this drive, much less a sufficient number for them to exercise their "innnate" propensity for variety.

A further and related error in the logic of this argument is also quite obvious, at least once it is pointed out. Even if, for the sake of the argument, we were to grant the point that men are biologically endowed with a drive for sexual variety, it does not at all follow that men should therefore attempt to acquire multiple wives. It rather follows that men should be interested in acquiring multiple *sexual partners*. As Leslie (1973:28-29) points out, men in most societies are usually quite able to get sex without marriage. The conception of sex as a right bestowed only by marriage is found in only a minority of cultures, one of which is ours. Consequently, even as social scientists, we have a culturally induced tendency to explain many aspects of marital phenomena in terms of the sexual component of the relationship. This is an error stemming from ethnocentrism. Young, unmarried men in polygynous societies are most unfortunate individuals indeed if they cannot find an outlet, or more likely many outlets, for sexual expression.

Since sex is not often an advantage singularly granted by marriage, although marriage always entails sexual privileges (Fox 1967: 54-55), it is quite certain that men in polygynous societies do not marry for the purpose of obtaining sexual partners. Indeed, since sex is available elsewhere, marriage would be a high price to pay for this advantage alone. The lot of the husband of several wives rarely if ever conforms to the American schoolboy stereotype of the Arabian shiek whose harem is ready and waiting to provide him his every pleasure. Linton (1936:183-187) feels that the polygynous husband should be pitied, not envied, by other men.

> . . . there are few polygynous societies in which the position of the male is really better than it is under monogamy. If the plural wives are not congenial, the family will be torn by feuds in which the husband must take the thankless role of umpire, while if they are congenial he is likely to be confronted by an organized female opposition. . . . If all a man's wives want a particular thing, they can work on him in shifts and are fairly certain to get what they want. (Linton 1936: 186-187)

It is now clear that Linton somewhat overstated the case here. However, his point is certainly worth considering.

If sex is not a particularly powerful motivation for marriage in polygynous societies, what is? Linton is led by his analysis to conclude that the popularity of polygyny "derives more from the general primate tendency for males to collect females than from anything else" (1936:185). From a social scientific point of view, this explanation borders on the unpalatable. It does not explain polygynous marriage, it merely categorizes the human version of it as a special case of a "general primate tendency," which is itself unexplained. Furthermore, if it is in fact a predisposition inherent in all primates, what would account for the instances of its nonoccurrence? Explanations of polygyny in terms of biological imperatives, primate tendencies, or any aspect of "human nature" simply will not do, because the pattern of its occurrence is variable rather than universal. We need, in this case, to look for the correlates of polygyny.

In an earlier study of this topic based on the 565 societies in Murdock's World Ethnographic Sample, Dwight Heath (1958) discovered one important correlate of polygynous marriage. He found that the greater the extent to which women contributed to production in a society, the more likely were the members of that society to favor polygyny. It is also the case that, where the labor of women is valuable, that of children is also. And polygynous marriages produce more children per family than any other form of marriage.[6] Polygynous marriages may therefore by favored where, from an economic standpoint, large families are advantageous and women can make substantial contributions to subsistence. These conditions are most likely to be found where the basis for the economy is subsistence horticulture. In such situations each agricultural worker can usually contribute more to production than he or she consumes. Each wife, together with her children, may have her own field which she works with occasional assistance from her husband on the heavier tasks. The more wives a man has, the more fields his family can tend, and the more food they can produce. Polygynous marriage is thus a subsistence advantage for the entire family.

This situation also exists when animal husbandry is a major means of subsistence. The daily care and feeding of the animals is usually the province of women and children. Thus, the more wives a man has, the more children he will have, and the larger his herds or flocks may be. An excellent example of this is the Siwai society, where the economy is based primarily on the raising of pigs. The Siwai ethnographer reports that polygynous marriages are desirable to Siwai men because of the potential they provide for enlarging the herds of pigs:

> It is by no mere accident that polygynous households average more pigs than monogamous ones. Informants stated explicitly that some men married second and third wives in order to enlarge their herds. They laughed at the writer's suggestion that a man might become polygynous in order to increase his sexual enjoyment. ("Why pay bride price when for a handful of tobacco you can copulate with other women as often as you like!") (Oliver 1955:352)

In a second study of the correlates of marital structure, Marie Osmond (1965) selected a sample of five hundred societies from the World Ethnographic Sample and from early reports on the subsequent Ethnographic Atlas. The societies were selected according to culture areas to minimize the effects of diffusion (see Chapter Two). Since this precaution was not taken in the Heath study, Osmond's results are somewhat more trustworthy. They are also slightly different.

Osmond did not find a correlation between polygyny and proportional female contribution to subsistence, at least at the bivariate level. She did find, however, that these two variables were positively related among societies whose economies were based on rudimentary horticulture and/or herding (1965:10-11). Since, as we argued above, potential female contribution to subsistence is greatest under precisely these conditions, Osmond's findings specify rather than contradict those of Heath. There may well be insufficient variance in female contribution to subsistence in other types of economies to allow this correlation to emerge (Aronoff and Crano 1975).

Osmond's analysis was more extensive than this, however. She incorporated several other variables which were found to be related to type of marital structure. In addition to the relationships already noted, she found that polygyny was disproportionately common in economies based on rudimentary horticulture and/or animal husbandry with little or no craft specialization, a stratification system based on hereditary aristocracy, a minimal state level of political integration, and a nomadic or dispersed settlement pattern with typically small communities of between one hundred and one thousand residents (1965:10). Monogamy was related to a different set of values of these variables: an economy based on intensive agriculture with a craft specialization of at least three distinct specialties; a complex stratification system of three or more social classes; a large state level of political integration; and a settlement pattern of towns or compound settlements with at least occasional large cities of fifty thousand population or more (1965:10).

How should these relationships be interpreted? Osmond suggests (1965:14-16) that, if one examines the variables related to marital structure as a set, it is clear that monogamy is favored by societies which are more "complex" than those which favor polygyny. The data indicate, therefore, a positive relationship between a cultural preference for polygyny and a composite variable which we might term "societal complexity," the components of which are those variables noted above as correlates of marital structure. The appropriate inference from the information presented thus far is that more complex societies prefer monogamy, with the less complex tending toward polygyny. This conforms with the commonsense observation that modern nation-states, the most complex societies of all, are uniformly monogamous.

This, however, is only a partial picture of the total relationship. Osmond constructed a scale of societal complexity based on the variables mentioned thus far, and examined the relationship between societal complexity as indexed by this scale and type of marital structure (monogamous or polygynous). She found that, while monogamy was clearly most common among the most complex societies, a preference for polygyny was most marked among societies at *intermediate* levels of the scale. The least complex societies in the sample were more likely than those at intermediate levels to be monogamous, although this tendency was less pronounced than among societies at the most complex end of the continuum. The overall relationship, then, is curvilinear, with polygyny least common among those societies at the extremes of the complexity dimension.

The most effective and concise interpretation of this pattern in the data seems to flow again from the role played by females in economic production. The least complex societies in the sample are those whose economies are based upon hunting and gathering; agriculture has not been developed. Here, women typically do make a very substantial contribution to the production of food, particularly by the gathering of fruits and other plants.

But large families are not an advantage here, and except in rare cases are probably a disadvantage, becuase small units produce (or rather find) more food per person than large units except when the environment is unusually lush. A polygynous marriage produces many children, and the family may easily grow too large, in terms of sheer numbers, to support itself off the land.

Additional evidence for this position comes from Boserup's (1970) study of women's economic roles, which focuses largely on Africa. After documenting the extensive contribution to subsistence in African horticulture made by women, she demonstrates the considerable economic advantages which accrue to families with multiple wives in horticultural societies (1970:15-41). This is not the case, though, in more densely populated regions where the plow has been introduced and where crops are grown on permanent fields, because here the labor required is heavier and thus tends to become the province of males (1970:47). Here, extra wives may be burdensome to support, and polygyny is infrequent and limited to the wealthy. Boserup summarizes her findings as follows:

> (T)wo broad groups may be identified: the first type is found in regions where shifting cultivation predominates and the major part of agricultural work is done by women. In such communities, we can expect to find a high incidence of polygamy. . . . The second group is found where plough cultivation predominates and where women do less agricultural work than men. In such communities we may expect to find that only a tiny minority of marriages, if any, are polygynous. (Boserup 1970:50)

Polygyny, then, is clearly related in a positive direction to the economic contributions which women, within the parameters of the subsistence system, can make. Men, because their additional wives and the children they produce are economic assets, can either increase their families' production or enjoy greater leisure. This situation is most likely in societies characterized by extensive or intensive horticulture and/or by animal husbandry. In other economic circumstances, polygyny is relatively unlikely. It is therefore also unlikely that the explanation of polygyny resides either in characteristics of the male sex drive or in the male's presumably inherent tendency to accumulate females (see Osmond 1965:16).

There is also a political factor which must be considered, at least as a part of the motivation for a male to take on multiple wives. In a great number of societies, virtually all social relationships are based upon, or mediated by, kinship, either consanguineal ("blood") or affinal (in-law). The more extensive one's kin network, the more potential allies one has in case of conflict, the more support in times of economic hardship, etc. Therefore, one may enter into marriage partly in order to obtain in-laws, who may be valuable assets in a variety of situations (see Oliver 1955:223-225 for the case of the

Siwai). This logic has not yet been developed to the point where we can employ it to explain cross-cultural variation in the preference for polygyny, since kin may be valuable resources in virtually any kind of society. But it does point out that there are many motivations for polygynous marriage other than sexual desires.

The widespread popularity of polygyny as an ideal or preferred marital form gives rise to several kinds of questions. Most of them center on the issue of how polygyny can possibly be viable in any society given (1) the usually balanced sex ratio, and (2) the obvious possibilities for conflict among co-wives. It would seem, at first glance, that these potential problems would render polygynous marital systems inherently unstable, both statistically and interpersonally. This, however, is not the case.

First, on the matter of statistics: how is it possible for every man to have two or more wives when the sex ratio (the number of males per 100 females) hovers near 100 in all known societies? The answer, of course, is that it's not possible. It is a virtual certainty that the great majority of marriages in any society will be monogamous, regardless of cultural preferences. (After all, most Americans would prefer to be rich, but few of us are.) Polygynous marriage, in many societies that favor it, is often an ideal attained only by the privileged few, as we noted above in our consideration of the causes of polygyny.[7] This in no way diminishes its status as an ideal, but does serve to compromise the ideal with the hard reality of the sex ratio.

In polygynous societies, then, wives are scarce resources. The question thus becomes, how are these scarce resources allocated? We have already partially answered this question when we indicated above that polygyny is generally a privilege reserved for older men. But this privilege is not simply bestowed upon men by virtue of their attaining a certain age. Rather, like any scarce resource, wives are difficult and "expensive" to obtain. There is first of all the matter of the "bride price," gifts or services which must be rendered to the bride's family by the groom or his family. This practice is quite widespread in polygynous societies; we shall have more to say about it later when we discuss marital formation (Chapter Seven). The bride price is usually quite difficult to accumulate, since it is rarely just a token payment. It is rather part of an exchange between the two families involved in the marriage which serves to further solidify their relationship and, not incidentally, help insure the stability of the marriage. Young men and their families do not often have the requisite capital for one bride price, let alone two or more. It is the older, more well-established and senior men, who have been able to accumulate sufficient resources to exchange for wives (see Patai 1959:39–40).

This economic problem in obtaining wives is related to another common feature of polygynous societies involving sex differentials in age at marriage. It is generally the case in these societies, as we have noted, that women marry for the first time shortly after puberty, or sometimes even before. The average age at first marriage for men, on the other hand, tends to be considerably higher (Murdock 1949:27; Murdock and Whiting 1951; Boserup 1970), partly because of the rigid economic prerequisites for marriage, and partly because the norms of polygynous cultures prescribe late marriage for men. One consequence of this is that, at any given point in time, the number of maritally eligible women in the population will be greater than the number of maritally eligible men, since women become eligible at an earlier point in their lives. Thus, while some men will have two or more wives, others (the younger ones) will have none, and still others (probably the majority) will have only one. The marital *system*, nonetheless, is usefully classified as polygynous if polygyny is preferred or valued by the culture.

So even in nominally polygynous marital systems, the practice of polygyny is almost certain to be characteristic of a minority, and is sometimes quite uncommon. But where polygynous marriages do occur, don't they present unique problems in the maintenance of interpersonal relations within the marriage? One would think (depending, of course, on one's cultural background) that jealousy among co-wives would be a practically insurmountable problem. And it is apparently the case that the members of multiple marriages do experience this problem with some frequency.

Stephens (1963:56-63) reports on numerous instances of jealousy among co-wives, and notes that consideration of the problem is built into the culture and folklore of many polygynous societies. It seems, however, that the ethnocentric tendency of many observers of polygyny is to err in overestimating the extent of the problem and the intensity of jealousy when it does occur.

It seems only "natural," to most Americans, that women should experience some feelings of intense resentment, rejection, and of course hostility if they are forced, or asked, to share their husbands with other women. But the evidence clearly points out that, while jealousy and hostility are always possible in this arrangement, they are in no way inevitable. The potential for jealousy between co-wives is hardly a deterrent to polygynous marriages in societies that encourage them, at least on any large scale. The relationships between a man's several wives may indeed be tense. But, as Linton (1936, 1959) points out, this may be a bigger problem for the husband than for the wives.

As this discussion has implied, ideas of sexual exclusivity between married pairs, or conceptions of marriage as a strictly dyadic union, are culturally developed. If one has not been raised in a culture which espouses these values, then one will probably not internalize them. This is not to say that jealousy and friction won't arise in polygynous marriages if only the culture approves of them, because any intimate association between two or more human beings is likely to generate its fair share of such tensions. It is to say, though, that there is nothing uniquely or intrinsically anxiety-producing about plural marriages. Numerous scholars have remarked, however, that jealousy between co-wives in polygynous marriages seems to be more common than jealousy between co-husbands in polyandrous marriages. This may seem somewhat suprising, in light of the typically greater value placed on female virginity in our society as well as most others (Reiss 1967; Kaats and Davis 1970), and in light of the common tendency of primate males to attempt to exercise complete sexual dominance over a number of females (Linton 1936; van den Berghe 1973). It is perhaps explained by the fact that marital decisions, in any kind of polygamous society, are generally made by males. Men enter together into polyandrous marriages primarily by their own volition; women usually have less authority to decide whether they will or will not share their husbands (Stephens 1963:56–57; Nye and Berardo 1973:38).

There are, as it turns out, two categories of factors which make polygynous marriages viable in an interpersonal sense. One consists of safeguards or precautions against conflict which are normally taken in polygynous societies. The other involves the advantages which accrue to the members of polygynous marriages by virtue of the fact that they contain several wives. Each factor is important.

Two conditions which probably tend to minimize interpersonal problems seem to go together in a way, at least in an either-or sense. Specifically, either (1) co-wives are sisters, or (2) each wife has a separate hut or residence for herself and her children. The practice in which all the wives of one man are sisters is called *sororal* polygyny, and is very common in polygynous societies. Murdock (1949:31) found that, of 193 polygynous societies, sororal polygyny was the preferred or sometimes required form in 70; he speculates that the proportion would be higher if the ethnographers were more explicit in reporting marital customs. It is quite reasonable to expect co-wives to get along better, and to feel less jealousy, if they are sisters than if they are strangers (Leslie 1973:29). Furthermore, it is usually true that where co-wives are sisters, they all live together in one household; this was the case in 44 out of 47 societies with sororal polygyny in the World Ethnographic Sample (Murdock 1957). But when nonsororal polygyny is practiced (co-wives are not sisters), each wife usually has her own household. The husband then visits each wife in rotation, not according to his particular preferences of the moment, but according to whose turn it is on an established schedule. Murdock feels (Murdock and Whiting 1951:20–21) that the practice of giving each wife a separate residence if the wives are unrelated is a concession to, and a means of minimizing, the possibility of competition and rivalry among wives. The practice of each wife's having her own household is sometimes called "hut" polygyny; when all wives live together, the term "harem" polygyny is often applied. Both sororal and hut polygyny would seem to minimize the potential for conflict in polygynous marriages. Since societies rarely combine these two procedures, we might infer that each one is probably fairly effective.

Another practice that is quite common, and which probably mitigates conflict, is the imposition of a clear status hierarchy among the wives themselves. In most polygynous marriages there is a "senior wife," usually the first, who is the head of the distaff side of the family. She has authority in certain areas over the other wives, assigns productive and maintenance tasks to them, and generally functions as the family's secondary leader, after the husband. This probably has an effect similar to that of the requirement that the husband sleep with each of his wives in rotation, according to a set schedule. Both reduce the number of things wives have to fight about. Where authority or procedures are clearly and firmly established, then they are removed from the field of competition. The more unequivocally each spouse's rights and obligations are specified by the rules, the less the ambiguity, and the less the overt competition for scarce rewards. Conflict between wives would not change the authority structure or bring a wife more sexual attention or favoritism from her husband, since these things are according to the rules not negotiable (see Murdock 1949:30; Nye and Berardo 1973:39).

The second kind of factor which probably operates to reduce tension in polygynous families and to minimize resentment between co-wives is that polygyny provides certain personal advantages to all concerned, especially in terms of economics and social status. As we have already mentioned, in polygynous societies wives are relatively scarce resources, and therefore difficult and expensive to obtain. But once they are obtained, they often have considerable value in the production of further resources. We noted the case of the Siwai (Oliver 1955; Stephens 1963:54–55), among whom pigs are the benchmark of wealth, where the task of maintaining these valuable delights is allocated to wives. The wives tend the gardens which produce food for the pigs. The more wives one has, the more gardens, and the more gardens, the more pigs. Large herds of pigs provide many economic advantages, both real and symbolic, to the families which own them. And Ronald Berndt (1965) speaks of the advantages, in terms of division of labor, care of indigent members, and diffusion of responsibility for care of children, which polygyny offers to the Murngin of North-eastern Arnhem Land. There are numerous other examples of the productive value of plural wives in many societies. This is hardly surprising in light of the fact that polygyny tends to be favored in societies where women have considerable productive value, and where large families are a resource. It takes a prosperous family to acquire more than one wife, but once wives are acquired they add to the family's prosperity. The work load of the senior wives is generally lightened by the addition of junior wives, so that each wife stands to benefit personally from increments to the ranks. In most polygynous households, wives are much more functional than ornamental.

Stephens (1963:53) reported on a small sample of societies on which he had rather extensive ethnographic reports. Of thirteen polygynous societies on which he had sufficient information, he found that being a member of a polygynous marriage was a mark of status and a source of prestige in eleven. Wives as well as husbands find their status in the community increased by the addition of other wives; this seems to be particularly true for senior wives. One author, in fact, is moved to construct an analogy between the accumulation of wives in polygynous societies and certain aspects of conspicuous consumption (a large house, domestic help, expensive vacations, etc.) in suburban America (Leslie 1973:27-28). He notes particularly the increments to wives' status which accrue by virtue of polygyny, and paints a picture of a status-conscious senior wife nagging her reluctant husband into finding a second wife. This can be carried too far, of course. But the basic point, and an important one, is that polygyny is not inevitably forced upon unwilling but subservient women by domineering, lecherous men. There are, in fact, many reports of women being the prime movers in the acquisition of more wives for their husbands.[8] It is obvious that, from the woman's point of view, being one of several wives has a number of distinct advantages. But, as Stephens points out in his own summary of this issue,

> . . . some co-wives are jealous and others apparently aren't. There appear to be great differences between societies as well as between individual co-wives within the same society. (Stephens 1963:62-63)

Perhaps the safest conclusion here is that reluctance to share one's husband is clearly not a feature of female human nature, whatever that is. Jealousy is not inevitable. Undoubtedly polygyny could not be superimposed upon an ongoing culture, such as that of the United States, which places a great premium on dyadic romantic attraction, sexual exclusivity and fidelity of married couples, and the social value of monogamous marriage without producing inordinate amounts of psychological stress. But in societies with cultural traditions which support the value of polygyny it probably works rather well, and is by no means as unwieldy as most Westerners would initially imagine it to be.

Polyandry

The World Ethnographic Sample (Murdock 1957) lists only four societies which are said to be characterized by polyandry, the marriage of one woman to several men. These are the Nayar,[9] the Marquesans, the Toda, and Tibet (see also Stephens 1963:33; Kephart 1972:34-35). Again it should be noted that this does not mean that polyandry is (or was) the dominant form of marriage in these societies in a statistical sense, for almost certainly most marriages in any society are monogamous. It means, rather, that the cultural definition of the "ideal marriage" in these societies specifies polyandry.

Polyandry has often been termed "unnatural" (see, for example, Stephens 1963:34) because of its relative rarity and because of the presumed tendency for men to collect women rather than vice versa. This seems to be a rather poor way to characterize a behavior which typifies entire societies, even if there are only four societies involved. A much more appropriate term, which is far less value-laden, would simply be "unusual." It appears that polyandry as a cultural practice is rare because it is engendered by economic and, perhaps, political circumstances which are themselves unusual.

Since there are so few documented cases of societies which practice polyandry, it is difficult to hazard generalizations about its causes which can be conceived as statistically valid. It is probably well, in this case, to think of the kinds of factors which *predispose* societies to adopt polyandry, rather than factors which determine its adoption. Leslie makes this point in conjunction with an hypothesis that "extreme societal poverty" is a predisposing condition (1973:32-33). That is, a polyandrous marital system may be a "coping mechanism" for societies whose members exist on the bare margins of subsistence; however, extreme poverty does not result in polyandry with any great frequency, because there are many very poor societies which do not practice it. Polyandry is one of a number of structural alternatives for societies which exist under harsh economic conditions.

How might polyandry serve to alleviate the hardships caused by limited resources? First, and most obvious, is the fact that polyandry is a very effective means of holding the population in check, or of preventing rapid population growth. Polyandrous marriages produce relatively few children, for the simple reason that a woman with four husbands can produce no more children than a woman with one in any given span of years. Thus polyandry has been found in certain societies where small families and little or no population growth might be deemed an advantage by virtue of the scarcity of resources. But obviously not all societies where resources are scarce practice polyandry; some additional factors must also be operative. My guess, and it is only a guess, is that polyandry is a viable option where resources are scarce *and* where there are few productive tasks which can be assigned to women and children. In many non-industrialized societies large families are advantageous: members can normally contribute more to production than they consume. But in some societies this is not the case. This situation might arise either in agriculturally based societies where arable land is at a premium, or economies based primarily on hunting where game is quite scarce.

The Tibetans studied by Prince Peter (1965) are an excellent example of the first circumstance. He reports (1965:200-201) that the economy of Tibet was primarily agricultural, and that farmland was a rather scarce commodity. This was true for two reasons. First, the climate in this region is quite harsh, and the high elevation and mountainous terrain made farming a difficult and chancy occupation. Second, according to custom and the legal structure, all land in Tibet was controlled by either the church, the government, or the landed aristocracy. The peasants, those who actually worked the land, did not really own their farms but, in effect, rented them from one of these three agencies. Rents amounted to perhaps two thirds of the annual produce of the farm (see also Winnington 1957), and the peasants retained their tenancy of the land only by the grace of the landlords. There was consequently little for a family to gain by expanding their lands and increasing production, because virtually any surplus went for rent and taxes. And there was considerable benefit in continuity of tenancy from one generation to the next, to secure the rights of the tenants to occupy the land.

Polyandry in Tibet was usually "fraternal." That is, the co-husbands of a single wife were normally brothers. The children borne by the wife were then the children of all the brothers. When the sons matured, they would take a wife and the family property would be passed on to them as a group. In this way, the property did not need to be subdivided, and the family was unlikely to grow too large to be supported by the land.

> Tibetans were very keen not to divide their property and anxious, also, not to let their family name die out. In order to attain these two objectives, they practiced polyandry. . . . Polyandry was practiced because in this way a number of brothers living on a family property could keep it undivided by taking one wife in common and sharing her, the land and the children among themselves. If there were no children, adoption was resorted to, so keen were the Tibetans to keep the property undivided and to hand down the family name. (Peter 1965:197-198)[10]

George Murdock supports the argument that polyandry is practicable "where women make an insignificant contribution to the economic life." He draws upon the Todas of India as an example of this point.

> The men, in addition to their political, religious, and ceremonial functions, do the herding, milking, churning, fuel gathering, building, trading, and cooking. In the absence of agriculture and important domestic arts, the female share in the division of labor by sex is confined to such comparatively minor activities as fetching water, mending and embroidering clothes, pounding and sifting grain, sweeping the floor, and cleaning the household utensils. (Murdock 1949:36)

The question remains, of course, of why it is that the Toda allocated so few productive tasks to women; this in itself is highly unusual (Aronoff and Crano 1975). But the fact is that they did, and it is not surprising that, in this society, several men could share one wife without severely overtaxing her energies.

The Kaingang of Brazil are a good example of a hunting society in which polyandry had a definite function. Although the Kaingang did not consider polyandry to be the ideal or preferred form of marriage, and are thus not mentioned among the four "polyandrous societies" listed above, their marital norms were quite flexible, and all forms of marriage were represented among them at least occasionally. Analyzing Kaingang genealogies for a one-hundred-year period, the ethnographer (Henry 1941:45) concluded that about 14 percent of all marriages were polyandrous. The primary means of subsistence for these people was hunting, an activity which is almost exclusively a male province in virtually all societies (Murdock 1937; Stephens 1963:282-283). Because women were permitted multiple lovers as well as multiple husbands, one of their principle values was their ability to attract hunters (men) to the small, wandering bands of which the society was composed.

> Even after her marriage a woman's amorous intrigues are of consider-able advantage to those around her—even to her own husband, for every time she attracts a man she has added a hunter to the band. ... His presence is welcome, of course, for another gun or bow and another knife and axe mean so much more meat and honey. (Henry 1941:33)

As for the Marquesans, a Polynesian group, Linton mentions that male labor was exceedingly valuable. Heads of families would often arrange marriages with women who already had lovers. The men would then join the family because of the women, and would contribute to the family economy:

> Households were graded in prestige. The basis of the grading rested primarily on man power; the more active adult males the household had, the more wealth it could accumulate. (Linton 1939:152-153)

So polyandry may be favored in societies where the labor of males is valuable, but that of females is not, or at least is much less valuable. This is undoubtedly an incomplete explanation of its occurrence, but it is a start.

Aside from the causes of polyandry, it would seem that the practice would be the source of considerable difficulties for the societies and individuals involved, at least to those of us not intimately acquainted with its workings. For example, Kephart (1972:54) concludes that polyandry "would appear to be detrimental to the best interests of both the individual and the larger group." He bases this on two assumptions. First, polyandry "runs counter to the presumed male desire for exclusive access to the female." This is the jealousy problem again, the same one we encountered in analyzing polygyny, but this time expressed from the male's point of view. Second, Kephart points to the sex ratio as a limiting factor, noting that "widespread polyandry would leave many women without husbands" (1972:54).

With regard to the jealousy problem, we have no evidence that there is any universal, inherent male desire for exclusive sexual rights to particular females. In fact, the mere existence of polyandry is evidence against such a disposition. Furthermore, we noted earlier that the ethnographic evidence indicates that co-husbands in polyandrous marriages are less likely to experience jealousy than are co-wives in polygynous marriages. But still there must be reasons why the problem of jealousy arises so rarely. There are probably several such reasons.

First, among the Tibetans, the Todas, and possibly other polyandrous groups, we know that polyandry is preferably fraternal. This, one might suggest, would minimize jealousy between co-husbands in the same way that sororal polygyny reduces friction between co-wives. The brothers have shared things all their lives, and are engaged in a common economic enterprise (staying alive) while they are co-husbands. Sharing a wife is simply one more manifestation of a much broader interdependence between them. Second, we have seen that polyandry is often an outgrowth of economic necessity. Jealousy may be a luxury that men in polyandrous societies can ill afford, since their very survival depends upon the solidarity and cohesiveness of the family unit.

Prince Peter (1965:206-207) combines these two facets of polyandry to construct a more or less psychological explanation of the viability of polyandry in Tibet. He believes that the harshness of the natural environment creates strong feelings of interdependence, affection, and solidarity among brothers, which is functional for their survival under these conditions. Close association between them, and sharing of all possessions and fortunes, is both essential and very highly valued. Sharing a wife is one specific case of this psychological closeness. Since much greater value is attached to the fraternal bond than to the marital (a situation almost unthinkable for Westerners, but quite practical and normal for Tibetans), sharing a wife with one's brothers carries positive rather than negative emotional loadings. Hoebel (1966:363-364) indicates that a similar phenomenon may occur among North American Indian tribes who practiced occasional polyandry or "wife-lending" between brothers.

Third, it is clear that polyandrous societies are likely to be very permissive regarding sexual relationships before, within, and outside of marriage (Stephens 1963:46). Apparently no great value is attached to chastity, fidelity, or any particular form of sexual exlusivity in any of these societies. And because sex is not a scarce resource (sexual relationships with a variety of partners are rather uniformly available to all categories of the population), there is little reason for sexual jealousy to arise between men over their joint sexual access to some singular woman. It is not as though the common wife were the only legitimate or possible object for their sexual proclivities. Sex, marriage, love and romance are clearly not bound up together in one inextricable package. Marriage is much more of an economic than a sexual or romantic union; both sex and romance may occur in the absence of, or outside of, marriage. This minimizes the jealousy-producing potential of polyandry.

Some of the "solutions" to the sex ratio problem are the same as those found in polygynous societies. First, for the usual obvious reasons most marriages in polyandrous societies are in fact monogamous; polyandry, even if preferred, will usually be in the minority (see Peter 1965:198, for the case of Tibet). Linton (1939) notes that only the higher-status Marquesan families were characterized by either polyandry or group marriage, and they were envied for this privilege by poorer households. This is, of course, connected with the economic advantages of plural marriage in these societies.

One solution to the problem caused by the generally balanced sex ratio which is employed by polygynous societies is apparently not workable in those which practice polyandry. This is the custom of differential age at first marriage for the sexes. For such a difference to work in reducing the differential availability of husbands and wives in polyandry, *men* would have to marry at younger ages. To my knowledge, there is no society where it is the case that men routinely marry older women. Perhaps this is because the status advantage which men have in virtually all societies (see Fox 1967:31-33) would be contradicted by an age reversal, since status also generally increases with age, at least in preindustrial societies (Cowgill and Holmes 1972:1-13). However, it is often the case that, with fraternal polyandry, one or more of the co-husbands will be younger than the wife, since the wife will probably be acquired when the eldest brother is of a marriageable age. Rivers (1906) reports that, among the Todas, even brothers who are unborn at the time of the marriage will, later on, be considered co-husbands. But this really doesn't answer the question of what to do with "excess" women.

Polyandrous societies sometimes do engage in a practice which results in a reduction of the imbalance in the ratio of available spouses. This is female infanticide: the killing of some newborn female children. The Todas and Tibetans clearly had this custom, and the Marquesans probably did (Stephens 1963:45). Since, as we have already noted, polyandrous societies generally exist on the bare margin of subsistence, the alternatives upon the birth of a female may be quite stark: let her die now, or let her die later. After all, if she does happen to survive childhood but then can't find any husbands, what is to be done with her? She would be a consumer whose productive potential would be extremely limited. The members of these societies may feel that they cannot afford to support nonproductive people without endangering the livelihood of everyone. This is perhaps especially true in polyandrous societies where, in addition to the surplus of eligible wives, female labor is low in value and there is no surplus produce to support marginal members.

In most polyandrous societies there are a variety of options open to women who are not married. Prince Peter discusses the situation in Tibet, which is reasonably representative of other polyandrous societies:

> Celibacy in Tibet was forced upon those surplus women who were unable to find husbands for themselves because of the high incidence of monasticism . . . and the practice of polyandry. Such women, if well-to-do, were able to live out their lives in the family circle of their married brothers. If indigent, they sometimes became nuns, but more often turned to prostitution, for which there was a great demand along the country's main arteries of trade. To be fair, it should however be said that some of the unmarried women were all the same absorbed by matrimony when they were united to widowers who had lost their wives through childbirth, a very usual cause of mortality among the female population. (Peter 1965:195-196)

A further interesting feature of polyandry, and one which also serves to minimize the sex-ratio problem, is that it occasionally tends to coincide with or slide into group marriage. In fact, in virtually all of the societies where group marriage is known to occur with any regularity, polyandry exists also. It is therefore appropriate at this point to examine some of the intricacies of group marriage.

Group marriage

According to the World Ethnographic Sample (Murdock 1957:686), there is no society which normatively espouses group marriage as the preferred marital form. This should not be taken as evidence of the total absence of group marriage, though, for two reasons: (1) it occurs as a minor variant, a possible but infrequently practiced alternative to more common forms of marriage, in several societies; and (2) the adequacy of Murdock's data analysis is in some question with regard to at least one case, the Nayar.

On the first point, Stephens (1963:44) notes that group marriage does occur, with varying degrees of frequency, in three of six societies in which polyandry is either preferred or allowed.[11] For the Tibetans, Stephens' source (Bell 1928) makes no mention of group marriage. But Peter (1965:198) indicates that group marriage did occur, although infrequently. After noting that polygyny was also practiced on occasion by the Tibetans, he goes on to describe an arrangement he calls "conjoint marriage":

> In them, a number of husbands, usually brothers, if they found their common wife to be barren . . . would get themselves another wife without divorcing the first, who would retain her status of elder wife. The

men then lived with the two women, sharing them among themselves as well as the children the second wife would bear them. (Peter 1965:198)

This does not mean, of course, that Tibet should be classified as a "group marriage society." Such marriages constituted a very small proportion of all marriages, and were (apparently) not regarded as preferable to polyandrous marriages except in the specific circumstance of barrenness of the first wife.

The failure to produce children is not the only cause for adding wives to an initially polyandrous marriage. Linton (1939) mentions that among the Marquesans, chiefs and men in other "well-to-do households" would have several wives. Although he is not specific as to the cause of this practice, it may have been simply a function of household expansion. The households of the higher strata would also contain a greater number of men, perhaps attached to the household through their association with one of the female members; the large supply of male labor would contribute to the status of the family. Among the Kaingang, large numbers of women were valuable to the wandering bands of hunters because they might attract men, whose skill as hunters would aid in the struggle for survival (Henry 1941).

Stephens (1963:47-49) also mentions two cases of societies whose ethnographers state clearly that group marriage was widely practiced: the Reindeer Chukchee (Bogoras 1909), and the Siriono (Holmberg 1950). But it is clear that the practices which are indicated by the use of this term involve, in both cases, socially legitimate but *nonmarital* sexual relationships. In one instance, the Chukchee, men may agree among themselves to exchange their wives as sexual partners; in the other, the Siriono, spouses acquire by marriage sexual rights to certain of their spouse's relatives. But married couples are still clearly distinguishable in these groups. The tendency to identify relatively "permissive" sexual relationships as instances of group marriage is a bit ethnocentric, stemming from the Western cultural tradition which equates sex and marriage. They are not at all the same thing. Stephens is quite correct in classifying these practices as instances of "sexual hospitality" and "sexual permissiveness," respectively, and certainly Murdock is on firm ground in not considering these two societies to be typified by group marriage.

The Nayar, however, pose a problem of a different order. They have been used as a counter-example to just about every empirical generalization regarding cross-cultural family uniformity ever offered. They have been quite extensively studied (Gough 1955, 1959, 1961a; Mencher 1965), perhaps because of the uniqueness of their marital practices and family system. The best way to delineate the difficulties in classifying Nayar marriage is to describe briefly the parameters of their marital structure.[12]

The Nayar do not constitute a society in the literal sense of the term, but are rather a Hindu caste living primarily in the Kerala province of South Malabar in India. Most of the Nayar men were employed as warriors, and thus were quite often away from home for long periods of time. The households, perhaps in consequence, were organized around women.

There were actually two types of marriage among the Nayar; they were not mutually exclusive, but rather one type was a prerequisite for the other. The first was called a "tali-tying" marriage, and was highly ceremonial. Girls went through this ceremony at some point prior to puberty, i.e., the onset of menstruation. These ceremonies would be performed individually for specific girls or collectively for several. During the ceremony, which lasted for approximately four days, the girl was united with a "ritual husband"; this union, however, lasted only for the duration of the ceremony and had little further significance.[13] The role of the husband, apparently, was simply to serve as a functionary in a "rite of passage" which symbolized the girl's transition from childhood to adulthood. After this ceremony was completed, the girl was defined as an adult by the culture. One of the rights bestowed by this designation was the right to enter into *sambandham* relationships with males of appropriate caste. This was the second type of marriage, often described by the term "visiting husband." Each adult female in the society was entitled to enter into sexual relationships with a male or males, which were apparently formed and dissolved at the discretion of the individuals involved. The people united in these "marriages" had sexual rights in each other, and on occasion the male gave the female certain small gifts symbolic of their relationship, but here the resemblance to other marital forms ends. Each spouse lived in his or her own household, with his or her family of orientation; the man visited the woman in the evening and returned to his own home before morning.

Nayar households, then, did not contain married couples. They were composed of individuals related to one another according to matrilineal reckoning—that is, through females. The households were called *taravads*.

A typical matrilineal *taravad* was composed of a woman, her children, her daughters' and her granddaughters' children, her brothers, descendants through her sisters and her relations through her dead female ancestors. (Mencher 1965:169)

Since men did not live with their wives, and children lived with their mothers, obviously fathers did not live with their children. But the father-child relationship was not at all significant in Nayar culture. In fact, since women could have many "husbands," biological paternity could hardly be determined with any certainty. This situation is common to polyandrous societies, of course, and it has often been suggested that this is one reason for the relative unpopularity of this marital form. The determination of paternity, however, was simply not an important isssue for the Nayar. Because of the flexibility of marriage, definitions of social legitimacy of children had to be quite broad. Therefore, any child was legitimate as long as there was some evidence that the child had not been fathered by a member of a lower caste. All that was required to establish this was for a man of the Nayar community to designate himself, or allow himself to be designated, as the father. His only responsibility was to provide certain small gifts to the midwife for her services in childbirth. From this time on, the adult male(s) responsible for the child would be the mother's brothers or other matrilineal kinsmen. These men, of course, would have children of "their own" residing in other households, but this was of virtually no significance. In fact, it was not important whether the socially designated father were or were not the biological father of the child.

Mencher (1965:174) calls the Nayar form of marriage polyandry. This is understandable, since each woman could have more than one "husband" at any given time. However, Mencher also notes that, obviously, each man could have many "wives." Gough (1959), therefore, says that the Nayar constitute a clear case of group marriage. In my opinion this characterization is more accurate than Mencher's. However, the set of males and females who may, at any particular time, be involved in an interlocking network of sexual relationships does not really constitute a group. They may not even know one another. "Visiting husband" relationships could exist for a period of time as short as one night. If a Nayar warrior were passing through another Nayar community, he could, with full social approval, find himself a "wife" for one night only. Whether or not this means that the term "group marriage" is inappropriate is a matter of some debate; it seems to be a judgment call. Gough argues that mating was not really promiscuous or random, and that legally established paternity was extremely important to the Nayar, at least in the collective sense that a child was fathered by a Nayar or a man of a higher caste. The latter point has been argued by many to be the ultimate criterion of the existence of marriage (see Gough 1959; Reiss 1971:187-196; for a contrary view, see Peter 1956). The Nayar, therefore, had a social institution that should probably be called marriage, and it seems to fit the nature of goup marriage more nearly than it does polyandry.

Are the Nayar, then, an exception to Murdock's generalization that no society is typified by the practice of group marriage? Strictly according to their marital customs, they probably are (or rather were, since they no longer follow the customs we have described). But the question, raised in several different connections, is whether or not the Nayar are a society. If not, Murdock says, they cannot be considered an exception. Reiss has debated this issue with Murdock with regard to the question of the universality of the family. Reiss' remarks, however, are also relevant here.

It is interesting to note here that Murdock, in correspondence with the author (Reiss), contended that the Nayar are not really an exception to his theory for they are but the old Warrior caste of the Kerala society and not really an entire society in and of themselves. There is reason to take issue with this defense. For one thing, few societies are entirely independent of other neighboring groups. . . . Equally important is the fact that Murdock had no doubts about the Nayar being a society when he included them as one of his 250 cultures in his 1949 book. . . . One can never be disproved if one can change the rules of proof to eliminate every negative case. (Reiss 1971:9)

The problem here is whether the unusual marital and family patterns of the Nayar are in some way dependent upon the fact that they were embedded in other components of Indian society which did not have these patterns. Would the practices in question have been developed, and could they have been maintained, if the Nayar had been a completely independent group? It is probable that the flexible marital arrangement originated in response to the problem of men being absent from the community for extended periods due to their occupation as warriors, which would not have occurred if the Nayar had not been a part of a larger society and specifically charged with this function. However, the system seemed to be quite stable and self-sustaining. Once established, it probably could have continued indefinitely, and without reference to the interdependence between the Nayar and other Indian castes, if pressure from outside the Nayar community had not been exerted to change their customs. It must also be remembered that the Nayar did maintain their own independent communities. They raised their own food and were in many other ways an autonomous social entity. Therefore, the argument that they were an example of a society characterized by group marriage seems defensible, although they do show a certain resistance to unambiguous classification.

But even if this contention is correct, it is nonetheless clearly true that group marriage is exceedingly rare. Reasons for this rarity must of necessity be quite general, because we have not had much opportunity to examine specific cases of group marriage to see why the practice might be less viable than, for instance, polygyny or monogamy. It may be that the complexity of interpersonal relationships becomes too great to handle, and that the tensions generated by large numbers of adults living together who all have sexual access to one another are rarely balanced by advantages proceeding from such arrangements. Kinkade (1973), reporting on an experimental "commune" in the contemporary United States, indicates that sexual competition and rivalry cause interpersonal problems, although most of them were successfully resolved in the commune in question. But communal living arrangements do not necessarily include completely open sexual access of each member to each other member, and therefore are not generally examples of group marriage. And most communes do not survive for a period in excess of the life span of their individual members, a necessary criterion of group independence. The closest thing to a large-scale exception to this generalization was probably the Oneida community in the nineteenth-century United States (see Kephart 1963, 1972:170–189; Carden 1970; and Robertson 1970). They very clearly did practice group marriage, but ultimately failed to survive the departure and death of their founder, John Humphrey Noyes. They therefore definitely cannot be described as a *society* characterized by group marriage, but only as a group which tried it. Other than Oneida, experiments in group marriage have been infrequent and short-lived.

Conclusion

Variation in marital structure is indeed quite considerable, although more than 99 percent of all known societies can be classified as either monogamous or polygynous. We should reiterate, though, that there is greater variation on the level of cultural ideals than on the level of the statistical frequency of individual marriages. Probably the majority of marriages in all societies are monogamous. But the causes of the statistical prevalence of monogamous marriage vary considerably across societies. Sometimes it is most common because it is eminently practicable, is functionally related to other structural parameters of the society such as its economic base, and is perhaps the only legal form. Other times, it is frequent by default: there are not enough women for every man to have two or more wives. But it is by no means the "natural" form of marriage; there is no such thing.

One obvious conclusion from this chapter is that marriage is not very effectively analyzed, particularly in the sense of marital structure, if it is conceptualized primarily in sexual terms. While sex is always a part of marriage, there are many other important components as well. Variation in type of marital structure seems to correspond rather well, although far from perfectly, to variation in the nature of economic conditions and constraints with which a society must contend. Where large families are economically valuable and where women perform important economic functions (these conditions, incidentally, tend to coincide), polygyny is likely to be favored. Where the opposite conditions obtain, polyandry sometimes emerges as the preferred form; this is likely when the environment is harsh and large families are difficult to support. Group marriage, although normatively preferred in only one society that we know of (and even that one is a questionable case), occurs sporadically in several societies, generally as an adaptation to problems of economic security which might be forestalled by greater numbers, or as a manifestation of unusual wealth in societies where it is allowed. None of the variations in marital structure we have discussed can reasonably be explained by sexual factors: cross-culturally, marriage is apparently more of an economic than a sexual relationship.

In fact, marriages do not inevitably contain a sexual component.[14] Evans-Pritchard (1951:108-109) reports on the practice of "woman marriage" among the Nuer, an African tribe. If a Nuer woman is believed to be barren, for whatever reason, she will be divorced from her husband and married to another *woman*. Homosexual relationships are not expected here; rather, the biologically female "husband" simply undergoes a social sex change and proceeds to behave as a man and a husband. She can then do anything Nuer men can do except, of course, impregnate her "wife." This task she simply hires out; when children are born, they refer to her as "father."

Practices of this sort indicate that marriage is not *always* a "socially legitimate sexual union" (Stephens 1963:5), although this characterization is usually quite accurate. Reiss proposes the following as the irreducible and culturally universal elements of marriage:

> (Marriage) is an institution composed of a socially accepted union of individuals in husband and wife roles with the key function of legitimation of parenthood. (Reiss 1971:192)

In other words, Reiss is saying that marriage consists of two interdependent social *roles*, which may be performed by varying numbers and kinds of individuals; it has as one of its consequences the social definition of the people involved as acceptable parents. This definition highlights the interdependence of spouses in aspects other than the sexual and points to the fact that marriages are embedded in broader family and kinship structures. Thus, although Reiss' definition is not nearly as descriptive as Stephens', it is probably more inclusive of the variety of marital practices across cultures.

In later chapters we will concern ourselves with many facets of marital relationships pertaining to interpersonal relations, power structures, practices of courtship and mate selection, and related topics.

Notes

1. Descriptions of the values these variables may take are given below where appropriate.

2. We now know (see Chapter Three) that this is not empirically correct, at least if we consider it to be a universal proposition as Murdock did. However, the several exceptions to this generalization are not immediately relevent to the current issue. Since we are now concerned with a primarily descriptive taxonomy, we may take advantage of the "virtual universality" of the nuclear family and proceed with the task.

3. The following discussion draws heavily on Murdock (1949:23-32).

4. There is a very important difference between the type of marriage preferred

by members of a given culture and the type of marriage which is, at any given point in time, characteristic of the majority of a society's married members. We'll discuss the importance of this distinction shortly. For the moment, though, we are interested in the normatively preferred rather than the numerically most common form of marriage.

5. This argument bears striking resemblance to several statements in classical sociological theory. Durkheim (1951:270–272) argued that monogamous marriage provides men with a source of regulation or discipline which they require to "tame their passions." Women supposedly possess an inherently different mental compositon and do not require external sources of stability.

6. Polygyny, of course, is the most effective marital structure for producing large numbers of children, since one man can impregnate many women.

7. In fact, in some societies in which polygyny is normatively endorsed, its practice is also normatively restricted to the "elite" minority.

8. See, for example, Lang (1946) on the Chinese and Bowen (1954) on the Tiv.

9. I believe that this characterization of the Nayar is inaccurate, or at least quite dubious. We will discuss their case below under "group marriage."

10. See also Linton (1936:183) for an earlier summary of Tibetan polyandry, which agrees with Prince Peter's account in all important particulars.

11. These three, together with their ethnographers, are the Kaingang (Henry 1941), the Todas (Rivers 1906), and the Marquesans (Handy 1923; Linton 1939).

12. The following account draws heavily on Gough (1959) and Mencher (1965). These two descriptions differ in certain of their particulars, since the authors are describing different communities, but they agree on the important points. Both of these accounts, we should note, are historical. That is, the system as they describe it no longer exists, but was prevalent among the Nayar for a long period of time, up until perhaps the end of the nineteenth century.

13. Mencher (1965:171) reports that one man might serve as the "ritual husband" for an entire cohort of girls, depending on regional variations in the custom.

14. There are probably individual cases of "virgin brides" or completely nonsexual marriages in all societies, but these are not at issue here. We are interested, rather, in culturally institutionalized practices, not specific instances of individual nonconformity to marital norms.

chapter five

Variation in family structure

Introduction

The central objective of this chapter is to review and synthesize attempts to explain cross-systemic variation in family structure. But, before attacking the question of the sources of variation, we must define the variable of interest and the values it may take. This issue proves to be rather perplexing.

Petersen (1969) has remarked that, in research on family and kin-group structure, there is great variability across researchers and studies in the conceptualization and measurement of the dependent variable. This is understandable, since the requisite definitions are of the nominal variety (see Chapter Three) and there is no "right" way of conceptualizing these variables, but it does make the cumulation of knowledge difficult (Freese 1972). A basic problem revolves around the issue of distinguishing the group to be labeled "family" from the network of kin in which it is (or may be) embedded.[1] In other words, for any given culture, how do we distinguish "family members" from "other relatives"?

Most researchers, up to this point, have operationally defined the family as the group of co-resident kin, those who share a household. This is largely because the indicators of family structure contained in cross-cultural data banks, principally the Ethnographic Atlas, are given by this criterion. However, several scholars (for example, Winch 1974; Yorburg 1975) opt for delineations of family composition based on considerations of economic interdependence, authority structure, daily contact, and "psychological interdependence" (see particularly Yorburg 1975:6), which may or may not correspond to the composition of the co-resident kinship unit.

It is important here to distinguish between operational indicators (empirical variables) and theoretical variables. As we proceed through this chapter, we will discover that most of the theoretical statements we examine implicate considerations of economic interdependence, authority structure, and so on as the defining characteristics of the various family types. However, it will often be necessary to employ the structure of the co-resident kin group as a surrogate variable or an operational indicator, because it is usually more readily available to researchers. Furthermore, the correlations between joint residence and the theoretical dimensions of family structure specified by Yorburg and others are undoubtedly positive.

If we take the structure of the co-resident kin group as our operational indicator of family structure, we may discriminate among the values this variable may take according to the number of distinct social positions within this unit. Theoretically, there can be an infinite number of possible values of this variable; however, for purposes of clarity it is useful to categorize them in some way. The least complex type of family structure will be labeled "nuclear," and may be diagrammed as in Figure 1.

Each of the positional designations in this diagram (the triangles and circles) refers to one social position, with one small exception we will note momentarily. They do not necessarily denote one individual. Thus the number of members of this family is not given by the diagram. The triangles refer to males, the circles to females.[2] In the most conventional interpretation of charts such as this, the diagram is taken to represent three social positions: hus-

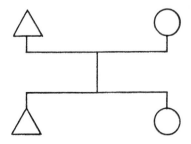

Figure 1:   The Structure of the Nuclear Family

band-father (upper left), wife-mother (upper right), and offspring-sibling (lower half). These terms designating positions may seem unduly cumbersome, but they are useful in that the term for each position specifies the relationship of the position incumbent to every other social position contained in the family structure. The children, for example, are the offspring of their parents and the siblings of one another. The convention of indicating all of a family's dependent children by the one term, rather than assigning a separate position for each sex, is due simply to the fact that it is rarely of theoretical importance in structural family analyses to distinguish between dependent children according to sex.[3] However, if a child marries, brings his/her spouse to live in the parental home, and raises children there, this child is then considered to occupy a unique social position in the family structure.

A few further words about the diagram are needed. Individual positions connected by a horizontal line running beneath the positional symbols are united by marriage; that is, they are husband-wife positions.[4] Those connected by horizontal lines above the symbols are siblings. Vertical lines indicate a parent-child relationship. Thus, all possible nuclear family positions and relationships are represented in Figure 1.

Although we now know that not all family systems do in fact contain the nuclear family within them (see Chapter Three), it is the usual practice to conceive of other kinds of families as extensions of this "nucleus." For most analytic purposes this works perfectly well. In practice, a family is generally defined as nuclear if it contains *only* the three nuclear positions or some subset thereof. A family which contains *any other social positions* is defined as "extended" (see Murdock 1949:32–40; Zelditch 1964:468; Nimkoff 1965: 19-23; Winch 1971:12; Leslie 1973:34–37; Nye and Berardo 1973:40–43). The emergence of an extended family depends upon what children do, or more precisely where they live, after marriage. If children of one sex or the other are expected to and actually do remain in their parents' homes after marriage, bringing their spouses to live with them and raising their children within this family, then the result is an extended family.[5]

One kind of extended family, and in fact the most limited kind in structural terms, is called the "stem" family. The stem family arises when *one* child, and only one, remains as a member of his or her parents' family after marriage, and all other children of both sexes leave the home to establish their own independent families. The stem family is shown in Figure 2.

In this situation, the male in the intermediate generation is simultaneously a member of two nuclear families: that of his parents, sometimes called his "family of orientation," in which he is a son; and his "family of procreation" in which he fills the position of husband-father. The stem family was once quite common in rural Ireland (Humphreys 1965, 1966), where it operated to keep family lands intact through the generations. Since only one

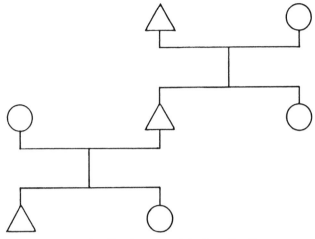

Figure 2: The Structure of the Stem Family

son could inherit the family farm, it was never necessary to subdivide the lands among many sons. Children other than the one inheriting the farm received some other form of compensation or inheritance.

The stem family is one type of extended family, since it is more complex (contains more positions) than the nuclear family. The next type, along the scale of increasing structural complexity, is called the "lineal" family (Murdock 1957:669; Chu 1969:311). Such families are also sometimes called "small extended families," and consist of the families of procreation of one member of the senior generation and two or more of the junior generation. They may arise when *all* children of one sex remain in their parents' household after marriage, bringing their spouses to live with them. If the cultural prescription is for males to remain in the home (this is called "patrilocal" residence), a lineal family would be diagrammed as in Figure 3.

I have deliberately left the daughters and sisters out of this figure because, in this system, they leave the family upon marriage to join another, and including them in the diagram would make it unduly complex.

Assuming that each married couple in this lineal family has only two sons who survive to adulthood, it is readily apparent that the possibilities for expansion in this type of system are enormous, at least up to the point where older generations are dying as fast as new ones are being born. If this lineal family were to expand until it contained the families of procreation of at least two individuals in each of at least two adjacent generations, it would cease to be lineal and would be called "fully extended." This is the fourth and most complex type of family delimited by Murdock (1957). If the sons in the third generation of our lineal family were to marry and begin raising their own children, this family would become fully extended.

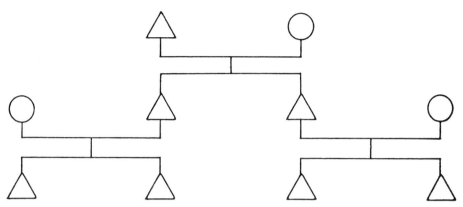

Figure 3: The Structure of the Lineal Family

Remember that family structural complexity is defined by the number of social positions contained in a family rather than the number of individuals who are members of the family. *Any* social position may, at any given time, have more than one incumbent, but it is still only one position. A polygamous marriage does not, then, make a family extended. It is reasonable to expect, of course, that family size and family complexity are positively related; the more positions there are, the more individuals can potentially fill them. But size and structural complexity are still two different variables.

It is common for analysts of family structure to simplify distinctions between family types into two categories, nuclear and extended. The latter type combines the three subtypes of stem, lineal, and fully extended. Murdock's World Ethnographic Sample allows classification of 549 societies on the family structure variable. Of these societies, 301 (54.8 percent) are typified by an extended family system, and 248 (45.2 percent) by independent nuclear families (Murdock 1957; Nimkoff and Middleton 1960). Not all analysts use this dichotomy, and Chu (1969; Chu and Hollingsworth 1969) has argued that the three subtypes of extended families are differentially related to other variables, particularly those involving stratification, and should be combined differently or not combined at all. There is no single "right" way of doing it, of course, and Murdock's original four categories are not the only ones possible. Now that we have the Ethnographic Atlas, with over 1170 cases, it is not always necessary to combine types to insure adequate cell sizes in tabular analyses, and the practice of collapsing categories should be avoided wherever possible. We will point to several instances later on of studies which obtained different results in part because of different methods of combining categories of family structure. The clearest conceptual distinction, though, seems to lie between nuclear and extended family systems, and we will employ this distinction in most of our general discussions.

At least brief mention should be made at this point of a few of the general differences between nuclear and extended family systems. Both kinds of systems are often said to have certain "advantages," counterbalanced by a set of "disadvantages." Distinctions along this dimension too often lead to value judgments, on the part of the reader if not the author, but it is nonetheless true that there are important practical differences between types of family systems that seriously affect the lives and behaviors of the people who live in each of them.

A nuclear family is one which is based upon, and begins with, a marriage. The marriage is the foundation of the family in the sense that, when two people are married, it signifies the beginning of a "new" family. The nuclear family is often said to be transitory in nature (Leslie 1973:35; Nye and Berardo 1973:40–41) because it has a definite beginning in marriage and, usually, a definite conclusion upon the death of one or both spouses.

In contrast, extended or "consanguineal" family systems are based upon relationships between parents and children rather than spouses. They tend to occur in societies in which kin relationships are of the utmost import. One derives one's "place" in society, one's network of affiliations, and one's life chances from parents and other kin. Marital relations are secondary to parent-child relations, to such an extent that parents are frequently vested with the sole authority to choose a spouse for their child (see Chapter Seven). Robert Winch (1971:30–41) gives as an example of the ideal type of extended family the system prevalent in traditional China. In this system, the individual's total identity depended upon his family connections. In our society the most important distinctions between adults have to do largely with occupation: who we are depends primarily on what we do. But in the Chinese extended family system (and others), the individual's location in the social structure was determined almost entirely by family considerations. Practically the only social positions an individual occupied were those connected with the family structure, and virtually all social roles were attached, in one way or another, to family positions.

> For perhaps twenty centuries there existed among the peasants of China a familial form that was just about as completely functional as is theoretically possible. All members of the family contributed their energies to the production of a common pool of wealth. The wealth was dispersed by the family head, who acted not as an individual with arbitrary power but as the responsible executive charged with the duty of looking out for the family as a whole and for all its individual members. It was taken for granted that the young would be indoctrinated by the family in the ways of the world, that the aged and the ailing would be cared for, and that the conduct of all members would be controlled by the overriding consideration of family welfare rather than individual gratification. (Winch 1971:31-32)

Winch goes on (1971:34-37) to say that the family in traditional China was the social structure primarily responsible for economic, political, educational, and religious functions as well as reproduction. Perhaps the most striking illustration of the power of the extended family in China is that, when a son was married, the marriage was contracted in the name of his parents who took a daughter-in-law, not in the name of the man who took a wife (Levy 1949:100-101; Winch 1971:38).

The advantages of the extended family, in a very general sense, are summarized effectively by Nye and Berardo (1973). It is clear from their remarks that extended families have important implications for the structure of societies as well as for the lives of their individual members.

> One advantage of the consanguineous family is that it ensures continuity over the generations by linking parental families with new families of procreation. Moreover, compared to the conjugal family the extended family is a more effective structure for maintaining family traditions and for transmitting family holdings intact from one generation to the next. Children in the extended family are exposed to a large network of kin relations. Other kin are immediately available who can assist the parents in the socialization tasks and who act as models for a variety of adult role behaviors. In times of crisis, such as the death of a parent, other kin are able to substitute in meeting the physical and emotional needs of the young. (Nye and Berardo 1973:41)

Goode (1964:50-55) argues that extended families provide certain important advantages to individuals in societies which do not have highly specialized agencies for the performance of specific functions. There are more people, and more categories or kinds of people, available to help in times of crisis and in daily tasks such as child care. Wealth can be maintained in the family across generations, and there are more people to contribute to the family's pool of resources. If one family member dies, others are available to take his or her place. Large families of several generations are also likely to have more political clout because of their many members, and because in societies where the technology is not changing so rapidly the experience of members of the senior generation is likely to be highly valued. On the other hand, the network of interpersonal relations in extended families is quite often difficult to manage, and individual relationships are likely to be less intense and personal and more diffuse. The family group exercises greater control over its members than is the case in nuclear families; individuality is less highly valued. And extended families can disintegrate if they lose their ability to effectively satisfy the economic and political needs and desires of their members.

Since the nuclear and extended family systems are in fact so different in terms of their implications for individual behavior and for social structure, it is important to inquire as to the antecedent conditions which lead to the emergence of one or the other type of family structure. For the remainder of this chapter, we shall be concerned with the tracing of research and theory on the sources of variation in family structure. We shall find, in general, that there is a correspondence between family structure and mode of subsistence. The constraints imposed by different ecological and economic systems have a great deal to do with family systems.

The emergence of the conjugal family in modern society

Industrialization and family structure

Social scientists have long observed that the nuclear family structure is characteristic not only of the United States, but of Western Europe and other "modern" nations as well. The definitive inquiry to this point into the causes of this state of affairs is William Goode's (1963) *World Revolution and Family Patterns*. Drawing heavily on earlier work by Parsons (1943), Goode assembled evidence from various regions of the world[6] to the effect that family systems are changing toward a common pattern which he designates by the term "conjugal." By this he intends to indicate the internal structure we have denoted as nuclear and several other characteristics which, he says, emerge along with this structure. Among them he includes the following (Goode 1963: 7–10; 1964:51–52):

1. The method of reckoning kinship, in societies with conjugal family systems, is bilateral; that is, kin ties are traced equally through both "sides" of one's family, and there are thus no unilineal kin groups (see Chapter Six). The marriage is the core of the family; ties with other kin are *relatively* attenuated. Family units are residentially separate, since children establish their own households upon marriage.
2. Parents and other kin have relatively little stake in marriages. Consequently, mate selection is "free" or autonomous rather than arranged, and it is usually based on interpersonal attraction.
3. Certain customs surrounding marriage in societies with extended families are absent. These include the dowry and bride price, the practice of the exchange of sometimes very valuable gifts between the families of the new spouses, and customs of "preferential mating" between cousins or other relatives.
4. The authority of parents over children and husbands over wives becomes less absolute; the balance of power within the family is more a consequence of negotiation than of inflexible rules. The social structure in general becomes more egalitarian, specifically with respect to relationships between the sexes and to rights of inheritance among all children.

The concept of the conjugal family thus implicates more than a nuclear family structure; these additional characteristics must also exist for the label to be appropriately applied. Goode also points out (1963:25-26) that, while family structures are generally changing in the direction of the conjugal system, they may be coming from considerably different directions. The basic problem, however, is to explain the perceived trend away from some form of extended family and toward the conjugal system.

Although he recognizes the importance of a multitude of causes, it is Goode's conclusions that the primary cause of the emergence of the conjugal family system in modern societies resides in the process of industrialization. He sees certain characteristics of industrial economies as antithetical to extended family structures. The most concise summary of his logic is contained in his concluding chapter, in which he accounts for the demise of extended families in industrial societies by noting five ways in which extended families are more or less incompatible with certain of the parameters of industrial economies (Goode 1963:369-370). While there are certain redundancies between several of his points, each one is nonetheless at least partially independent of the others.

First, Goode points out that one important characteristic of an industrialized society is the high degree of geographic mobility of its population. People must often move to find employment or advancement. Since the unit of labor is the individual rather than the family, and since the employee is compensated for his labor in liquid form (money rather than crops or other produce), it is efficient for the domestic unit to be as small as possible. Moving one's spouse and children to a new community, because of one person's employment or prospective employment in that community, is much less cumbersome than attempting to move a three- or four-generation fully extended family. In Goode's terms, industrialization

> . . . calls for physical movement from one locality to another, thus decreasing the frequency and intimacy of contact among members of a kin network. . . . (Goode 1963:369)

Contrast this to the residential stability usually found in societies whose economies are based on agriculture. Here wealth is given by land, a nonmobile resource. The members of a family work the land that, in one way or another, "belongs to" the family; their compensation for this labor takes the form of the produce of the land. One pursues one's career on the family's land, which rather conveniently stays in one place. This permits proliferation of family size and complexity up to some saturation point, beyond which the productivity of the land is insufficient for the maintenance of the family. If farms are small and/or the land is relatively infertile, the stem family is likely to be the typical structure. If the land is more extensive and productive, the fully extended family may well characterize the society; as family size expands, the family will be segmented with some members moving away periodically to begin new farms or to enter trades in urban areas. But in any case, geographic mobility is much more characteristic of industrial than agricultural economies, and conjugal families are better suited to high rates of geographic mobility than are extended families.

A second kind of mobility also becomes prevalent in industrialized societies: social mobility. This concept indicates movement in the socioeconomic structure rather than movement in physical space. It is very possible, and quite common in industrialized nations, for the employed members of two adjacent generations to have vastly different occupations. These occupations may differ not only in the nature of the tasks performed, but also in the prestige and income they command and in the education they require for their acquisition and successful performance. In other words, an adult man or woman may, by virtue of education, occupation, and income, belong to a different socioeconomic stratum than his or her parents. This is called "generational mobility." It is important because sociological research has documented many differences between strata in life styles, attitudes, preferences, and behaviors of all varieties. If generational social mobility does in fact occur in any given family, the members of the various generations are perhaps pursuing different career paths, may have different interests and proclivities, and in general have less in common with one another than do members of the same social stratum. In agricultural societies, on the other hand, one's occupation is generally rather rigidly fixed by one's parents' occupation. In the Hindu caste system, occupation is quite literally inherited. Among the Chinese peasantry in preindustrial times, the individual had virtually no choice of occupation because there were no existing opportunities other than succeeding to a position of authority in the family's farming enterprise. Class differences between generations of the same family are exceedingly rare in agricultural societies because successive generations generally make their living in the same way—usually, in fact, on the same farm. Thus the relative infrequency of both geographic and social mobility combine to make extended families feasible in agricultural societies, but in industrial societies they work to divide and separate the generations.

Two other points that Goode makes are intimately tied to the issue of social mobility. One is that, in an industrial economy with a great variety of highly specialized occupations, it is unlikely that one's kinship connections are going to be of much direct value in securing a job. Nepotism, of course, is far from unheard of, but most people make their way in the occupational world by virtue of their own skills, qualifications, experiences, and luck. This is not intended to deny the very important social placement function of the family in industrialized societies; for instance, one's chances for a college education and one's socialization for achievement are considerably enhanced if one is born to upper-middle-class parents in the United States rather than to impoverished farm laborers. But this situation does not at all compare with that in agricultural societies, where one's father is also almost automatically one's employer, and where the individual's entire economic future is tied to the fate of the family enterprise. In industrial societies, one's family connections may be more or less valuable in job placement; in agricultural societies, one's family and one's career are often the same thing. The value to the individual of maintaining a place within the family structure throughout the life cycle is much greater in agricultural than in industrial economies.

Along with high rates of social mobility and the more limited (or perhaps less direct) relevance of kin to job placement, Goode reemphasizes in a separate point the fact that socioeconomic positions in industrial nations are *achieved* rather than inherited or "ascribed" by birth. Although a surprising amount of mutual aid is exchanged between related conjugal families in industrial societies (see Sussman and Burchinal 1962a, 1962b; Sussman 1965; Adams 1968, 1970; Troll 1971; Lee 1977), in most cases related conjugal families are economically independent of one another in the sense of economic survival. One's primary source of livelihood, for most of the life cycle, comes from either one's own occupational endeavors or those of one's spouse. Most people are not primarily dependent on consanguineal kin for subsistence, although they may receive help in times of crisis, expensive gifts on special occasions, and other more or less sporadic assistance from relatives. These kin exchanges may make life easier,[7] but they do not provide a livelihood. This minimizes the power of the kin network to control the individual's behavior and means that each person *can* make his or her way without depending on relatives for status and security. Goode interprets this as a distinctive feature of the value systems of industrialized societies:

> Industrialization creates a value structure that recognizes achievement more than birth; consequently, the kin have less to offer an individual in exchange for his submission. He has to make his *own* way; at best his kin can give him an opportunity to show his talent. (Goode 1963: 369-370)

The last three points of Goode's argument that we've mentioned are highly interdependent. They might all be summarized by the statement that in industrial societies kin are to a large extent economically independent of one another. Goode, in a sense, has isolated three somewhat distinct dimensions of this economic independence. The central facet of this logic is that, in industry, the individual is the unit of labor, and the worker receives a level of compensation which is insufficient to support several generations of dependents except in the most unusual cases. Since the careers of related workers are most often independent, there is considerable value in a high degree of independence among them in terms of residence, socioeconomic status and life style, and mutual responsibility for one another, and correspondingly less value in several generations uniting, or remaining united, as an economic unit.

A final, but very important, component of Goode's explanation of the rise of the conjugal family in industrialized societies has to do with the increasing structural complexity and functional differentiation or specialization of social systems which generally occur concurrently with industrialization. He observes that many (perhaps most) of the political, religious, and educational as well as economic functions of extended families and corporate kin groups in agricultural societies are gradually taken over by more specialized social structures as societies industrialize. In fact, the tendency toward increasing specialization of social structures as well as individual occupations has been taken as a benchmark of societal complexity by sociologists from the period of Spencer (1876-96) and Durkheim (1893) to the present. The logic here is that industrialization requires such things as education for specialized occupations, political integration at a high collective level, and extremely elaborate coordination of production and distribution which are beyond the scope of family structures. Consequently, specialized social structures emerge to handle these specialized functions, and the family becomes less crucial as an economic, political, and educational unit.

As other structures are developed around these specific functions, membership and participation in family organizations becomes less vital, from the individual point of view, in economic, political and educational terms. The individual's economic roles are performed in specifically economic social structures and are components of these structures rather than of the family. One need not be a member of a family in order to survive, since economic and family roles are largely independent. The same logic applies to roles in other kinds of social institutions: the family is no longer the locus of "instrumental" role performance. Individuals pursuing economic advancement, for example, have many reasons for leaving their parents' families and few for remaining in them. The consequence of this structural differentiation on the societal level is therefore a decrease in the complexity of the family structure as societal complexity increases.[8]

The central point of Goode's argument, in summary, is that family units become structurally simplified (i.e., the conjugal family arises) and functionally specialized as societies undergo the process of industrialization (see also Winch and Blumberg 1968). This is because the conjugal family system is more congenial to the demands of an industrial economy than an extended system would be. These demands or constraints include pressure for high rates of geographic and social mobility and emphasis on achievement as opposed to ascription or heredity in the occupational structure, and the development of specialized social structures which come to perform many of the functions associated with the extended family in more "traditional" agricultural societies.

There are several other recent attempts to explain the rise of the conjugal family in modern societies, most of which are quite similar to Goode's theory. Zelditch (1964:492-497), reviewing primarily the work of Ogburn and that of Parsons (1943), comes to the conclusion that the extended family can persist as the dominant family form only where the extended family is the basic task unit or unit of labor in the society. This occurs, for example, in a society based on family farms, where "estates" are indivisible or impartible, and where occupational specialization is based on kinship positions. Each of these features is characteristic of agrarian societies but not of industrial ones. Mogey (1964:504-511) also posits a series of conditions antecendent to the conjugal family which agree, in most respects, with those specified by Goode, although the two analyses are inconsistent in that some of the factors labeled causes by Mogey are considered to be components of conjugal family systems by Goode. These include such things as bilateral kindreds and neolocal residence. But, while Mogey's conceptual distinctions are somewhat different from Goode's, the logic is essentially similar. The process of industrialization, through its effects on the occupational system and related social institutions, operates to decrease the prevalence of extended families and to increase the relative frequency of conjugal families in comparison to the situation found in agricultural societies.

Problems with the theory

An article by Sidney Greenfield (1961) challenges the logic which relates industrialization and the conjugal family.[9] Greenfield bases his attack on two kinds of evidence. First, he points to several societies which do not fit the pattern hypothesized by Goode and others: that is, either societies with industrial economies which are characterized by extended families or societies with nonindustrial economies in which the conjugal family predominates. Second, he points out that the "small nuclear family," according to many students of European history, predated industrialization in Northern and Western Europe by hundreds of years. Since causal logic is based upon the premise that a cause must precede an effect,[10] it is not reasonable to assume that industrialization was the cause of the conjugal family in Europe. These points merit some intensive consideration.

Greenfield cites several examples of societies with clearly industrial economies which, in his interpretation, have viable extended family systems. These include Japan (E. Johnson 1960), Canada (Garigue 1956), Brazil (Wagley 1960), and Britain (Young 1954; Shaw 1955; Firth 1957). However, it is now clear that the Japanese family has experienced considerable change in the direction of the conjugal system (Goode 1963; Vogel 1963, 1965; Blood 1967). Greenfield's other examples draw on research which indicates, in each case, the existence of social and some economic relations between related families, but the family structure of these societies is generally nuclear, and their systems manifest many other characteristics which conform to Goode's conjugal type. No one is disputing the existence of functional kin networks in industrial societies; they are clearly important even in the United States (Adams 1968; Klatzky 1973; Lee 1977). But the issue here is the presence and predominance of extended families in industrial societies, not the existence of viable social relations between related conjugal families.

As an example of a society in which the conjugal family form is dominant but the economy is based upon agriculture, Greenfield chooses Barbados, a small, densely populated island in the Caribbean. Here he points out that the conjugal family is the ideal form, although actual family structures may differ from this ideal because of poverty, high rates of illegitimacy, and low rates of legal marriage. But Greenfield documents quite extensively the similarities between the family systems of Barbados and the United States, as well as the : differences in their economic bases, and argues that this constitutes evidence against the hypothesis that industrialization is the cause of the conjugal family.

In one sense, Greenfield has an excellent point here. He argues persuasively that social scientists have erred in confounding two meanings of the term "industrialization," one having to do with machine technology and the other with patterns of social organization which are often found in conjunction with machine technology. But while machine technology is clearly not the cause of the conjugal family in Barbados, it is apparent that many of the processes which Goode specifies as consequences of industrialization and causes of the conjugal family are also present in Barbados. They result, however, from the particular characteristics of the Barbadian agricultural system. The most important of these features are geographic mobility and economic independence of kin.

Farms in Barbados are not family-owned subsistence farms, but rather cash-crop plantations. The economy is based on the raising and exporting of sugar. The masses of the population are wage-earning laborers who work in the sugar fields, which are owned and managed by the "aristocracy." They are paid in cash for their services. Men, who are the primary breadwinners, must move in pursuit of work. Furthermore, social mobility is an important feature of the occupational system, and comes from individual advancement through the occupational hierarchy:

> Each nuclear family is ascribed a place in the system of stratification which is based upon the social class of the family of orientation of the adult male subject to the mobility he may achieve in his occupational pursuits. Mobility is a driving force in both societies (Barbados and the United States). Kinship relationships are generally divorced from the occupational system, thus permitting conjugal units to be socially mobile, independent of kinship ties. Nuclear families striving for mobility are often best able to do so by almost total denial of kinship claims,

which, of course, leads to the isolation of the conjugal unit. (Greenfield 1961:319)

Greenfield also points out that, in a wage-labor type of economy (whether agricultural or industrial), the wage earner is generally paid only enough to support a rather small set of dependents—that is, a conjugal rather than an extended family. Thus, the causal logic by means of which Goode and others relate industrialization to the conjugal family is not really being disputed by Greenfield; rather, he is observing that the specific causes of the conjugal family (social mobility, geographic mobility, economic independence of kin, emphasis on achieved status) may follow from cash-crop farming as well as from machine technology.

The case of Barbados provides a valuable extension of Goode's logic rather than an exception to it. Since the agricultural base of the Barbadian economy is a cash crop, and since individuals are paid for their labor in wages rather than in a share of the produce, it is not unreasonable to conceive of Barbados as an industrial economy whose primary industry is agriculture. This is admittedly stretching the meaning of "industry" beyond a simple equivalence with machine technology, but the similarities of cash-crop agriculture with industrial economies are clearly greater than the similarities between cash-crop and subsistence farming. Thus Greenfield's argument does not cause rejection of Goode's theory; it is rather an extension of it, particularly in terms of expanding the meaning of the independent variable, type of economy.[11]

What Greenfield has accomplished is a procedure often called "negative case analysis," in which cases which do not conform exactly to a hypothesis or empirical generalization are investigated more intensively to determine precisely *why* they do not conform. Greenfield, it seems, has succeeded in explaining the apparent counter-instance of Barbados by an extension of the same basic logic employed in Goode's theory. The theory designed to account for the emergence of the conjugal family in modern societies is therefore modified and extended, but certainly not disproven, by Greenfield's study.

However, Greenfield also brings up an important issue bearing on the causal ordering of the variables in the theory. He points out (1961:320–322) that according to many authorities on family organization throughout European history (for example, Arensberg 1955, 1957), the small family unit has been characteristic of most of Europe and North America since long before the industrial revolution. Thus, while societies which are currently characterized by industrial economies also evince the conjugal family as the predominant family form, it is not at all clear which variable is the cause and which the effect. This is a very important theoretical issue, since most explanations for the correspondence between industry and the conjugal family are premised on the assumption that causal priority resides in the economic system.

In attempting to resolve the problem of causal order,

two avenues of inquiry suggest themselves. First, it may well be the case that the economy-family relationship is reciprocal rather than recursive: that is, each variable may be both a cause and an effect of the other. Goode explicitly recognizes this possibility in many of his discussions of the issue, and often speaks of "the fit between industrialism and the conjugal family" (1964:109–110) rather than, for example, "the effects of industry on family structure." Second, and equally likely, it is quite reasonable to assume multicausality with respect to the determinants of family structure. The conjugal family may have a variety of antecedents, only one set of which may be summarized by the term "industrialization." These possibilities are obviously complementary rather than contradictory: some as yet unknown factor may cause the emergence of the conjugal family, which then facilitates the process of industrialization because it is amenable to industry's demands for mobility, etc.

Further evidence has been accumulating since the publication of Greenfield's article to the effect that family structures similar to the modern conjugal type may in fact have existed considerably prior to the industrial revolution. Two of the more interesting studies in this regard are those of Furstenberg (1966) and Laslett (1973), both of whom analyzed historical data. Furstenberg, in a very interesting piece of work, studied carefully selected accounts of family practices in the United States taken from the writings of foreign travelers between 1800 and 1850. This was, as he documents, clearly prior to the period of industrialization. He drew upon 42 such accounts, selected according to the extent of observations on family behavior they contained. He concluded that the American family in the preindustrial period was not that different, in many respects, from its current form. During this period of American history, courtship and mate selection were relatively autonomous, the marital relationship was fairly close and intimate as well as quite egalitarian in terms of the power structure, and extended families were rare. In Furstenberg's opinion,

> Changes in the American family since the period of industrialization have been exaggerated by some writers. The system of mate selection, the marital relationship, and parent-child relations in the preindustrial family all show striking similarities to those in the family of today. (Furstenberg 1966:337)

What are the implications of Furstenberg's findings for Goode's theory? They are less clear than one might imagine at first glance. For one thing, Goode himself is quite cognizant of the fact that many characterizations of the family in earlier times are heavily distorted by ideological biases and inadequacies in the descriptive data. He speaks of "the classical family of Western nostalgia" (1956:3), which is

> ... a pretty picture of (family) life down on grandma's farm. There are lots of happy children, and many kinfolk live together in a large rambling house. Everyone works hard. ... All boys and girls marry,

and marry young. Young people, especially the girls, are likely to be virginal at marriage and faithful afterward. Though the parents do not arrange their children's marriages, the elders do have the right to reject a suitor and have a strong hand in the final decision. After marriage, the couple lives harmoniously, either near the boy's parents or with them, for the couple is slated to inherit the farm. No one divorces. (Goode 1963:6)

This type of family, of course, never existed on any significant scale. It is a myth. Goode, though, is not claiming that changes in the United States in family patterns since preindustrial times have been that drastic. There are many reasons why the extended family was not, and could not have been, all that common in preindustrial America. Some of these reasons, like the explanations of the family system in Barbados, are extensions of the logic of the basic theory.

Even though industrialization was not yet a factor in the social structure, the United States at the time of these observations was nonetheless very much characterized by geographic mobility. It was a frontier society. The early nineteenth century was a period of very extensive westward movement, and geographic mobility, whatever its cause, tends to minimize family structural complexity. Furthermore, a substantial proportion of the population at that time consisted of first-generation European immigrants, many of whom had left their families in the "Old Country" to come to America. These migration factors would tend to produce conjugal families.

Second, Furstenberg notes that most of the travelers' accounts to which he had access were accounts of essentially middle-class families. These consisted largely of urban dwellers (small businessmen and professionals), who actually constituted a very small proportion of the population. Where the accounts dealt with farm families, they generally pertained to "prosperous landowners" who were raising cash crops and participating in a market economy. Thus, while the United States certainly had an economy based on agriculture at this time, Furstenberg's material is primarily about the nonagricultural segment of the population. The subsistence farmers, who are the most likely category to evince extended families, were clearly underrepresented in his sample of observations.

Third, as Furstenberg notes (1966:334), ". . . less than 4 percent of the population was over 60 years old" during the historical period in question. One very important factor which limits the statistical frequency of the extended family even in societies where it is clearly the cultural ideal is the age distribution of the population. Relatively young populations cannot have too many extended families, because for a family to extend over three generations the life span of the first generation must overlap significantly with that of the third generation. In 1850, less than half of the American population survived until age 50 (Metropolitan Life Insurance Company 1952). By 1973, life expectancy in the United States had risen to 71.3 years, including an expectancy of 67.6 years for males and 75.3 years for females (U.S. Department of Health, Education, and Welfare 1975a:2). Yet even today many of us never know our grandparents. Clearly, in the nineteenth century, the relatively low life expectancy placed a severe limitation on the statistical prevalence of extended families.

Furthermore, contrary to popular opinion, people probably married at later ages in the nineteenth century than they do today. In 1890, the earliest year for which we have reliable statistics, the average age at marriage was 26 years for men and 22 years for women. As of 1972, the average ages had dropped to 23.3 and 20.9 for men and women, respectively (U.S. Bureau of the Census 1972:2). Thus, low life expectancies, in combination with late marriages, meant that few people were likely to survive beyond the birth of their grandchildren. The possibility of forming extended families was severely restricted by demographic reality.

So there are reasonable explanations for the apparent absence of extended families in Furstenberg's data on preindustrial America, some of which are derivable from Goode's theory, and some of which are attributable to the nature of the data. This analysis, like that of Greenfield, leads to the conclusion that there is considerable merit in the set of particular causes of the conjugal family which Goode and others have summarized (mobility, achievement, etc.), but that these factors may themselves stem from causes other than industrialization, in the strict meaning of that term.[12]

A fascinating series of articles leading to somewhat similar conclusions is contained in a volume edited by Michael Gordon (1973) entitled *The American Family in Social-Historical Perspective*. In the first of these articles, Peter Laslett (1973) reports on the proceedings of a conference held at Cambridge University in 1969 (the product of which is published in Laslett 1972). Through the study of various historical and demographic statistics, the members of this conference determined that the extended family had *never* been common in preindustrial England. Speaking of the period prior to the colonization of America, Laslett says:

> All the evidence went to show that the extended household was uncommon, indeed quite rare, in the preindustrial England of this era. Some three-generational households existed, just about the same number as in the England of the 1960s, but neither vertical nor lateral extension was at all frequent. Parents did not live with their married children, nor bachelors or spinsters with their married brothers or sisters, all that much more often than they do today. (Laslett 1973:21)

Furthermore, similar conclusions were reached about family structure in preindustrial France, Holland, Italy, Japan, and the United States (see Laslett 1972). And, apparently also in contradiction to the theory we are investigating, Laslett's data show that the historical period in which the English household attained its peak of structural complexity was between 1850 and 1880, which was *during* the industrializing period.

> In those communities where we have so far been able to compare their composition in preindustrial times with their composition during the process of industrialization itself, it can be shown that households became *more*, not *less*, extended. (Laslett 1973:23)

Can we conclude, then, that the change in family structure which Parsons (1943) and Goode (1963) speak of did not really occur at all, and that the family has been characterized by constancy across all varieties of economic bases? No. The next two articles in the same volume indicate that such a conclusion would be very much unwarranted, although Laslett does introduce some very important qualifications to the theory.

Berkner (1973) does not actually claim that Laslett's conclusions are wrong, but rather that they are somewhat overgeneralized, and that he and his collaborators failed to take certain important variables into account in their analyses. The most important of these is the life cycle of the extended family. Berkner documents the point with an example of family structure among the eighteenth-century peasantry of the Waldviertel, an area in Lower Austria. In this region, the dominant family form was the stem family, the operation of which was very similar to that in rural Ireland (Arensberg and Kimball 1940; Humphreys 1965, 1966). In a stem family system, one son would inherit his parents' farm, and other children would receive a fair share of the inheritance in cash or some other form of compensation.

> From this point of view, the extended family is merely a phase through which most families go. . . . (W)hen a young couple marries, they begin their marriage in an extended family. In time the parents die, and the now middle-aged couple spend their years in a nuclear family. When one of their sons marries and brings his wife into the household the family becomes extended again. (Berkner 1973:41)

This means that, *at any given time*, the clear majority of families in a stem family system must necessarily be nuclear in structure. But the system is still a stem family system.[13]

Other authors have argued that, because of the effects of stage of life cycle, life expectancy, average age at marriage, and other demographic variables on family structure, it is not possible for more than thirty percent of the families in any preindustrial society to contain three generations at any point in time even if very generous assumptions are made concerning population parameters on the relevant variables (Glick 1957; Levy 1965; Burch 1967, 1970). But this does not mean that the family *system* is not extended, just as a low statistical frequency of polygamous marriage in a society does not mean that the marital system is monogamous (see Chapter Four).

Therefore, because Laslett did not control for stage of the family life cycle in his analyses, Berkner argues that he considerably underestimates the prevalence of extended families in preindustrial England and Europe. Another problem with Laslett's analysis which Berkner points out is that extended families in general, and stem families in particular, are not associated theoretically with simply the absence of industrialization, but with the presence of sedentary subsistence agriculture. But Laslett's data come largely from urbanized areas and pertain to a significant extent to classes of people who were never assumed to have had extended families:

> (W)hile the literature on stem families has always assumed its link to specific social strata, in particular the landed peasantry, only half of Laslett's sample is made up of agricultural households, and many of these would not fit the category of landed peasants. Since the sample is so heavily weighted against the peasantry, it is not surprising that the proportion of stem families is so low. (Berkner 1973:44)[14]

The existence of some form of extended-family *system* in preindustrial Europe cannot, then, be easily discounted. But the point that most of Europe was not, at any recent time, characterized by strong, omnipresent families such as the "ideal type" described for traditional China is also important. The prevalence of stem and nuclear families, as opposed to the fully extended variety, in Northern and Western Europe may have facilitated the early adoption of an industrial economy in that region of the world.

Goode (1964:114-116) reviews differences in the process of industrialization between Japan and China. Japan's industrialization process was much more rapid, and was accomplished with considerably less social strain and disruption, than was the case in China. According to Levy (1955), many of the differences between these two nations are attributable to the different family systems operative in them prior to industrialization. In Japan, with the stem family system, the inheritance was, in effect, impartible. This meant that family property could be kept intact through the generations, and wealth (capital) could be accumulated which could then be invested in industrial enterprises. In China, though, all sons inherited equally, and accumulation was much less possible. China was also characterized by a cultural emphasis on family loyalty, such that the Chinese

> ... regarded nepotism as a duty. A man could not reject his family if he improved his station in life, and he was expected to carry upward with him as many members as he could. (Goode 1964:115)

This, of course, operated against the allocation of occupational positions on the basis of talent and personal achievements, which is held to be essential for industrial development. The Japanese, in contrast, were not subject to the demands of "filial piety" to the extent that the Chinese were, and consequently were more able to place their most able people in the positions for which their skills best qualified them, with much less regard for family connections. A stem family system such as characterized Japan and much of Europe in the immediate pre-industrial period also produces a substantial migration of young people away from the farms and into urban centers, since only one child inherits the farm. These "excess children" go into crafts, trades, and other urban occupations, and collectively constitute a ready source of labor for newly developing factory systems. The stem family, then, although we have nominally placed it in the extended family category, differs from fully extended family systems in that it may in fact further the industrialization process. Habakkuk (1955) makes a similar point with regard to differing patterns of inheritance systems in industrializing Europe: impartible inheritance customs, associated with stem families, produced an urban migration which provided the labor for industry, whereas partible inheritance suppressed industrial growth by the reverse process.

A point which needs further discussion here is Laslett's observation (1973:23) that English households evinced a tendency toward *increased* extension during the peak of industrial development, between 1850 and 1880. In another article in the same collection, Anderson (1973) makes the same observation for the English community of Preston in 1851. He found that a larger proportion of households in Preston, a developing industrial center, contained extended kin than was true for either a rural area sampled for the same time period or for Laslett's data for the period 1564 to 1821 (Laslett 1969). To what extent is this finding inconsistent with our theory?

Anderson contends that the explanation for the high rate of residential sharing that he observed is to be found in the economic advantages this arrangement offered to people in the particular situation of an industrializing town. Welfare and pension systems were as yet undeveloped at this period in history, and older retired workers' chances of surviving in relative comfort were greatly increased if they could share a household with their adult children. The advantage for the children in this arrangement was, in Anderson's words, that

> . . . the relative could also substantially increase the family income, not usually by seeking employment in the labor market, but by caring for the children and home while the mother worked in the factory. In this way the mother could have child and home looked after better, and probably more cheaply, than by hiring someone to do so, and the income she brought in kept the relative and gave a considerable surplus to the family budget. (Anderson 1973:71-72)

This situation pertained particularly to people in a relatively impoverished condition; as the general economy and specific workers gradually became more prosperous, the material advantages of co-residence with kin slowly became fewer. The result of this process is a *temporary* increase in family complexity in urban areas corresponding to the early stages of industrialization. As Gordon says in his introduction to this article:

> Anderson is arguing that kin ties and kin contact will be maintained only where these kin can perform reciprocal services. Family life during the beginnings of industrialization may, then, represent a distinctive transitional stage, rather than a full-blown picture of later patterns. (Gordon 1973:59)[15]

A study by Handwerker (1973) leads to conclusions similar to those of Anderson's study. Handwerker investigated family structure among the Bassa, a Liberian tribe, concentrating on those who were in the process of migrating from rural areas to a developing urban-industrial center, Monrovia. He found a great variety of family and household structures among Bassa in Monrovia, rather than a clear tendency toward conjugal family units, and concludes from this that family structure cannot be predicted or explained by the characteristics of technological systems. However, he did find that nuclear family structures were most common among those with high incomes; various forms of extended families predominated at lower income levels, and were explained as adaptations to the economic exigencies of migration. His evidence, then, indicates that family structure during the *process* of industrialization may well be different from family structure in a fully industrialized system, not that type of economy has no explanatory power with respect to family structure. Those who have "successfully" dealt with the process of urbanization and industrialization (that is, those with high incomes) tend overwhelmingly to evince nuclear families. Also, extended families are most likely to appear where subsistence is based upon the possession of property (1973:191). It seems reasonable to hypothesize that, as the economy of Monrovia stabilizes and as the pressure of high rates of immigration eases, nuclear families will become increasingly common. (For evidence that the transition from extended to conjugal families during industrialization may be quite direct and immediate, see Roy 1974.)

"Doubling up" with relatives in terms of residence has of course been a very common pattern of dealing with some of the problems caused by rural-to-urban migration in industrial societies, including the United States (Lee 1977). These arrangements, though, are usually temporary. They do not involve a drastic change in a society's family structure, nor do they mean that extended family households are likely to be typical of urban-industrial centers for any significant period of time.

Summary

The theory that an industrial economy and a conjugal family structure are functionally interdependent, for the reasons expressed primarily by Goode (1963), has not come through this analysis unchallenged. The two most serious forms of objection, however, were well anticipated by Goode and incorporated into his logic. These are the problems of causal order and of the actual extent of change.

It is clearly a rather serious distortion of reality to view the family as simply a passive agent in this relationship, a reactor rather than an actor, or an effect to the exclusion of its causal implications. I have elsewhere argued that the tendency for sociologists to view family phenomena as "more likely to adapt to changes in other institutional structures than to effect changes in them" (Nye and Berardo 1973:625), although in part scientifically defensible (see Nimkoff 1965:33–35; Vincent 1966), may also be partially a result of the expressive or gratification value which our culture assigns to family relations (Lee 1974:523–525). At any rate, Goode's explication of this theory clearly specifies the relationship between economy and family as reciprocal. The observation made by Greenfield, Laslett, and others that the conjugal family to a certain extent predates industrialization in some parts of Euopre and the Americas does not, therefore, disprove the theory or any of its component propositions. It does, though, indicate clearly that there are other causes of the conjugal family system besides industrialization, a point which is not at all contrary to the theory, but which constitutes a basis for its possible extension. Goode, in fact, forcefully recognizes the independent role of the spread of conjugal *ideology* across cultures, emanating from industrialized societies and affecting those in lesser stages of industrialization. While a great portion of the explanation of conjugal family systems involves a functional relation between such systems and an industrial economy, cultural diffusion also plays a role.[16] A good example of this may be Thailand, where according to Smith (1973) the conjugal family is now considered the ideal form, largely due to Western influence, but extended families provide such advantages to the subsistence farming activities characteristic of the country that ". . . the vast majority of newly married couples spend at least a few years as part of a limited extended family" (Smith 1973:140).

The second objection to the theory, that family structures do not really change that much in correspondence to the industrialization process, also deserves serious consideration. This is clearly a matter of degree. Marion Levy (1965) argues that, regardless of the *ideal* family system which prevails in any given society, the majority of all families in all societies are and have been nuclear in structure (see also Burch 1967, 1970). We will detail his argument below. But, as we have pointed out, the historical data which have led certain researchers to this conclusion are inadequate in several ways, particularly in that they pertain more to family size than structure or composition, and that the family life cycle has generally not been taken into account in these analyses. Nonetheless, we do not wish to perpetuate the myth of the "classical family of Western nostalgia." The use of primarily cross-cultural data, in which societies are classified according to their "typical" family structures and intrasocietal variation is at best indirectly considered, makes it easy to overrate intersocietal and temporal differences in family type. But differences do exist in both ideal and actual systems, and these differences do correspond to a considerable extent to differences in the economic bases of societies.

The theory of correspondence between industry and the conjugal family is reasonably well documented, and the associations between economy and family type which have been observed are quite readily subject to explanation by reference to the theory. But in one very important sense the theory is quite partial. It was the objective of Goode and other proponents of this theory to explain why industrial societies are increasingly characterized by conjugal family systems. Although they generally took, as a baseline for comparison, societies with sedentary agricultural economies and extended families, the range of variation in the types of societies they examined was actually quite limited. The problem they addressed is not really the general question of the determinants of family structure, but rather the specific issue of why industrial societies have conjugal families. This is only one part of the broader theoretical problem. Do all types of nonindustrial societies tend toward extended families? What are the causes of the extended family in agricultural societies? These and other similar questions remain largely unanswered within the framework of Goode's analysis. They are addressed in the next section.

The broader perspective: determinants of family structure

The independent variable

We have thus far reviewed evidence to the effect that conjugal family systems are generally typical of industrial societies, and, at least by implication, that agricultural societies are more likely to be characterized by extended families. An empirical generalization which fairly accurately expresses this relationship is that as the level of industrialization increases, family structural complexity decreases. But what about societies at the preindustrial, or even preagricultural, level of economic development? Are all such societies homogeneous in terms of family structure? The generalization we have just stated might seem to imply that this is the case. But in fact it doesn't. It simply says nothing about variation among societies at the preindustrial level, beyond the single observation that agricultural societies are more likely than industrial societies to evince an extended family system.

One of the problems here is that the term "industrialization" is not sufficiently abstract to permit the formulation of general propositions which will include all types of societies. (We have already pointed out that it is inadequate in certain other respects as well.) We need a more general concept, which will include the phenomenon of industrialization, but which is more abstract and will permit the inclusion of a greater range of societies.

Marsh (1967:33-37) suggests the concept of societal "differentiation." Such a variable should permit the researcher to theoretically and empirically rank societies according to their degree of internal differentiation. As component indicators of this variable, Marsh includes population size of the operative political unit, degree of stratification, and (for "contemporary national societies") percentage of males employed in nonagricultural occupations and annual per capita energy consumption.[17] The higher the score, the more differentiated the society.

Robert Winch and his associates (Winch 1974; Winch and Blumberg 1968; Blumberg and Winch 1972; Freeman and Winch 1957) have employed a concept which they term societal "complexity." Its basic premises are quite similar to those of "differentiation," but the operational indicators are somewhat different. In a recent empirical analysis (Blumberg and Winch 1972) the variable was operationalized by a combination of measures of technology and social organization. Their measure of technology ranks societies according to type of subsistence economy. From lowest to highest, the index includes (1) gathering, (2) hunting, (3) incipient agriculture, (4) horticulture or extensive agriculture, and (5) intensive (sedentary) agriculture. This takes us up to the point of "incipient industry," where another scale takes over (see Adelman and Morris 1967; Blumberg and Winch 1972:914-919). On the social organization dimension, they employ a scale based upon a theoretical discussion by Goldschmidt (1959), which includes:

> (1) mean size of local community; (2) permanence of settlement (the nomadic-sedentary dimension); (3) stratification (ranging from none to a system based on social classes); and (4) political complexity (number of levels of jurisdictional hierarchy beyond the local community). (Blumberg and Winch 1972:904)

In terms of theoretical meaning, the concepts of societal differentiation and societal complexity are virtually identical, or at least interchangeable. Assuming that industrialization is an indicator of societal complexity, Blumberg and Winch phrase Goode's conclusion in the more abstract terms we have been looking for:

> . . . Goode studied developing and developed societies from nomadic Arabs to urban-industrial Japan and the United States. He concluded that, as societies modernize, their diverse but relatively complex family systems converge on a simple, less-extended form which he called conjugal. That is, Goode's study documented the point that the relation-

ship between complexity of societies and extended familism (family complexity) was negative. (Blumberg and Winch 1972:899)

But, as these authors go on to point out, empirical support for this generalization is far from unequivocal. It is relevant here to inquire into the extent of support for Goode's conclusion from other studies, and the causes of differences between the results of the various investigations.

Related evidence

Three years prior to the publication of Goode's study in 1963, a study of the relationship between family structure and type of economy appeared (Nimkoff and Middleton 1960) which was based on the World Ethnographic Sample. In terms of societal complexity, the range of societies in this sample begins with those where subsistence depends on hunting and gathering at the low end, and extends to societies based on agriculture and animal husbandry. Nimkoff and Middleton included nine economic types between these two extremes, representing the complete range of societal complexity contained within the World Ethnographic Sample. Family structure was dichotomized into categories of "independent" and "extended."[18]

Nimkoff and Middleton were able to classify 549 of the 565 societies in the World Ethnographic Sample according to both economic and family structure. Their conclusion, phrased again in abstract terms, was that the relationship between societal complexity and family complexity is *positive*. Of the 24 least complex societies in the sample (those whose economies were based on hunting and gathering), 20 (83.3 percent) were characterized by independent families. Of the 18 societies in which agriculture and animal husbandry were "codominant" (the most complex societies), only two had independent families and 16 (88.9 percent) were categorized as having extended families (Nimkoff and Middleton 1960:217). The positive relationship between these variables was maintained throughout the intermediate categories of societal complexity.

At first glance, it appears very much as if these results contradict those of Goode. Is the correlation between societal complexity and familial complexity positive, as the results of Nimkoff and Middleton indicate, or negative, as Goode contends? The key to the resolution of this apparent conflict lies in an examination of the range of the independent variable, societal complexity. If we consider societal complexity, measured by type of economy, as a continuum ranging from hunting and gathering at the lower extreme to industry at the upper, with sedentary agriculture and animal husbandry intermediate, it is clear that the two studies in question took their observations from different points on this scale. Nimkoff and Middleton studied societies in the lower ranges of complexity, while Goode studied those at higher levels. On the single point on this continuum where their observations correspond, the primarily agricultural societies, the results of these two studies agree: extended families predominate. Goode points out that independent families characterize industrial societies, whereas Nimkoff and Middleton show that this same family structure is typical of hunting and gathering societies at the opposite pole of the continuum.

The results of these two studies are complementary rather than contradictory. The appropriate conclusion is that the relationship between societal complexity and familial complexity is *curvilinear.* The highest levels of family complexity (that is, the highest frequencies of extended family systems) are found at the intermediate levels of societal complexity. This point corresponds to economies based on intensive agriculture and animal husbandry. Any change in societal complexity from this point, in either direction, corresponds to a decrease in family complexity.[19]

This conclusion was not at all unanticipated. Nimkoff and Middleton, in fact, point out quite explicitly that industrial societies are virtually unrepresented in the World Ethnographic Sample, but that a great deal of other data indicate that the independent family predominates in them:

> While it is possible for extended families to exist with separate dwellings for the component conjugal units, nevertheless the family in most industrial societies is in fact, as field studies indicate, organized along independent, not extended, lines. (Nimkoff and Middleton 1960:225)

The existence of this curvilinear relationship was also posited, on theoretical grounds, by Marsh (1967:73) and by Winch and Blumberg (1968), and later documented (Blumberg and Winch 1972) by data from the Ethnographic Atlas supplemented by a sample of 43 industrial societies collected by Adelman and Morris (1967). In this study (Blumberg and Winch 1972), the highest frequency of extended families was found among societies with either extensive or intensive agriculture (80 percent). One can discern this "inflection point" even in the Ethnographic Atlas; societies characterized by "intensive agriculture with irrigation," a technological advance over nonirrigated agriculture, are less likely (65 percent) to have extended family systems. For the 25 most complex societies in the Adelman-Morris sample, only three (12 percent) have extended family systems. Thus it is clear from these data that a curvilinear relationship does exist. Our problem now is to explain it.

An integrated explanation

The explanation of a curvilinear relationship must, almost necessarily, come in two parts. We have already reviewed Goode's explanation for the affinity between an industrial economy and a conjugal family system, and none of the evidence for the curvilinear relationship causes us to modify our earlier conclusions about his theory. The task that remains is to explain why the nuclear or independent family should characterize hunting and gathering societies, and why the advent of agriculture should be associated with an increase in family structural complexity.[20] Nimkoff and Middleton give us an excellent starting point.

These authors provide three succinct explanations for the positive association between societal and familial complexity in the lower part of the societal complexity scale. The first, and probably most important, explanatory variable is the size and stability of the food supply. Drawing on earlier work by Steward (1955), they argue that the members of societies which depend on hunting and gathering for subsistence must disperse in order to most effectively exploit the food-producing capacities of the environment. Large collections of people who are spatially and temporally proximate overtax the productive capacities of the land. Hunting and gathering societies have always had very low population densities. Part of the dispersal process results in small, relatively independent family units, which achieve the highest per capita production of food:

> When game and wild plants are limited and dispersed, the members of a hunting or gathering society will generally scatter to achieve their optimal exploitation. . . . Participation of many persons in seed- or root-gathering generally not only fails to increase the per capita harvest but decreases it. (Nimkoff and Middleton 1960:218)

On the other side of the coin, agricultural societies usually produce a more abundant and stable supply of food. This enables larger concentrations of individuals to reside together, on one plot of land, for much longer periods of time if not indefinitely. Furthermore, in an agricultural system based upon human labor, it is generally the case that each worker can produce as much as, or more than, he or she consumes. There is, at least, a productive task for virtually everyone. The family can exploit the productive capacity of the land to a greater extent because of the number of available workers, and also because the variation in age, sex, and social position within the extended family lends itself well to an efficient division of labor in the agricultural enterprise.

A second component of Nimkoff and Middleton's explanation involves spatial or geographic mobility. As we argued in an earlier section, when the environment is such that the individual is the unit of labor, and when the individual is required to be mobile by the subsistence pattern, extended families are difficult to maintain. Nimkoff and Middleton (1960:219) observed that ". . . the extended family system is found least often among purely nomadic or migratory bands and is most common among sedentary peoples with a fixed residence." Not surprisingly, hunters and gatherers are very likely to be nomadic, and agriculturalists are almost uniformly sedentary. It turns out, therefore, that the variable of geographic mobility has no *independent* explanatory power; its effects are statistically explained by type of subsistence economy (Nimkoff and Middleton 1960:219). But it does help interpret the economy-family relationship. Hunters and gatherers are typified by nuclear family structures because, in part, mobility is required by their mode of subsistence, and extended families are cumbersome to maintain under conditions of high mobility. Also, a large extended family would be forced to move more often, because they would exhaust the resources available in a particular location more rapidly. The source of livelihood in an agricultural society, the land, stays put. Agriculturalists are therefore enabled, by the fixed nature of their wealth, to live in extended families, and as we have already seen these extended families provide them with certain advantages in terms of division of labor and, therefore, productive capacities.

      This points out an important parallel between the causes of the "independent" (nuclear) family in the least and the most complex societies. On the abstract level, the causal factors overlap to a certain extent. Geographic mobility is involved in each case. Nimkoff and Middleton point this out explicitly:

> The modern industrial society, with its small independent family, is then like the simpler hunting and gathering society and, in part, apparently for some of the same reasons, namely, limited need for family labor and physical mobility. The hunter is mobile because he pursues the game; the industrial worker, the job. (Nimkoff and Middleton 1960:225)

      The third component of the explanation, which overlaps conceptually with the first two to some extent, is property ownership (Nimkoff and Middleton 1960:219-220). The possession of some specific parcel of land, on either an individual or a family basis, is clearly more important to farming populations than to hunters and gatherers. The latter, of course, require rights to the use of land, but this generally involves tribal or group rights to range over large expanses of territory in pursuit of food. The agricultural family enterprise, though, requires in most cases the allocation of specific property to specific economic units, often families. Since the family's property is the source of survival for the individuals belonging to the family, successive generations are understandably reluctant to part with it. This results in a residential compounding of the generations on the family property, and hence in extended families.

      Nimkoff and Middleton's work in this area has not gone unchallenged, in spite of the clarity of their analysis. Another study of the economy-family relationship, which was also based on the World Ethnographic Sample, came to a very different conclusion. Marie Osmond (1969) argues that a type of family which she terms "limited," and which includes the nuclear family as one subtype, is *more* common among societies based on intensive agriculture than among hunting and gathering societies, and that a "general" type of family is characteristic of less complex societies. How can the same data lead to two such different conclusions?

The answer lies in the two explicitly different measurement logics employed, and specifically in the categorization of the family structure variable. Nimkoff and Middleton, as we noted, combined Murdock's stem, lineal, and fully extended types into a composite "extended" category. The other classification, "independent," encompassed ". . . familial groups which do not normally include more than one nuclear or polygamous family (Nimkoff and Middleton 1960:215). Osmond, however, uses a different criterion for categorization. She is interested in the potential number of economic dependents which the head of a family household might have in various types of family structures. She argues that the number of such dependents is potentially greater in fully extended and "compound" families—that is, families related through multiple (polygynous) marriages—than in simple nuclear, stem, or lineal families. Osmond's two categories of family structure are, therefore, the "limited" (nuclear, stem, and lineal) and the "general" (fully extended and polygynous).

It is this difference in classification that produces the unique results of Osmond's study. For example, using her classification scheme, she found that of the 111 "intensive agriculture" societies in her sample, 70, or 63 percent, had "limited" families and only 41 (37 percent) had "general" family systems. Thus it appears that the limited family is very common under the condition of intensive agriculture—much more common, in fact, than under any other type of subsistence economy represented in the World Ethnographic Sample. But if her data are reclassified according to the Nimkoff-Middleton categories, the percentages are exactly reversed for intensive agricultural societies: 63 percent have extended families and 37 percent have independent families. The same kind of reversal occurs in her other two categories of the subsistence economy variable.

The disagreement here, then, is over the "proper" method of categorizing types of family structure. There is obviously no inherently right or wrong way of doing it, but this doesn't stop us from expressing a preference according to the criterion of usefulness in the construction of explanatory theory. We think[21] that the classification scheme used by Nimkoff and Middleton is preferable from a theoretical point of view, for two reasons. First, Osmond's classification combines marital with family structures. We have argued previously that these constitute *two* relevant variables for theoretical purposes, not one, unless it is empirically shown to be most fruitful to combine them. This has not been demonstrated. Second, Nimkoff and Middleton and others have demonstrated that the family structure variable behaves empirically in ways that are both predictable and explainable according to a rather well-developed (for sociology) theory. The main criterion for determining the value of any scientific construct is whether it can be used effectively in theoretical statements (see Lee 1975b). The family structural complexity variable has demonstrated theoretical utility. Dropping it in favor of Osmond's alternative construct would not, at this particular juncture, be justifiable theoretically.

But the information which Osmond provides is valuable in its own right. The important thing to recognize is that her conclusions do not correct or supplant those of Nimkoff and Middleton. She is approaching a slightly different issue from a different point of view, and the variables she employs differ, slightly but significantly, from those used by other researchers. The reason that Osmond's answers were different from those of Nimkoff and Middleton is that she asked different questions. Petersen (1969) has argued strongly in favor of comparability of measurement in kinship research, and with very good reason: varying measurement procedures can cause a greal deal of confusion in the interpretation of results which may appear to conflict, but actually do not.

It becomes clear from our synthesis of these empirical studies that what needs explaining is not the high frequency of conjugal families in industrial societies or nuclear families in hunting and gathering societies, but the prevalence of extended families in agricultural societies. There has been no pattern of unilinear evolution toward some "higher" or "more civilized" family form as societies develop or modernize. Rather, the development of agriculture apparently led to an increased tendency toward extended families, as compared to the situation in societies where food is obtained by foraging and/or hunting. But further technological development and social differentiation beyond the point of intensive agriculture is associated with a family system very similar to (but not identical with) that found in hunting and gathering societies.

An interesting illustration of the relationship between subsistence pattern and family type, on a very immediate level, is the case of the Papago Indians of the North American desert Southwest. This people follows a yearly cycle of about four months farming and eight months hunting and gathering, depending on the timing of rainfall. During the four farming months they live in villages which consist almost entirely of patrilineally related kinsmen, may of whom banded together into extended families:

> Each lineal family gathered in a collection of domed huts, with its progenitor at its head. . . . He shared with his sons (and sometimes his brothers) a plot of land which received floods during the rainy season. Here all the men worked on crops which were kept in a common store-

> house. . . . When the father died, the sons still lived as neighbors, each
> one collecting about him his own children and grandchildren. (Under-
> hill 1965:154–155)

But when the dry season began the extended families apparently broke up into independent units, most likely nuclear in structure, which roamed the desert hunting game and gathering vegetation. Thus, in the space of a year, the Papago illustrate the relationship between economic and family structures.

The processes which culminate in the various forms of family structure have, we hope, been clarified to a certain extent by this analysis. It is important to recognize, though, that the type of subsistence economy is not the only variable which is systematically associated with family structure, nor can we perfectly predict type of family from type of economy at the cross-cultural level of analysis. There are some hunting and gathering societies with extended families, and some sedentary agricultural societies with conjugal or nuclear families. Nimkoff and Middleton point out (1960:221–225) that many of these "deviant cases" may be explained by a rather simple refinement of their basic theory. For example, although it is *generally* true that agricultural economies produce a more adequate food supply than hunting and gathering, societies of the latter type which live in an environment of abundance don't have to be mobile, and larger collections of people can be supported by a small amount of land. Extended families may thus develop in these situations.

This observation, together with points made earlier in this analysis, leads to an important conclusion which is actually a modification of the general theory being evaluated. The critical variables involved in the explanation of family structure are not economic types *per se*, but rather the set of conditions which tend to coincide with them. Specifically, nuclear family structures emerge where ecological and technological constraints make for high rates of geographic mobility and high valuation on individual achievement, where the unit of labor is the individual, and where most people depend for subsistence on labor rather than on property. The fact that these conditions occur most frequently in hunting-gathering and industrial economies produces a correlation between economic types and family types, but the immediate causes of nuclear family structures reside in the intervening variables. The opposite values of these variables tend to occur in horticultural or agricultural economies, and are associated with extended family types. But where the ecological environment is such that, for example, it is possible for hunting and gathering groups to remain sedentary, these peoples may well evince extended families. As we have found in many other analytic cases, the development of a theory often requires us to "disaggregate" omnibus variables such as type of economy into their component parts, and to investigate the independent impact of each component on the dependent variable. Future research in this area will hopefully proceed in that direction. Meanwhile, we need to examine two further factors which are, cross-culturally, associated with family structure.

Stratification and family structure

Nimkoff and Middleton (1960:219–221) found that the type of family system characteristic of a society was related to the extent of social stratification. They trichotomized 512 societies in the World Ethnographic Sample into those with little or no stratification, those with distinctions of some importance based on wealth, and those with hereditary social classes and/or slavery predominant. Their conclusion was that "... the greater the degree of social stratification, the greater is the tendency for the extended rather than the independent family system to become established" (Nimkoff and Middleton 1960: 219).

It might be supposed that the more complex societies in terms of subsistence economy (those with intensive agriculture) would also be the most likely to evince complex stratification patterns, and thus that the relationship between stratification and family structure would be spurious. But according to Nimkoff and Middleton's tabulations this is not the case. They found that the relationship in question obtained within categories of subsistence economy, although the differences in family structure according to stratification were somewhat less in the more complex societies.

Although Nimkoff and Middleton do not advance a highly developed explanation of this association, they do suggest (1960:219) that "societies with appreciable stratification will generally have more family wealth than those with little or no stratification." That is, if there are considerable status distinctions between the members of a society, based at least in part on wealth, then there must be some segment of the population which is relatively well-to-do. They may own more land, or possess more material advantages of whatever sort, than the remainder of the population, and may therefore be able to establish and maintain extended families. Since they would be the most visible segment of the society, their family patterns would be likely to be taken as "typical" and in fact other categories of people may attempt to model their own behavior after that of the "elite."

Chu and Hollingsworth (1969), also using the World Ethnographic Sample but employing different categorization procedures for the relevant variables, obtained results which essentially support those of Nimkoff and Middleton. They trichotomized Murdock's types of family structure, combining the stem and lineal types in one category. They found that the independent (nuclear) family system predominated in the absence of significant social stratification, the lineal-stem system was positively related to a complex stratification pattern with three or more distinct social classes, and the extended family was most likely to appear under hereditary aristocracy systems of stratification (1969:326). They did not, however, institute controls for type of economy or other possible relevant variables.

The authors of this study point out that, according to their reading of previous research and theory,

> . . . the importance of finding the positive relationship between the independent family and absence of significant social stratification seems to be that it contradicts much contemporary sociological thinking. (Chu and Hollingsworth 1969:327)

The contemporary thinking they are referring to appears to be the observation that "the independent family is more closely associated with industrialized societies in which complex class systems exist" (1969:323). What they are actually pointing to is not a contradiction, but rather a generalization to the effect that the relationship between stratification and family structural complexity is either curvilinear, having the same form as that between type of economy and family structure, or that the positive association they observe pertains only to societies with nonindustrial economies. The choice between these alternatives would depend upon whether industrial stratification systems are more complex than those of agricultural societies, which is an empirical and conceptual question beyond the scope of our task.

A third inquiry into the relationship between stratification and family structure is that of Blumberg and Winch (1972:907-909). Their findings differ from those of the previous two studies. Using a four-part categorization of degree of stratification, they find the relationship to be curvilinear, with highly complex families most common among societies with hereditary aristocracy (this agrees with Chu and Hollingsworth), but less frequent where social classes have developed. Their findings, however, are not directly comparable with those of the earlier studies, partly because they distinguished four categories of stratification instead of the five used by Chu and Hollingsworth or the three used by Nimkoff and Middleton. Also, their measure of family structural complexity is a dichotomy, including nuclear families with frequent polygyny in the "highly complex" category along with the stem, lineal, and fully extended family systems.

Blumberg and Winch also found (1972:912) that the association between stratification and family structure was largely explained by type of subsistence economy. Thus, they interpret degree of stratification as simply one among several manifestations of societal complexity, the primary indicator of which is type of subsistence economy (1972:910-911).

All three studies we have reviewed suggest that the statistical relationship between extent of stratification and family complexity is curvilinear, with the peak of family complexity at intermediate levels of stratification. However, they differ to a certain extent in the explanations attached to this relationship. The proffered explanations, in turn, differ according to the measurement and categorization of key variables. We may conclude that the relationship in question is in fact curvilinear, but the question of whether or not stratification has explanatory power independent of type of economy shall have to await further analyses for a definitive answer.

Internal causes of family structural change

Marion Levy (1965), in the context of a discussion of conceptual distinctions between ideal and actual family structures, argues that extended family systems contain within themselves certain strains which make their long-term continuation problematic. While not denying the existence of considerable variation in ideal family types across cultures, Levy contends that the variation in actual structures is much less:

> The general outlines and nature of the actual family structures have been virtually identical in certain strategic respects[22] in all known societies in world history for well over 50 percent of the members of those societies. (Levy 1965:41-42)

The type of family which is and has been common to virtually all societies, in this argument, approximates the nuclear type. Levy is contending, in other words, that extended family systems have never been the statistically dominant family form in any society.[23]

In developing this point, Levy conceptually distinguishes between three types of societies: those which do not have a modern medical technology; those complex societies which have developed such technology as part of the "modernization" process; and "transitional" societies which have imported modern medicine but which are not modernized in other ways. He then inquires, theoretically, into the correspondence between ideal and actual family structures in each of these three types of societies.

As we know, industrialized societies are almost uniformly characterized by the conjugal family system as the ideal type. According to Levy,

> There is little to prevent high correlation between the ideal and actual family structures as far as vertical and horizontal proliferation are concerned. (Levy 1965:49)

In societies which do not possess modern medicine, which would include virtually all hunting and gathering societies as well as most of those which are dependent on agriculture, Levy recognizes that there are "radical variations in ideal family structures from one society to another" (Levy 1965:49). But, he argues, uniformly high death rates in these societies make the actual attainment of an extended family very rare.[24] Therefore, correspondence between ideal and actual structures will be frequent only when the ideal structure is nuclear (1965:49-54).

The third category of society, those which are currently "modernizing," requires the most complex explanation of the three types. Extended family systems are quite common among these societies in the ideal sense. And, since modern medicine is being imported by most of them at the present time and death rates are dropping accordingly, a high prevalence of extended families is demographically possible. But Levy contends that there are certain internal structural features of extended families which work against their continuity:

> Paradoxically, perhaps, it may be suggested that the actual closure of the gap between ideal and actual family units may itself be one of the major factors creating pressure for a change in the ideal family type— that change always being in the direction of a smaller ideal unit. (Levy 1965:56)

These factors include, most notably, the complexity of administering a family of three or more generations, and the obvious difficulty of maintaining inheritance systems which would keep families together across generations without expanding their size beyond the capacities of their land to support them. Levy recounts (1965:57-58) the problems which occurred in the traditional Chinese extended family when more than two sons survived to maturity. These included problems of inheritance and insufficient land, the raising and controlling of inordinately large numbers of children, and the transmission of authority between generations.

> It is the hypothesis here that much of the stability of the large scale ideal family structures inhered in the fact that those ideal conditions were not in fact approximated much more often than was compatible with special levels of kinship administrative virtuosity. . . . A good part of Chinese literature is concerned with the difficulties of maintaining stability when the really large ideal family was in fact attained. The family head who could run such an aggregation and keep it stable was regarded as having a special virtuosity. (Levy 1965:58)

Thus the very existence of extended families on the empirical level may be a source of change toward the conjugal family system at the ideal level.

Does Levy's argument regarding the statistical prevalence of small or conjugal familes, even in societies with norms specifying extended families, make the issue of the determinants of family structure superfluous? No, not at all. Levy is simply pointing out that there has probably been less variation, cross-culturally and historically, in actual family structures than we have sometimes assumed. But there is no doubt that considerable variation in ideal family structures does exist, and that this variation in cultural content has many important ramifications for behavior. Levy points out (1965:60-63) that variation in ideal family structure affects authority structures, the allocation and distribution of economic goods, inheritance, and fertility. Furthermore, in a culture in which extended families are normatively preferred, most people will *attempt* to form extended families where conditions permit. But for a variety of reasons, depending in part on medical technology, they don't always succeed. (Our earlier discussion of the effects of the family life cycle on family structure is also relevant here.) A family *system* may reasonably be classified as extended even though a statistical majority of all families may be nuclear in structure.

Conclusion

In the course of this analysis, we have discovered that family structural complexity is related, on the cross-cultural level, to several other kinds of abstract variables: societal complexity and extent of stratification seem to be the most important, at least theoretically. In both cases, the relationship is curvilinear. Although most "modern" industrial nations are characterized by the conjugal family, family structure is not simply an inverse linear function of "modernization." There is, rather, a more intricate and theoretically meaningful association between family structure and societal complexity or differentiation; industrialization is simply one value of the latter variable.

We should also reiterate some important qualifications which pertain to the theory we have discussed. First, problems of causal priority among the variables involved have not been clearly resolved, but it is not particularly useful to view family structure as a dependent variable only. The process undoubtedly involves reciprocal causation. Second, the relationship between societal complexity and family structure, while fairly well documented empirically, has not been completely explained in any final sense. The explanations we have offered here should be considered tentative and plausible, based on what we know at the moment, but not definitive. Third, there are many exceptions to the generalizations we have stated, on both the societal and the individual levels. We have dealt, of course, with cross-cultural and cross-societal data exclusively. Not all individual families in extended family systems are, *ipso facto*, extended families. There is a great deal of intrasocietal variation in family structures, some of which we shall investigate in later chapters by means of cross-national data.

Up to this point, we have investigated family structures as if individual families were the largest possible unit of analysis. Empirically, this is clearly not the case. In virtually all societies families are bound together into larger units by ties of kinship of one sort or another. This is true even in societies with conjugal families: kinship ties are not absent in such systems, they are simply different than in other societies. In the next chapter, we will define and discuss the basic parameters of the various kinds of kinship systems, their causes, and their consequences.

Notes

1. Contrary to superficial appearances, we did not settle this issue in Chapter Three where the universality of the family was discussed. Reiss' (1965) definition was constructed for the purpose of determining the existence of a universal association between family structure and function. The problem here is to determine what kind of conceptualization of the family structure variable will be most efficient in the construction of a particular explanatory theory. Since objectives are different, the definitions appropriate in each instance also differ.

2. One should be able to decipher the Freudian symbolism of this convention without a detailed explanation.

3. The categorization scheme and terminology employed here are taken directly from Robert Winch (1971:11-12; Winch and Blumberg 1968:75).

4. Some social anthropologists prefer to use an equal sign to indicate marriage in their kinship charts. Classroom experience, however, has shown that this symbol currently carries ideological implications which I do not at all intend, and would very much like to avoid at the moment. Hence the horizontal line.

5. See Chapter Six for a discussion of postmarital residence.

6. The West, Arabia, Sub-Saharan Africa, India, China, and Japan.

7. Blood (1969) reports a positive correlation between mutual aid exchanged with relatives and marital solidarity for a sample of American wives.

8. The "declining functionality" of the family has been a major thesis for several very influential scholars in the twentieth century. Ogburn (1922, 1938, 1955) and Zimmerman (1947, 1970) have taken this process as indicative of family disorganization and general social disorganization, respectively. Their arguments, however, are premised upon some clear value judgments; this is particularly true of Zimmerman. See Leslie (1973:224–230, 237) for a summary of their positions. Bardis (1964:458-459) expresses a point of view similar to Ogburn's. Goode's logic, while closer to Ogburn's than to Zimmerman's, bears greater affinity to Parsons (1959; Parsons and Bales 1955; Rodman 1965b) and other functional analysts who argue that the family is becoming more specialized, in a functional sense, rather than "disorganized." The family in highly differentiated societies is more restricted in function as it is restricted in structure.

9. Greenfield is obviously not attacking William Goode's argument specifically, since Goode's first and most important work on this subject did not appear until two years after Greenfield's article was published. But as we noted, Goode was by no means the first scholar to espouse this logic. Greenfield

actually launches his thesis from a generalization by Ogburn and Nimkoff (1950:469) to the effect that the "consanguine" (extended) family is replaced by the conjugal form as industrialization proceeds.

10. This is actually a bit of an overgeneralization. Under some circumstances it is reasonable to conceive of causes as being chronologically subsequent to their effects; in other words, teleological causal theories are not necessarily wrong because they are teleological. See Hempel (1959). However, in this case the conditions necessary for the application of a teleological explanation do not appear to obtain.

11. Another problem with Greenfield's logic is that correlational hypotheses are never rejected by examples of counter-instances.

12. A series of studies by Lantz et al. (1968, 1973, 1975) involving content analyses of preindustrial American magazines from 1741 to 1850 also indicate that many of the elements of conjugal family systems were present in American families prior to industrialization. These elements include romantic love as a basis for mate selection and a trend toward more equalitarian (less overtly patriarchal) power structures in marriage. The implications of and limitations on these findings are similar to those of Furstenberg.

13. Another example of a type of family which varies in cyclical fashion, from nuclear to extended and back again, over the course of the family life cycle, is the Hindu "joint family." In this system, brothers live together for as long as their parents are alive and, after the death of their parents, until their own children are "launched." At this point the joint household is divided, with each brother and his spouse forming their own residential unit. See Gore (1965:211–213).

14. For evidence of the greater frequency of stem families among rural farming populations than urban dwellers see Sweetser (1964) for Finland, Drake (1969) for Norway, and Winch and Greer (1968) for the United States.

15. For a more detailed account of Anderson's findings and explanations, see Anderson (1971). The methodological techniques employed for the collection and analysis of these sociohistorical data are summarized in Anderson (1972).

16. See Chapter Two for a detailed discussion of the concept of diffusion.

17. The method of index construction, along with the scores of particular societies on this scale, is given in Marsh (1967:329–374).

18. Independent families here are defined as "familial groups which do not normally include more than one nuclear or polygamous family." Extended families are all other types, including Murdock's categories of stem, lineal, and fully extended. (Nimkoff and Middleton 1960:215)

19. This should not be taken to imply that hunting and gathering societies are typified by *conjugal* family systems. Nimkoff and Middleton measured only internal family structure as the criterion variable; they did not investigate type of mate-selection system, postmarital residence patterns, or any of the other factors which Goode stipulates as criteria of conjugal families.

20. Our phraseology here might imply that we have settled on a causal order, with type of economy as the cause and family structure as the effect. In fact, as in the case of Goode's argument, the causal directionality of the relationship in question is not at all settled. But, since Nimkoff and Middleton adopt this order, and since it facilitates communication, we shall continue for the moment to speak of economy as the cause and family as the effect.

21. The "we" here is purely editorial. "We" do not know the extent of consensus among comparative researchers on this matter.

22. Levy is referring here to (1) size of membership, (2) age composition, (3) sex composition, (4) generational composition, (5) number of married couples, and (6) number of siblings. See Levy (1965:41).

23. In addition to his review of existing literature on the prevalence of extended family systems, Levy's own research makes him very well qualified to address this issue. He is the author of probably the most definitive work on the traditional Chinese family (Levy 1949), long regarded as the "ideal type" of extended family system.

24. For a demonstration of the statistical probabilities of occurrence of extended families under a range of reasonable demographic assumptions, see Ansley Coale's appendix to Levy's article in Coale *et al.* (1965:64-69). Thomas Burch has supported, elaborated upon, and qualified Levy's argument in certain important respects. See Burch (1967, 1970).

chapter six
Kinship structure

Kinship, interaction, and organization

Kinship and interpersonal behavior

Of all the chapters in this book, the current chapter is clearly the most introductory. While it is not the case that the study of kinship is more complex or advanced than other branches of the social sciences, it is nonetheless true that there is a vast amount of material available to the student of kinship. The data are extensive, the perspectives employed by scholars in the area are extremely diverse, and the terminologies are often quite complex.[1] We will not pretend here to give the field full coverage (which would be impossible in an entire volume on the subject), but will instead attempt to explicate certain basic concepts in kinship analysis and introduce some of the empirical content of these concepts.

This disclaimer of a complete treatment of the subject should not, however, imply that we consider kinship unimportant. On the contrary, kinship is of the utmost importance in any study of comparative social organization, in many ways that residents of industrialized nations may initially find difficult to comprehend. For many of the world's societies the study of kinship is synonymous with the study of social organization as a whole. It is this equivalence that enabled the anthropologist George Peter Murdock to publish his book, in 1949, entitled *Social Structure,* which dealt in its entirety with kinship and family systems. This is a useful illustration of the point that, in many of the world's societies, kinship structure *is* social structure.

What are the implications of this equivalence for societies in which it obtains, and for the members of these societies? In societies where kinship is the basic organizing principle, it is often the case that no other kinds of groups or social structures exist independently of the kinship structure.[2] In an "undifferentiated" society, the kin group is the unit within which economic, political, educational, and religious interaction occurs. In a differentiated society such as the contemporary United States, the individual makes his living by participating in the economic or occupational structure, is trained for this participation by an educational system, has his rights protected and his interests expressed and defended by the political structure, and achieves a religious identity by virtue of his membership in an organization which specializes in this function. In a kinship-based society, though, all of these things follow from membership in a single group; entrance into such a group and one's position within that group depend entirely upon kinship relations.

> For the longer period of human development, mankind lived for the most part in societies in which kinship-based groups were *the* constituent units. A man's health and security, his very life and even his chance of immortality, were in the hands of his kin. A "kinless" man was at best a man without social position: at worst, he was a dead man. (Fox 1967:15, italics added)

The individual in such a society, then, is almost totally dependent on his kin for his social position or place in society. He has no position other than that which he occupies in the kin group. Virtually all of his relationships with other people will be based upon or mediated by kinship.

The anthropologist Radcliffe-Brown gives a fascinating illustration of this phenomenon and its implications from his experience as an ethnographer in Western Australia. He was guided in his travels by an aboriginal Australian. Each time they came upon a band of people, the first and absolutely necessary step in establishing lines of communication was to determine the kinship connections between the visitors and the hosts. This was one important function of the guide. His kinship relations with the various camps were instrumental in gaining access for the anthropologist. In one case, however, no kin relationship between the guide and a band could be discovered. Radcliffe-Brown was apparently able to establish some rapport anyhow, but the guide refused to enter the camp.

> . . . I found that he was frightened. These men were not his relatives, and they were therefore his enemies. . . . If I am a blackfellow and meet another blackfellow that other must be either my relative or my enemy. If he is my enemy I shall take the first opportunity of killing him, for fear he will kill me. (Radcliffe-Brown; quoted in Stephens 1963:100)

The general principle regarding the importance of kinship among this tribe (the Kareira) which Radcliffe-Brown infers is as follows:

> It is impossible for a man to have any social relations with anyone who is not his relative because there is no standard by which two persons in this position can regulate their conduct towards one another. I am compelled to treat a person differently according as he is my "brother," "brother-in-law," "father," or "uncle." If I do not know which of these he is, all intercourse is impossible. (Radcliffe-Brown; quoted in Stephens 1963:101)

There is a small logical inconsistency in Radcliffe-Brown's interpretation: a relationship of enmity is a kind of social relationship, so some kind of interaction between nonkin is in fact possible. But the point here is that the Kareira divide the social universe into two categories, relatives and enemies. The reason that nonrelatives are defined as enemies is that virtually all norms for regulating interaction are attached to kinship positions. If a kin relationship cannot be defined, then there are no norms by which the behavior of the parties to the interaction may be governed, anticipated, or understood.

But kinship can affect interpersonal relations to a much greater extent than simply allowing a distinction between "friend" (relative) and "foe" (nonrelative). People who are connected to one another by virtue of their locations in a common kinship structure are able to interact with one another because they can systematically anticipate each other's behavior; there are, in other words, norms which govern and regulate their relationship and which are commonly or jointly understood. The exact content of these norms depends upon the kind of kin relationship that obtains. People behave differently toward different kinds of relatives, and expect different kinds of responses in return. In some cases the norms are very general and pertain simply to the class of people defined as kin: one may, for instance, expect hospitality from one's relations in a distant community through which one is traveling. Other kinds of norms, however, are quite specific to individual kin relationships. This means that, in a kinship-based society, one may predict the form and content of interaction between two individuals with considerable accuracy provided that one knows (1) the parameters of the kinship system, and (2) the exact kin relationship that obtains in the case of interest.[3]

Stephens attests to the importance of "patterned" kin behavior in defining and regulating modes of interaction between relatives:

What do I mean by *patterned* kin behavior? One thing I mean by "patterned" is that behavior between a pair of kinsmen is fairly predictable and stable. One kinsman knows—in some details, at least—how another kinsman will act toward him. He can predict his behavior, or some aspects of it, in advance. The second thing I mean by "patterned" is that the kin behavior is not stable and predictable merely because of the known individual traits of the persons involved, as in a nonkin friendship relationship. Instead, the behavior is predictable because it is *culturally standardized.* (Stephens 1963:83)

Interpersonal kin relationships tend to be patterned, in the manner described by Stephens, where kinship and kin groups predominate as the bases of social structure. And the extent to which kin relationships are patterned is highly related to the importance of kinship as a structural or an organizational principle (Stephens 1963:99).

When we speak of social organization, we generally mean the various ways in which the members of a society are organized into groups, and the ways the various groups are related to one another. According to Marvin Olsen (1968:3), social organization is ". . . the process of merging social actors into ordered social relationships, which become infused with cultural ideas." In societies where kinship is the basis of social organization, kinship is the primary and perhaps exclusive principle by which order is imposed on social relationships. One important implication of this is that individuals are organized into groups according to kinship. Patterned kin relationships occur within the context of organized kin groups. In the next section we discuss the nature of these groups.

Kinship and group membership

In a discussion of the principles of kin group formation, residents of Western societies may have a rather partial impression of exactly what a kin group is.[4] In the contemporary United States, there is a tendency to think of kin groups as simply groups of people who are related to one another. This is not the meaning of the concept of kin group as it is employed by anthropologists. In comparative research, it is most useful to conceive of a society with kin groups as one in which each individual is unambiguously assigned, by virtue of parentage, to one and only one group. Each individual, then, knows clearly the group to which he or she belongs, and knows who the other members of the group are. No one belongs to more than one group.[5]

This is quite different from the situation which obtains in most Western societies. In the American system, each person is related by birth to each of his or her parents and to all of the people to whom they are related. Theoretically, the number of people to whom an individual is related is

infinite. Furthermore, each one of the members of one's kin network is also related to a theoretically infinite number of other individuals. Except for full siblings, no two people share exactly the same set of relatives. The collection of
persons to whom any given individual is singularly related is usually called a
"kindred." However, a kindred does not possess the properties of a kin group. If,
for instance, several members of one kindred behave as a group in certain situations (they play cards together regularly, or they jointly operate a business), they
still do not constitute a *kin group* in the anthropological sense. They may be a
sociable group of relatives, or an economic unit which happens to consist of kin,
but they are not a kin group. While a group of kin may congregate at regular times
for particular purposes, a kin group is a unit defined by the cultural rules of
social organization, which has an existence independent of its individual members, and where membership is given by birth.

In the United States, kinship is reckoned according to
the facts of genealogy as we know them. These facts include a stipulation that
the individual is related equally to each parent, and to all relatives of each
parent. Each individual's own kindred is unique to him or her (and to full siblings). Because we recognize kinship with both "sides" of one's family, our
method of reckoning descent is termed *bilateral*. Bilateral descent by itself cannot produce kin groups; it produces, rather, sets of overlapping kindreds.

The key difference between societies with kin groups
and those without them is that, in the former, descent through *one parent only*
is recognized for purposes of group membership. This is the principle of unilineal
descent. It means that, in effect, an individual "inherits" membership in a kin
group from one of his or her parents. If one belongs to one's father's descent
group, the appropriate term is *patrilineal;* if it is the mother whose group membership is passed on to the children, the system is called *matrilineal.*[6]

The members of those societies which practice one or
the other form of unilineal descent are not necessarily ignorant of the biological
realities of procreation. They may "know" perfectly well that they are biologically related to both parents and thus to both sets of kin. However, biological
reality is selectively applied to social life. Kinship is a social phenomenon, particularly when it comes to group formation. These groups may form along lines
which are at least partially drawn by selected facts of biological relationships,
but kin group membership is not completely determined by genetic relations. A
member of a society with patrilineal kinship groups may indeed recognize his
mother's relatives as his own relatives, at least up to a certain degree of relatedness, but he simply does not belong to their kin group. They, in fact, will belong
to many different groups, since each person's group membership comes from his
or her father.

There are, then, three basic methods of reckoning de-
scent: patrilineal, matrilineal, and bilateral. (There are also several kinds of modi-

fications or combinations of these, some of which we will point out briefly below.) The first two of these result in the formation of unilineal kin groups; the last does not, at least not without special provisions. Obviously, societies in which kinship is an important basis of social structure are likely to practice one or the other of the unilineal methods, because of the possibilities for group formation inherent in them. One way of apprehending the importance of kinship for social structure cross-culturally is to examine the relative distributions of unilineal and bilateral kinship systems across the world's societies.

Out of the 1170 societies in Murdock's (1967) Ethnographic Atlas, there is sufficient information on 1153 to permit classification according to type of descent system. Of these, 741 (64.3 percent) are characterized by one or the other type of unilineal descent; 581 (50.4 percent of the total) are patrilineal, and 160 (13.9 percent) are matrilineal. Three-hundred seventy-nine societies (32.9 percent) have no operative unilineal principle of descent, and are therefore bilateral. Another term for bilateral descent is "cognatic affiliation." This is the term Murdock uses in the Atlas. (The meaning of this term is actually a bit more general than that of "bilateral descent," but the difference need not concern us here.)

There are, in addition, 33 societies (2.8 percent) which have institutionalized *both* forms of unilineal descent, patrilineal and matrilineal. This seems to contradict the generalization we made above that unilineal descent assigns the individual unambiguously to one and only one kin group. A simple modification is all that is required to take account of this. In a society with double descent, each individual will be simultaneously affiliated with one patrilineal descent group and one matrilineal descent group. Each kind of descent group will serve a different set of functions. For example, among the Yako of Nigeria, a man receives rights to the use of land by virtue of his membership in a patrilineal descent group. The patrilineage, in other words, "owns" some segment of land, and the members of each patrilineage have the rights to the produce of that group's land. But all movable goods are inherited matrilineally. According to Fox,

> ... for an individual (Yako) man inheritance is divided; he gets his house and land and all other immovables from his father, but it is from his mother's brothers that he gets money and livestock and all movable property. Looked at another way, on a man's death his land and house go to his own sons or other close agnates, while his money and cattle will go to his sisters' sons or other close uterine (matrilateral) relatives. (Fox 1967:136; see also Forde 1964)

Thus, in societies with double descent, both kinds of unilineal descent groups exist, but they operate in different ways. An individual, upon birth, is simply provided with two group memberships instead of one. This is clearly very different than the situation in a society with bilateral kinship, where individuals "recognize" relatives on both sides but belong to no distinct kin groups, because kin groups as such do not exist.

The quotation from Fox above brings out another very important point about matrilineal descent. Note that he traces the inheritance of movable goods among the Yako from mother's brother to sister's son, not from mother to daughter. It might appear, from the discussion to this point, that matrilineal and patrilineal descent systems are mirror opposites of one another, differing only in the manner of determining group membership. Although true on a superficial descriptive level, this generalization results in serious distortions if carried too far. Regardless of the means by which descent-group membership is determined, the formal authority positions within kin groups are virtually always held by men. Matriliny does not at all imply matriarchy, or anything close to it.[7] Regardless of the principle by which individuals are assigned to kin groups, these groups are organized around their male members (see Fox 1967:31-33). In patrilineal descent groups, the "key relationship" is between father and son: property, authority, and so on flow directly down the line. But in matrilineal societies, father and son are members of different groups; one inherits property and position from one's mother's brother. This creates certain organizational problems for matrilineal societies, which we will discuss shortly.

How important are unilineal descent groups in those societies in which they are found? We have already said that they usually constitute the "basis of social structure" in these societies, but what exactly does that mean? Stephens (1963:107-125) lists eight characteristics or attributes which unilineal kin groups (whether patrilineal or matrilineal) usually possess. These include such things as corporate property ownership and corporate enterprise within the economic sphere. That is, these groups either own or hold rights to land, and the members of the group cooperate in working or exploiting the land. The economic security of the individuals who belong to the group depends in large part upon the welfare and prosperity of the group as a whole. The families of which such groups are comprised, whether independent or extended, join together in certain kinds of economic endeavors, and share land and other valuable property among themselves. The kin group is also likely to possess an internal political structure or "government," with positions of authority often allocated according to seniority in the kinship structure. As a governmental unit, the kin group

> . . . may act as a unit of social control, enforcing its rules and punishing infractions (by its members). . . . Also, the kin group may be held accountable—by some larger political grouping—for the conduct of its members. (Stephens 1963:117)

Kin groups are frequently internally integrated by virtue of common religious obligations, particularly where the worship and propitiation of ancestors is a focal point of the religion. Each kin group has its own set of ancestors, who (it is often believed) watch over the welfare of the group and its members, and whose ranks each individual will join upon his or her death. The religious and political functions of kin groups are often very closely intertwined. Religious sanctions may be employed as a means of social control over group members, and authority figures within kin groups legitimate this authority by virtue of their seniority among the living and, therefore, their proximity to the ancestral ranks. The roles of political leader and religious priest are often vested in the same individual, who is accorded this position by virtue of his seniority within the kin group. This obviously makes him a very powerful person, and increases his ability to exert control over other members of the group.

The members of a kin group are bound together by other kinds of interdependencies as well. Some of them are very general and diffuse, such as reciprocal obligations of aid and hospitality. Others are fairly specific, such as obligations to unite for the protection of the rights of an individual member when they are threatened by the actions of a nonmember or another group. The group, according to Stephens (1963:120-121), may act as a "military unit," engaging in combat with other kin groups for the protection of members, vengeance, retaliation, and so on.

Thus the members of a given kin group are bound together by a network of economic, political, and religious interdependencies. It can be readily seen that unilineal kin groups are extremely important as agents of social integration, uniting individuals into collectivities with common goals, interests, and experiences. But the parameters of unilineal kinship systems do more than just integrate individuals into groups. They also integrate the groups into larger social systems: that is, societies. This is possible primarily because of one further characteristic of unilineal kin groups, which is very nearly a universal feature of social structure: kin group exogamy. That is, in societies with unilineal kin groups, a member of one such group cannot marry another member of the same group.[8] In any given society, therefore, the various extant kinship groupings will be related to one another, either directly or indirectly, by ties of affinity or marriage.

The fact that the parties to a marriage must be members of two different kin groups is much more significant than it may initially appear. It has many crucial implications for the structure of kin groups, the nature of marriage and mate selection, and the relationships between distinct kin groups. Many of these implications follow from the residential behavior of married couples subsequent to the marriage. The continuity, and therefore the long-term welfare, of any descent group depends largely upon two considerations: first, obtaining or recruiting spouses for the unmarried members of the group from the ranks of other groups, since rules of exogamy prohibit any given group from being reproductively self-sufficient; and second, retaining some measure of control over at least a portion of the married members of the group after they marry. The second point here means that the residential location of the married couple is of vital importance to a kinship system. In a kinship-based society (one structured around kin groups), postmarital residence behavior is generally patterned according to some cultural rule. The subject matter of this residence rule is not simply the physical location of the married couple, but rather the more general question of the group in which the couple as a couple will participate.

There are four logically possible options here. The newly married couple may reside with the husband's kin, the wife's kin, both (usually in some sequence), or neither. The potential for the formulation of extended families and localized kin groups obviously depends upon continued residence after marriage with or near one or the other set of kin. Almost by definition, in societies without functioning kin groups married couples do not systematically reside with either family of orientation, but rather typically establish a new, independent household. This is called, logically enough, *neolocal* residence. In the United States, for example, it is rather unusual for couples to begin their married lives by residing with one set of parents. When it does happen, it is almost invariably regarded as a temporary, and perhaps unfortunate, response to financial exigencies. The couple is expected to establish a separate residence as soon as possible. While it may be near one or both sets of parents, there is no cultural rule specifying that this should be the case, or that one set of parents should be preferred over the other as "neighbors."[9]

In societies with descent groups, though, there is usually some kind of cultural rule specifying the group with which a couple should reside. If the expectation is that the couple should live with or near the husband's parents, residence is *patrilocal;* residence with or near the wife's kin is termed *matrilocal.*[10]

There are two other general categories of postmarital residence which require a little further explanation. One is termed *ambilocal.* It obtains in societies where the couple is expected to reside with one or the other set of kin, but where the expectation does not specify which one. In these cases, the couple is free to choose the group they wish to join, based on considerations such as which group has the greatest surplus of resources at the moment. Davenport (1959) points out that bilateral kin groups are in fact possible under the rule of ambilocal residence. The rule of descent specifies equal kinship relatedness to the relatives of both parents, but membership in a kin group is then given by the residential choice. Our earlier generalization that kin groups cannot be formed by the principle of bilateral descent must therefore be slightly qualified: societies with bilateral descent systems may have modified kin groups if they also have a rule of ambilocal residence. Murdock (1968) also points out that any unilocal rule of residence may cause the emergence of a localized group of relatives even in a society with bilateral descent, and these relatives may behave as a group under certain circumstances. Since patrilocal residence is very common among bilateral societies (see Table 1), this is an important qualification.

There is a fifth general category of residence rule, denoted by the term *avunculocal,* which requires some rather extensive explanation. Its existence also highlights certain problematic features of matrilineal descent, which show that matrilineal systems are not simply opposites of patrilineal ones but have certain distinctive features of their own.

As one would expect, rules of residence and rules of descent are quite highly associated (Table 1). Societies with patrilineal descent systems tend overwhelmingly to have patrilocal residence; only 2.6 percent of all patrilineal societies have some other residence rule. This is relatively easy to explain if one remembers two general principles of kinship systems: (1) men, regardless of the method of tracing descent, occupy the positions of authority within kin groups; and (2) men and women who belong to the same descent group cannot mate, because of the role of exogamy. Thus the men of a given patrilineal descent group must find wives from other groups; the children these wives bear, however, will belong to their fathers' groups. The male children, particularly, will eventually succeed to positions of importance and authority within this patrilineal group. It is therefore quite important that the group retain control over the children of its male members and incorporate them early

Table 1:   Rules of Residence and Rules of Descent[a]

Type of Residence	Type of Descent				
	Patrilineal	Matrilineal	Double	Bilateral	Total
Patrilocal	558 (97.4%)	28 (17.8%)	31 (93.5%)	190 (50.7%)	807 (70.9%)
Matrilocal	1 (0.2%)	51 (3215%)	0 (0.0%)	81 (21.6%)	133 (11.1%)
Neolocal	6 (1.0%)	6 (3.8%)	0 (0.0%)	32 (8.3%)	44 (3.9%)
Avunculocal	0 (0.0%)	50 (31.8%)	1 (3.0%)	0 (0.0%)	51 (4.5%)
Ambilocal	5 (0.9%)	18 (11.5%)	1 (3.0%)	72 (19.2%)	96 (8.4%)
Duolocal[b]	3 (0.5%)	4 (2.5%)	0 (0.0%)	0 (0.0%)	7 (0.6%)
Total N	573	157	33	375	1138
Total %	(100)	(100)	(100)	(100)	(100)

[a]*Computed from the Ethnographic Atlas (Murdock 1967).*
[b]*In these seven societies, spouses continue to reside with the families of orientation after marriage. This may also be called "natolocal."*

into group processes. The most effective means of doing so is to insure that sons remain firmly located within the domain of the group, and to "import" wives for them from outside. The daughters of the group, on the other hand, can leave it upon marriage with no loss to the group in terms of its continuity or sphere of control, for their children will belong to other patrilineal groups.

There is much greater variability in residence rules among matrilineal societies (Table 1). Only about one third of all matrilineal societies are matrilocal; nearly one fifth are patrilocal; and almost one third have institutionalized avunculocal residence. Avunculocality is the practice of residing with the husband's mother's brother after marriage. It is the exclusive province of matrilineal societies; out of 51 societies with avunculocal residence, 50 are matrilineal. The other is characterized by double descent, and thus also has matrilineal descent groups.

This diversity of residence rules among matrilineal societies is indicative of the problematic nature of kin-group control over male members under matriliny. This control is problematic because no cultural rule of residence serves to keep all male members of a single matrilineal group in the same place (see Richards 1950). We can see why by looking at each alternative residence system.

It would seem logical for the members of a matrilineal society to take up residence with the wife's kin after marriage, since the couple's children will belong to her descent group. This, however, removes the husband from the group of which he is a member. He would not reside with the group in which he has economic, political, and religious positions and rights. The group would lose some measure of control over him, and he would find it much more difficult to implement his rights with respect to his group. His wife's group is also unlikely to simply incorporate him into their own structure, since that group is organized around her male relatives: her father, brothers, and other males to whom she is related through her mother. Thus, in matrilineal societies, matrilocal residence results in the geographic dispersal of the male members of the group after their marriage.

Patrilocal residence might seem at first to obviate this situation. All of a woman's sons (the male members of the group in any single generation) could remain as members of the group residentially, bringing their wives to live with them. However, the same problem crops up again in the next generation. The children fathered by the co-resident males are not members of the local kin group, but of their mothers' groups. The members of this group in the next generation are the children born to the *sisters* of the group, who have gone their various ways to reside patrilocally with their husbands. Thus patrilocal residence, like matrilocal, results in the dispersal of male members rather than in their geographic concentration.

This brings us to the third possibility, avunculocal residence. In such a system, a man takes his wife to the home (or at least the village) of his mother's brother, from whom he will inherit his wealth and position, and to whose group he belongs under the matrilineal principle. Here, the male resides with his father's group (of which he is not a member, of course) until marriage, or at least until puberty, when his own descent group (his mother's brothers) reclaims him. In Fox's terms,

> The resulting local group will consist of a series of matrilineally related men with their wives and dependent children, but without their adult children. (Fox 1967:107)

They do have, though, the adult male children of their sisters, who constitute the membership of the group in the next generation.

The great diversity of residence types in matrilineal societies is due, then, to the inherent impossibility of devising some single residence rule which will keep all male members of a descent group together. This is not the only unique organizational feature of matrilineal descent, but it has certainly attracted the most analytic attention. Although less than 15 percent of the world's societies trace descent matrilineally, these kinship systems have been of considerable interest to students of social structure, largely because of the special problems these systems encounter regarding the reconciliation of male dominance with the principle of tracing kin group membership through females. One wonders why the matrilineal option is ever "chosen" by societies, since the patrilineal system is so much simpler. This, however, is part of the broader question of the antecendents of descent systems in general, which is our next topic.

Antecedents and correlates of descent systems

Evolutionary theory

We have given brief notice to various forms of evolutionary theories in previous chapters. These theories also pertain, in part, to hypothetical sequences in the evolutionary predominance of the forms of reckoning descent. There are several distinct theories of such sequences which might be classified as evolutionary, but which posit different progressions. Two of the most prominent, both of which first appeared in 1861, were directly contradictory. They were the source of considerable intellectual controversy for quite some time.

J.J. Bachofen (1897) operated under the assumption that human social organization arose from a state of original promiscuity, random mating, and the virtual absence of ordered relationships and structured social groups. The logical next step, he argued, was some form of organization premised on the mother-child relationship, since the connection between these two positions is biologically obvious whereas the determination of genetic paternity is problematic, especially under conditions of "promiscuous" mating. This led, he believed, to a matriarchal authority structure as well as to matrilineal descent. Later, as human relationships became more structured, patriarchal power structures and patrilineal descent systems gained predominance.

Henry Sumner Maine (1885), on the basis of his study of the legal codes of ancient societies, came to an opposite conclusion. His inferences from these data favored the earlier development of male-dominated forms of social organization. He concluded that the earliest human societies were organized around males, implying both patriarchy and patriliny, and that the subsequent development of "civilization" was in the direction of moderating this male dominance.

So much logic and evidence has been marshaled against unilinear evolution in general that the scant attention currently paid to Bachofen and Maine seems justified. There is no particular reason to assume that all human societies shared any common "starting point" or that they proceeded from such a point in similar directions. Kinship systems do undoubtedly change over time, and to the extent that these changes stem from technological advances or the structural differentiation of societies kinship systems may even be said to "evolve." However, this should not be taken to imply that there is any invariant sequence of stages through which all kinship systems must pass on their way toward "civilization."

Neither Maine nor Bachofen, however, was engaged in totally unfounded speculation. Maine's generalizations were based on very interesting and valuable data, but they pertained to societies which were sufficiently advanced to leave some record of their legal codes. The earlier human groupings to which he extrapolated could hardly be expected to have possessed legal codes, much less any means of recording them. Maine's extrapolation was clearly over-enthusiastic, but his information on legal codes and his inferences from these codes to norms and behaviors are nonetheless valuable.

In terms of cross-cultural comparative data, Bachofen's argument that matriliny preceded patriliny at first appears to have some merit. In one of his earlier studies, Murdock (1937) tested hypotheses to the effect that matrilineal customs were associated with "lower cultural levels," and patrilineal customs with "higher" levels. He found some statistical support for such hypotheses. Patrilineal descent, for example, is strongly correlated with such indices of cultural development as the domestication of animals and the emergence of written language (see also Marsh 1967:50). But if societies developed in invariant unilinear sequences, one would expect virtually no exceptions to these correlations. There is some relationship between type of descent and level of cultural development according to multiple indicators of each variable, but these associations are not nearly strong enough, in Murdock's opinion, to constitute support for any kind of evolutionary theory. From the patterns of correlations in his data, Murdock infers that matrilineal descent is not in fact characteristic of the most "primitive" societies, but is rather ". . . a special adjustment to a somewhat exceptional set of social and economic circumstances on a relatively advanced level of cultural development" (Murdock 1937:469).

While unilinear evolutionary theory does not adequately account for differences between societies in type of descent system, there are certain aspects of change in the features of kinship systems which seem to be regular and sequential. A particular kinship system may experience "evolution" in the sense that a change in some relevant feature of the environment or the system itself will have predictable and sequential ramifications on other aspects of the system. Murdock (1949:221–222) has argued that, if change is introduced into a previously stable kinship system, "such change regularly begins with a modification in the rule of residence" (1949:221). Other features of kinship systems follow from rules of residence, which thus have some measure of causal priority. According to Murdock, a change in the rule of postmarital residence will have most immediate consequences for the form of extended families, such that their composition will reflect the new residence rule. This, in turn, produces a change in the structure of consanguineal kin groups in the same direction, which ultimately affects the kinship terminology employed to symbolically represent the kinship structure.[11] Driver and Massey (1957) expand this logic and subject it to a rather ingenious test on data from 280 North American Indian societies. They hypothesize that postmarital residence depends upon the division of labor between the sexes in subsistence pursuits. A change in the rule of residence then affects the method of determining rights to the use of land, which is followed by changes in the rule of descent. As in Murdock's system, a change in kinship terminology is hypothesized to follow the other changes.

Since the hypotheses here involve sequences of change among various aspects of kinship systems, it would seem that longitudinal data would be required for their adequate evaluation. The ethnographic data available, however, were synchronic: that is, they pertained to social systems at only one point in time. But Driver and Massey argued that (1) if each of the relevant variables were coded into the categories of "matridominant," "patridominant," and "balanced," and (2) if their hypothesized sequence of change were correct, then (3) correlations between adjacent "stages" should be greater than correlations between stages which were hypothesized to be nonadjacent. One would expect to find positive correlations between all "matricentered" traits, for example, but the correlation between "matridominant division of labor" and "matrilocal residence" should be of greater magnitude than that between "matridominant division of labor" and "matrilineal descent." This is in fact what they found (Driver and Massey 1957:432-434).

To estimate the implications of these findings they must be placed in proper perspective. First, it is important to recognize that Driver and Massey did not hypothesize or find an evolutionary sequence between patrilineal, matrilineal, and bilateral kinship systems or traits. But once external forces act to change the kinship structure of a society, that change appears to follow a certain systematic order. Of particular interest to us is their inference that the nature of the descent system is dependent upon the rule of residence (through an intervening variable, land tenure) which is in turn dependent upon the division of labor by sex in subsistence activities. Second, the idea of a chronological sequence of changes, with implied time lags between changes in various traits, is important in helping to explain the absence of perfect correlations between traits which would appear to be functionally related. For instance, according to their argument, patrilocality is a cause (or at least an antecedent) of patrilineal descent, but according to Table 1 there are 249 societies in the Ethnographic Atlas which have patrilocal residence customs but lack patrilineal descent. Driver and Massey are not, however, positing a chain reaction, but a developmental cycle which may extend over indefinite periods of time. Different societies may be in different stages of a change cycle, accounting in part for the lack of perfect correspondence between residence and descent systems.

The reader may already have noted a marked parallel between the arguments we have evaluated here on the sequence of changes in kinship systems and those of Goode and others regarding sources of change in family structure. Driver and Massey, Murdock, and others have argued and demonstrated that type of descent system depends on type of residence rule, which in turn is contingent upon variables involving the division of labor. Goode (1963) contended that industrialization (division of labor) demands high geographic mobility (neolocality) which produces a conjugal rather than an extended family system. With regard to family and kinship structure, then, there seems to be some theoretical consensus on the causal efficacy of ecological and technological variables, the effects of which are partially mediated by variables pertaining to the spacial or geographic distributions of individuals in pursuit of subsistence. We shall follow up on this logic below.

To summarize: There is no empirical or theoretical reason to believe that the several kinds of kinship systems in existence stand in any evolutionary relationship to one another. However, the hypothesis that there are systematic chronological relationships between changes in the various components of each type of system seems quite plausible. The theory and data provided by Driver and Massey indicate that rules of residence are chronologically (and thus, presumably, causally) prior to rules of descent, and that the division of labor by sex is antecedent to both residence and descent variables. If this is correct, we should look for the causes of residence/descent systems among those factors which influence the division of labor by sex, particularly with regard to subsistence activities. These variables fall under the rubric of ecological and economic factors.

Ecological and economic factors

Quite some time ago, Lowie (1920) speculated that the type of descent system operative in a society would depend to a large extent on the division of labor by sex in primary subsistence activities. If the economic tasks which provided the greatest portion of subsistence, or at least a fairly large and stable portion, were pursued primarily by women, the kinship system was likely to be matrilineal. If the labor of men were the major source of subsistence, on the other hand, patrilineal organization would be more likely. Research in subsequent years has generally supported this argument, and has also clarified the causal process involved.

The question logically arises here as to the kinds of work that fall under the headings of "women's work" and "men's work." Stephens (1963:282-283) presents a table adapted from Murdock (1937) on the division of labor by sex for the societies available to Murdock on 46 kinds of work, coded into five categories ranging from "men always do it" to "women always do it." Some of the kinds of labor represented in the table would appear to be major subsistence activities (hunting, gathering, crop tending and harvesting, etc.), while other kinds (house building, basket making) are clearly supplementary to or supportive of the basic subsistence tasks. In the first category, major subsistence activities, women predominate in only one: crop tending and harvesting.[12] Of the 143 societies with important agricultural components of the economy on which Murdock had sufficient information, men always take primary responsibility for these tasks in 10, whereas crop tending and harvesting is defined as exclusively women's work in 44. If the "always" and "usually" categories are combined for each sex, crop tending and harvesting is "men's work" in 25 societies (17.5 percent), and "women's work" in 83 (58.0 percent); in the other 35 societies this labor is divided about equally between the sexes.[13] One might therefore hypothesize that agricultural societies would show a tendency toward matriliny, while others would be more likely to have patrilineal descent systems.

According to Murdock's (1937) data, this is in fact the case (see also Murdock 1949:204-205). Subsequent analyses have both supported and qualified this hypothesis (Steward 1955; Aberle 1961; Stephens 1963:126-132; Nimkoff 1965:39-44). But in order to explicate the causal processes involved, it is necessary to recall that residence rules intervene between ecological/

economic causes and their effects on descent systems. Subsistence activities, particuarly as they relate to the division of labor by sex, affect rules of postmarital residence; these, in turn, result in the *de facto* emergence of different descent systems. The processes work differently in societies with different bases of subsistence, so it is perhaps advisable to analyze hunting and gathering societies and agricultural societies separately.

According to the World Ethnographic Sample (Murdock 1957), over one half of all societies with economies based on hunting and gathering have bilateral descent systems. Among the remainder, patrilineal systems are twice as common as matrilineal ones (Nimkoff 1965:41). We have already noted, in Chapter Five, that extended family systems are relatively rare in hunting and gathering societies, largely because of the instability of the food supply and the necessity of considerable geographic mobility in search of food. Probably for the same kinds of reasons, extensive localized kin groups are also rare. Since the food-producing units in these societies are generally individuals or small groups, larger collections of kin are economically functional only under unusual circumstances or, perhaps, on special occasions. Thus kin-group membership is not necessarily crucial for the individual, and there is not often a clear need for some unilinear principle of kin-group formation. However, under certain conditions a particular rule of postmarital residence will become operative, sometimes giving rise to a system of unilineal descent.

Julian Steward (1955) has delineated the conditions which may lead to the development of "patrilocal bands" among hunting-gathering peoples, based in part on the earlier ethnographic work of Radcliffe-Brown (1930) in Australia. According to his argument, there are two interrelated ecological conditions which increase the probability of patrilocal residence and thus, by extension, patrilineal descent among societies in which hunting is a major source of food. These are (1) scattered, nonmigratory and scarce game, in areas which consequently have (2) low population densities (see also Stephens 1963: 127-130; Fox 1967:92-95). Men, of course, are the principal or only hunters, and hunting under these conditions is at best a chancy and difficult business. The hunter is at a considerable advantage, however, if he possesses intimate knowledge of and long experience with the territory in which he hunts. Because such land will support only small groups of people, localized bands are almost necessarily exogamous: men must find wives from other groups. But if, upon marriage, a man were to join his wife's group, he would have to begin learning the idiosyncracies of a new territory all over again. The general skills of a hunter may be readily transferable from one locale to another, but knowledge of the territory, which is of crucial survival value, is not. Patrilocal residence is obviously advantageous, since it enables men to remain in the same area all their lives, which greatly increases their efficiency as hunters.

If localized groups are composed of residentially stable, related males and their in-marrying wives, it is relatively easy to see how the propensity to trace descent patrilineally can develop. But, as Fox emphasizes, the descent groups which arise are *de facto* rather than *de jure:*

> In the patrilocal situation, there is no "rule" of patrilineal descent determining membership in a band. All there is is a combination of circumstances which produce bands of males. These males—because of exogamic restrictions—cannot marry the females that they breed, so they must look elsewhere for mates. . . . The result is an approximation to a patrilineal situation. (Fox 1967:93-94)

If, on the other hand, game is more abundant, population densities are higher, and some significant proportion of subsistence is provided by gathering vegetation (almost exclusively the province of women), the matrilocal option is at least possible and matrilineal descent may result. The matrilocal pattern, however, does not appear to have positive survival value for hunting and gathering groups under these conditions in the same sense that patrilocal residence does in less hospitable environments.

The most extensive cross-cultural study of variation in descent systems according to ecological and technological variables is probably that by David Aberle (1961), which was based on Murdock's World Ethnographic Sample. This study focused particuarly on matrilineal systems. The central conclusions of Aberle's investigation are the following: (1) matrilineal descent systems rarely occur in combination with animal husbandry, hunting and gathering, or fishing as the principle subsistence base (1961:664); (2) among nonextractive (that is, agricultural) economies, all subsistence types except "dominant horticulture" tend to select against matriliny (1961:702); and (3) among societies characterized by dominant horticulture, the factors which account for variation in type of kinship system are as yet undetermined.

How does this fit with our hypothesis that type of descent system is contingent upon the division of labor by sex? First, it is important to determine what Aberle means by the category "dominant horticulture." He defines this type of subsistence essentially as a residual, having first delineated "plough agriculture," in which an agricultural base with concomitant use of the plow is dominant, and "African horticulture," in which nonplow agriculture is combined with the domestication and husbandry of large animals such as cattle. The "dominant horticulture" category, then, includes societies which depend almost exclusively on the raising of crops for subsistence, but where the technology has not developed the plow (1961:671-674). The substitute for the plow, in many of these societies, seems to be the female. That is, women often take primary responsibility for the tending of the fields. Through the intervening variable of matrilocal residence, which is generally considered a necessary condition for the development of matrilineal descent (Murdock 1949:209–210; Driver and Massey 1957; Gough 1961b:552), this can result in the *de facto* emergence of a matrilineal system.

Robin Fox (1967:86–90) offers a concrete example of how this might occur drawn from the Shoshone Indian tribe of North America and a branch of this tribe which later became known as the Hopi. The Shoshone were a wandering band of hunters and gatherers living in the inhospitable, desert-like environment of the American Southwest. In this situation, their kinship structure consisted primarily of nuclear families bound together by ties of marriage. Kinship was apparently traced bilaterally, and groups of related nuclear families would occasionally combine for cooperation in hunting or for ceremonial purposes. These periods of cooperation, however, were rather sporadic, because the relatively unproductive environment would not support groups larger than the nuclear family for long periods of time. The basic cooperating unit, then, was the nuclear family.

Some of the Shoshone, in the course of their wanderings, migrated toward the southern reaches of their territory. They found land which was a bit more suitable for agriculture because of the availability of river water for small-scale irrigation. Here, according to Fox,

> The amount of agriculture—the cultivation of maize largely—was still limited, and so the men had to supplement this with hunting. A sexual division of labor was established, with the women tending the crops and the men doing the hunting. The ideal set-up . . . was the matrilocal residence group. A small group consisting perhaps of an old grandmother, her daughters, and their daughters, lived in a house or group of connected houses and looked after the plots of corn. To these houses came husbands who spent most of their time away in hunting or warfare or religious activity with other males of the band. (Fox 1967:88)

So women did most of the working of the land, and were consequently permanently resident on it. Probably the most obvious method of transmitting rights in land from one generation to the next was through women. Men, being hunters, did not require specific parcels of land on which to pursue their economic activities. Insofar as the labor of males was required for agricultural purposes, their skills were transferable from one plot of land to another. The skills of women were also transferable, of course, but the prosperity of the agricultural enterprise required their virtually continuous presence on the land. Land thus came to be identified as the property of women and was inherited matrilaterally. The property-based groups of females became the focal points of households, and this led ultimately to the adoption (or rather, emergence) of the matrilineal method of reckoning descent group membership. This kind of process probably operated in most of the "dominant horticulture" societies in the world which developed matrilineal kinship systems.

Our explanation of the relationship between agricultural and descent systems is still quite partial, in at least two ways. Aberle leaves two important questions to be answered with his summary statement that

> ... all nonextractive subsistence types except "dominant horticulture" tend to select against matriliny. Horticulture itself does not select *against* patriliny and bilaterality, but all other nonextractive types select *for* one or the other. (Aberle 1961:702)

The obvious questions here are (1) in what ways do other bases of subsistence select against matriliny? and (2) what factors distinguish between those "dominant horticultural" societies which adopt different kinds of descent systems? Aberle has shown that it is quite plausible for matrilineal systems to develop under conditions of dominant horticulture, but he also demonstrates that dominant horticulture is not sufficient to cause matriliny. Other nonextractive subsistence types, however, make matriliny highly unlikely. What factors select against matriliny in societies with other kinds of agricultural bases, and what factors distinguish matrilineal from patrilineal or bilateral systems in societies with dominant horticulture?

The answer to the first question is not too difficult, at least in an abstract sense. In societies where subsistence depends on the use of the plow and/or the tending of large animals, the labor of males is crucial in productivity (see Stephens 1963:282-283). These systems tend to be more productive than those based upon horticulture alone (Aberle 1961; Gough 1961b), but they also require "heavy" tasks such as handling the plow as a vital part of the production process. These heavier tasks are normally allocated to men (see Boserup 1970). Animal husbandry or pastoralism further requires some degree of mobility on the part of those tending the herds, and women are likely to be confined to a small geographic area by the requirements of child-bearing and child-rearing. Thus men assume a dominant role in the subsistence technology of plow-based agricultural or pastoralist economies. Where the primary productive labors are those of males, rights to land tend to be vested in males and inherited in the male line. This produces a patrilocal tendency, which is strongly associated with patrilineal descent (see Aberle 1961:677, Table 17-4).

A similar logic may explain the observation by Gough (1961b:551) that "in matrilineal societies ... which rely very predominantly on cultivation, dominantly matrilocal residence will be found among those with lower productivity, and dominantly avunculocal or duolocal residence among those of higher productivity." Increased productivity may be concomitant with successively greater incorporation of males and their labor into the agricultural enterprise. The greater the involvement of males in cultivation, the less the advantages of vesting rights to land tenure in females. Avunculocal residence, at least, is regarded as a step in the metamorphosis of a kinship system from matrilineal to patrilineal (Murdock 1949:207; Gough 1961b:552). Avunculocal residence emerges from prior matrilocal residence systems, after matrilineages have already developed. Thus, matrilocal/matrilineal systems are found within a relatively narrow ecological range (Aberle 1961:702). As a society develops a more productive technology it is likely to shift away from such a system, with the change in descent type foreshadowed or precipitated by a shift away from matrilocal residence. This does not imply, however, that matriliny is a specific stage of general evolution, but rather that the ranges of economy and productivity in which it is likely to occur are more restricted than those of other descent systems.

It is important to note that, throughout our interpretations and reconstructions of processes which lead to the adoption of the various systems of descent, we are employing the causal logic explicated by Driver and Massey (1957), in which descent is dependent upon land tenure, land tenure upon postmarital residence, and residence upon division of labor by sex in subsistence pursuits. This logic not only fits their data well, but provides the most readily interpretable and parsimonious logical structure by means of which variation in descent systems can be explained and understood.

Aberle (1961:702) offers no speculation as to the factors that might operate to bring about different types of descent systems in societies with "dominant horticulture" subsistence bases. His contribution was to show that matriliny is more likely under this ecological condition than any other. Stephens (1963:130–131) suggests that matrilocal residence, and thus matriliny, may be more common in societies with the custom of "bride service." Here, a prospective husband provides service or labor to his wife's family in exchange for the privilege of marrying her, and this would obviously predispose toward matrilocal postmarital residence. But, as Stephens points out, this may be a better explanation of the development of matrilocal/matrilineal systems in hunting and gathering societies than in horticultural ones. In his logic:

> In a society with capital goods, they (wives) will be paid for in whatever the local currency happens to be—baskets of yams, or dogs' teeth, or cows, or sea-shells, or gongs. But most bands of hunting nomads cannot accumulate capital goods, so these people frequently barter their own labor and hunting skill in return for wives. (Stephens 1963:130)

This may in part account for the occasional appearance of matrilocal residence and matrilineal descent among hunting and gathering societies (Aberle 1961: 677), but the argument would not apply as well to societies with some sort of agricultural subsistence base.

I suspect that some of the variation in type of descent system among "dominant horticultural" societies may be attributable to the types of communities which are permitted by ecological conditions, particularly along the dimension of population density. Anthropologists almost universally recognize that, in patrilocal societies, a woman may often be required by her marriage to move to a community which is quite far removed from her natal group; in matrilocal societies, however, men are rarely if ever expected to move more than a short distance away from their families of orientation after marriage. Stephens (1963:132) speculates that this may be due to pervasive male dominance. No one really wishes to move a long way from his or her own kin, but men have the power to implement their wishes. My own explanatory preference here is a modification and elaboration of Stephens'. Regardless of the extent to which males in general dominate females, men universally occupy positions of authority and responsibility in their own kin groups, whether membership in these groups is allocated according to patrilineal or matrilineal principles. In a patrilocal/patrilineal system a woman can leave her own kin group forever upon marriage and the group, as a group, will be none the worse off. But in a matrilocal/matrilineal system, the alienation of a man from his own descent group when he "marries out" of that group will constitute an important loss to both the individual and the group. The extent of alienation, or removal from group properties and processes, will be directly proportional to the distance of the move. Distances in postmarital mobility will thus be minimized in matrilocal societies. Matrilocal residence (and, by extension, matrilineal descent), should occur only in societies where the distances between the territories occupied by the localized segments of descent groups are minimal, such as when the members of multiple groups live in one village. In a society where subsistence depends upon horticultural activities without the aid of the plow, matriliny, as Aberle demonstrated, is a possibility. Its actual emergence may depend on the degree to which ecological conditions permit the occurrence of communities of sufficient size to contain multiple lineage groups. This is somewhat problematic, because it would imply relatively high productivity on rather small parcels of land, and productivity is limited by the definitional absence of the plow (Gough 1961b). In situations where a population must remain widely dispersed, it is probable that the disadvantages of matrilocal residence would prevent the development of matriliny in any kind of economic system.[14]

Finally, it is important to reemphasize here the point that, in postagricultural or industrializing societies, the economic base tends to select against *any* form of unilineal descent, probably for the same reasons that extended families are uncommon (see Chapter Five). The emergence of industry removes much of the functional significance of extended kin groups. In the absence of important functions for such groups to perform, the advantages of the structural principles (unilocal residence, unilineal descent) upon which they are based are also diminished, and kinship systems become bilateral.

It is obvious that ecological and economic variables have important effects upon the type of kinship system prevalent in any given society. There are, however, the inevitable qualifications which must be made. We have ignored possible reciprocal influences of descent systems on technology and other facets of social organization. The premise behind this is that the causal ordering posited by Driver and Massey (1957) is correct. However, it is undoubtedly true that the descent system, once established, has important implications for many aspects of social organization and behavior. We shall investigate some of these possibilities in the next section.

Kinship and polity

One aspect of political behavior which has attracted the attention of sociologists and anthropologists over the years, and which is clearly associated with variation in kinship structure, involves the extent to which political interaction consists of the socially approved pursuit of special interests, as opposed to political integration based upon consensus, total group cooperation, and the minimization of conflict. The kind of political system in which special interest groups compete for the enhancement of their own particular interests has been termed "factional," and a political system in which conflict is avoided, special interest groups de-emphasized, and overall consensus promoted is labeled "communal" (Paige 1974:301-302). A rather strong correlation exists between this dimension of the polity and the type of unilineal descent principle operative, in societies without complex political systems beyond the level of kinship organization. Specifically, cross-cultural data indicate that factional polities tend to occur jointly with patrilineal descent systems, and communal polities are more likely to be found in societies which trace descent matrilineally (Swanson 1968, 1969; Paige 1974).

The current debate over this issue does not focus on the existence of this correlation, which is well documented, but rather on how it should be explained. Swanson (1968, 1969) has developed a theory in which the type of descent system is regarded as the dependent variable, and type of polity as independent. He argues that the maintenance of a communal political system requires the inculcation of certain behavioral traits in the participants, such as willingness to cooperate and compromise, and other socioemotional skills which would minimize the "combative" propensities of participants in the political process. These kinds of personality traits are, in general, identified with the female social role. The adoption of matrilineal rules of descent, then, symbolically represents the predominance of feminine traits in socialization values. Tracing descent through females emphasizes the desirability of personality traits with

which they are identifed; this is held to be functional with respect to the maintenance of the communal polity, which depends upon the successful inculcation
of these traits in each generation. Matrilineal descent symbolizes the primary
socialization principle in societies with communal polities.

Successful participation in factional political structures,
on the other hand, demands traits such as aggressiveness, independence, and
instrumental task orientation. These are presumably "masculine" traits. Patrilineal descent arises in societies with factional polities as, again, a symbolic
representation of the behavioral principles which constitute the objectives of
socialization, given the prior existence of a factional polity.

Paige summarizes Swanson's causal logic as follows:
> The fundamental function of descent rules is to represent the charac-
> teristic emotional style of parents of both sexes. Political organization
> leads to socialization techniques, which in turn lead to symbolic repre-
> sentations (of the political structure). (Paige 1974:303)

But Paige goes on (1974:303–304) to point out that Swanson's theory does not
take account of the well-established relationship between rules of descent and
rules of residence (Nimkoff 1965; D'Andrade 1966), and the evidence that rules
of descent are causally prior to variation in descent systems (Murdock 1949;
Driver and Massey 1957), which we have already reviewed. Paige argues that, if
the assumed causal direction in Swanson's theory is reversed, an explanation
results which takes account of residence as an antecedent variable, and also
allows the integration of this theory with previously developed explanations
of political behavior in industrial societies.

Paige's theory, in summary, is that the type of descent
system institutionalized in a society is antecedent to the development of a factional or communal political structure. It is a well-established principle in political sociology that the extent of intergroup conflict or factionalism is directly
related to the degree to which group ties are overlapping rather than cross-cutting (see, for example, Lipset and Rokkan 1967). That is, in a society in which
the same set of individuals is bound together by numerous kinds of connections
and relationships, each set will come to constitute a self-contained interest group
and will act for the furtherance of these interests. But in a society where each
individual is a member of several distinct kinds of groups, and where these
groups do not share a common set of members, the opportunities and motivations for the formation of factions are reduced. In Paige's terms,
> Cross-cutting group ties occur when political actors owe allegiance to
> groups with conflicting special interests. The pattern of conflicting
> loyalties in such a situation prevents the actors from expressing any
> single position and consequently reduces conflict and cleavage between
> the groups themselves. Overlapping group ties occur when patterns of

interest group allegiance reinforce one another and there are few ties of loyalty between groups. In such situations, political opponents share no bonds of group loyalty, and factionalism and intense conflict are encouraged. (Paige 1974:304-305)

Paige then points out that, as we have seen, a patrilineal descent system produces overlapping group ties among males when combined, as it virtually always is, with patrilocal residence. All the male members of one descent group are enabled to reside together, or at least in the same area. The local group and the descent group are the same. We also know that there is no residence rule which can be combined with matrilineal descent to produce localized kin groups of males. For men in a matrilineal society, the local group and the descent group are different, at least at some points in the life cycle. Patrilineal descent produces overlapping group ties and, therefore, factional polities, whereas matrilineal descent leads to cross-cutting group ties and communal polities.[15]

Paige hypothesizes (1974:309) that fraternal interest groups of various kinds are more common, and assume greater political importance, in societies with patrilineal descent than in those with matrilineal systems. Fraternal interest groups are indicated by such variables as the presence of monolineage communities (localized communities composed of the members of only one descent group) and small extended families under a single male head. Both of these types of groups are indeed more common in patrilineal societies (Paige 1974:311). He also uses data from Swanson's sample of societies to show that decision-making units are much more likely to be kinship groups in patrilineal than matrilineal societies (1974:313). Furthermore, he extends the theory (1974:315-318) to show that, in societies with bilateral descent, factional polities are associated with patrilocal residence rules and communal polities with matrilocal (or at least nonpatrilocal) residence. This is subject to explanation by the same logic, since the imposition of unilocal residence rules in societies with bilateral descent frequently results in groupings quite similar to those found in unilineal societies (Davenport 1959; Murdock 1968).

Paige's theory might also be extended to account for an association observed by Ember and Ember (1971) between patrilocal residence and the occurrence of intrasocietal warfare. Ember and Ember argue that, given the existence of internal warfare, kin groups naturally keep their fighters (men) immediately available for defense, and consequently adopt a patrilocal residence rule. This is quite plausible. However, it is also possible that the existence of localized patrilineal groups of males would promote intergroup conflict through the operation of overlapping kin ties.

Swanson (1974), in a rejoinder to Paige's article, argues that the data presented by Paige do not clearly support Paige's theory and/or disconfirm his own. He points out that the correlation between patrilineal descent and the presence of kin-based decision-making units, on which Paige bases part of his argument, is at least partly spurious. This is due to the fact that, on the average, patrilineal descent tends to occur at higher levels of societal complexity than matrilineal descent in the relevant samples, and the less complex matrilineal societies do not have decision-making political units at all. Thus, Paige's distinction between kin-based and non-kin-based political units is actually in large part a distinction between the presence and absence of complex political organization (Swanson 1974:322-323). In the more complex societies, Swanson shows that there is in fact no association between kin-based political units and type of descent.

This does not, as Swanson clearly stipulates, disprove Paige's theory. But neither does Paige's argument disprove Swanson's explanation of the correlation between political types and descent systems. We know that the relationship exists, but there are at least two competing explanations for it, and the data do not permit an unambiguous choice between them. While Paige shows that the same theory of political behavior may be applicable to both preindustrial and industrial societies, Swanson's theory is consistent with an explanation of associations between political and religious structure which may be equally important (Swanson 1967, 1974:326-327). For the time being, then, we must regard the issue of causal priority in the relationship between descent system and type of polity as unresolved.

Summary and conclusions

We have found, in the preceding discussion, that the type of kinship structure prevalent in any given society is related to certain ecological, economic, and political variables. The economic and ecological variables may most probably be regarded as the causes of kinship structure; there are arguments to the effect that the political variables are both antecedents and consequences of the kinship system.

Bilateral descent is most common in hunting and gathering societies as well as industrial societies. Those in between (primarily with agricultural economies) are likely to have one or the other type of unilineal descent. Patrilineal descent is much more common than matrilineal, perhaps because it presents fewer difficulties in the local organization of the male members of descent groups. Matrilineal descent occurs disproportionately among societies with nonmechanized agriculture ("dominant horticulture") and where the ecology permits relatively dense concentrations of the population. All other nonextractive ecological types tend to select against matriliny. Factional political structures tend to coincide with patrilineal descent systems, and communal polities with matrilineal systems. The causal order here is as yet undetermined; coherent arguments have been advanced for each variable as the causal factor.

In addition, although "evolutionary theory" has been discounted as an explanation of variation in type of kinship structure, there are important sequential relationships among the components of kinship systems. Specifically, it appears that type of descent is contingent upon residence rule, which in turn depends upon the division of labor by sex in subsistence activities. This depends, logically enough, upon the basis of subsistence in a society. Because matrilineal descent is apparently workable only within a relatively narrow ecological range (dominant horticulture), technological developments such as the introduction of the plow work against matriliny, and it therefore occurs most often in the early stages of the development of agriculture. This does not, however, constitute evidence in favor of general evolutionary theory, as Aberle (1961) clearly points out.[16]

We will discover, in succeeding chapters, that kinship systems have important consequences for many aspects of interpersonal relations, including such diverse areas as mate selection, marital power, divorce rates, and socialization practices. It has often been argued that, in the United States and similar industrial societies, the effects of kinship are most remarkable for their absence. Parsons' (1943) position that the American nuclear family is "isolated" from extended kin has been very influential in the discipline of family sociology (see also Gibson 1972). However, most family scholars now agree that his characterization of the "isolated nuclear family" was somewhat overdrawn. It is certainly the case that the typical conjugal family in the contemporary United States is more independent of relatives than are families in societies with unilineal kin groups; this, in fact, is stipulated in Goode's (1963) conceptualization of the characteristics of conjugal family systems. But this does not mean that kinship is sociologically unimportant in societies with these family systems. The study of kinship relations, and the causes and consequences of variation in their characteristics, will undoubtedly continue to be a central focus of family sociology as well as of anthropology.

Notes

1. Terminological complexity does not necessarily imply theoretical complexity or an advanced science. Robin Fox makes this point clearly in his explication of the "Rumpelstiltskin philosophy" in anthropology (Fox 1967:50).

2. The argument I am about to make is couched in avowedly functionalist terms, because of the heuristic value of these concepts for the explication

of this particular point. For similar statements, see Freeman (1958), Stephens (1963:141-145), and, for a more elaborate version, Winch (1971: 3-29).

3. See Stephens' (1963:78-102) discussion of deference, avoidance, and joking relationships and how they are differentially attached to particular kin relationships.

4. The following section draws much descriptive material from Fortes (1959a), Stephens (1963:102-107), and Fox (1967:36-53).

5. This generalization is a slight distortion of reality, as the reader familiar with the principle of double descent will immediately recognize. For the moment, however, the explication of the concept of unilineal descent must take precedence over an exact replication of empirical reality. The appropriate qualification will be made below.

6. This statement implies that one's father and one's mother will be members of different groups. This is, in fact, virtually always the case. We will discuss the causes and implications of this fact below; for the moment, it may be treated as an assumption upon which subsequent arguments are premised.

7. But see Chapter Eight for qualifications to this generalization.

8. Unfortunately, considerations of space prevent a discussion of the various attempts to explain the origin and persistence of incest taboos and rules of exogamy. This is, however, a fascinating topic with many important theoretical implications. For the reader concerned with further inquiry in these matters, some of the best works currently available on the topic (which, incidentally, represent a great variety of viewpoints) include Goody (1956), Levi-Strauss (1956), Slater (1959), Middleton (1962), Talmon (1964), Fox (1967:54-76), Lindzey (1967), Bagley (1969), and Livingstone (1969).

9. There does appear, however, to be a weak statistical trend toward greater proximity to and interaction with the wife's relatives in industrialized societies (Komarovsky 1967; Sweetser 1968; Adams 1970:581; Troll 1971: 269-270; for contrary data, see Adams 1968). This statistical tendency, however, has no direct implications for the cultural rule of neolocality.

10. There is a small logical inconsistency in the construction of these terms. The prefix "patri-" refers to "father" rather than "husband," of course, and "matri-" to "mother" rather than "wife." Some anthropologists prefer the terms "virilocal" and "uxorilocal," respectively, which are technically more correct. However, the former set of terms still seems to be more common, and we shall continue to use them with the stipulation that their meaning should be interpreted according to custom rather than literal translation.

11. We will not deal here with the analysis of kinship terminologies, beyond simply indicating that there are systematic variations in the type of terminologies employed, and that the study of these terminologies can provide significant insights into the social structure of the societies in which they are employed. The interested reader will find useful treatments of the subject in Murdock (1949), Fox (1967), and Needham (1971), among many other sources.

12. This is actually a bit of a distortion. In 101 societies where the gathering of herbs, roots, seeds, etc., is an important source of subsistence, women are exclusively responsible for this in 74. However, gathering tends to coincide with hunting as a major subsistence activity, and men heavily predominate in hunting. For reasons we will discuss shortly, most hunting and gathering societies are patrilocal and patrilineal.

13. Recall also our discussion of the economic roles of women in horticultural societies in Chapter Four, and the references cited in that connection.

14. This hypothesis is by no means original with me. Schneider, for example, apparently had a similar idea in mind when he posited that "isolated communities (or smaller groups) consisting of matrilineal core and in-marrying spouses are extremely difficult to maintain" (Schneider 1961:27).

15. See also Murphy (1957), Van Velzen and Van Wetering (1960), and Otterbein (1968).

16. We have concentrated, in this section, upon correlates of descent systems which have relatively clear causal implications with respect to other types of systems. There are many other correlates of type of descent which we have ignored because of this criterion. For example, Murdock (1949) points out that patrilineal descent is correlated with nonsororal polygyny. It is clear that nonsororal polygyny would be extremely cumbersome to maintain under any condition other than patrilocal residence, and this probably accounts for the correlation observed by Murdock. The theoretical implications here, however, seem relatively minimal, and we have consequently bypassed the issue.

part three
Family interaction

In the next three chapters we will leave the subject of the structure of marital, family, and kinship systems, and concentrate on the processes of interaction which occur within these various systems. In Chapter Seven we will investigate premarital relationships, concentrating particularly on patterns of mate selection and on premarital sexuality. Chapter Eight focuses on the marital relationship itself; we will investigate variations in marital role performance, marital power, and marital dissolution. In Chapter Nine we turn to the study of the parent-child relationship; topics include antecedents of parental values in socialization, sex differences in socialization, and consequences of parental behaviors for child and adult personality development.

In this section we make extensive use of cross-national studies for the first time in the book. This means that the focus of our attention will be primarily on the extent to which correlations between variables measured on the intrasystemic level are similar or different across systems. If they are different, then systemic characteristics are indicated as important in any resulting explanation. However, cross-societal and, particularly, cross-cultural data will also be investigated. Studies which are reviewed in these chapters have been selected, as in the earlier parts of this book, not because they cover the field of comparative family sociology in any exhaustive sense, but because they demonstrate how comparative research can contribute to the development of theoretical explanations of human behavior.

We begin, in Chapter Seven, with a look at premarital heterosexual relationships in a comparative context.

chapter seven
Premarital relationships

Systems of mate selection

Arranged marriage and autonomous mate selection

> Americans marry for love. . . . Other reasons such as economic gain, status achievement, rebellion against parents, escape from loneliness, "everyone else is doing it," and sexual gratification are either culturally unsupported or actually shameful. (Udry 1974:131–132)

If anything, Udry is understating the case here. Love and marriage are so highly intertwined in modern American culture that it is difficult for many people to conceive of any motivation for marriage except love. It comes as a considerable shock to many students to find that the cultural concepts of love and marriage were not associated until relatively recently in Western history. In fact, the anthropologist Ralph Linton once argued that American society is virtually unique in making love a prerequisite and basis for marriage:

> All societies recognize that there are occasional violent, emotional attachments between persons of opposite sex, but our present American

culture is practically the only one which has attempted to capitalize these and make them the basis for marriage. (Linton 1936:175)

It is now recognized that Linton's statement is too extreme; there are in fact a fair number of societies in the world in which marriages are, or are supposed to be, based on the kind of emotional attachment we call romantic love. But there are also many societies in which love and marriage are culturally unrelated, and some which apparently lack any recognition of or allowance for the regular occurrence of romantic love as an emotion (Stephens 1963:204).

The latter two situations often occur in societies where marriages are, in common parlance, "arranged." In its most extreme form, this means that the parties to a marriage (the prospective spouses) have no voice in the selection of the spouse. This decision falls within the province of family elders. The opposite situation is what Reiss (1971:49–51) calls "autonomous" or "participant-run" courtship. In ideal-type form, an autonomous mate-selection system would be one in which marital choices may be entirely explained by reference to the behavior of prospective spouses: that is, where the people who are to be married have complete control over the outcomes of the selection process. In reality, of course, we are talking about a continuum rather than a dichotomy. Neither polar type is perfectly represented by any one society, although traditional China comes very close to the arranged type (Lang 1946; Levy 1949; Winch 1971:37–39), and modern America clearly approximates the autonomous variety.

William Goode (1959), in a seminal paper on this subject, argues convincingly that the capacity to love is a universal psychological potential. However, there is considerable cross-cultural variation in both the extent to which romantic love is an important cultural theme and the degree to which mate selection is premised on romantic attraction. Goode maintains that, in *any* society, some control over the process of mate selection must be maintained by adults and family elders. As we have seen in previous chapters, marriage plays a crucial role in structuring social systems. A marriage is virtually always more than the union of two (or more) individuals in an economic and sexual alliance. Marriage serves to unite two families or kin groups—to establish new alliances or reinforce existing ones. The nature of the kinship relations established or maintained by marriage are often of paramount concern to the families of the spouses. Thus, Goode maintains that there is no society in which all, or even most, marriages are based on uncontrolled emotional attachments:

> Kinfolk or immediate family can disregard the question of who marries whom, only if a marriage is not seen as a link between kin lines, only if no property, power, lineage honor, totemic relationships, and the like are believed to flow from the kin lines through the spouses to their

offspring. Universally, however, these are believed to follow kin lines. Mate choice thus has consequences for the social structure. But love may affect mate choice. Both mate choice and love, therefore, are too important to be left to children. (Goode 1959:42-43)

Goode goes on (1959:43-46) to explicate five ways in which family elders and other representatives of "adult society" can exercise control over the mate-selection process. These methods of control vary from more to less direct. The first four are variations of arranged marriage patterns. Mate selection may be controlled by parents by means of (1) child betrothal; (2) rules of kinship which narrowly specify the field of eligible mates, such as preferential cross-cousin marriage; (3) physical segregation of potential mates during late childhood and adolescence; and (4) a value system which de-emphasizes romance as a basis for marriage, often found in combination with close supervision of unmarried people by elders of the family. These four methods either vest the right of choice directly in parents, or severely restrict the options of maritally eligible persons and their opportunities to interact with potential spouses.[1]

The fifth type of mate-selection system, according to Goode, is formally or nominally autonomous, but is in actuality a set of more indirect forms of parental control. Romantic love is encouraged in this type of system, but a variety of manifest and latent processes operate to channel the romantic inclinations of participants in the system along lines which are acceptable to their elders. This is the type of system which is often designated as "autonomous." Goode is not quarreling with that designation, but is rather pointing out that such systems are premised on indirect control rather than complete freedom. Here, parents

> . . . seek to control love relationships by influencing the informal social contacts of their children: moving to appropriate neighborhoods and schools, giving parties and helping to make out invitation lists, by making their children aware that certain individuals have ineligibility traits (race, religion, manners, tastes, clothing, and so on). Since youngsters fall in love with those with whom they associate, control over informal relationships also controls substantially the focus of affection. (Goode 1959:450)

The result of this process is not that parents choose spouses for their children, but rather that children choose spouses from among a "pool of eligibles" whose composition is determined largely by parental behavior. Thus parents directly influence the *type* of mate that their child is likely to select. This influence is generally in the direction of similarity of traits and social characteristics (class, race, religion, etc.), and a great number of studies have documented strong tendencies toward "homogamy" in mate selection in the contemporary United States.[2]

The existence of this extensive variation in the distribution of decision-making power and influence in mate selection gives rise to at least two interrelated questions. First, what causes the variation? What are the conditions under which one or another type of mate-selection system is likely to emerge? Second, what factors cause maritally eligible people to put up with situations where their right to choose their own spouse is either limited or virtually nil? In other words, how can arranged marriage systems operate without producing enormous amounts of intergenerational and, ultimately, intramarital, resentment and friction?

The answer to the first question appears to lie in the characteristics of family and kinship systems, and specifically in the extent to which kinship is, in any given society, the basis of social structure. Freeman (1958) expressed this logic in functionalist terms, arguing that the greater the role of the family in the social structure, and the more crucial family membership and welfare to the well-being of the individual, the greater the family's control over mate selection (see also Winch 1971:37–39, 69). Freeman and Winch support their arguments with examples. Stephens (1963:198–199), however, has demonstrated the existence of a cross-cultural correlation between parental arrangement of marriage and two variables which index the structural importance of kinship: the existence of unilineal kin groups and the prevalence of extended families. A society characterized by unilineal kin groups and extended-family households is not likely to have an autonomous or participant-run system of mate selection.

The explanation of this correlation seems relatively clear-cut. If, for example, a son in a patrilocal extended family is to be married, he will be bringing his wife into his parents' household following the marriage. She, and the children she bears, will be members of a family headed by her husband's parents. In such situations, marriage does not constitute the formation of a new family, but rather a means of recruiting a new member to an existing family. This new member will have several critical roles within the family, including most importantly child-bearing. Because her husband's family cannot produce new members without enlisting the cooperation of females who are not already family members (remember the incest taboo), the continuity of the family depends upon the reproductive capacities of the new wife and other in-marrying women (subsequent wives her husband may take, or the wives of his brothers). She must also be able to pull more than her own weight in productive enterprises; since the family is likely to be highly self-sufficient in economic respects, other members are likely to be unwilling and perhaps unable to support a nonproductive adult member. Furthermore, the marriage to which she is a party will probably be important to both her new family and her family of orientation in terms of the interfamily alliance it establishes or maintains, since marital ties are crucial to social integration in kinship-based societies. For these reasons, the choice of a spouse for a child in an extended family is a very important *family* decision. As such, it is likely to be made by those who have primary decision-making authority within the family: the family elders.

As extended-family systems break down, then, with the onset of industrialization, we should expect to observe successively smaller proportions of marriages being arranged in societies where this has previously been the custom.[3] In a study of marriages in Tokyo, Japan, Robert Blood fails to observe any such trend in his sample, but argues that his study is too limited in its time frame for such a trend to appear (1967:36–37). He does, though, review more extensive studies of social change in Japan which show that arranged marriages are decreasing in frequency and that the nature of the arrangement is changing (1967:7–12). A study of mate-selection practices in Ankara, Turkey (Fox 1975) shows that arranged marriages are relatively less common among the most urbanized, industrialized segments of the population (long-time residents of urban areas, those with higher educational levels, etc.). It is among these people that extended families and corporate kin groups may be expected to be the least frequent and the least salient (see Chapter Five). Lobodzinska (1975) documents a shift from arranged marriages to autonomous mate selection based on inter-personal attraction in twentieth-century Poland. She attributes this change to the influences of urbanization and industrialization, and particularly to the de-clining role of the family in economic production.

So where family and kinship predominate in the social structure, marriages are most likely to be arranged. This fact also helps, in part, to explain how and why it is that young people (those who are to be married) allow such "interference" in their lives by parents. It is important to recognize here that, while in American society the choice of a spouse by one's parents would be defined as perhaps the epitome of parental interference in the lives of their children, this is not at all the case under the conditions which give rise to the practice of arranging marriages elsewhere. Mate choice is generally recog-nized to be family business, and parents, when choosing mates for their children, are exercising legitimate authority rather than arbitrary power. The spouses-to-be are often not at all eager to take the initiative in selecting a mate.[4] Fox (1975) discusses the importance of "family honor" in Turkey, based on the work of Dodd (1973). Family honor is highly valued according to the traditional culture, and it depends very heavily upon the reputations, modesty, and chastity of the female members of the family. Participation in an autonomous courtship system would require girls to compromise the honor of their families by being more aggressive, less modest, and less retiring than the culture deems appropriate. The value placed on family honor is greater than any value placed on independence in mate selection, even in the urbanized segment of Turkey from which Fox's sample was drawn. Consequently, nonarranged marriages ("love matches") in Turkey are rare; less than 30 percent of the marriages in Fox's random sample of Ankara were classified as love matches.

The desire for autonomy in mate selection can also be held in check by factors other than values such as family honor. Goode (1959) points out that, in virtually any kind of mate-selection system, those who have the greatest stake in the formation of "proper" or advantageous marriages are the upper strata. These people control the greater proportion of resources, and they depend on the willingness of family members to use their wealth in the best interests of the family. Consequently, Goode (1959:46-47) hypothesizes that mate choice is in fact less autonomous in the upper strata of any society, including our own. (For a review of evidence on this point, see Lee 1977). Upper-class parents are more motivated than others to control the marital choices of their children, and they are also more able to do so. This is partly because of their greater ability to segregate their children from those of other classes. But also, because of the magnitude of resources controlled by upper-class families, their young are likely to find it in their own best interests to conform to the wishes of the families in mate selection as well as in other matters. In Goode's words,

> The upper strata have much more at stake in the maintenance of the social structure and thus are more strongly motivated to control the courtship and marriage decisions of their young. Correspondingly, their young have much more to lose than lower strata youth, so that upper strata elders *can* wield more power. (Goode 1959:46-47)

Marriage is not necessarily regarded as the ultimate romantic, intimate, emotional relationship; in fact, in most cultures the concept of marriage is associated with few such ideas. George Theodorson (1965) studied cross-societal variation in romanticism among college students in the United States, Chinese Singapore, Burma, and India. He found that romantic ideals such as trust in one's spouse, equality in marriage, and emotional intimacy within the marital dyad were by no means universally accepted or valued among even these college students, who probably represent the most "Westernized" segments of their respective societies. Acceptance of romanticism was clearly greatest among American students and least among Indian (the most "traditional" culture), with the Singapore Chinese and Burmese intermediate. Theodorson found, furthermore, an interesting association between acceptance of romanticism and motivation to marry in his samples. On the cross-societal level, he found a perfect rank-order correlation between average romanticism and desire to marry. In India, for example, he found that over 28 percent of the females in his sample (37 percent of all those answering the question) would prefer *not* to marry if given the choice. Only 1.4 percent of the American women expressed a similar sentiment. In the three Eastern cultures in this sample, Theodorson maintains that the traditional practice of arranged or "contractual" marriages is declining. The relative absence of a romantic ideology in these societies may foretell a corresponding decline in marriage rates: in the absence of parental pressure and initiative in mate selection, the young people themselves are relatively less motivated to marry at all in comparison to their counterparts in societies with highly developed romantic complexes such as the United States.

Obviously, the criteria employed in selecting a mate vary widely between societies with autonomous and arranged mate-selection systems. In societies with autonomous systems, love is virtually always given as the justification or rationale for a particular choice. But, as Goode's (1959) thesis would lead us to expect, the characteristics of a "good spouse" are quite different in arranged-marriage systems, and involve primarily considerations pertaining to kin-group membership, intergroup relations, and economics. Stephens (1963:190-197) contends that the most important selection criteria here are factors such as the size of the marriage payment (typically a "bride price"), the reputation and status of the kin groups involved in the exchange, levirate and sororate obligations, and the maintenance of continuous traditions of marriage between kin groups. A cross-cultural study by Rosenblatt and Cozby (1972) lends credibility to this argument. They found that free or autonomous mate selection is positively correlated with selection criteria which they term "impractical." This category was apparently defined in residual fashion; practical grounds included ". . . food-getting skills, value of alliances created by the marriage, just plain proximity, rank, personality, food preparation skills, strength, health. . . ." (Rosenblatt and Cozby 1972:693). Cultures permitting free choice of spouse were also characterized by other elements of the "romantic love complex": idealization of chosen spouse, emphasis on affection in the relationship, traditional practices of courtly love, and an important sexual component in mate-selection criteria.

Another study by Coppinger and Rosenblatt (1968) helps to specify the kinds of circumstances under which romantic criteria will be important in mate selection. They argue that marital stability has adaptive advantages in virtually all societies, and that therefore some social or cultural elements will be present in all societies to make marital stability rewarding or advantageous for individuals. Perhaps the most powerful motivation for stability would be spousal interdependence in subsistence. That is, if each spouse were highly dependent upon the other for certain kinds of subsistence, marriages would be highly stable because the costs of dissolution to the individuals involved would be great. In societies with lesser degrees of economic interdependence between spouses, some other factors must operate to promote marital stability.

One such factor might be strong romantic attachment between spouses: if economic interdependence is low, emotional interdependence might develop to take its place. Coppinger and Rosenblatt thus hypothesize the existence of a negative relationship between marital interdependence in subsistence activities and the prevalence of a cultural romantic love complex.

Fifty-five ethnographic reports of societies with some variety of unilocal postmarital residence were rated for the prevalence of romantic love as a criterion in mate selection. Spousal economic interdependence was measured indirectly by the use of two variables contained in the Ethnographic Atlas: the society's proportional reliance on a particular mode of subsistence for food (for example, hunting, fishing, agriculture); and the proportional contribution of each sex to each kind of food-producing activity. The sum of the products of these proportions gives the relative contribution of each sex to the society's supply of food. Coppinger and Rosenblatt found that, for their 55 societies, women contributed an average of approximately 40 percent of the total food supply.[5] The authors reasoned that any departure from this average indicated high economic dependence of one spouse on the other, whereas divisions of labor approximating the average indicated a balanced subsistence contribution and high spousal interdependence. The working hypothesis therefore took the form of a positive correlation between deviations from the mean female contribution to subsistence, in either direction, and the prevalence of a romantic cultural complex. This is in fact what they found; the correlation, although relatively small, was positive and significant.

In combination with Theodorson's (1965) study of romanticism and motivation to marry, the work of Coppinger and Rosenblatt leads to an hypothesis about the conditions under which a romantic love complex will develop as an important element of culture. Specifically, it appears that a romantic ideology will emerge and become an important set of criteria for mate selection when "instrumental" reasons for mate choice (food-producing ability, kin-group connections, etc.) are absent or unimportant. When such instrumental criteria are important, marriages will usually be arranged, according to criteria other than romantic attraction. This is likely in societies with unilineal kin groups and extended families, because in these situations marriage serves important instrumental functions—functions which are of extreme import to persons other than the spouses themselves. Where marriage does not have these instrumental consequences, people can afford to marry for reasons of personal gratification, happiness, and satisfaction, and it is under these conditions that romantic ideologies are most likely to develop and become relevant in courtship and mate selection. William Stephens expresses this logic concisely in attempting to explain the central role of romantic love in modern American courtship:

... in our country romantic love serves as a rationale for mate choice; it is the reason one gives, in our society, for his choice of a spouse. In societies with arranged marriages, such a rationale for mate choice is of course unnecessary, since the individual does not choose his own spouse. One possible reason, then, for the apparent frequency of romantic love among ourselves, is that the *notion* of romantic love—used as a *rationale* for marriage—has filled an ideological vacuum, caused by the dissappearance of arranged marriage. (Stephens 1963:206)

To summarize: Mate selection is controlled or supervised in some way by family elders in all societies, but there is a great deal of variation in the directness of the control and the decision-making power formally allocated to parents and children. In societies with extended families and important kin groups, marriages tend to be more directly arranged by parents, because the consequences of mate selection are instrumental and accrue largely to existing families rather than to the individuals between whom the marriages are contracted. In societies with bilateral kinship and conjugal families, the consequences of marriage for the families of the principals are much less instrumental. Here, the choice of spouse is formally the prerogative of the individuals involved, although parents both intentionally and unintentionally influence the composition of the "field of eligibles" for their children by the transmission of cultural norms of homogamy, their choice of residence, etc. When mate choice is formally free or autonomous, a romantic ideology tends to develop. This ideology establishes criteria for mate selection which revolve around personal gratification, as well as a rationale for particular marital choices.

While this reasoning seems logical, there are at least two studies whose findings are partially inconsistent with it, and which thus necessitate some qualifications. First, it is clear that this logic implies that romantic love should be a more central focus of culture in societies with conjugal families than in those with extended families. Conjugal families, furthermore, occur under conditions of neolocal residence; nonneolocal (unilocal) postmarital residence patterns produce extended families. We should therefore expect to find a positive correlation, on the cross-cultural level, between neolocal residence and the presence of a romantic cultural ideology. However, according to Rosenblatt (1967), romanticism is positively correlated with nonneolocal residence. This correlation is inconsistent with the theory we have thus far developed.

Employing functionalist logic, Rosenblatt shows that one can construct alternative hypotheses regarding the relationship between romantic love and postmarital residence. First, one might argue that romantic love should be more functional, and thus more prevalent, in neolocal societies because (1) love could serve to keep marriages intact in the absence of pressures from localized kin groups; (2) the economic interdependence of spouses may be greater when they maintain their own residence and household, and this could lead to greater emotional interdependence;[6] and (3) since the married pair live apart from their kin, more of their emotional needs must be satisfied by one another.[7] On the other hand, love might be more prevalent under conditions of nonneolocal residence because (1) it could serve to strengthen the conjugal unit in the face of divisive pressures from co-resident kin;[8] (2) love is needed to promote marital stability in the absence of direct spousal economic interdependence; (3) conjugal love smooths relations between the unilineal kin groups of the spouses; and (4) the high economic interdependence of spouses residing neolocally increases the importance of more objective or "practical" criteria in mate selection (Coppinger and Rosenblatt 1968). The study in question (Rosenblatt 1967) was designed to determine which of these two contradictory lines of reasoning would receive empirical support. Since romantic love is positively related to nonneolocal residence, the second logic is obviously more valid according to Rosenblatt's data.

There is, however, a significant problem with these data which certainly qualifies the utility of the results. Of the 75 societies in the sample, only 6 were clearly characterized by neolocal residence; 10 more had neolocal residence "as a significant alternative" (Rosenblatt 1967:476). The remaining 59 societies (79 percent of the sample) fell into the nonneolocal category. There is therefore some doubt about the extent to which the neolocal residential situation is adequately represented by the 6 neolocal societies in the sample. The interpretation of these results should thus be quite cautious, particularly since they contradict the findings of Stephens (1963:199) on the relationship of autonomous mate selection to extended family households and unilineal kin groups.[9] Rosenblatt, in effect, has shown that romantic love *may* play a significant role in mate selection in societies with nonneolocal residence rules, which are likely to have extended families (see Chapter Six). Furthermore, nonromantic criteria *may* be important where mate choice is autonomous.

Further support for the latter point is given by Fox (1975). On the basis of Goode's (1959) argument that parental control over mate selection serves to maintain existing stratification patterns, Fox hypothesized that, for her Turkish sample, couples whose marriages were arranged would be more homogamous than love-match couples on criteria such as education, father's education, and residential background. However, there were no differences in homogamy between the two groups. Fox concludes that education and earning potential are important criteria for mate selection in love matches as well as in arranged marriages in the Middle East, and that love matches therefore do not *necessarily* disrupt existing stratification patterns (Fox 1975:192).[10]

We have, it seems, three empirical generalizations which are to some extent theoretically inconsistent: nonneolocal residence is positively related to the prevalence of extended families; extended families and arranged marriages tend to occur jointly; but romantic love as a criterion for mate choice is positively related to nonneolocal residence. The first two generalizations, plus the positive correlation between romantic love and autonomous mate selection (Rosenblatt and Cozby 1972), would lead us to expect a negative relationship between nonneolocal residence and romantic love. Instead we find the opposite. Research has not yet provided an explanation of this inconsistency. We clearly need a study of the relationship between residence and romantic love with a more broadly based sample than was employed in Rosenblatt's (1967) investigation, to better estimate the empirical validity of the third generalization.

It is clear at least that, even when individuals are allowed to choose their own spouses, the most relevant bases for choice are not always romantic. Rosenblatt's observation that couples who reside neolocally are more dependent upon one another for subsistence is a key point here. In this situation of high interdependency, instrumental or "practical" criteria for mate selection may be of paramount importance because the married couple is not enmeshed in a localized group of economically supportive kin. This reinforces the point that the members of most nonindustrial societies marry to survive, not to love.

There are, it seems, two important kinds of "survival criteria" which influence mate selection, particularly in societies where marriages are arranged. First, as we discussed in Chapter Six, marriages create and solidify alliances between kin groups which have survival value in terms of the cooperation, economic and otherwise, which they enable. Second, marriages often involve the direct transfer of property between the kin groups of the new spouses. Goode (1959) and Stephens (1963) have pointed out that the form and size of these property transfers are often of critical importance in the arrangement of marriages. In Murdock's World Ethnographic Sample, about 70 percent of the societies included have some form of marriage payment. Of these, by far the most common is the "bride price," where the groom's family transfers some property (usually tangible and nonperishable) to the bride's family, presumably as compensation for the loss of their daughter's services when she joins her husband's kin group. This practice is most common in Africa (Goody 1970: 53). Payments from the bride's family to the groom or his family are much less common. Stephens (1963) calls these transfers "dowry." Goody (1970), however, uses the term "groomwealth," and restricts the referent of "dowry" to those situations where the bride receives wedding gifts from her family. He points out that this practice has important implications for systems of descent and residence, and that it foreshadows the development of conjugal family systems. Since the dowry, in Goody's sense of the term, militates against the maintenance of property by unilineal kin groups, and since the practice was most common in preindustrial Europe, it may have been partially responsible for the early development of conjugal family systems in Europe. These, perhaps, promoted the early development of industrial technology (see Chapter Five).

Two studies reviewed by Marsh (1967:67-72) illuminate the causes and correlates of the various forms of marriage payment. Richards (1950), in a sample of Bantu societies in Central Africa, found that the size of the bride price or "bridewealth" is correlated with the prevalence of patrilocal residence. That is, the bridewealth is more likely to be practiced, and likely to be of relatively greater magnitude, when the bride is residentially removed from her parents and her natal kin group. And Heath (1958), working with the World Ethnographic Sample, found a systematic relationship between the form and size of the marriage payment and the female's contribution to subsistence. Groom-wealth is most likely where the female's subsistence contribution is quite low; the greater her contribution to subsistence the greater the size of the bride price tends to be. If a woman's labor is valuable, her family is likely to receive substantial compensation for transferring the rights to her productivity to her husband.

There is also an association between property transfers at marriage and the existence and elaborateness of marriage ceremonies. Rosenblatt and Unangst (1974) classified 44 societies according to the importance of marriage ceremonials. They found that these ceremonies were most likely to exist, and most likely to be highly elaborate and visible affairs, where marriage involved the transfer of valuable property. This situation is most common in societies based on herding and/or agriculture, because in these kinds of societies wealth and well-being depend upon the possession of tangible, cumulative property (cattle or land or both). The authors argue that the marriage ceremonies publicly represent and solidify the commitment of each kin group involved to the property arrangements contingent on the marriage. Consequently, the more important the property transfers the more important and elaborate are the marriage ceremonies.

Considerations of property, then, are often very important criteria in mate selection. In some societies bride prices may be extremely high relative to typical accumulations of wealth. The economic stability of entire families may be largely contingent upon the negotiation of favorable "exchange agreements" in the marriages of their children. Stephens (1963:214-215) reports, not unexpectedly, that marriage payments are more common in societies with unilineal kin groups (the same, of course, is true of the practice of arranged marriage). He also argues (1963:214) that the economic relationships established between kin groups by marriage payments have consequences for the integration of the families of spouses with one another, and that marriage payments help to promote marital stability. If, for example, a man divorces his wife without good reason (such as barrenness), he loses the bride price which his family has paid. Economic considerations thus often override romantic or emotional criteria, both in the selection of mates and in the maintenance of marriages.

A functional analysis of romantic love

We have established that marriages are likely to be based on romantic criteria in industrial societies, although this practice is not restricted to industrialized nations.[11] There has been considerable debate as to the consequences of employing romantic criteria in mate selection for the adjustment and stability of individual marriages (see Udry 1974:148-149, for a review of arguments on this issue), but empirically it appears that in conjugal family systems there is no correlation between attitudinal romanticism and subsequent marital adjustment (Kephart 1970; Spanier 1972). The consequence of an autonomous courtship system based on romantic attraction for *societies* is, however, a different matter. We have thus far treated romanticism as a kind of a "default option," a criterion for mate selection which is implemented when there are no other immediately relevant criteria. But this may be an inadequate explanation.

Sidney Greenfield (1965) has argued that the romantic love complex has extremely important consequences for the entirety of American society, and particularly for the economic institution. He contends that our economic and occupational systems are based upon achievement rather than ascription. That is, individuals survive, and survive more or less well, depending on the contribution which they are able to make to the production and distribution of goods and services, and the value of that contribution to the economic system. Individuals are compensated for their contributions, according to their value, in liquid form (money); they then turn this money into the goods and services they require and/or desire by participating in the market as consumers. One's ability to consume is thus premised upon one's productive capacities as a member of the labor force.

But access to the labor force is limited. In particular, adult males have advantages in acquiring these positions, and in the acquisition of prestigious and high-paying positions, by virtue of greater training, less limited mobility, and numerous other competitive advantages with which our culture has provided them.[12] The essential point is that all members of a society must consume, but only a fraction of an industrial society's members can have direct access to the productive roles in the labor force which make this consumption possible. In our society, women and (especially) children are relatively unlikely, as compared to adult males, to participate in the labor force. In Greenfield's terms, the analytic problem is this:

> For the system to work, then, there must be a means by which women and children are provided with the necessary and highly valued goods and services—both in terms of absolute survival requirements and culturally defined prestige wants. Another way of phrasing this is to ask: How are women and children articulated with the industrial sector that

produces and distributes the material items in the culture? (Greenfield 1965:372)

Greenfield's answer to this question is, predictably, the family. Most families consist of producers (members of the labor force) and dependents. The husband-father is almost always expected to play a productive role and to receive compensation for it. The wife-mother may also play such a role, although it is usually secondary to her husband's occupational position, or she may assume the role of economic dependent.[13] The children are invariably dependents. So the family, because it typically consists of workers and dependents, allows people who do not play productive roles in the labor force to consume goods and services.

What role does romantic love play in all of this? Greenfield argues, quite correctly, that Americans are highly motivated by the desire to acquire and accumulate wealth (see also Merton 1968:185-248). We place high value on the acquisition of material goods far beyond mere subsistence requirements. He argues further that any given worker or potential worker is probably at an objective advantage over others in the consumership game if he or she is not encumbered with a family. The family limits mobility and the amount of time and effort that could otherwise be devoted to resource-producing activities. Furthermore, when an individual enters into a marriage he or she is running a substantial risk of acquiring dependents who will use up resources: possibly the spouse, and certainly subsequent children. Almost any adult would have a better chance of economic success, as an individual, by remaining unmarried, participating in the labor force, and keeping the resources generated by this participation for himself or herself. But the industrial economic system would break down in the face of such pressure on the labor force. Some people must adopt the role of economic dependent in order for the system to work. Others must, somehow, be motivated to provide for these dependents even though this results in a decrease in their own standard of living.

Greenfield contends that the romantic love complex in industrial societies provides such a motivation. It establishes a set of values, alternative or complementary to the value of economic success, which most people pursue in spite of the personal economic disadvantages such pursuit entails. If such a value system did not exist, the economic system could not operate as it does. Greenfield concludes that:

> ... the function of romantic love in American society appears to be to motivate individuals—where there is no other means of motivating them—to occupy the positions husband-father and wife-mother and form nuclear families that are essential not only for reproduction and socialization but also to maintain the existing arrangements for distributing and consuming goods and services and, in general, to keep

the social system in proper working order and thus maintain it as a going concern. (Greenfield 1965:377)

Greenfield's theory shares certain analytic problems with other functional analyses (see Hempel 1959), including the absence of an objective definition of what constitutes a "social system in proper working order," and an incomplete or possibly circular causal logic. Demonstrating that the romantic love complex has important consequences for societal stability does not, in itself, illuminate the causes of its existence. But the logic employed here fits well with Theodorson's (1965) study of romanticism and motivation to marry. It leads, furthermore, to an empirical hypothesis that romantic love is more likely to be a mate-selection criterion in industrial than in nonindustrial societies, where families are the productive economic units and individuals must, in general, belong to families or functioning kin groups in order to survive.

The analysis here indicates that, as a cultural element, the romantic love complex is far from superfluous. It articulates well with other aspects of the American social system. It provides a motivation to marry in the absence of incentives involving economic subsistence. But the association between love and marriage is hardly universal, and in some ways is a relatively recent innovation in Western cultures.

Conclusions

Marriage is not always a romantic alliance. In fact, romance is rarely associated with marriage. Other criteria for mate selection are often of paramount importance; romantic love justifies marriage primarily when instrumental justifications are lacking. But romantic love may be a central component of a cultural system even if the criteria for mate selection in that culture are instrumental. Romance may be associated with homosexual, extramarital, or other nonmarital relationships.

It is important to recognize that, even where mate selection is formally the prerogative of the individuals who are to be married, parents and other adults exercise both direct and indirect controls over the mate-selection process. It is a sociological truism that one can only fall in love with people one has met. Parents play a critical role in placing or locating their children in particular social environments. These environments usually contain other individuals whose social characteristics are quite homogeneous. From this follows the marked tendency of individuals in autonomous mate-selection systems to marry homogamously—in other words, to marry others who are similar to themselves in characteristics such as race, ethnicity, socioeconomic status, education, and religion. In industrial societies such as the United States, parents rarely if ever arrange a marriage or dictate the selection of a particular spouse for their child. But parents, both intentionally and unintentionally, structure the set of potential spouses from which the final choice is made. No system of mate selection is completely free.

In our culture, the concepts of love and marriage are both associated with a third concept: sex. For us, sex is most often viewed as a concomitant and expression of love, and for generations marriage has been the single legitimate arena for sexual expression, although this is certainly changing. But in all societies sexual relationships do occur both before and outside of marriage, sometimes as part of the courtship process and sometimes as an activity completely unrelated to mate selection or marriage. In the next section we will review some of the major comparative studies of premarital sexual relationships, attitudes, and behaviors.

Premarital sexuality

Love and sex

The concepts of love and sex have been associated in Western cultures, and many others, for a very long time. Everyone knows that. It is less often recognized, however, that the nature of the association between these concepts has not always been conceived in the same way. Today in America, a value position which Reiss (1967) calls "permissiveness with affection" is increasingly common, particularly among the younger and better-educated segments of the population. This attitude set holds that a sexual relationship between an unmarried couple is morally justifiable if it occurs as part of a strong mutual affectional relationship. Love, then, justifies sex. Goode (1959:41) defines love as ". . . a strong emotional attachment, a cathexis, between adolescents or adults of opposite sexes, with at least the components of sex desire and tenderness." Sex is therefore a part of what is probably the most widely accepted sociological definition of love.

But it has not always been this way. Love and sex have sometimes been held to be antithetical. Several decisions of the "courts" of medieval England decreed that love could not exist between married persons. Part of the logic of this position seems to be that love is created by a combination of curiosity and mystery. Marriage, however, involves (ideally at least) almost complete intimacy and sharing of all aspects of one's self and person. The mystery upon which love is based breaks down in the face of the mutual self-revelation of the spouses. A central part of what one reveals to one's spouse is, of course, sexual. The perceived incompatibility between love and marriage was thus based, in large part, upon a perceived or presumed incompatibility between love and sex, a virtually inevitable concomitant of marriage. (For descriptions and analyses of the situation in medieval England, see Hunt 1959; Bernard *et al.* 1959; Reiss 1960; and Udry 1974:131.)

This logic did not die with the middle ages. In the twentieth century, Freud (1922:72) defined love as "aim-inhibited sex." Waller (1938:187-209) helped popularize a similar argument among sociologists; Udry (1974:140) summarizes Waller's theory with the statement: "Love is an idealized passion which develops from the frustration of sex." Freud and Waller mean, briefly, that the emotion of love arises as a response to an unsatisfied desire or drive for sex. By implication, then, when the sex drive is satisfied, the emotional response to its blockage or frustration, namely love, disappears.

There have been two different kinds or levels of hypotheses which have been developed from this logic. One is the rather obvious hypothesis that the romantic and ideational qualities of a heterosexual relationship defined as "love" by the participants in it should be obliterated, or at least seriously diminished, by sexual intercourse. This hypothesis has been tested rather extensively on American college students (see Burgess and Wallin 1953: 239-242; Kirkendall 1961; Kanin and Davidson 1972), and has found virtually no support.[14]

A slightly different form of this hypothesis has also been rendered on the cross-cultural level, most explicitly by Robert Blood (1952). Blood argued that, given a presumed incompatibility between sexual intercourse and romantic love, the "romantic love complex" as a cultural element should be incompatible with a high degree of premarital sexual freedom. That is, in societies which permit great freedom to adolescents with regard to sexual behavior, the sex drive is rarely blocked, and love (the emotional reaction to sexual frustration) should thus be an insignificant part of the cultures of such societies. Where premarital sexuality is culturally restricted, however, many people should experience the frustration of sexual impulses, and love should become a cultural focus. Blood adduced several examples from ethnographic work which, he contended, supported this hypothesis.

There is evidence, however, that Blood chose his examples rather selectively. There may be a very small negative relationship between sexual permissiveness on the cultural level and the cultural importance of romantic love (Stephens 1963:207), but there are too many exceptions to lend credibility to the thesis that love *is* "aim-inhibited sex." Furthermore, Rosenblatt and Cozby (1972) found that autonomous mate selection was positively related to both romantic love and the importance of sex in mate selection in their sample of ethnographic reports.

It is clear that many cultures have associated the concepts of romantic love and sexual intimacy, although in widely diverging ways.

Objectively, it appears that sex and love are neither inexorably linked nor mutually exclusive, on either the individual or the cultural level of analysis.

Cross-cultural variation in premarital sexual behavior

Although norms regarding premarital sex are changing with considerable rapidity in the contemporary United States (see Reiss 1960, 1967), most people still regard the American normative system as rather restrictive in a comparative sense. Opinions and personal values regarding the legitimacy of sex before marriage, or between unmarried people, are highly variable in American society. There are, however, many societies which have virtually no normative sanctions against premarital sex, although all normative systems proscribe sexual relations between certain categories of people.

Murdock, in the sample of 250 ethnographic reports which he analyzed in *Social Structure*, had sufficient information on 158 to estimate the extent to which premarital sexual relations were proscribed by the norms. He reported that

> . . . nonincestuous premarital relations are fully permitted in 65 instances, and are conditionally approved in 43 and only mildly disapproved in 6, whereas they are forbidden in only 44. In other words, premarital license prevails in 70 percent of our cases. (Murdock 1949: 265)

Stephens, on his much smaller sample of ethnographic studies, found a similar distribution. Out of 39 societies, 20 fully permitted premarital sex and only 6 ". . . have a strict and apparently effective rule against premarital sex" (1963: 246). In the classification systems employed by Murdock and Stephens, the United States would probably rank near the "restrictive" pole of the continuum, although this may be changing somewhat.

In contemporary cross-national comparisons Americans also appear to be rather conservative on both attitudes and behaviors. This is most demonstrably true among college students. Luckey and Nass (1969) compared sexual attitudes and behaviors of samples of college students from the United States, Canada, England, Germany, and Norway. On attitudinal questions involving such things as the appropriateness of premarital intimacy and the value of virginity in a prospective spouse, they consistently found the English students to be the most liberal, followed rather closely by the Norwegians. Students in the United States and Canada, particularly the Canadians, were markedly more conservative. The frequency distribution for the percentage of students experiencing premarital sexual intercourse was very similar, ranging from a high of 74.8 percent for English males to a low of 35.3 percent for Canadian females (1969:374-375). The researchers do not attempt to explain this variation. They simply observe that North American college students are generally more conservative than European students in sexual matters, and that their results show an increase in premarital permissiveness for all countries in their sample when compared with the results of earlier studies (1969:378).

Harold Christensen and his associates have made extensive comparisons of sexual attitudes and behaviors between Danish students and two samples of college students in the United States, one from the Midwest and another from the Mormon culture of the Intermountain region. Samples from these three areas were drawn in both 1958 and 1968. Christensen has consistently found the Danish students to be most liberal both attitudinally and behaviorally (see Christensen and Gregg 1970), with the Mormon respondents most conservative on both kinds of measures. Christensen also documents a trend over the 10-year period in the direction of greater permissiveness in all three culture areas. Attitudinally, acceptance of nonvirginity in a spouse increased for both sexes in all three samples, as did approval of premarital coitus under conditions of mutual love and responsibility (Christensen and Gregg 1970:619–620). To check on the possibility that the "changes" observed might be artifacts of employing different samples in 1968 than 1958, Christensen and Gregg constructed a subsample from their 1968 Midwestern data in which respondents were matched with the 1958 Midwestern subjects on sex, year in school, church attendance, and courtship involvement. Analyses of this matched sample yielded results consistent with the trends observed for the total sample. The differences observed over the 10-year period are thus probably due to change rather than sampling effects.

On the behavioral level, Christensen and Gregg found that the percentage of respondents with premarital coital experience increased, in general, for all three culture areas, but their relative ranking remained constant: the Danes were most permissive, the Mormons most conservative, with the Midwesterners intermediate but a bit closer to the Mormons than to the Danes (Christensen and Gregg 1970:621). They thus show that norms and behaviors with regard to premarital sex vary systematically and in the same fashion across the cultures in this study. However, like Luckey and Nass (1969) they do not offer an explanation of why European college students are more permissive than American students.[15]

Indeed, causal analysis of cross-societal variation in sexual behavior has been exceedingly rare, even though descriptive material abounds. The systemic correlates of sexual permissiveness have rarely been investigated. One thing we do know in this area is that societies in which polygyny is practiced tend to be more restrictive in their premarital sexual norms than nonpolygynous societies (Ford and Beach 1951; Whiting and Child 1953; Whiting 1961). D'Andrade, in reviewing this research, allows that no clear explanation for this relationship is immediately obvious (D'Andrade 1966). To

an extent this association seems contrary to common sense: restricting premarital sexual activity seems somehow incongruous with the practice of permitting males to have multiple wives and, thus, multiple marital sexual partners.
But on another level the association does make sense. Polygyny, as we know
(see Chapter Four), occurs frequently in conjunction with patrilocal residence
and patrilineal descent. The determination of paternity is problematic and
important in these societies, since children belong to their father's kin group.
Therefore, even though the male is permitted a variety of sexual partners, he is
often restricted in terms of the circumstances under which he may engage in
sexual relations. If a woman bears a child out of wedlock, the child's paternity
is uncertain. Since paternity determines kin-group membership, which is crucial
to both the individual and the social structure, uncertainty with regard to
paternity must be minimized. One way of doing this is to restrict legitimate
sexual relations to marriage; if such a restriction is effective, then each child will
have a sociological father. In matrilineal societies paternity is not nearly so
problematic. Children belong to their mother's descent group, and maternity is
biologically obvious. Matrilineal societies are relatively less likely to practice
polygyny than are patrilineal societies, so this may account for at least part of
the association between polygyny and premarital sexual restrictiveness. This
relationship, furthermore, is not terribly strong. There are quite a few polygynous
societies which do allow, or even encourage, premarital sexual relations, especially for males.

Stephens (1963:256-260) has provided some interest-
ing data on the common observation that "primitive tribes" allow greater
premarital sexual freedom than do "civilized societies." This empirical generalization provides fertile ground for ethnocentrism, particularly if the variables
involved are left undefined or relatively ambiguous. Stephens, however, clearly
defines a "civilized community" as ". . . a community which is part of a society
that embraces cities" (1963:256). When civilization is operationalized as the
presence of urban or urban-like concentrations of people, it shows a marked
negative relationship to premarital sexual permissiveness (see Table 2). Although
exact causal relations between these variables are of course difficult to determine, Stephens speculates that the association is due to variation in type of
political organization. He points out that, until relatively recently, most civilized
communities have been incorporated into autocratic agrarian states or kingdoms,
in which political power is concentrated in the hands of a ruling elite. Most
primitive tribes are stateless. Stephens argues (1963:258-259) that an autocratic
state is associated with "autocratic" family customs, including restrictive sexual
norms along with other relatively "conservative" features such as high degrees of
deference between family members. In this conception, the state and the family
tend to be governed according to similar abstract principles: where the state is

Table 2: The Relationship Between "Civilization" and Nonmarital Sexual Permissiveness

Civilization[a]	Nonmarital Intercourse			
	Effectively Restricted	Ineffectively Restricted	Allowed	Total
Present	3	2	2	7
Absent	1	6	24	31
Total	4	8	26	38

[a] *"Civilized" societies are those which include cities.*
Source: Stephens (1963:256). In this tabulation Stephens does not discriminate between premarital and extramarital intercourse; hence, I use the term "nonmarital intercourse." There is, however, no evidence that rules concerning premarital and extramarital intercourse should be differentially distributed according to the "civilization" variable, and Stephens' logic seems to pertain equally well to both.

autocratic, family norms (including sexual norms) also operate to restrict individual autonomy (see Stephens 1963:26-339, for a more complete explication of this logic). And as the state develops beyond the "kingdom" stage, Stephens argues that family norms also change:

> When the kingdom, the autocratic agrarian state, evolves into a democratic state, these family customs seem to gradually liberalize: family relationships become less deferential and more "democratic," and sex restrictions loosen. (Stephens 1963:258)

We should point out here that Stephens' theory is quite consistent with the observation that polygyny is correlated with sexual restrictiveness: both polygyny and autocratic states are more common in patrilineal than in matrilineal societies, since matriliny tends to appear in societies based on subsistence horticulture in which the political state is not highly developed (see Chapter Six and Schneider and Gough 1961).

The explanations of sexual permissiveness which we have developed here do not, however, help us explain why European college students are more permissive sexually than their North American counterparts. None of the societies involved in the cross-societal comparisons we have reviewed (Luckey and Nass 1969; Christensen and Gregg 1970)[16] practice polygyny, and all have relatively democratic polities on the national level. Since there is some obvious geographic clustering in the values of the variables involved, a partial diffusionist explanation (see Chapter Two) is indicated: Denmark and Norway are more similar to one another than to the United States in part because of their proximity and the consequent higher levels of cultural exchange than would occur between two less proximate societies. But this doesn't help us get at the original cause of greater sexual permissiveness among Europeans. To answer this question, we need to know more about the analytic variables which cause variation in sexual permissiveness, and more about how these causal variables may be differentially distributed in European and American societies. The kind of cross-national study which would shed light on this subject has not yet been done.

Male-female differences in sexuality

The study by Luckey and Nass (1969) and several reports by Christensen and his associates not only document differences in premarital sexuality between North Americans and Europeans, but also highlight several regularities across these societies. One important regularity noted by virtually all researchers in this area is that women tend to hold more conservative attitudes, and to engage in premarital sexual behavior less often, than do men (see, for example, Christensen 1962, 1966; Christensen and Carpenter 1962a, 1962b). This sex difference has repeatedly been documented in North American studies (Reiss 1967; Clayton 1972; Teevan 1972; Vener *et al.* 1972), and cross-cultural investigators have often commented on the fact that female sexuality is more likely to be restricted, normatively and behaviorally, than is male sexuality (Murdock 1949:265; Ford and Beach 1951; Stephens 1963:246-249; D'Andrade 1966:186-187).

Numerous explanations have been offered for the greater sexual conservatism of females. Murdock (1949:265) is of the opinion that sexual restrictions on females are more prevalent than those on males because females bear the children, and because illegitimate birth is negatively valued in virtually all societies. By restricting female premarital sexuality, the probability of illegitimacy is reduced. This is consistent with Reiss' argument that the primary and universal function of marriage is the legitimation of parenthood (Reiss 1971:187-196). Stephens (1963:246), however, contends that according to his reading of the ethnographic literature precautions against illegitimate birth are rarely mentioned as the "reason" for restrictions on female sexuality. Instead, he notes that most societies place high value on female virginity at marriage; virginity is of course a different thing than avoiding the birth of an illegitimate child.

I think Murdock probably has the more useful point of view on this issue, although his explanation doesn't account for the entirety of the difference. There are at least three important problems with Stephens' opinion that female sexuality is restricted because of the premium placed on virgin brides. First, why is female virginity more highly valued than male virginity?[17] It could well be because of the negative implications of illegitimacy. Second, the reasons given for a particular norm or behavior do not necessarily coincide with its causes. Stephens does not say whether the reason in question (the value of female virginity) was most frequently proffered by ethnographers or by their subjects. This, of course, is an important point: were people explaining or rationalizing their own behavior, or were motives imputed to actors by observers? But in either case, reasons or motives for behaviors do not constitute scientific explanations of those behaviors. Third, Stephens (1963:246-247) points out that the justification given for restricting female sexuality was often in considerable disaccord with actual behavior: many cultures which ostensibly valued female virginity at marriage nonetheless permitted or encouraged considerable premarital sexuality on the part of women, although generally less than for men.

Murdock's explanation of the widespread existence of the sexual "double standard" (the practice of allowing greater latitude in sexual behavior to males than to females) is undoubtedly too facile and simplistic to explain the entirety of male-female differences in sexuality. It does, however, tie in rather well with certain theoretical explanations of differences between male and female sex roles, and also helps to make sense of some current changes in premarital sexual behavior. Kingsley Davis (1966) has argued that different kinds of sexual behaviors will be normatively proscribed in direct proportion to the extent to which these behaviors are perceived to interfere with the continuity of the marital and familial institutions. Thus homosexuality usually encounters more normative disapproval than premarital sex because it does not presage marriage or child-bearing, whereas premarital sex is often just that: premarital.[18] By extension, it could be argued that premarital sexual activity by females is a more direct threat to the "integrity" of marriage and family than is such activity by males, because it is the female who runs the risk of pregnancy out of wedlock. Thus the female is more likely to be condemned for engaging in premarital sex. Reiss (1971:40-43, 174-177) extends this argument by noting that, by virtue of traditional sex-role differences and divisions of labor between the sexes, the female sex role is more directly tied to the family than the male sex role. The woman's primary functions, in most societies, have been child-bearing, child-rearing, domestic maintenance, and the care of the family. Men, on the other hand, have been more involved in extrafamily economic and productive roles, at least in leadership capacities. Female sexuality prior to or outside of marriage is thus a more direct threat to the family than male non-marital sexuality, because she is more involved than he in the maintenance and continuity of family affairs. As we argued in Chapter Three, this probably stems in part from the female's biological abilities to bear and nurse children; her more central role in other, related family activities may be attributable to a "generalizing" of these capacities (D'Andrade 1966:178). Further credence is lent to this thesis by the findings of Luckey and Nass (1969) and others, to the effect that the double standard regarding sexual behavior is relatively uncommon among people who devalue sex-role differentiation in other arenas of behavior, such as occupation, education, and political leadership.

If, as Murdock contends, the widespread existence of the double standard may be attributed to the negative valuation of illegitimacy, certain consequences should follow which are empirically testable. In particular, if restrictions on female sexuality have their roots in precautions against illegitimate births, then if sex and conception are dissociated, we should observe a greater relaxation of prohibitions against female sexual behavior than of those on male sexuality, and differences in sexual behavior between the sexes should be reduced. This hypothesis is subject to partial test in modern societies where the technology of contraception has been most thoroughly developed, and where contraceptive information and materials have recently been disseminated to large segments of populations. The resulting ability to dissociate conception from sex means that premarital pregnancy can be prevented without prohibiting female participation in premarital sexual activity. Thus we should observe more rapid increases in premarital sexual behavior by females than by males, such that differences between the sexes on participation in premarital intercourse should be less in recent years than they were, say, a generation or so ago.

This hypothesis, it turns out, conforms quite well to the data. Over the past decade or so, there is considerable evidence that the gap between American males and females in terms of premarital coital experience has been drastically reduced, and perhaps virtually eliminated (see Bell 1966; Bell and Chaskes 1970; Smigel and Seiden 1968; Robinson et al. 1972; Vener et al. 1972; Vener and Stewart 1974; among many others). Among the most convincing studies is the cross-societal investigation by Christensen and Gregg (1970). For their two United States samples of college students (Intermountain and Midwestern) they found virtually no change between 1958 and 1968 in the proportion of males who had experienced premarital intercourse, but a significant increase in the percentange of experienced females. The most dramatic increases for both sexes occurred among the Danes, who had the highest rate of premarital coital experience in 1958 (64 percent of the males and 60 percent of the females). In the 1968 data, 95 percent of the Danish males had experienced premarital coitus; the figure for females was *97 percent* (Christensen and Gregg 1970:621–622). These authors point out that the more permissive the norms regarding premarital sex, the less the differences between the sexual behavior of males and females (see also Christensen 1962, 1966; Christensen and Carpenter 1962a).

Thus the "sexual revolution," in the United States and elsewhere, has had much more profound implications for the sexual behavior of females than that of males. This is consistent with Murdock's thesis on the cause of the double standard, although this consistency by no means constitutes "proof." A further qualification, however, is very much in order. It would be a drastic error, in addition to a massive oversimplification, to attribute the totality of the variation in female premarital sexual behavior in industrialized societies to

the differential availability of "The Pill." Evidence from early studies of premarital sexuality in the United States (Terman 1938; Kinsey *et al.* 1948; Burgess
and Wallin 1953) uniformly indicates that rates of premarital intercourse for
females increased suddenly and dramatically shortly after the beginning of the
twentieth century. This increase for females was *not* accompanied by a corresponding increase for males. From this point to the mid-sixties, rates for both
sexes seem to have remained relatively constant, although attitudes about
premarital sexuality continued to liberalize. The increased rates of premarital
intercourse for American women in the past several years, again without a
corresponding increase for men, is the second such change in this century (see
Kaats and Davis 1970).

      Increased availability of contraceptives may have had
a great deal to do with the recent jump in female sexuality. However, it is
doubtful that the increase in the first couple of decades of this century can be
attributed to the same cause.[19] Furthermore, it does not seem tenable to argue
that increases in the permissiveness of norms and values regarding premarital
sex, which have been occurring throughout the century, are due to contraceptive
advances. The latter factor is more usefully viewed as a *precipitant* of increased
premarital sexuality among women than as an ultimate or final explanation.
Contraceptives have, in other words, allowed many people to engage in behaviors
in which until fairly recently they would not have wished to participate. My
speculation is that the fundamental cause of these changes lies in the changing
set of positions occupied and roles played by women in industrial societies.
Their participation in extrafamily social structures, particularly the economic
and occupational, has increased dramatically in this century. They are gaining
access to, being recruited for, and achieving success in many occupational and
other positions which have traditionally been filled almost exclusively by males.
Sex differences are gradually being minimized in almost all areas of human
behavior, and differences in sexual behavior are similarly showing reductions.

      The changes in female roles are also related to the
changing nature and functions of the family system in industrial societies. Marriage, as we have noted repeatedly throughout this book, is now primarily an
affectional, emotionally supportive relationship rather than one of economic
interdependence at the subsistence level. Marriages are contracted on the basis
of emotional and romantic attraction, and are increasingly dissolved when this
attraction dissipates. Spouses are more nearly able to play companionate and
partner roles in marriage (Burgess *et al.* 1963; Leslie 1973); the instrumental
significance of the family has decreased, but its emotional significance has
increased.

      Since marriage is now based primarily on affection, and
survival is or can be insured by participation in nonfamily systems, sex is increasingly justified by affection rather than marriage. This is well documented

by Reiss' (1967) study of premarital sexual standards: the traditional beliefs in either sexual abstinence before marriage or the double standard are being generally superseded by adherence to the standard Reiss calls "permissiveness with affection," which almost necessarily implies a similar set of criteria for evaluating and judging the sexual behavior of males and females. According to this standard, mutual affectional relationships justify premarital sexual relationships. Since affection is reciprocal, the rights of men and women to engage in sexual relations are almost necessarily equal under this set of values.

Another way of looking at this is that sex is now justified by mutual or dyadic *commitment*, particularly in the sense of an intention to continue in a relatively permanent relationship. Commitment to marry has legitimized sexual relations for a long time; in preindustrial Europe and America, when engagements were broken only in very rare circumstances, engaged couples were commonly expected to have intercourse. Thus the normative approval given to premarital coitus increases with the level of commitment or courtship involvement of the couple (Reiss 1967), and this appears to be true cross-societally as well (Christensen 1962, 1966; Christensen and Carpenter 1962a; Luckey and Nass 1969). Marriage, of course, is one extremely important form of commitment, but it is less often assumed to be completely permanent (see Farber 1964:103-133, for his concept of "permanent availability"). Other forms of commitment are increasingly recognized as justifiable grounds for engaging in sexual relations, for both sexes.

These changes are made possible by the change in the basis of marital relations from instrumental interdependence based on a sexual division of labor to mutual affectional interdependence. This has accompanied the "liberation" of women from virtually complete involvement in family roles and allowed them to join men in the pursuit of educational, occupational, and even political achievement. In combination with the gradual removal of the risk of premarital pregnancy by the "contraceptive revolution," this has resulted in important changes in the sexual aspects of female sex-role performance.

Dyadic commitment and sexual behavior

Reiss' work on the increasing popularity of the "permissiveness with affection" standard for premarital sexual behavior directly implies that, although the proportion of unmarried people (especially women) participating in sexual relations is on the rise, the behavior often labeled "promiscuity" should be declining. That is, premarital sex is increasingly an approved or accepted behavior, but only under conditions of mutual love. Reiss' (1971: 137-138) analysis of some of Kinsey's data shows that, while female participation in premarital coitus definitely increased in the early part of the twentieth century, most of the overall increase was accounted for by greater proportions of women who had premarital intercourse with the man they eventually married. Other data show that the percentage of American women who had premarital intercourse only with men they did *not* marry actually declined during this period (Terman 1938:321; Reiss 1971:136-137). Thus the "sexual revolution" appears to have involved a change from a situation where a large number of men had intercourse with a small and select number of women (who must have been rather busy) *outside of the courtship system*, to a situation where sexual relations became a more usual and expected prelude to marriage, usually involving couples who eventually married or at least expected to do so.

This logic implies that, as standards for sexual behavior liberalize, we should observe a progressively greater proportion of premarital coitus occurring within the context of relationships that are clearly preliminary to marriage. Increases should therefore be observed in variables such as the percentage of sexually experienced unmarried people who have intercourse with only one partner, and whose first sexual experience is with a partner with whom they are "going steady" or engaged. Because they permit comparisons across cultures as well as across time, the data analyzed by Christensen and Gregg (1970) are highly appropriate for testing these hypotheses.

They found (1970:624-625), however, a trend toward "permissiveness with commitment" only for their Midwestern respondents. For the Mormons and the Danes, 1968 respondents were *less* likely than those in 1958 to have confined their experience to one partner, or to have their first sexual experience with a steady or fiancé(e). Certain other patterns in these data indicate that Reiss' hypothesis may be appropriate only for certain values of the attitudinal permissiveness variable. For example, in 1968 normative approval of premarital sex was greater in the Midwest than in the Intermountain (Mormon) sample, but Midwesterners were also more likely to limit their (more frequent) sexual experiences to one partner. This supports the hypothesis. The Danes, on the other hand, held the most permissive values, but were *least* likely of any cultural group to have had only one sexual partner. This contradicts the hypothesis, and is also in partial contrast to earlier data (Reiss 1967:87-88; Christensen 1962, 1966; Christensen and Carpenter 1962a), which showed that normative approval of premarital coitus increases with level of courtship involvement, particularly for females.

This suggests that increased sexual permissiveness may be associated with commitment to permanency up to a point. But as sex becomes an increasingly accepted part of premarital commitment, the definition of what constitutes sufficient commitment may begin to liberalize. That is, the existence of *affection*, whether or not this affection is manifest by any kind of formal or informal commitment, may come to be the defining criterion of the acceptability of sexual relations. Whether or not this will happen in the American courtship system on any large scale remains to be seen, but data from Europe, where norms are more liberal, clearly support this hypothesis. In addition to Christensen's Danish data, Luckey and Nass (1969) found that their English respondents were much more likely than those from countries with more conservative norms to indicate that being "casually attracted" was sufficient grounds for engaging in intercourse. They also found that, for European respondents, "Even having several sexual partners before marriage was not judged particularly detrimental to the marriage" (1969:372). Analysis of cross-societal data, then, shows that the relationship between permissiveness in attitudes and behavior, on the one hand, and dyadic commitment, on the other, may be limited to the lower ranges of the permissiveness variables. This is not evident from American data alone.

Throughout this discussion, the importance of values in the determination of sexual behavior has been emphasized, but not analyzed in detail. The implications of values for behavior are neither as clear-cut nor as obvious as one might initially expect, however, Several scholars, most notably Christensen and Rodman, have paid considerable attention to these implications via comparative research, and their work now merits attention.

Values and behavior

Premarital sexual behavior tends to a large extent to be congruent with values and standards regarding premarital sex on the individual level (Reiss 1967:117, 120-124; Christensen and Gregg 1970:624). But this congruence is far from perfect. We have already pointed to Stephens' observation (1963:246-247) that many cultures place a premium on virgin brides but still allow great latitude in premarital sexual behavior for females as well as males. And Christensen (1969; Christensen and Carpenter 1962b; Christensen and Gregg 1970) has done a great deal of research on attitude-behavior discrepancies with regard to premarital sexuality, much of which is cross-national in nature. His 1968 data indicated that there was considerably less variation in behavior than in attitude. Where standards were conservative (the Mormon or Intermountain culture), many more students had engaged in premarital coitus than approved of it. Where standards were permissive (Denmark), on the other hand, attitudes were more permissive than behaviors. By 1968, however, cross-societal differences had been minimized by increasingly permissive attitudes; of his three samples, only Mormon females were more likely to experience intercourse than to approve of it (Christensen and Gregg 1970:622).[20] And attitudes were better predictors of behavior in 1968 than 1958 (1970:624).

Why is the relationship between attitudes and behavior important? Christensen has shown that many consequences of premarital sex which are generally evaluated negatively depend more upon the attitude-behavior relationship than upon the behavior itself (see particularly Christensen and Carpenter 1962b). In his own words, Christensen

> has demonstrated from cross-cultural data for 1958 that—even more than the act itself—it is the discrepancy between what one values and what he then does that determines guilt, divorce, and related negative effects. (Christensen and Gregg 1970:623)

In an article summarizing the findings of analyses of the 1958 cross-societal data, Christensen (1966) reports that under conditions of restrictive or conservative values regarding premarital sex (that is, in the Inter-mountain sample), premarital intercourse was much more likely to be accompanied by feelings of coercion and guilt (Christensen and Carpenter 1962b), and premarital pregnancy was much more likely to eventuate in forced marriage (Christensen 1960, 1963a) than in Denmark with its more permissive norms. Furthermore, the relationship between premarital pregnancy and divorce was markedly stronger in the Mormon sample than in the Danish (Christensen 1960, 1963a, 1963b). In each case the Midwestern sample, with moderately conservative sexual norms, was intermediate between the Mormons and the Danes.

Christensen (1969) has summarized these findings in two propositions which form part of his "theory of relative consequences" of premarital coitus. These propositions represent the relationship among premarital sexual attitudes and behaviors and the consequences of the behaviors for the individuals who engage in them. These propositions are, first:

> Deviations from actual sex norms, as these are prescribed by existing societies and internalized within their constituent members, increase with the restrictiveness in the culture. (Christensen 1969:218)

In other words, the more restrictive the norms, the more likely are individuals to deviate from them in behavioral terms. Second:

> Negative consequences deriving from premarital coitus are positively related to these behavioral deviations from norms, which means that they increase with restrictiveness in the culture. (Christensen 1969: 218)

So even though Danish students are much more likely to experience premarital coitus than are American students, the Danes are less likely to feel guilt or remorse, less likely to be coerced into an unsatisfying or undesired marriage if premarital pregnancy does result, and if premarital pregnancy is a factor in the marriage it is relatively less likely to result in divorce.

In his 1968 survey, Christensen found that the "value-behavior discrepancy" had decreased, as compared to 1958, in all three cultures. That is, a smaller proportion of those who actually engaged in premarital coitus had violated their personal standards by doing so. This is attributable to a more rapid liberalization on the attitudinal than the behavioral level. Significantly, the percentages of students reporting that their first coital experiences were occasioned by coercion and/or followed by feelings of remorse also declined in all three cultures. The declines in these "negative consequences" of coitus were greatest among the Mormons, who had had the most restrictive standards. But the ranking of cultures on these consequences remained the same: the greater the restrictiveness of normative standards, the more likely that premarital coitus would be accompanied by negative consequences (Christensen and Gregg 1970: 626). Christensen's comparative data, by maximizing the variation in both attitudinal and behavioral variables beyond the extent possible in intrasocietal research, make these relationships more evident and clearly facilitate their explanation (see Chapter One).

However, the fact that Christensen's data come entirely from college students is a serious limitation on the generalizability of this theory. One wonders, of course, whether his hypotheses would receive equal support among nonstudents, or among different age categories. The use of college-student samples, while facilitating comparisons across cultures, does restrict the variance on certain variables that might be of some importance to the "theory of relative consequences." In particular, Christensen's samples are undoubtedly quite homogeneous according to most social class indices, with a clear bias toward middle-class respondents. Recent comparative work on the relationship of values to behaviors in the lower classes indicates that Christensen's theory may be less appropriate for this segment of societies than for college-student populations.

Christensen's theory of relative consequences takes, as its point of departure, the extent of congruence between values and behavior. The greater the extent to which behavioral permissiveness in sexual matters exceeds the normative standards for such behavior, the greater the likelihood that the behavior will culminate in negatively valued consequences. This assumes that both behaviors and values are, first, objectively quantifiable and thus comparable, and second, comparable along a single dimension. These assumptions, it appears, may be less justifiable in lower-class subcultures.

There has been considerable controversy in the social science literature over the proper classification and explanation of remarkably high rates of illegitimacy which have been observed in many Caribbean societies. Rodman (1971:177), for example, reports that 41.1 percent of all births in 1967 in Trinidad and Tobago were illegitimate: that is, the fruits of premarital or nonmarital intercourse. There is, furthermore, a strong inverse relationship between illegitimacy rates and social class; we would expect rates in the lower classes to be much higher than national averages. Cutright (1971a:34) points out that several factors other than premarital sexual permissiveness influence illegitimacy rates. These include, in general terms, the degree to which the members of various groups are able and motivated to control conception and gestation (the availability of birth control and abortion), and health-related factors which influence the abilities to conceive and bear children. However, high rates of illegitimacy clearly imply high rates of premarital sexual intercourse, even though other factors must be considered in a complete explanation.

The evidence shows, then, that lower-class residents of Caribbean societies have high rates of premarital sexual intercourse. The question of relevance to the theory of relative consequences is whether or not this behavior is in accord with the values held by these people; the consequences of the behavior theoretically depend upon the extent of this accord. Rodman (1961) has shown that, for a lower-class Trinidad village which is probably quite representative of lower-class Caribbean culture, most "premarital" intercourse occurs in one of two kinds of socially recognized heterosexual relationships. These relationships are termed "friending" and "living":

> The "friending" relationship is one in which a man visits a woman at intervals for sexual intercourse, and in which he has certain limited obligations to the woman and to any children of his that she may bear. . . . The "living" relationship is one in which the man and woman live together under one roof, but in which they are not legally married. (Rodman 1965a:225)

The question, then, comes down to the extent to which lower-class residents of Trinidad regard these quasi-marital relationships as deviant: to what degree are "living" and "friending" conforming rather than deviant behaviors? Several students of the phenomenon have argued that these relationships are contrary to operative social norms (see especially Goode 1960; Blake 1961). If this is true, then Christensen's theory would lead us to expect frequent feelings of guilt and remorse, a strong impact of premarital pregnancy on the probability of divorce, and other "negative consequences" of this non-normative behavioral permissiveness.

However, Rodman has argued convincingly that this conclusion is based on an overly simplistic view of the nature and role of values in determining behavior. He has introduced a concept called the "lower-class value stretch" which, he believes, enables a more accurate analysis of lower-class marital behavior (see Rodman 1963, 1966, 1968, 1971:190-200). In brief summary, Rodman contends that most lower-class people do in fact accept the majority of middle-class values, including those which place negative value on premarital ("promiscuous") sex and premarital pregnancy. However, the realities of their economic situation, highlighted by his Trinidad data, make behavioral adherence to these values difficult or impossible. The Trinidad village which Rodman studied was composed of lower-class people whose day-to-day ability to subsist was always tenuous. Men were ostensibly expected to provide for their families by selling their labor, but wages were very low and rates of unemployment exceedingly high. Job security was practically nonexistent. Men could hardly count on having jobs from one day to the next. One "solution" to this problem of economic uncertainty was, in Rodman's terms, "marital fluidity" (1965a:226-227). When a man marries, he assumes obligations for the support of his wife and any subsequent children which are difficult to repudiate, legally if not socially. With high uncertainty about this economic future, however, it is unwise for a man to assume such obligations since he may not be able to fulfill them. Men, therefore, are hesitant to enter legal marriages, and would prefer less formal ties such as those which characterize "friending" and "living" arrangements, at least in the absence of certain and secure ability to fulfill the responsibilities of legal marriage. But this is not simply an example of male irresponsibility; women too are better able to cope with the vagaries of subsistence in the quasi-marital relationships than in legal marriages. Since they and their children are heavily dependent on the labor of a man to provide a livelihood, and since the stable employment of any given man is highly problematic, it is unwise for the woman to foreclose her options by making herself permanently dependent on a single man for support. The quasi-marital unions are easily made and easily broken. A man can leave one such relationship when he finds himself out of work (men must often move in pursuit of employment), and a woman can dissolve a relationship with an unemployed man and form another with one who has a job with relative ease, thus helping to insure more continuous support for herself and her children.

Rodman sees this marital fluidity or flexibility as crucial to the survival abilities of his subjects. His data show that these people ultimately prefer legal marriage—it is accorded high cultural value. But "living" and "friending" are not defined as objectively wrong, only as less preferable but often necessary alternatives to legal and permanently binding marriage (see Rodman 1971:120-121). And while children born to "living" or "friending" couples are *officially* illegitimate, since their parents are not legally married, they are not regarded as such by the community. Thus the "premarital" sexual relations which give rise to the high official illegitimacy rate are not contrary to community values; these values, instead, have "stretched" to accommodate the objective realities of economic existence in the lower classes.[21] If Rodman is correct, Christensen's theory of relative consequences should not be directly applicable to this lower-class population.

Rodman furthermore argues that the "lower-class value stretch" is generalizable beyond the confines of Trinidad and the Caribbean area, to the lower classes of virtually all societies.[22] The economic circumstances faced by lower-class people, particularly in a wage-labor economy, give "marital fluidity" the same adaptive advantages in the United States:

This fluidity of the marital bond is, I believe, characteristic of lower-class families generally. Within the United States the higher rates of divorce and desertion within the lower class, as well as of "common-law" unions and illegitimacy, are indicative of such fluidity. If, as I am suggesting, these lower-class patterns are responses to the deprivations of lower-class life, and if they are functional for lower-class individuals, then we can see the sense in which many of the lower-class family patterns that are often regarded as problems are actually solutions to other, more pressing, problems. (Rodman 1965a:227)

Middle-class people have less trouble in behaviorally conforming to their values in sexual and marital terms; thus Rodman conceives of the "value stretch" as a distinctively lower-class phenomenon. To the extent that he has correctly analyzed the premarital (or quasi-marital) sexual behavior of the lower classes, it would appear that Christensen's theory of relative consequences would be inappropriate for these social strata, or would at least require substantial modification. Another important implication of Rodman's analysis is that the definition of what does and what does not constitute marriage is culturally variable (see also Stephens 1963:5-7, 10-12; Reiss 1971:187-196), and distinctions between premarital and marital behaviors, in sexual matters as well as others, need to be informed by this definitional variability in order to achieve maximal theoretic utility. Rodman's Trinidad subjects obviously considered "living" and "friending" to be forms of marriage, albeit not identical to our more usual form. The government employees responsible for census records obviously did not share this definition. But for most sociological purposes these relationships may clearly be considered marital.

Conclusions

We have discussed several ways in which comparative research and theory have helped to illuminate patterns of mate selection and premarital sexuality. Certainly one major function of this material is that it may help to mitigate ethnocentrism. Premarital interaction patterns vary considerably across societies, and these variations are comprehensible according to logical explanatory principles of human behavior. This discovery helps put our own system in perspective.

Once again, it is clear that variation in systems of mate selection is explicable largely in terms of variation in economic and ecological factors. Whether a social system is characterized by autonomous courtship or arranged marriage depends upon the structure of family and kinship systems; these, as we found in Chapters Five and Six, are heavily dependent on mode of subsistence. In the next chapter, we shall discover that many aspects of marital interaction processes are also contingent, directly or indirectly, upon economic variables.

Notes

1. We should point out here that we are discusssing first marriages only. In societies where polygyny is practiced, a man (with, often, his first wife) has the right to choose second and subsequent wives for himself even if first marriages are arranged in one of the above ways. However, his negotiations will often be with the parents of the potential wives.

2. For recent reviews of the role of homogamy in American mate selection, see Kephart (1972:293-316), Eshleman (1974:279-327), and Udry (1974: 154-167).

3. The reader will recall (see Chapter Five) that Goode lists autonomous mate selection as a defining criterion of a conjugal family system, which, according to his theory, emerges when industrialization produces differentiated social structures which remove certain major functions from the family.

4. For a vivid illustration, see Mace and Mace (1960:144-145).

5. The societies in this sample appear to be quite representative of all those contained in the Ethnographic Atlas, at least on this variable. Aronoff and Crano (1975) report an average female contribution to subsistence of about 44 percent for the entire Ethnographic Atlas using a similar method of computation.

6. Note the inconsistency between this hypothesis and the findings of Coppinger and Rosenblatt (1968), reported above.

7. This hypothesis is consistent with the work of Bott (1957) on the relationship between conjugal roles and social networks, to be reviewed in Chapter Eight.

8. There is a great deal of research on the tensions between conjugal and generational relationships in extended families. See Levy (1949) on China and LeVine (1965) on Africa, among many others.

9. We must, of course, recognize that Stephens and Rosenblatt investigated different variables. Stephens studied variation in the locus of control over mate selection, Rosenblatt the extent to which romantic criteria are employed in the process of choice. Although these two variables are undoubtedly correlated, they are not definitionally identical.

10 This, of course, is quite consistent with Goode's (1959) argument that

parents channel mate choice by delimiting the alternatives even where mate selection is formally "free."

11. We should point out that it has not been until relatively recently in Western cultural history that romantic love and marriage have been culturally associated. Treatments of the historical development of the concept of romantic love may be found in Hunt (1959), Bernard *et al.* (1959), Reiss (1960, 1971), and Udry (1974).

12. As Greenfield observes, the male's advantage over the female in the labor market is progressively decreasing. But the general point behind his argument still holds, and probably always will: no industrial society can provide productive roles in the labor force for all of its members. Any such society must employ selective or discriminitive criteria in allowing access to the labor force; whether age and sex are the relevant criteria is immaterial to this basic point.

13. This is not at all intended to imply that the housewife has no economic value. This is obviously false. But she does not independently contribute new resources to the family's pool of funds which can be used for consumption. She rather manages the allocation of these funds and the maintenance of consumer goods which resources provided by some other source (usually the husband-father) have purchased.

14. Some have argued that evidence of declining romantic and sexual interests among married couples (Pineo 1961) constitutes support for the Freud-Waller theory (see, for example, Udry 1974:140–141). But, as Udry recognizes, Pineo studied couples over twenty years of marriage. The decreases in romance and sexuality in this sample were not evident after the first three years of marriage (Burgess and Wallin 1953). If love were due to the frustration of sexual desires, it would hardly have taken twenty years for this frustration to be overcome even if we were to assume that sexual intercourse did not commence until marriage, an assumption clearly contrary to the data for many members of this sample.

15. Christensen does, however, provide a series of very interesting causal analyses in which premarital sexual norms and behaviors are employed as independent or explanatory variables in the explanation of related phenomena. Some of this material will be reviewed below.

16. In the terminology we have adopted here, both of these studies are closer to the cross-societal than the cross-national type with regard to the question of the causes of premarital sexual permissiveness. Both report variation in permissiveness measures by society and by sex, but neither one explicitly examines and compares the intrasocietal correlations of these measures

with possible causal factors other than sex. The crucial distinction is whether comparisons between societies are made on univariate distributions of variables (cross-societal) or bivariate or multivariate patterns of association (cross-national). Christensen's research is cross-national in many respects, as we will discover below, but not on the issue of the determinants of premarital sexual permissiveness.

17. This difference is common to industrial as well as nonindustrial societies. Kaats and Davis (1970:394) found that male American college students were significantly more likely than females to value virginity in a prospective spouse, but much less likely to be concerned about their own virginity at marriage. Christensen and Gregg (1970:619) found a similar difference for their American and Danish samples with the exception of the 1968 Danish data where males and females were equally likely (92 percent) to accept nonvirginity in a mate.

18. This is very much in accord with the observation by Murdock (1949:270–273) and Stephens (1963:250) that permitted premarital sexual relations often follow the lines of preferential marriage customs. For example, where cross-cousin marriage is preferred, premarital sex between a man and his father's sister's daughter (his cross cousin) may be permitted or even encouraged. In societies that practice the levirate, a male is very often allowed sexual privileges with his brother's wife.

19. There was, however, a marked advance in contraceptive technology and availability in the latter part of the nineteenth century, which undoubtedly had an important effect here. See Reiss (1972:170–171).

20. One may wonder, as do Christensen and Gregg, why some people who approve of premarital intercourse do not engage in it. They point out that approval of premarital intercourse is generally conditional upon some level of affection or commitment such as engagement, and the respondent may not himself or herself satisfy the condition. This is clearly quite plausible. It is also possible that many of these "permissive" respondents have not had sexual intercourse because they have not been able to find a willing partner.

21. Rodman's work is obviously and explicitly informed by Robert Merton's "anomie theory" of deviant behavior. See Merton (1968:185-248).

22. A great deal of research on lower-class family behavior in the United States is interpretable within this framework. See particularly Cohen and Hodges (1963), Rainwater (1960, 1966b), and Rainwater et al. (1959). For evidence that the association between socioeconomic status and divorce in the United States may be decreasing, see Glick (1975).

chapter eight
The marital relationship

Sex roles in marriage

Instrumental and expressive roles

The issue of socially defined behavioral differences between men and women has been of almost continuous concern to us since our discussion of the origins of the family in Chapter Three. As D'Andrade (1966) and others have argued, the direct implications of primary physiological sex differences for behavior are probably rather small. However, human beings have a propensity to generalize stimuli, to classify and organize cognitions in consistent ways. Thus, as we have seen, sex differences *as socially defined and prescribed* are at the root of much variation in family structure, kinship structure, and premarital sexual behavior. There are remarkable cross-cultural consistencies in behavioral sex differences, virtually none of which are *directly* attributable to physiological sex differences. Many of them, though, may be attributable to generalizations from these primary differences.

As we saw in Chapter Two, comparative research may be employed in the search for universal, or at least highly general, relationships between variables. Many such inquiries have involved attempts to find culturally invariant behavioral differences between the sexes. One such attempt, which has had a very considerable impact on family sociology, was a theory of sex-role differentiation emerging from the work of scholars such as Parsons, Bales, Slater, and Zelditch at Harvard in the early 1960s. Their research focused around a distinction between "instrumental" and "expressive" role behavior; these concepts require some brief explication before we can apply them directly to sex differences and family relations.

Bales and Slater (1955) observed the behavior of 14 separate groups of Harvard male undergraduates in a laboratory setting. The groups ranged in size from three to six persons. Each group was assigned an identical task of proposing a solution, as a group, to an administrative problem. The experimenters, of course, were interested in the nature of group interaction rather than in the proposed solutions. Each group met four times and was presented with a similar task on each occasion. At the end of each session, each subject was asked several questions about his reaction to the group performance and to other members of the group. These questions included (but were not limited to) the following:

> Who contributed the best ideas for solving the problem? Please rank the members in order. Include yourself.

> How well did you personally like each of the other members? Rate each member on a scale from 0 to 7, where zero means "I feel perfectly neutral toward him," and 7 means "I like him very much." (Bales and Slater 1955:262)

Among a great variety of findings, Bales and Slater discovered that the same person was rarely rated as both the "best-idea man" and the "best-liked man." Instead, there was a tendency toward role specialization. They summarize their results by noting that

> . . . the specialization seems to appear most clearly between one person who achieves prominence in relation to the task demands made upon the group, and another person upon whom more liking is bestowed who presumably meets more social and emotional needs. (Bales and Slater 1955:302)

They further suggest (1955:299–306) that, even though their experimental groups were structured quite differently than are families, the same kind of role differentiation should occur within family systems. In particular, they argue that the husband-father often behaves as a task leader or "idea man," and the wife-mother plays the complementary role of socioemotional leader.

This logic was extended by Morris Zelditch (1955) and tested via cross-cultural data. Zelditch (1955:309–312) distinguishes between task or "instrumental" leader and "sociometric star," or "expressive" leader. He argues that, because certain common factors impinge upon all social groups, any group will exhibit a tendency toward role differentiation along these lines. But families are distinct from other social groups by virtue of their composition. They include associations between two or more opposite-sex adults (the marrige) and associations between these adults and dependent children. The female adult, by virtue of her distinctive physiology, bears the children and, under most ecological conditions, is the only family member who is capable of feeding infants. This has important implications for social relations with the family:

> In other societies necessarily—and in our own for structural reasons which have *not* disappeared with the advent of the bottle—the initial core relation of a family with children is the mother-child attachment. And it follows from the principles of learning that the gradient of generalization should establish "mother" as the focus of gratification in a diffuse sense, as the source of "security" and "comfort." She is the focus of warmth and stability. Thus, because of her special initial relation to the child, "mother" is the more likely expressive focus of the system as a whole. (Zelditch 1955:313-314)

The husband-father, meanwhile, is not so occupied by the rearing of children. According to Zelditch, his role involves ". . . first, a manipulation of the physical environment, and consequently a good deal of physical mobility" (1955:314). The father, then, provides for the family; he is responsible for instrumental tasks. Furthermore, since he is relatively unencumbered with strong emotional attachments to the children (at least as compared to his wife), the father may also play the role of objective authority figure or disciplinarian. This logic leads to two related hypotheses. First, roles in nuclear families will be differentiated along the instrumental-expressive axis. Second,

> If the nuclear family consists in a defined "normal" complement of the male adult, female adult and their immediate children, the male adult will play the role of instrumental leader and the female adult will play the role of expressive leader. (Zelditch 1955:315)

Note that the instrumental and expressive roles, as Zelditch employs them, directly involve leadership. He does not say that women never behave in instrumental ways, or that men do not relate to other family members expressively, but rather that leadership in each capacity resides with the specified sex. His criteria for measurement (1955:317-320) involve specific information to the effect that the role-incumbent whose performance is being analyzed plays a leadership role in the management of family enterprise (instrumental), or is *the* person who is charged with mediating or resolving hostilities in the family (expressive).

Zelditch first tested the hypothesis that nuclear families do differentiate family roles along the instrumental/expressive axis. Of the 56 ethnographic cases which formed his sample, he found that 46 did evince such intrafamily role specialization (1955:320). Most of the counter-instances were cases in which the nuclear family was embedded within a larger kin group (matrilineal in half of those cases). Instrumental and expressive roles were in fact differentiated, but family members performed these roles with respect to members of other nuclear families: for example, a male ego might be, in a matrilineal system, the primary disciplinarian with respect to his sister's children, and his own children would be disciplined by his wife's brother.

The hypothesis that instrumental leadership is the province of the husband-father and expressive leadership that of the wife-mother was also strongly supported by a conservative test: cases in which information was insufficient to indicate positive conformity to the hypothesis were counted as negative. Of 19 matrilineal societies, the wife-mother was classified as the expressive leader in all of them. Of the remaining 37 nonmatrilineal societies, 29 clearly conformed to the hypothesis for both sexes. The remaining 8 were accounted for largely, but not entirely, by either the nuclear family's embedment in the kin group as noted above, or by insufficient data in the ethnography. Only 1 society, the polyandrous Marquesans (Kardiner 1939), appears to constitute a clear reversal of the hypothesized sex roles.

Zelditch's argument, as we have noted, is that these intrafamily differences in role performance are due to the ways in which adult men and women are differentially related to (1) children, and (2) economic activities. These are the same factors which many authors (Washburn and DeVore 1961; Hockett and Ascher 1964; Gough 1971) have speculated to be responsible for the origin of the family and its persistence as a prominent feature of social structure (see Chapter Three). The facts of complementarity between the sexes in the division of labor, and of variation in the nature and extent of this complementarity, have proven to be crucial explanatory variables in relation to a great number of family phenomena. One must, however, guard against the overuse of variables of this kind. It is easy to fall into the trap of attempting to explain virtually everything in terms of "innate" or "natural" differences between the sexes. In fact, it appears that there are very few biologically based sex differences among humans (van den Berghe 1973). Most behavioral differences between males and females, even those which exhibit great consistency across cultures, can more realistically be attributed to human generalization from physiological differences which are in reality rather minimal (D'Andrade 1966). The conclusion of Zelditch's study, therefore, is not that men are "naturally" instrumental creatures and women "inherently" expressive ones, but rather that the specialization of leadership capacities in these two spheres of action according to family position is consistent with the set of economic and family roles which are regularly ascribed to husbands and wives across cultures.

A recent study (Aronoff and Crano 1975) has reported information which, the authors feel, seriously challenges or perhaps disproves Zelditch's hypothesis about role differentiation according to sex. Employing Murdock's Ethnographic Atlas, Aronoff and Crano contend that food production is by definition an instrumental activity. By employing two variables contained in the Atlas which estimate the proportional reliance of each society on five types of subsistence activities, and the proportional contribution of each sex to each type of productive enterprise, they constructed estimates of the proportion of each society's food supply which is contributed by the labor of women. They found that, across all societies in the Atlas, the female contribution to subsistence averaged almost 44 percent (Aronoff and Crano 1975:17).[1] This contribution varies according to culture region, from a low of 32 percent in the Circum-Mediterranean area to a high of nearly 51 percent in the Insular Pacific, but societies in which less than 30 percent of the food supply is attributable to women are quite rare, and the female contribution exceeds that of males in nearly one quarter of all societies in the Atlas (1975:18). Aronoff and Crano infer from these data that the predominance of men in instrumental activities is marginal at best; although no data on expressive role performance was available, the extent of female instrumental activity casts doubt on the utility of the instrumental-expressive distinction, at least in relation to sex roles in the family. They conclude:

> Considering direct subsistence activity as a whole, the principle of task specialization within the family, with women confined to the household arena by assumed biological factors, clearly seems to be incorrect. The second principle of role segregation, with males assuming the role of instrumental specialist in the family, seems equally incorrect. (Aronoff and Crano 1975:18-19)

While the data on differential contribution to food supply by sex which Aronoff and Crano provide are clearly valuable, their rejection of Zelditch's thesis on the basis of these data is much too facile. The central problem here is their failure to recognize that Zelditch was concerned with leadership rather than labor.[2] Zelditch notes explicitly at many points in his study that all family members do perform instrumental roles, and that men are virtually always involved in expressive relationships to some extent. This, however, is not crucial to his thesis. His conceptualization and measurement of instrumental role performance involves the extent to which the husband-father (note: *not* males in general) is "boss-manager of the farm" (1955:318), not the extent to which he is an agricultural operative. His hypothesis simply does not imply that men should predominate in productive labor; it implies, rather, that leadership and authority in instrumental tasks are allocated to adult male members of families. As Aronoff and Crano recognize, the Ethnographic Atlas does not provide data on instrumental leadership or on any aspect of expressive role performance. The proportional-contribution-of-food-supply variable which they use as a surrogate for instrumental leadership is not, however, an indirect indicator of those variables on which they had no data, but is instead a quite different variable altogether, one which is not implicated by the theory which they purport to evaluate. It has been widely recognized since the publication of Murdock's (1937) study of the sexual division of labor by type of activity that the female contribution to instrumental and productive tasks is virtually always extensive. There are many productive tasks which, cross-culturally, are more likely to be performed by women than by men. These include such important food-producing activities as crop-tending and harvesting in horticultural societies and the gathering of fruits, herbs, etc., in societies with hunting-and-gathering technologies (see Murdock 1937; Stephens 1963:282–283). But this means that women produce food, not that they are likely to be instrumental leaders within the family.

While the data reported by Aronoff and Crano do not give sufficient reason to reject Zelditch's hypothesis, other studies have provided grounds for qualifying it heavily. One of the most important of these is a study by Robert Leik (1963) which, while based exclusively on American data, indicates that the hypothesis in question may be much less applicable to intrafamily relations in modern societies than it is at the cross-cultural level. Leik studied the interaction behavior of members of nine families, each of which consisted of a father, a mother, and a college-age daughter, in a laboratory setting. As part of his study, Leik observed and coded the interaction of each member of his sample when acting as a member of a *family-like group* (consisting of a father, a mother, and a daughter who were unrelated to one another), and when participating in their own families. He discovered that fathers were indeed more likely to manifest instrumental behaviors, and mothers and daughters expressive behaviors, when participating in the family-like groups. These differences were much reduced, however, when the subjects interacted with other members of their own families. Most of the change was due to increased participation of mothers in instrumental activities within their own families; fathers increased their expressive behavior only slightly in the same circumstance.

What are the implications of this for Zelditch's theory? They are obviously considerable, but at the same time do not negate its value. A crucial difference between ethnographic research (and subsequent cross-cultural comparisons using ethnographic data) and more structured observational techniques of data collection must be reiterated here. The ethnographer is concerned with describing regularities in behavior; the laboratory experimentalist is concerned with describing and explaining variation. Zelditch may well have found an important cross-cultural regularity. Leik has specified the circumstances under which this regularity will be manifest in the behavior of American family members, and conversely the circumstances under which it will not be manifest. Leik's data indicate that instrumental/expressive role differentiation according to sex may be a cultural stereotype: prescriptions for role behavior which are likely to be implemented in interaction among strangers, who are not known to one another personally. But in interaction with intimate associates such as family members, the stereotypes break down. Here, interaction involves more of the complete personality. Role behaviors within the family do not conform precisely to the normative guidelines for these roles as they are represented in the general culture. However, in interaction with strangers, stereotypical norms are much better predictors of behavior.

Thus Zelditch's hypothesis appears to be of greater utility in the explanation of cross-cultural variation in sex role definitions than in the analysis of role behaviors within family systems, particularly in industrial societies. On the other hand, Leik's data also do not deal directly with the leadership dimension which is crucial to Zelditch's hypothesis. Differentiation of leadership in instrumental and expressive activities may still proceed along sexual lines, although the probabilities are that such differentiation is less in the family systems of industrial than nonindustrial societies.

Sex roles and spousal interdependence

One of the most thought-provoking concepts in family sociology in recent years has been a distinction developed by Elizabeth Bott (1957) between "joint" and "segregated" modes of conjugal role performance. Unlike Zelditch's distinction between instrumental and expressive roles, Bott's conceptualization pertains to the behavior of spouses as couples rather than as individuals. Conjugal role performance is defined as *joint* to the extent that spouses (1) engage in leisure and recreational activities together rather than separately, and (2) perform household and other marital tasks interchangeably. Couples who pursue leisure activities separately and who evince a rigid division of labor are said to have a *segregated* mode of conjugal role organization.[3]

A great many studies, in a variety of cultures, have documented an increasing tendency toward marital norms and behaviors which conform rather closely to the "joint" patterns described by Bott, and away from the "segregated" type of relationship. It appears that this trend is related to changes in two broad categories of variables, economic and familial. Specifically, joint conjugal role organization, at both the normative and the behavioral levels, becomes more common as societies industrialize and as the family system becomes more "nucleated" or conjugal.[4]

Kerckhoff (1972:62-65) argues that the primary causal variable in this process is industrialization, with family structure operating as an intervening variable. As we noted in Chapter Five (see also Goode 1963), industrialization means the separation of family and productivity. The family is no longer the unit of production, and families depend for their livelihood upon the endeavors of some of their members in the occupational system. This results in the increasing prevalence of the nuclear or conjugal family type, and a corresponding decline in the frequency and functional signifiance of the extended family. The conjugal family becomes increasingly independent of relatives in economic, occupational, residential, and even sociable terms. (Kerckhoff argues that, while industrialization *per se* promotes the emergence of independent family systems, a *strong* industrial economy is necessary to insure that most conjugal families will actually be independent.) Furthermore, following Parsons (1943) and Goode (1963), Kerckhoff contends that industrialization brings about a value system which stresses achievement, universalism, and egalitarianism. The independence of married couples means that spouses are more dependent upon one another for the fulfillment of both instrumental and expressive needs than is the case in other types of economic and family systems. The emerging value system causes spouses to reject "traditional," "arbitrary" definitions of sex roles, and to tend toward flexibility in their marital role expectations and behaviors. Emotional intimacy and support, companionship, and communication become more central foci of marital relationships and more important criteria by means of which marriages are evaluated.

Pearlin (1971), in an analysis of the causes of companionship in Italian marriages, comes to a very similar conclusion:

> . . . it seems likely that such factors as the romantic selection of mates, the physical separation of the household from the extended family, the segregation of work and family, the freeing of time from the logistical demands of home and the more equal participation of women in social institutions—educational and political—are among the concomitants of an urban-industrial setting that turn spouses toward each other for support and companionship. (Pearlin 1971:162)

The identification of joint conjugal role organization with industrial development is so strong that many researchers (for example, Theodorson 1965; Podmore and Chaney 1972; Conklin 1973; Fox 1973, 1975) have employed measures of "jointness" in marital roles as indicators of "modernization" in marriage. There is also considerable evidence that certain changes representing modernism, such as trends away from arranged marriage toward autonomous mate selection, are positively correlated with indicators of joint marital role organization (Blood 1967; Fox 1973, 1975; Lobodzinska 1975).

If the increasing prevalence of joint conjugal norms is a consequence of the greater independence of married couples in industrial economic systems on the cross-cultural level, then it should be the case that conjugal independence and joint marital role performance are positively related if individual marriages are taken as the units of analysis. That is, the greater the extent to which a married couple is independent of friends and relatives, the more joint (or less segregated) their conjugal role performance. On the basis of her intensive study of 20 London families, Bott (1957) hypothesized that the degree of segregation in conjugal role organization depends directly upon the "connectedness" of the couple's social network. If each spouse is a member of a "close-knit" network of friends and/or relatives, the members of which are all connected to one another by sociometric ties, then marital roles will tend to be segregated. This situation is likely to occur when the spouses have lived in the same neighborhood for all or most of their lives, including the period prior to marriage. Each spouse will continue to be drawn into the activities of the network, and its other members will exert pressure on the spouse to continue the performance of his or her role as a network member as it was performed prior to the marriage. Furthermore, each spouse will find that many of his or her instrumental and expressive needs are satisfied by the network, as they were before the marriage. Spouses are less dependent upon one another because the close-knit network performs many functions that would otherwise be relegated to the spouse. If, on the other hand, the social networks are "loose-knit" (consisting of disparate associates who are unrelated to one another except by virtue of their common relationship to "ego"), then the married pair will be more dependent upon one another for companionship, emotional support, and help in instrumental task accomplishment. The result will be joint conjugal role organization. The causal variable here, according to Bott, is not simply the extent to which each spouse has available friends and relatives, but the extent to which these associates constitute an integrated, cohesive social network which has an existence independent of the individual, and which can thus exert organized pressure on the individual to continue as a network member in spite of the marriage. In Bott's words,

> If both husband and wife come to marriage with . . . close-knit networks, and if conditions are such that the previous pattern of relationship is continued, then the marriage will be superimposed on these preexisting relationships, and both spouses will continue to be drawn into activities with people outside their own elementary family. (Bott 1957:60)

Bott's thesis has received more or less direct empirical support from studies in both the United States (Nelson 1966; Blood 1969) and

Britain (Turner 1967). However, other investigations (Udry and Hall 1965; Aldous and Straus 1966; Wimberley 1973) have failed to support her hypothesis. These discrepant results seem to be due in large part to differences in sampling, measurement, and conceptualization, particularly regarding the independent variable, network connectedness. It now appears possible that the causal variable is not the extent of network connectedness (whether social networks are close-knit or loose-knit), but rather the extent to which each spouse is integrated into a same-sex peer group (see Harris 1969: 165–175; Wimberley 1973; Lee 1977). All of the studies which have been taken as supportive of Bott's hypothesis are also consistent with this interpretation due to the nature of their measurement procedures, and those studies which have failed to uncover any association between social networks and conjugal roles have measured the independent variable strictly in terms of network connectedness.[5] Thus, the most appropriate hypothesis appears to be that there is a negative relationship between joint conjugal role performance and the integration of each spouse into same-sex peer groups, which include groups composed of relatives.

This version of the hypothesis is consistent with our logic here. The greater the extent to which conjugal units are independent of, or isolated from, supportive social networks such as extended families or same-sex peer groups, the more the spouses are dependent upon one another for the gratification of emotional and instrumental needs, and the greater the tendency toward joint conjugal role organization. Industrialization, with its concomitant nucleation of family structures, promotes this spousal interdependence on the societal level, such that marital role performance in industrial nations is likely to be more joint and less segregated than in nonindustrial societies. And within industrial societies, joint conjugal role performance is directly related to the independence of the conjugal pair from social networks, especially same-sex peer groups.

Summary

We have evidence to the effect that in industrialized societies with conjugal family systems, joint conjugal role organization is relatively more common than in societies with extended family systems. This also helps to explain why Zelditch's (1955) hypothesis of male leadership in instrumental roles and female leadership in expressive roles is less viable in conjugal family systems than in those of preindustrial nations. Although there is considerable variation between individual families in any system, the trend toward conjugal family systems seems to be accompanied by a convergence of marital sex roles.

What are the implications of this role convergence for power and authority relations within the family? It is relatively clear that conjugal family systems tend to be characterized by relatively equalitarian norms regarding the distribution of marital authority. Does this mean that traditional sexual inequality is breaking down with the advent of industrialization? Are cultural and normative systems changing from patriarchal to equalitarian, and do such changes imply actual behavioral changes in male-female power relationships? These issues are pursued in the next section.

Sex roles and conjugal power

Sex differences in power and authority

Since the inception of the discipline, anthropologists have contended that a virtually universal difference between the sexes involves a power imbalance: authority tends to be held by men over women, and deference is owed by women to men (see Hobhouse et al. 1915:173-174). We have commented upon this observation, in various forms, in the reviews of anthropological research and theory by scholars such as Murdock (1949), Stephens (1963), Fox (1967), and many others. In this conception, women are seen as almost inevitably subservient and subordinate to men in just about every field of endeavor. While the greater physical size and strength of the male are occasionally perceived as one source of this inequality, it is more often attributed to woman's roles in reproduction and child-rearing and her supposedly consequent restriction to the domestic domain. Some scholars argue that even technological advances which might free women from full-time responsibility for children will not alter "basic" male-female differences in social positions or roles. For example, Clellan Ford concludes his summary of sex roles and sex differences with the projection:

> It does not seem likely that changes in technology or conscious striving for an equality of the sexes with respect to the roles they play will make any really fundamental changes in the forseeable future. Many theorists are prone to overestimate the relativity of culture and the malleability of human behavior. . . . The differences arising from their reproductive roles alone imposes a basic cleavage between the sexes with respect to the kinds of lives they can live, and there are limits to the modification that can be tolerated if the social group is to survive. (Ford 1970:42)

Other summaries of comparative research on sex differences have reported some clear regularities in behavioral differences between the sexes (for example, D'Andrade 1966; Draper 1975). Most studies indicate that men are more aggressive, egoistic, and peer-oriented, and less responsible, nurturant, and compliant than females. Exceptions to these generalizations have been noted, even on the cultural level;[6] these indicate that most sex differences in behavior may not have direct and complete biological explanations, because people everywhere share pretty much the same set of biological characteristics, But, as Brown (1970) clearly points out, women's roles everywhere must be compatible with the demands of child-bearing and child-rearing. This means, much more often than not, that women are restricted to the domestic sphere of activity, that they are often dependent upon men for support for themselves and their children, and that they are consequently subject to the authority, and perhaps the outright domination, of men.

One study of a conscious and explicit attempt to change this situation is Melford Spiro's (1956) observation of an Israeli kibbutz. The founders of this kibbutz were motivated by an ideology favoring complete equality, and sex differences were perceived as a major source of inequality, particularly as these differences were manifest in "traditional" families. Women, therefore, were to be "emancipated" from their domestic confinement by the institutions of collective living. Most of the tasks which are commonly identified as having to do with household maintenance and child care were transformed to the community level. These tasks, along with those involving economic productivity, were then assigned to men and women equally.

However, the results of this experiment as reported by Spiro (1956:221-230) seem to support Ford's (1970) conclusion that sex roles are not completely malleable. Residents of the kibbutz discovered that women were not generally as efficient as men in many of the productive tasks for which sheer physical strength was a prerequisite. Furthermore, although child-rearing was indeed made a collective responsibility, women needed to take time from productive tasks to bear and nurse children. This resulted in the increasing assignment of women to tasks in or near the nurseries, and their progressive removal from "productive" sectors of the economic system and insertion into "service" positions. Consequently, women found themselves once again performing tasks associated with conventional female roles (cooking, cleaning, child care, etc.), but performing them at the community rather than the family level, as occupational rather than as family roles. Spiro contends that kibbutz women found less satisfaction in the performance of these occupational obligations than they did in their family roles, and commonly wished that they had not been "emancipated" at all.[7]

This example shows that "improvements" in the status of women are not at all insured by a simple ideological commitment to egalitarianism. Neither does the abolition of traditional family structures guarantee that sex differences in role behavior will be obliterated. Nonetheless, many eminent scholars have argued persuasively that the changes in family systems which coincide with industrialization and "modernization" are in fact serving to relieve the woman of her domestic and household duties, are allowing her to assume positions of prestige and responsibility in the occupational and political spheres, and consequently are promoting equality between the sexes in social roles and social power (see, for example, Goode 1963, 1968a, 1971; Bernard 1968, 1972; Rossi 1964). These arguments, in general, are premised on the assumption that differences in power and authority between the sexes depend upon the sexual division of labor, which in turn depends upon the type of economic and technological system prevalent in the society. As women are increasingly allowed access to positions in the productive sector of the economy, they become less and less dependent upon men for subsistence, and their power and authority relative to men increase.

Resource theory

The empirical basis for much current theory comes from a seminal study of marital relations conducted in the Detroit metropolitan area by Blood and Wolfe (1960). On a probability sample of wives from 731 Detroit-area families, they measured decision-making authority by asking the wife which spouse typically made each of eight kinds of decisions which American families must recurrently make, including such things as which job the husband should take, where to go on vacations, and how much of the family budget should be spent on food (Blood and Wolfe 1960:19).

Blood and Wolfe proposed two hypothetical explanations of variation in conjugal power structure (1960:12-15). First, they argued that American society, like most others, has a clear patriarchal tradition. That is, it has been normative throughout our culture's history for the man to be the ultimate decision-making authority within the family. But this appears to be changing. Therefore, categories of the population which are more identified with "tradition" should be more husband-dominated than those more removed from tradition. They hypothesized that husband-dominance should be disproportionately found among ". . . those families which have been less exposed to urban, industrial, and educational influences" (1960:24), including families of farmers, immigrants, the older segment of the population, those with low education, and Catholics. These hypotheses, however, were not supported by their data (1960:24-29).

Blood and Wolfe then turn to what they initially call "pragmatic" theory. In this logic, the relative power of the two spouses is hypothesized to be a function of their "comparative resourcefulness," or the extent to which each spouse contributes valued resources to the family. Resources consist of skills or qualifications possessed by one spouse which enable him or her to contribute to the fulfillment of the other's needs and the gratification of the other's desires. For example, education, occupational prestige, and particularly income contributed by one spouse increase the family's status in the community and also add to the material comforts of life. And membership in community organizations brings knowledge and skills pertinent to the resolution of family issues as well as contributing to the family's status in the community. Therefore, the general hypothesis of this theory is that the greater the relative contribution of resources by one spouse, the greater that spouse's authority in marital decision-making.

This leads to a variety of more specific hypotheses (Blood and Wolfe 1960:30–44). They discovered, for example, that husband's power is positively related to his occupational status, income, and general social status. This is quite consistent with "resource theory": the higher the husband's status, the more resources he is providing to his family. When the resources of husbands and wives were compared along dimensions such as education, organizational participation, and labor force participation, they found that comparative decison-making authority was directly related to the comparative resources of the spouses. For example, the husband's power was greatest when he worked more than 40 hours per week and the wife was not employed outside the home. Conversely, the husband's power in the family was lowest where he was unemployed but his wife was employed (1960:40). The authors conclude that

> . . . the power to make decisions stems primarily from the resources which the individual can provide to meet the needs of his marriage partner and to upgrade his decision-making skills. (Blood and Wolfe 1960:44)

This theoretical perspective on conjugal power has a clear affinity with exchange theory, rendered explicit in the work of David Heer (1963). Heer maintains that each spouse, overtly or covertly, compares the benefits he or she is deriving from the marriage with those derivable from possible alternatives. The greater the benefits or rewards provided by one's spouse, and/or the less available are satisfactory alternatives to one's current marriage, the more dependent one is upon one's spouse for the provision of rewards and the satisfaction of needs. Dependency is inversely related to power; to "alienate" a provider of scarce resources is to risk possible loss of those resources. The more dependent one spouse is upon the other, the greater the power of the spouse who is depended upon.

This logic has come to be known as the "resource theory" of conjugal power. Its central premise is that decision-making authority is determined by a process of negotiation and bargaining between spouses, with ultimate authority residing with the spouse whose resources are greatest. This implies that women have entry into the competition for marital authority.

> Whereas in the past, custom often dictated that all families should be patriarchal, today the rise of women produces considerable variation

between families (and even within families with the passage of time). . . .
Under these circumstances, power in American marriages is not a
matter of brute coercion and unwilling defeat so much as a mutual
recognition of individual skills in particular areas of competence and of
the partners' dual stake in areas of joint concern. (Blood and Wolfe
1960:45)

Resource theory in cultural context

To what extent is the resource theory of marital power
applicable across varying cultural conditions? A series of investigations into the
determinants of conjugal power, measured in roughly the same fashion as by
Blood and Wolfe, was conducted in Yugoslavia (Buric and Zecevic 1967), France
(Michel 1967), and Greece (Safilios-Rothschild 1967). The results of these
studies were compared with one another, and with the original results of Blood
and Wolfe, by Rodman (1967). As a consequence of these comparisons, resource
theory was both supported and modified.

The primary hypothesis tested in each of these societies
was that husband's authority is positively related to husband's socioeconomic
status, as measured by education, income, and occupational prestige. We know,
in general terms, that such a relationship does exist in the United States (Blood
and Wolfe 1960; McKinley 1964; Centers et al. 1971; Kandel and Lesser 1972a;
Cromwell et al. 1973). The hypothesis was also supported for France (Michel
1967), and has been found applicable, in varying degrees, to Belgium (Leplae
1968), Denmark (Kandel and Lesser 1972a), Germany (Konig 1957; Lamouse
1969; Lupri 1969), Ghana (Oppong 1970), Japan (Blood 1967), Mexico (Cromwell et al. 1973), and Turkey (Fox 1973). But in Greece (Safilios-Rothschild
1967) and Yugoslavia (Buric and Zecevic 1967), the relationship between husband's socioeconomic status and husband's marital authority was found to be
negative: high-status husbands had the least decision-making authority, and their
wives the most. This directly contradicts the hypothesis.

Rodman (1967, 1972), in the process of summarizing
these results, has inductively developed an explanation for these cross-national
discrepancies which he terms the "theory of resources in cultural context." The
central premise of this theory is that comparative spousal resources do determine
conjugal power through the process of social exchange, but only if cultural
norms are sufficiently flexible to allow resources to operate. In each of the
societies where husband's status and husband's conjugal power are positively
related, the cultural or normative context may be characterized as relatively
equalitarian with respect to marital power. Norms specifying the propriety of
male dominance have been replaced, or are in the process of being replaced, with
norms which uphold the value of equality, mutuality, and sharing. In other

words, the more equalitarian the norms, the better resource theory seems to work: that is, the more clearly its predictions on the distribution of marital power are supported.[8] In Greece and Yugoslavia, however, the norms are markedly patriarchal in character. Here, Rodman argues, the various indices of husband's status (education, income, occupational prestige) do not operate as resource variables, but rather as cultural variables indexing exposure to nontraditional, equalitarian norms. Education is thought to be particularly important in this regard. Patriarchal norms attain greater flexibility among the higher strata in these societies, especially the more educated. Rodman summarizes this as follows:

> It appears that there are two conflicting tendencies operating. . . . To the extent that a man's higher status operates as a valued resource that gives him more leverage within the marital relationship, it increases his power. To the extent that it operates to place the man in a patriarchal society in closer touch with equalitarian norms, it decreases his marital power. (Rodman 1972:58)[9]

Rodman (1972) also points out that, by taking normative systems into account as a conditional variable, the explanatory power of resource theory may be increased with regard to intranational variation in conjugal power. For example, several studies conducted in the United States show that the typical positive relationship between husband's status and husband's power is not perfectly linear (for example, Blood and Wolfe 1960:33; Centers *et al.* 1971; Kandel and Lesser 1972a). In a study of American working-class marriages, Komarovsky (1967:220–235) found that husband-dominance in decision-making was notably greater in the lower-blue-collar class than among upper-blue-collar workers (high school graduates). This negative relationship, she feels, represents the greater tendency of less-educated people (both men and women) to endorse patriarchal norms (1967:225–227).

Rodman (1972) takes this as evidence that subcultural variations in normative systems also affect the applicability of resource theory. Resource theory yields useful explanations of conjugal power where norms are predominantly equalitarian. Where the norms are patriarchal in character, a reverse logic is more appropriate. Here, variables such as education do not constitute resources, but rather index relative access to equalitarian normative systems. The result of this interaction between resources and the normative system is that the association between husband's status and husband's power is slightly curvilinear but predominantly positive in equalitarian societies, and negative in patriarchal societies (see Rodman 1972:65–67, for an elaboration of this point).[10] Resource theory is differentially applicable depending upon the extant normative system, which tends to be more equalitarian in industrial societies (thus allowing for the operation of resource variables), and more patriarchal in agrarian systems.

A further modification

Does resource theory in cultural context mean that women have more conjugal power in industrial societies? This would appear to be the case, since in a patriarchal normative system the culture dictates that husbands will make important family decisions, and no contribution of resources by the wife will change these norms. Resource theory might seem to imply that women cannot gain family power until the cultural system shifts toward equalitarian norms, which comes with industrialization. Thus the "status of women" should improve with industrialization and correspondent modernization.

Recent anthropological research, however, has shown that this model of linear improvement in female status with modernization may be a gross oversimplification of reality, and that the authority and status of women may actually decrease with industrialization. In particular, two recent ethnographic studies (Bossen 1975; Rogers 1975) have seriously challenged the argument that women's status is uniformly low in horticultural societies and improves as these societies modernize. Both of these authors contend that the assumption that males dominate females in nonindustrial societies (see Fox 1967; Patai 1967; Michaelson and Goldschmidt 1971) is based upon an analysis of formal, visible, culturally endorsed norms rather than upon intensive observations of the conduct of everyday life. In fact, the wife's authority in marriages in nonindustrial societies may be quite high, and for a variety of reasons industrialization may result in a decrease in the wife's conjugal power. Interestingly, both Bossen and Rogers employ the logic of resource theory in their arguments. This issue actually involves two related questions: how is it possible for women to be in an advantageous authority position in societies where the cultural norms are clearly patriarchal? and, how can the emergence of industry and more equalitarian marital and sex-role norms eventuate in a decrease in female authority?

It has often been observed that, in preindustrial economic systems, women are rather completely tied to the home and the domestic arena by child-care responsibilities (see Evans-Pritchard 1965; Chapter Three above). The family is based upon a division of labor along sexual lines in which men exploit the external environment to support the home-bound women and children. But what does it mean to say that the woman is tied to the home? Of what does her domestic sphere of activity consist? Many ethnographers have pointed out that the "home" to which the woman is tied often consists not only of the household, but also of a set of economic tasks which involve food production. Particularly in horticultural societies, women are likely to tend the fields which actually provide the bulk of subsistence; we have made this observation in several previous chapters. Thus women may indeed be tied to the domestic arena, but this happens to be the arena in which most of the food is produced (see Boserup 1970). Furthermore, since horticultural societies tend to evince a rather rigid sexual division of labor, men and women are highly dependent upon one another for the performance of their respective tasks. Women clearly contribute valuable resources in this kind of economic arrangement. Furthermore, both Bossen and Rogers argue that, because women have primary responsibility for domestic activities (including substantial food production), they actually make most of the important decisions in the domestic arena. And because the household is an economic as well as a family unit, many if not most important decisions are in fact domestic decisions. The decision-making authority of the wife in horticultural societies should not be underestimated; this authority, furthermore, appears to be based upon her contribution to family resources.

There are numerous recent reports of the extent of female authority in horticultural societies based upon ethnographic observations. Riegelhaupt (1967) shows that Portuguese women have a great deal of power because of a rigid division of labor between spouses in which the wife is charged with the responsibility of allocating family resources. Friedl (1967) shows that a similar process occurs among Greek peasantry. Women receive land from their families as dowries when they marry, thus they contribute important resources to the marriage; they also manage domestic affairs, which include many important areas of family decision-making. And Rogers' (1975) research on a French peasant village showed that women's contributions to subsistence were such that it was quite possible for a woman to survive, and even support children, without a husband, but if a man lost his wife she would have to be replaced. Although women's tasks might be categorized as "domestic," they were of such importance that men were heavily dependent upon them for subsistence; consequently, the balance of power in peasant families resided with women.

How, then, does the coming of industry operate to reduce the wife's power in the family? Essentially, the man's dependence upon his wife's contribution to subsistence is reduced. Industry brings a money economy. Money is earned by wage labor. Men are more likely to be recruited into the labor force than women, particularly for the more prestigious supervisory positions. Bossen (1975) argues that this is partly because those industrial nations which export industrial technology have labor forces which are dominated by males, and their representatives assume that men should be the recipients of the skills and jobs in industrializing nations. Boserup (1970) has shown that this can happen even in the introduction of modern farming techniques. She points out that in most of Africa, subsistence horticulture has been the province of women (see Chapter Six). However, when Europeans introduced new agricultural technology, they introduced it to men. The woman's role in food production was substantially reduced because the men were recruited for cash-crop farming, given technology which increased their productivity, and placed in positions where their dependence on women was minimized (see also Wheeler 1967). Bossen's research in the Guatemalan community of Tecpanaco shows how the economic predominance of the male can be greatly increased by the introduction of modern technology. She points out that women were systematically excluded from positions in the labor force above the most menial work, and that the advantageous occupational positions allocated to men have implications for their marital and family power. Bossen feels that the differential opportunities afforded men and women in industrializing societies are largely attributable to the characteristics of those industrialized nations which export modern technology. She concludes that

> These differences suggest that in Tecpanaco, as in our other examples, modern technology does not make its appearance as a neutral factor; it tends to support the structural interests and priorities of the system that introduces, or imposes, it. . . . One of the structural characteristics of Western capitalist societies is a priority for males in all productive activities and particularly in captial intensive occupations. There is a corresponding preference to assign women to domestic, dependent, and marginal economic roles. (Bossen 1975:599)

Thus the theory of resources in cultural context argues that industrialization brings with it the emergence of equalitarian marital and sex-role norms. Under this condition, marital power is a function of the relative contribution of the spouses to family resources. But this does not necessarily mean that the wife's power is increased above that typical in societies which are normatively patriarchal, because women usually find themselves at a marked disadvantage in the competition for resources. The difference in conjugal power between patriarchal and equalitarian societies is not that wives have more power in the latter, but that the processes by which the conjugal balance of power is determined may be different.

However, this material presents a bit of a dilemma for the theory of resources in cultural context, or at least for the interpretation of a part of its data base. Bossen (1975) and Rogers (1975) are arguing that women's decision-making authority may be reduced in the process of industrialization because the resources available to women, which give them "bargaining power," may be greater in horticultural than industrial economic systems. This makes good sense within the context of resource theory. But how can this observation be reconciled with the data from Greece (Safilios-Rothschild 1967) and Yugoslavia (Buric and Zecevic 1967) to the effect that the association between resources and conjugal power in these relatively patriarchal societies is negative?

There is an important measurement issue involved here. The measurement of marital power is very complex (Safilios-Rothschild 1970, 1972; Turk and Bell 1972; Olson and Rabunsky 1972; Sprey 1972; Bahr, 1972, 1973), and its cross-national measurement is even more difficult (Blood and

Takeshita 1964; Safilios-Rothschild 1969; Blood and Hill 1970; Cromwell and Wieting 1975). All of the sociological researchers involved in the cross-national testing of resource theory have asked their respondents to tell them who makes decisions of certain kinds or in specified areas, along the lines of the original Blood-Wolfe index. The areas of decision-making about which respondents were questioned varied across societies (it is useless to ask people who decides what car to buy when most of them will never buy a car), but the structure of the power measure has been the same in all of these studies. However, Rogers' (1975) research shows that responses to this kind of question may have variable meanings across cultures. She found, in the French peasant village she observed, that both men and women joined in the perpetuation of a "myth" of male dominance. Men, she argued, were willing to trade actual decision-making authority for the public *appearance* of authority. Therefore, even though most important decisions were made by women, both sexes would be likely to report that final authority resides with men. The "myth of male dominance" is an established and tenacious institution in peasant society because both sexes benefit from it:

> The perpetuation of this "myth" is in the interest of both peasant women and men, because it gives the latter the *appearance* of power and control over all sectors of village life, while at the same time giving to the former *actual* power over those sectors of life in the community which may be controlled by villagers. . . . Neither men nor women believe that the "myth" is an accurate reflection of the actual situation. However, each sex group believes . . . that the opposite sex perceives the myth as reality, with the result that each is actively engaged in maintaining the illusion that males are, in fact, dominant. (Rogers 1975:729)

In this kind of situation, a researcher asking who makes what decisions may get an answer in accord with public mythology rather than with actual practice. This would seem to be a particular problem in societies where women control extensive resources but have little normative power, and thus may not directly affect the results of the studies summarized by Rodman (1967, 1972). Nonetheless, Rogers points out that we need to be cognizant of measurement problems in evaluating and interpreting, as well as executing, research.

It is important to note that Buric and Zecevic (1967) and Safilios-Rothschild (1967) studied primarily the association between *husbands'* resources and husbands' power, which they found to be negative in Yugoslavia and Greece, respectively. Fox (1973) investigated the relative contributions of husbands' and wives' resources to the explanation of husbands' power in Ankara, Turkey, where the culture is clearly patriarchal. As in the other studies in patriarchal societies, the relationships between husbands' resources and husbands' power were found to be negative. But the relationships between *wives'* resources and husbands' power were also negative. In Rodman's terms, this implies that resources operate as cultural variables for men, but as resource variables for women.[11] Resource theory may therefore be selectively applicable even in societies with patriarchal cultural systems (Fox 1973:726).

What are the implications of these studies for the theory of resources in cultural context? Rodman (1967, 1972) argued that resource theory has predictive and explanatory value with regard to marital power only when cultural norms are relatively equalitarian, thus permitting resources to operate. It would appear that this limitation on resource theory may be a bit severe; the studies of Fox (1973), Bossen (1975), Rogers (1975), and others indicate that a modification of the cultural context theory is in order. Conjugal power is a function of resources *either* (1) where cultural norms are relatively equalitarian, *or* (2) where the sexual division of labor is such that spouses are highly interdependent in subsistence activities. Only where patriarchal norms occur jointly with male-dominated division of labor can actual power structures be predicted by cultural variables alone.

This modification of the theory indicates that the original resource theory of conjugal power may be more broadly applicable than we had earlier expected. Specifically, hypotheses derived from resource theory may be useful in predicting and explaining marital power even under the most patriarchal normative system, provided that both sexes contribute to production. The theory in this form is of considerable use in interpreting the results of studies such as that by Gouldner and Peterson (1962), who employed cross-cultural data originally assembled by Leo Simmons (1945) on 71 preliterate societies. Gouldner and Peterson (1962) found that variables labeled "subjection or inferiority of women" and "patripotestal family authority" were positively correlated with patrilineal descent and inheritance practices and patrilocal residence, and negatively correlated with matrilocal residence, matrilineal descent, and matrilineal inheritance. The explanation for these correlations is certainly not that matriliny implies matriarchy; contrary to the assumptions of early writers, it doesn't. Matriliny has to do with criteria for membership in kin groups, not with authority structures within these groups. The appropriate explanation, rather, may involve resource theory. We have seen (Chapter Six) that matrilocal residence and matrilineal descent occur in conjunction with horticultural subsistence economies, where most food is produced by manual labor in the fields, and where women are likely to be the primary horticultural laborers. The relatively large female contribution to subsistence eventuates in matrilocal residence and matrilineal descent, and also means that women provide a substantial proportion of the family's resources. It is this contribution of resources to the family that increases female power in matrilineal and matrilocal societies, not the fact that descent-group membership is determined along female lines.

One clear conclusion from this body of research is that the relationship between norms and behaviors is much more complex than it might seem to be on the surface. Equalitarian cultural norms regarding marital sex roles do not at all imply that authority is equally divided or shared syncratically in all, or even most, marriages. The appropriate implication, rather, is that factors other than the normative are operative in the determination of actual authority structures. Gillespie (1971), for example, on the basis of a review of research on marital power, concludes that in an "equalitarian" system wives attain authority over their husbands only by *exceeding* them in resources, and that women's access to external resources is culturally blocked as compared to the access afforded males:

> The equalitarian marriage as a norm is a myth. Under some conditions, women can gain power vis-à-vis their husbands; i.e., working women, women with higher educations than their husbands have more power than housewives or women with lesser or identical education as their husbands, but more power is not equal power. Equal power we do not have. Equal power we will never get so long as the present socioeconomic system remains. (Gillespie 1971:457–458)

Similarly, patriarchal norms are not directly transferred from the cultural to the behavioral level.

Other evidence exists to show, more indirectly, that changes brought about by various aspects of "modernization" do not immediately culminate in greater female authority in marriage. Studies comparing arranged marriages with "love matches" (nonarranged marriages) in Tokyo, Japan (Blood 1967) and Ankara, Turkey (Fox 1975) both find that overall differences in conjugal power between these two kinds of marriage are quite minimal. But effects of normative systems are still evident. Blood (1967:61–63) found that husbands in arranged marriages were more powerful in areas such as determining when to have intercourse and where to go on vacations; they tended to exercise unilateral power in these areas. But they were *less* powerful than husbands in love matches in the child-care area. Blood attributes this (1967: 63–65) to a blurring of the traditional sexual division of labor in love matches. In arranged marriages wives are unilaterally responsible for child care, whereas in love matches both spouses tend to participate. The lack of significant difference in total power scores is due to the existence of unilateral power in specific decision-making areas for each spouse in arranged marriages, as compared to greater sharing of authority in most areas by spouses in love matches.

Fox (1975:188) finds that decision-making in arranged marriages is both more husband-dominated and more sex-segregated. However, these differences are due largely to asssociations between marriage type and certain background characteristics which index exposure to traditional norms: spouses in arranged marriages are more likely to be rural, to have low education, and to marry young. Furthermore, Fox suggests that traditional norms favoring wifely subservience may still be so strong in Turkey that, although love-match spouses may hold more equalitarian attitudes, their behavior cannot conform highly to these values:

> Thus, while the type of marriage, whether love-match or arranged, may well distinguish among women in terms of their subsequent attitudes on traditional sex roles and views of the world, marriage type may not account for behavior variation, simply because love-match wives and arranged marriage wives are not allowed to differ in terms of wifely behavior. Both sets of wives may be constrained to play the role of wife in the traditional mold: obedience and subordination to the husband. (Fox 1975:191)

Contrary to Gillespie, the equalitarian norm of marital authority is not a myth; its translation to behavioral levels, though, is indirect. Equalitarian norms do not directly imply equalitarian marriages, as Gillespie points out, but the characteristics of the normative system have important effects on the processes by which conjugal power structure is determined. In the analysis of conjugal power, as in many other areas of investigation, these normative factors are more usefully employed as system-level conditional variables than as independent variables which directly determine behavior.

Summary

The change from patriarchal to equalitarian normative structures which appears to accompany industrialization and "modernization" does not imply a corresponding change in marital power structures at the behavior level. This is because norms do not directly determine behavior. Patriarchal norms are apparently manifest in patriarchal behavior only where women make very little contribution to subsistence. This situation, as we know (Aronoff and Crano 1975), is quite rare. Under conditions of relatively equalitarian norms, or where women make important contributions to subsistence regardless of the norms, marital power is determined largely by the spouses' contribution of resources to the family.

The emergence of equalitarian norms may mean, though, that marital decision-making in particular areas becomes, in Bott's (1957) terms, more a product of joint rather than segregated conjugal role performance. That is, each spouse is empowered to participate in the making of decisions which, under more "traditional" norms, were the exclusive province of one spouse only. But again, this does not mean that the wife's overall authority increases. She may participate in decisions which were formerly the unilateral prerogative of the husband, but she must also share with him authority over matters which formerly fell in her exclusive domain. And as Gillespie (1971) and others point out, equalitarian norms will not eventuate in equalitarian marital power structures unless and until the resources upon which power is based are equally distributed between spouses. This is not yet the case.

Marital dissolution

Introduction

It is commonly believed that industrialization, and the conjugal family system which accompanies it, operate in such a way as to drastically increase the frequency of divorce over that prevalent in nonindustrial societies. A further implication of this line of reasoning is that marriages in modern societies are less harmonious and gratifying to the individuals involved than is the case in the more "traditional" societies. Both of these points are serious misconceptions; reality is much more complex.

The United States currently has the highest divorce rate among industrialized nations, although others have had higher rates in the past (Goode 1966b:498). Furthermore, the rate in the United States has increased dramatically since about 1960. In 1974, there were 4.6 divorces per one thousand population in the United States; by September of 1975, this rate had climbed to 5.2 per thousand. As recently as 1958, there were only 2.1 divorces per one thousand population. The sharp increase in the divorce rate actually began about 1963; the rate exactly doubled in 11 years.[12] Although the increase in divorce is obviously substantial in the United States, some other industrialized nations such as Sweden have experienced even more rapid increases. However, the United States rate is clearly the highest among industrial societies (Goode 1966b:497–498).

But in cross-cultural and historical perspective, modern American divorce rates are rather modest. In one of the more systematic cross-cultural descriptive studies of divorce, Murdock estimated that rates of divorce in about 60 percent of the world's preliterate societies exceeded contemporary U.S. rates (Murdock 1950:197).[13] Of the 40 societies in Murdock's sample, only the Incas had no apparent provision for divorce. It appears that virtually all societies do permit divorce, or some institutionalized means of dissolving marriages, but only in extremely rare instances is divorce positively valued by the culture. The most famous of these instances, and possibly the only one, is the Crow Indian tribe of North America, among whom

> ... public opinion, instead of exerting its usual stabilizing influence, actually tends to undermine the marital relationship. Divorce is exceedingly frequent, and a man subjects himself to ridicule if he lives too long with one woman. (Murdock 1950:197)

There is obviously, then, a great deal of variation across cultures in the extent to which married couples are allowed or encouraged to, and actually do, resort to divorce as a solution to marital problems. (There is also considerable variation in the kinds of things which are defined as marital problems.) Some of the antecedents of this variation have been determined, in both cross-cultural and cross-societal investigations.

Affiliations and divorce

One very important determinant of cross-cultural variation in divorce rates is the method of reckoning descent-group membership. Max Gluckman (1950, 1955) shows, with examples from African kinship systems, that divorce is considerably more common in matrilineal than in patrilineal societies. The explanation for this lies in the more direct and obvious biological connections between mother and child than between father and child. In patrilineal systems, children belong to their father's kin group. But the father is related to his children most clearly through the mother. For this reason, it is important that the descent group maintain control over in-marrying females, for their children constitute the membership of the group in the next generation. In Gluckman's terminology, the husband acquires, by virtue of his marriage, rights in his wife's child-bearing capacities as well as rights in her as a wife. She produces children for his group.

In matrilineal societies, on the other hand, rights in a woman's procreative capacities remain inalienably with her natal kin group. The key relationship here is between mother's brother and sister's son, not between father and son. Thus a divorce has virtually no ramifications for the generational continuity of matrilineal descent groups. A woman may be separated from her husband and his kin by virtue of divorce, but in matrilineal systems there are no procedures by means of which she can be officially alienated from her brothers. Her children belong to her own group. A divorce means that she will have to find another husband (or sexual partner) if she is to produce more children, but the attachment of her existing children to their descent group is not at all threatened by the removal of their father. In turn, the father is not particularly concerned by the structural alienation of his "own" children occasioned by divorce, because his most important relationships with the succeeding generation are those with the children of his sisters, not with the children of his wife.[14]

So rates of marital dissolution tend, on the average, to be higher in matrilineal than in patrilineal societies, because in the former the kin-group attachments of children are not affected by divorce. This does not, however, account for the entirety of cross-cultural variation in divorce rates. In a cross-cultural study of ethnographic reports from 62 societies (60 of them contained in the Human Relations Area Files as well as the World Ethnographic

Sample), Charles Ackerman (1963) attempts to develop a more generally applicable theory by employing the concept of differential affiliations of spouses. Ackerman interprets anthropological research on divorce, including Gluckman's and that of others (cited above), to say that divorce rates depend largely on the extent to which the kin-group affiliations of spouses are either overlapping and supportive, on the one hand, or diverse and divisive, on the other. He further notes that a great deal of sociological research in the United States (specifically Burgess and Cottrell 1939; Goode 1956; Zimmerman 1956; see also Zimmerman and Cervantes 1960) has shown that homogamy is positively related to marital stability. That is, spouses who are relatively homogeneous on social characteristics such as race, socioeconomic status, religion, and so on, are less likely to divorce than spouses who differ on such characteristics.[15] Furthermore, Zimmerman's research in particular shows that married couples whose social networks are characterized by homogeneity are less likely to divorce than those whose networks contain members with more diverse or heterogeneous characteristics (see also Lee 1977).

Ackerman hypothesizes that these two lines of reasoning may be related by emphasizing the extent to which spouses are involved in networks of social relations which are overlapping or "conjunctive," as opposed to "disjunctive." Involvement in conjunctive networks could foster the internalization of similar norms and values by married couples, reinforcing the solidarity of the marriage. But disjunctive affiliations mean that spouses receive reinforcement from, and respond to the expectations of, different groups; their own norms and values may differ in consequence, and the solidarity of the marriage may thus be tenuous.

> If we can grant that the behavior and expectations of members of collectivities are affected by the norms and values of the collectivities, it is clear that when the affiliations of both spouses are *conjunctive,* that is, overlapping or identical, the behavior and expectations of both spouses are affected by the same norm and value sets. The affiliations of the spouses can, on the other hand, be *disjunctive;* that is, each spouse may maintain membership in different collectivities. In such a situation, the behavior and expectations of the spouses are affected by different norm and value sets. . . . The more disjunctive the affiliations of the spouses, and the more disparate the norm and value sets of their affiliations, the higher the probability of divorce. (Ackerman 1963:14)

In testing this proposition, Ackerman found that the means of reckoning descent was more appropriate as a conditional variable than as an independent variable. Specifically, different indicators of the conjunctiveness or disjunctiveness of affiliations are employed for bilateral societies than for unilineal societies.

In societies which trace their descent bilaterally, Ackerman found that those societies which practice community endogamy (that is, marriages are usually formulated between members of the same community) and consanguine endogamy (marriages typically occur between kin) have low divorce rates relative to societies which practice community and/or consanguine exogamy. Divorce rates are lowest when community and consanguine endogamy are practiced in combination (Ackerman 1963:17). In line with this theory concerning the effects of affiliations on marital stability, Ackerman interprets endogamy as an indication of conjunctive affiliations.

> Whereas community exogamy unites spouses from different communities, community endogamy unites spouses who have a common community background. It seems fairly apparent that the probability of conjunctive affiliations is greater in the latter case. Further, whereas consanguine exogamy unites spouses whose kin affiliations must be different, consanguine endogamy unites spouses with overlapping kin affiliations. (Ackerman 1963:15-16)

This line of reasoning, however, turned out to be appropriate only for societies with bilateral descent. In societies with unilineal descent groups, no relationship was found between divorce and any kind of endogamy. Ackerman interprets this not as a failure of the theory, but as an indication that different measures of conjunctive and disjunctive affiliations are necessary in unilineal societies.[16] In unilineal societies, the best single indicator of conjunctive affiliations was found to be the existence of the levirate. This is the practice of requiring a widow to marry one of her deceased husband's brothers. In Ackerman's logic, the levirate indicates that the wife is so completely severed from her own kin group, and incorporated into her husband's, that she remains a member of his group for the rest of her life even if her husband dies. Her affiliations with her natal kin group are entirely subordinated to the affiliations with her husband's kin which she acquires upon marriage. Regardless of the disjunctiveness of the affiliations of spouses prior to marriage in unilineal societies, the levirate, where it exists, insures that their affiliations after the marriage will be conjunctive. Hence divorce rates are lower in unilineal societies which practice the levirate than in those which do not (Ackerman 1963:18-19).

There were, in Ackerman's sample, six unilineal societies which did not practice the levirate but which nonetheless were judged to have low divorce rates. In at least four of these, Ackerman found evidence of practices which served either to (1) sever the premarital affiliations of one of the spouses and incorporate that spouse into the other's social network, or (2) extend the affiliational network of each spouse to include the affiliations of the other. In the societies with high divorce rates, postmarital affiliations almost uniformly were, in Ackerman's judgment, disjunctive.

Ackerman has discovered a variable which is an important source of variation in marital stability under a great variety of cultural conditions. The extent to which spousal affiliations are conjunctive is a highly abstract variable, and therefore one which must be operationalized in different ways under different kinds of conditions. However, this abstractness also means that its explanatory power is considerable. It helps to explain why divorce is more common in matrilineal than in patrilineal societies, since spousal affiliations are clearly more disjunctive in the former case. It also sheds light on research in industrial nations which has shown that the incidence of divorce is negatively related to variables such as homogamy, "generational continuity" (Aldous 1965), harmonious relations with in-laws (Duvall 1954; Blood and Wolfe 1960), and equal rather than unilateral relationships with kin (Farber 1966; Mindel 1972). All of these empirical generalizations are subject to at least partial interpretation in terms of the extent to which spousal affiliations are conjunctive. Furthermore, since spousal affiliations are known to be more disjunctive in the working classes of industrial societies (Young and Willmott 1957; Rainwater 1965, 1966b; Komarovsky 1967; Lee 1977), Ackerman's proposition may in part explain the relatively higher divorce rate among working-class than among middle-class couples.

There may also be a relationship between the conjunctiveness of spousal affiliations and the observation (Stephens 1963:235–236) that the presence of children is, cross-culturally, one of the most widespread and effective impediments to divorce. Stephens notes that many ethnographers report that divorces are much more common in the early years of marriage, particularly before children are born. There is considerable cross-cultural variation in the disposition of children following a divorce; sometimes (if there are two or more) they are divided, sometimes they go with their father, and sometimes with their mother. Stephens surmises, by inference from the tendency toward early divorce, that parental love for children is "the most widespread effective obstacle to divorce" (1963:236).[17] But if children do prevent divorce, at least in some societies, it may be because they constitute a focus of conjunctive affiliations for their parents. Both parents relate to the child; this common relationship may operate like other conjunctive affiliations to increase the stability of marriage.[18]

In summary, cultural practices which result in, or maximize the probability of, conjunctive spousal affiliations are associated with low divorce rates. These factors include community and consanguine endogamy in societies with bilateral kinship systems, and the levirate and other mechanisms of severance/incorporation or extension/inclusion in unilineal societies. On the other hand, disjunctive affiliations are associated with high divorce rates. Matrilineal societies have higher divorce rates than patrilineal societies, partly because divorce does not threaten the kin-group membership of children in matrilineal societies, and partly because spousal affiliations are more likely to be disjunctive in the matrilineal case (see Chapter Six). The relationship between conjunctive affiliations and marital stability is also useful in explaining differential divorce rates within industrial societies in a variety of ways.

Divorce in conjugal family systems

Goode (1963) says that conjugal family systems are characterized by *relatively* high divorce rates. He attributes this to the comparative isolation of the conjugal unit from kin, and the consequent mutual dependence of spouses upon one another for emotional support.

> Since the larger kin group can no longer be counted on for emotional sustenance, and since the marriage is based on mutual attraction, the small marital unit is the main place where the emotional input-output balance of the individual husband and wife is maintained, where their psychic wounds can be salved or healed. . . . Thus, the emotions within this unit are likely to be intense, and the relationship between husband and wife may well be intrinsically unstable, depending as it does on affection. Consequently, the divorce rate is likely to be high. (Goode 1963:9)

However, this does not mean that as the conjugal family system becomes increasingly prominent divorce rates will inevitably increase. Goode did find evidence of rising divorce rates in Western societies, Sub-Saharan Africa, India, and China. But in Arabic Islam (1963:155-162) and Japan (1963:358-365), he found that divorce rates were decreasing rather than increasing, although the family systems in these areas showed signs of becoming increasingly conjugal along other dimensions. This was because, in each case, divorce rates were exceedingly high before the change toward the conjugal family system began. In preindustrial Japan, rights to divorce a wife resided largely with the husband's parents; if she displeased them she could be, and often was, sent back home. This was particularly common in rural areas. In Arabic Islam, a husband could divorce his wife by unilateral verbal decree; since World War II, however, Arabic laws have made divorce increasingly difficult to obtain. This information, in combination with Murdock's (1950) observations on preliterate societies, shows clearly that divorce rates in industrial societies with conjugal family systems are not necessarily higher than those of other types of societies. As with other aspects of the family system, the direction of change in the divorce rate as the system becomes conjugal depends upon the characteristics of the system prior to the onset of change (Goode 1963:368-369). But Goode also points out that all *Western* societies appear to be experiencing a substantial increase in divorce rates (1963:367). Why is this the case?

Part of the answer undoubtedly lies, as we have seen, in the increasing independence of the conjugal unit from extended kin. The married couple experiences less pressure from the kin group or network, and less organized and immediate pressure, to remain together. And the children produced by marriages are no longer of such vital concern to the kin group. They are the children of the married couple, not the succeeding generation of a lineage or extended family. Kin have less stake in marital stability; there is no organized group other than the immediate family whose continuity is threatened by marital dissolution. Furthermore, the criteria by which mates are selected and marriages are evaluated have changed considerably, generally from instrumental to interpersonal. Marriage (and family, for that matter) has become increasingly functionally specialized; it is, in a conjugal system, the source of emotional gratification rather than of economic survival. In the immediate preindustrial and industrializing periods of Western history, families were rarely fully extended in structure (Laslett 1969, 1972), but were nonetheless highly self-sufficient economic and productive units. The cooperation of family members, including most centrally spouses, was crucial for the economic well-being of all members in both urban (Anderson 1973) and rural (Berkner 1973) areas. Divorces were legally difficult to obtain, and the disruption of the cooperating economic unit had more serious implications for economic security than is the case in a fully industrial society such as the contemporary United States.

Expectations regarding marital behavior are also changing considerably. People have come to expect their spouses to provide companionship, intimacy, and emotional support. There is evidence from such diverse cultures as Japan (Blood 1967), France (Michel 1970), and Turkey (Fox 1973, 1975) that women who have been exposed to "modern" marital norms, through education, travel, or employment, have come to expect more from their husbands in terms of these dimensions of interpersonal relations. This may well result in a decrease in marital satisfaction, because these higher expectations are less likely to be met or exceeded by the spouse's behavior. The norms of the more traditional marriage systems did not foster such expectations, so spouses were less likely to be disappointed by relatively low marital intimacy.

Two cross-societal analyses of divorce rates (Day 1964; Kunzel 1974) highlight some of the structural factors related to divorce in industrial and industrializing societies. Day analyzed the divorce rates in the United States and Australia, and found the rate in Australia to be approximately one half that in the United States. He determined that this difference could not be attributed to differences in legal impediments to divorce between the two countries.[19] Instead, he argued that there are three structural features of the economic and marital systems of these two societies which are in part responsible for the lower divorce rate in Australia. First, the average age at first marriage is older in Australia than in the United States. We know (Bumpass and Sweet 1972) that age at marriage is negatively related to probability of divorce; therefore Australians are less likely to divorce because they are less likely to marry young. Second, although Australians marry later, the interval between marriage and the birth of the first child is, on the average, shorter than in the United

States. We have already established that childless couples are statistically at a somewhat greater risk of divorce than couples with children, and American couples spend a greater proportion of their family life cycle in the childless stage. Third, Day argued that economic and occupational opportunities for women in Australia are less than in the United States. This makes women, once married, more dependent on their husbands for support, since their chances of self-sufficiency are lower. They, presumably, are more willing than American women to put up with a marriage which does not fulfill their expectations, and husbands also may be relatively hesitant about the prospects of providing long-term support for a divorced wife, and possibly children, who have no other likely means of support.

An analysis by Kunzel (1974) of 13 fully industrialized and 15 industrializing European nations lends credibility to Day's conclusions. Kunzel discovered that divorce rates are higher in the fully industrial societies, and attempted to determine more precisely why this is the case. She related the relative frequency of divorce in her two groups of societies to certain features of the family life cycle, which she found to be related to both level of industrialization and divorce. These features included a decline in average age at marriage, a decrease in the number of children per family,[20] and an increase in life expectancy, all of which accompanied full industrialization and were positively related to the frequency of divorce. Two of these factors (age at marriage and number of children) correspond closely to those which Day found instrumental in the explanation of differential divorce rates between the United States and Australia. In addition, Kunzel found that fully industrial societies made greater use of women in the labor force, and particularly married women. This means that women have a greater opportunity for self-sufficiency in industrial societies, lessening their economic dependence upon their husbands. Divorce thus entails less potential economic insecurity for women in industrial societies; like Day, Kunzel concludes that this results in an increase in the frequency of divorce as industrialization proceeds.

There is also a very important self-perpetuating feature of rising divorce rates, which Day (1964), in particular, emphasizes. That is, as the divorce rate rises, divorce becomes progressively more common and visible. Since it is less unusual, less social stigma comes to be attached to divorce and divorced persons. Divorce comes to be regarded as a more "normal" type of solution to marital discord, and thereby becomes more "available" in a cultural (although not necessarily legal) sense. This may account, in part, for the continuing rise in divorce rates in societies, such as the United States, which have been fully industrialized for some time. Trite as it sounds, a major reason for the relatively high divorce rate in the United States in 1975 was the high divorce rate in 1974 and previous years.[21] Divorce, as it becomes more common, engenders more divorce.

Day also, in the course of his analysis, makes explicit the logic of a relationship between divorce and conjugal role organization. Kerckhoff (1972), as we have noted, has argued convincingly that marital roles tend to be jointly organized, rather than segregated, in conjugal family systems. Day (1964) contends that joint role performance is less characteristic of Australian, than American marriages. He describes Australian spouses as relatively independent of one another in terms of companionship; he also notes that Australian males have an institutionalized "mateship" or buddy system, whereby many of their emotional needs are met through close friendships with other males. We have already found that Australian wives are relatively unlikely to be members of the labor force and share the provider role with their husbands. Day concludes:

> It seems likely . . . that the "partnership" type of marriage is less common in Australia than in the United States. The strength of such marriages is that they permit richer, fuller relations between a husband and wife well suited to one another; their weakness, that they maximize the chances of difficulty arising between those who are not. Compared with American couples, the Australian husband and wife seem to share fewer activities and to participate less often in joint decision-making. The consequence is a reduction in the opportunities for friction. (Day 1964: 521)

Thus joint marital role performance, more characteristic of marriages in conjugal than in extended family systems, may contribute to the high divorce rate in industrialized societies by increasing the potential for conflict between spouses.[22]

Finally, we need to note that the structural determinants of divorce operate differently depending on the characteristics of the legal system. Goode (1962; 1963:85–86) notes that in Western societies, divorce rates are now typically higher in the lower socioeconomic strata.[23] Cutright (1971b) has demonstrated convincingly that income is the primary causal variable in this association. Low income places strains on marital relations due to mutually low evaluations of role performance, particularly involving the husband's performance of the provider role; and high income results in the accumulation of assets which would be seriously fragmented by divorce. But Goode demonstrates that in historical perspective, this has not been the case until quite recently. The historical tendency has been for divorce to be more common among the more privileged classes of Western societies.

This does not at all mean, however, that prior to full industrialization middle- and upper-class marriages were more susceptible to conflict or strain than others. The causes of marital disharmony and dissolution, particularly those related to socioeconomic position, have probably remained rather constant throughout the industrialization process. It means, rather, that divorce as a solution to marital discord has until recently been more readily available to the higher strata. Most societies have liberalized their divorce laws as they have industrialized. This has made divorce increasingly available to, and economically feasible for, the lower socioeconomic strata. Goode (1962) has shown, on the basis of an analysis of family law and divorce rates in 17 Western societies, that the correlation between social class and divorce is positive where divorce laws are restrictive, but negative where the laws are more liberal. Thus, he concludes:

> In the West, as divorce proceedings were liberalized and made econom-
> ically available to all, the normal difficulties of lower-class family life
> were permitted an expression in divorce. . . . For all Western countries,
> then, a gradual shift in the class distribution of divorce should occur,
> from a positive correlation between class and divorce rate, to a negative
> one. (Goode 1963:86)

Segre (1975) elaborates on this argument in a recent review article, which also serves as a partial summary of our logic here. He contends that although divorce may be quite common in preliterate societies (Murdock 1950), this does not indicate high family instability because stability stems from the extended family and the continuity of the kin group. In industrial societies, however, family stability depends upon marital stability, which consequently becomes a dominant cultural value. The upper, middle, and working classes strive to attain this value, but they are differentially successful. Where divorce laws are relatively liberal, the greater strains which the working classes experience result in higher rates of divorce. The lower classes, however, are subject to such severe strains that dominant cultural values represent virtually unattainable goals; they are therefore irrelevant to the lower classes. The divorce rate in the lower class, while high, is a less appropriate index of the extent of marital disruption than it is at higher socioeconomic levels, because lower-class people are unconcerned about "respectability" and are more likely to resolve their marital problems by extralegal means such as desertion.[24] Furthermore, they are less likely to formalize heterosexual relations by marriage in the first place (recall our discussion of Rodman's concept of "marital fluidity" in Chapter Seven). Consequently, rates of illegitimacy as well as desertion are likely to be highest in the lowest socioeconomic stratum in industrial societies. It is also reasonable to surmise, from this argument as well as Goode's, that the proportion of the desertion rate attributable to the lower class is even greater in societies with restrictive divorce laws.

Conclusions

As we noted in Chapter Five, describing a family system by the adjective "conjugal" implies that families in such systems are organized around marriages rather than around consanguineal relationships. This is certainly true of the contemporary United States, although it is an error to assume that kinship affiliations and networks have no effects on family behaviors.

Marital relations in conjugal family systems are different, in a variety of ways, from marital relations in extended family systems. Many of these differences are incorporated in Goode's (1963) delineation of the components of conjugal systems. Distinctions between instrumental and expressive role performance, particularly in leadership capacities, are probably less viable as characterizations of husband and wife roles. Conjugal role performance is probably more joint and less segregated than is the case in most other family systems. The balance of marital power is heavily influenced by the relative (and absolute) contributions of resources by spouses rather than traditional patriarchal norms, although this does not mean that wives are necessarily more powerful than they are in other systems. Finally, divorce rates tend to be relatively high in conjugal systems, but probably no higher than in societies which reckon kinship relations matrilineally, and perhaps no higher than in many patrilineal societies.

The relatively high divorce rate in the contemporary United States is often taken as evidence of a "disintegration" of our family system, and as an indication that marriage as a social institution is on its way out. There is no comparative evidence which justifies such a conclusion. It is the case, though, that in the absence of severe legal impediments to divorce, industrial societies with conjugal family systems are likely to evince relatively high divorce rates. But the stability of a marital *system* is not contingent upon the stability of the individual marriages which comprise that system. The political, religious, and particularly economic and familial structures of modern societies provide few instrumental impediments to marital dissolution, at least compared to the situations typically found in preindustrial societies. One apparent consequence of industrialization is the increasing prevalence of marriages based on interpersonal attraction. A consequence of this development is that if the original basis for the marriage dissipates over time, the inducements for remaining in the marriage are rather weak. But none of this implies that the conjugal family system, or the institution of marriage itself, is "threatened" by a rising divorce rate. Marriage is as popular as ever, although the average age at marriage as well as the divorce rate is rising in the United States (Glick 1975). It is true that conjugal family systems have high rates of marital instability; it is not true that such systems are, in any relevant sense of the word, unstable.

Notes

1. This is not entirely new information. See Coppinger and Rosenblatt (1968) and Chapter Seven, note 5 above.

2. Aronoff and Crano are aware of this shortcoming, as indicated by a con-

cluding footnote to their article (1975:19). But they do not qualify their analysis or conclusions in light of it.

3. For a similar distinction, which is useful in similar ways, see Jessie Bernard's (1964:687-688) discussion of "parallel" versus "interactional" patterns of marital role performance. See also Platt (1969) and Oppong (1971) for criticisms and extensions of this conceptualization.

4. Recent studies of the emergence of "joint" marital organization concurrent with, or related to, industrialization include Michel and Feyrabend (1969), Michel (1970), Podmore and Chaney (1972), Young and Willmott (1973), Hutchison (1974), Rapoport et al. (1974), and Ginsberg (1975) among others.

5. For a complete review and synthesis of these studies, see Lee (1977).

6. For examples, see Mead (1935), Barry et al. (1957), Ember (1973), Whiting and Edwards (1973), and Chapter Nine below.

7. See Hacker (1975) for an analysis of why experiments to bring about full sexual equality in Israeli kibbutzim, the Soviet Union, Communist China, and Sweden have not as yet been completely successful.

8. For a relatively explicit example of this involving a comparison between Mexico and the United States, see Cromwell et al. (1973). Resource theory is useful in both cultures, but more so in the United States where norms are more equalitarian. See also the five-culture study of Buehler et al. (1974). Here resource theory was supported, but relatively weakly. The equivocality of the results here may be due to intracultural sample homogeneity, and also to the fact that the data base involved adolescents' perceptions of marital power distributions in their parents' marriages. However, Buehler et al. clearly found that resource theory led to more accurate predictions of conjugal power in industrialized nations, where norms are presumably more equalitarian.

9. The data collected by Cromwell et al. (1973) support the existence of normative differences between social classes in the direction hypothesized. They measured marital power in normative terms; that is, they asked who *should* make particular decisions rather than who *does*. They found that endorsement of patriarchal norms was inversely related to socioeconomic status for men in both Mexico and the United States, but the relationship was markedly stronger in Mexico.

10. Interestingly enough, Blood anticipated this modification of resource theory based on his analysis of Japanese marriages. He concluded that ". . . resource theory of marital power must be limited in its application to modern, emancipated social conditions" (Blood 1967:168-169).

11. It should also be noted that in both Greece and Yugoslavia, wives had

higher marital power scores when they were employed than when they were not (Buric and Zecevic 1967:331; Safilios-Rothschild 1967:347), and in Yugoslavia wives had more power when they had more education than their husbands (Buric and Zecevic 1967:329).

12. These figures were taken from U.S. Department of Health, Education, and Welfare (1975b, 1975c, 1975d). The rates include legal annulments as well as divorces.

13. This study was based on ethnographic reports (most of which, of course, lacked precise statistical data) of 40 societies. It must also be recalled that Murdock was employing the American divorce rate as of 1949, which was about one-half the current rate per one thousand population.

14. For elaborations of this line of reasoning, which lead to essentially similar conclusions, see Fallers (1957), Fortes (1959b, 1959c), and Mitchell (1961). An excellent illustration of the process which leads to and maintains high divorce rates among matrilineal peoples may be found in Richards' (1956) study of the Bemba of Africa.

15. There is some evidence now that earlier researchers and theorists may have overestimated relationships between homogamy and marital stability. For a comprehensive summary of American research on this subject, see Udry (1974:240-260).

16. This is because in unilineal societies, the basis for affiliations is the descent group rather than the community or the kindred. An endogamous community consisting of several distinct kin groups which are exogamous "is not structurally analogous to the endogamous bilateral community" (Ackerman 1963:17).

17. It is not at all clear that this is the case in the United States. Jacobsen (1959:134) found that divorce rates are higher among childless couples than those with children for the first 30 years of marriage. However, he speculated that children did not prevent divorce; rather, "both divorce and childlessness result from more fundamental factors in the marital relationship" (1959:135; see also Monahan 1955). But divorce is nonetheless proportionately more common among childless couples. In 1973, 40 percent of all divorcing couples had no children under 18 years of age. The average number of children affected by each divorce decree was 1.17 in the United States in 1973; this is a decrease from the peak of 1.36 per divorce in 1964 (U.S. Department of Health, Education, and Welfare 1975c).

18. There is a very important qualification to Stephens' generalization that children constitute obstacles to divorce. In many societies, the fact that most divorces occur before children are born may well be attributable to

the childlessness itself, which is a very common justification for divorce cross-culturally (see Murdock 1950).

19. There is one possible exception to this. Australian law required a three-year waiting period, in most instances, before divorces could be finalized (Day 1964). In the United States, where such periods vary across states but are much shorter, most divorces occur in the second and third years of marriage. The Australian system, though, eliminates this "peak" in the relationship between divorce and marital duration.

20. This variable was measured indirectly by the population growth rate, which was, on the average, higher in the industrializing societies (Kunzel 1974).

21. See Stinchcombe (1968:101-129) for a study of historicist causal imagery.

22. This generalization is appropriate at the systemic level of analysis, but not at the individual level. We know (Udry and Hall 1965; Aldous and Straus 1966; Lee 1977) that joint conjugal role organization is more prevalent among the middle classes of industrial societies. We shall also establish below that, in most of these same societies, the divorce rate is inversely related to social class. Thus, to transfer this generalization to the individual level would be to imply a false correlation, and to fall victim to the ecological fallacy. The proper interpretation is that marital *systems* characterized by joint conjugal role organization tend to have higher divorce rates than systems where conjugal roles tend to be segregated.

23. But see Glick (1975) for evidence that this correlation is decreasing.

24. This logic is similar to Rodman's (1965a, 1966, 1971) description of the "lower-class value stretch" noted in Chapter Seven.

chapter nine
Socialization

Introduction

Socialization of children has long been regarded as one of the primary functions of the family, and has often been considered to be the defining functional characteristic of family structures (see Chapter Three). While it is not always the case that biological parents are responsible for all aspects of the care and training of their offspring (recall the cases of the matrilineal Nayar and the children's houses in the Israeli kibbutz), it does appear that, in all societies, at least one adult of each sex is involved in both the care of children and the socialization process (Lynn 1974:32). But societies vary widely in the extent to which the responsibility for socialization is allocated to families, in the traits which adults attempt to instill in the succeeding generation, in the techniques of socialization employed, in the extent to which boys and girls are treated differently, and ultimately in the outcomes or products of socialization.

The scientific literature on socialization is voluminous, and comes from many diverse disciplines. We will not pretend here to cover all the issues involved. But there are many instances in which comparative social research has been able to contribute to the explanation of differential socialization behaviors. Our strategy here will be to explicate those explanatory theories which comparative research has helped to develop, paying particular attention to the knowledge of the effects of systemic factors which has been generated by the comparative method.[1]

We will begin our investigation of socialization with a discussion of variation in the values or goals which guide parents and other socializing agents in the process. While it is certainly not the case that individuals invariably act in accord with their values, it is nonetheless useful to consider values as important, if not necessarily perfect, predictors of behavior. In the socialization process, the values held by socializing agents mediate the effects of structural variables on socialization behavior and the outcomes of socialization (Kohn 1959a). We are therefore interested in investigating the dimensions along which parental values vary, the structural antecedents of such variation, and the consequences of these values for socialization behavior and outcomes. We will see, once again, that type of economic system and the differential locations of individuals within economic systems are among the most important determinants of socialization values and behaviors.

Parental values in socialization

From the sociological point of view, socialization refers to the process whereby individuals acquire the personal system properties—the knowledge, skills, attitudes, values, needs and motivations, cognitive, affective, and conative patterns—which shape their adaptation to the physical and sociocultural setting in which they live. . . . The critical test of the success of the socialization process lies in the ability of the individual to perform well in the statuses—that is, to play the roles—in which he may later find himself. (Inkeles 1969:615-616)

Most definitions of the socialization process emphasize the strong connection between socialization practices and the performance of "adult" roles. But parents do not simply pass on a unitary and static culture to their children. Their behavior is in part determined by their own experiences in the various institutions of their societies. In particular, the experiences of adults in the competition for resources, and their observations of and generalizations about the kinds of behaviors which are likely to result in successful competition, are crucial determinants of the values which direct their socialization behavior. These values are not always consciously recognized, nor are they necessarily intentionally inculcated in children,[2] but they nonetheless influence socialization techniques and, ultimately, outcomes. Characteristics of the "physical and sociocultural setting" in which people live are important antecedents of the content and method of socialization. Because the characteristics of social and ecological environments differ, the personal properties requisite for successful adaptation to these environments also differ. These differences are reflected, to a considerable extent, in the socialization process.

Socialization and type of economy

Parents socialize their children in accord with values which they have found to be important or useful in guiding their own behavior. Economic behavior appears to be particularly crucial in this regard. Barry, Child, and Bacon (1959), in a landmark study in this area, discovered a theoretically crucial association between certain dimensions of subsistence patterns and socialization values. They were interested in the extent to which cultures emphasized, in the socialization process, behaviors which might be characterized as "compliant" (obedience, nurturance, responsibility), versus the extent to which "assertive" behaviors (achievement, independence, self-reliance) are valued as outcomes of socialization. They reasoned that a major determinant of the relative emphasis on compliance versus assertion is the extent to which ecological and technological factors permit food to be accumulated. In societies where food can be easily accumulated, group welfare depends heavily upon long-term group planning, a complementary division of labor, and interpersonal cooperation. Individuals need to follow certain established routines in their work behavior, the benefits of which will not accrue to them for perhaps many months. Barry *et al.* (1959:53-54) argue that pastoralist or herding economies offer the greatest possibility of food accumulation short of industry, with agriculture slightly lower but still high on potential for accumulation. In these situations welfare depends upon group cooperation, a division of labor, and some form of centralized authority.[3] Therefore, ". . . adults should tend to be conscientious, compliant, and conservative in societies with high accumulation of food" (1959:53).

But where food cannot be accumulated and stored, survival depends upon day-to-day success in the struggle for subsistence. Aggressiveness, self-reliance, and individualism may thus be highly valued traits. This is most likely to occur in societies which depend on hunting and/or fishing. Here rewards or punishments are immediate; success depends upon individual skill and initiative; requirements for cooperation are minimized. Thus, "in societies with low accumulation of food resources, adults should tend to be individualistic, assertive, and venturesome" (Barry *et al.* 1959:53). The personal characteristics appropriate for each level of accumulation potential should, the authors reasoned, be emphasized in the socialization process.

To test these hypotheses, Barry *et al.* employed a sample of 104 ethnographies on primarily nonliterate societies. They used Murdock's (1957) classifications of subsistence type for these societies, contending that pastoralist societies represented the high extreme of the accumulation continuum and societies dependent on either hunting or fishing the low extreme. In addition, agricultural societies with no animal husbandry were considered to be intermediate in accumulation. These were subdivided into two intermediate categories according to their degree of secondary dependence on hunting and fishing. Agricultural societies whose dependence on hunting and fishing was less than the average (median) were considered to be relatively high on accumulation; those with greater than average dependence were defined as relatively low. Comparisons of socialization practices were then made between the two extreme categories and the two intermediate categories separately.

Six dimensions of socialization practices were conceptualized as relevant to the research problem. These included the extent to which children were trained to be (1) obedient, (2) responsible, (3) nurturant, (4) achievement-oriented, (5) self-reliant, and (6) generally independent and self-directed. Ratings on each dimension were made by judges who examined each ethnographic report in detail (see Barry *et al.* 1957 for the exact method). The theory obviously implies that the first three dimensions of socialization listed above should be positively related to food accumulation, and the last three negatively related.

When the extremes of the accumulation dimension were compared, responsibility and obedience training were found to be most strongly emphasized by the high-accumulation societies (pastoralist, with or without agriculture), whereas the low-accumulation societies (hunting and/or fishing) train their children most heavily for self-reliance, independence, and particularly achievement. Only the nurturance variable does not behave as expected; it is not significantly correlated with accumulation in any direction. Comparisons of the intermediate categories of food accumulation yielded similar results, although the correlations were lower. The authors then combined their dependent variables, leaving out nurturance, into an index of "compliance" versus "assertion." They found, predictably, that accumulation was strongly correlated with compliance and negatively correlated with assertion (1959: 59-60). A check for possible spuriousness according to variables such as size of settlement units, complexity of stratification, and type of descent system produced negative results (1959:59-62).

It is clear from this study, then, that certain types of economic and ecological conditions require different kinds of personal properties in the adults who participate in the systems, and that socializing agents attempt to instill these properties in succeeding generations. Barry, Child, and Bacon conclude their article with a concise summary of their findings, which

> . . . are consistent with the suggestion that child training tends to be a suitable adaptation to subsistence economy. Pressure toward obedience

and responsibility should tend to make children into the obedient and responsible adults who can best insure the continuing welfare of a society with a high-accumulation economy, whose food supply must be protected and developed gradually throughout the year. Pressure toward self-reliance and achievement should shape children into the venturesome, independent adults who can take initiative in wresting food daily from nature, and thus insure survival in societies with a low-accumulation economy. (Barry *et al.* 1959:62-63)

This line of research has not been extensively pursued in the cross-cultural arena, in part because the documentation of the theory which Barry *et al.* provided was so extensive and complete.[4] However, while those researchers were investigating the relationship between socialization and subsistence economy on the cross-cultural level, a theoretical and empirical orientation to the relationship between socialization and socioeconomic status was developing within the United States which evinces many parallels with the cross-cultural research, and which was later to have some important comparative ramifications. The primary originator of this inquiry was Melvin Kohn (1959a, 1963).[5]

Socialization and socioeconomic status

Although Kohn pursued his own research within the boundaries of the United States, and although he did not take the work of Barry *et al.* as an explicit basis for his theory, the parallels between his work and the cross-cultural research which preceded it can be readily seen.[6] Kohn contends that values mediate the effects of social structure on behavior. With reference to socialization, this means that the values which guide parents in their child-rearing behaviors have their origin in the location of the parents within their society's various institutional structures. He focuses particularly on the socioeconomic structure, which he conceptualizes in terms of social class.[7] He argues that members of different social classes in an industrial society are subject to different sets of experiences, are reinforced (positively or negatively) for different kinds of behaviors, and consequently develop differing perspectives on the way the world works and on how to cope with life effectively. These class differences, he contends, have their roots in the differential characteristics of occupations.

Kohn contrasts middle-class or white-collar occupations with working-class or blue-collar occupations. He points to three primary kinds of distinctions between them. First, in white-collar jobs the worker is typically involved with the manipulation of symbols, ideas, or people; interpersonal skills are both required and developed by these jobs. Blue-collar workers, on the other hand, deal primarily with physical objects; they make things, fix things, or distribute things. While these jobs may require considerable technical expertise, at least at the operative level, interpersonal skills are not usually crucial to work. Second, blue-collar work tends to be highly standardized or routinized; a skill is learned or developed, and then repeatedly applied to objects which may be identical, as in assembly-line work, or which at least have a common set of relevant properties, as in mechanical repair work. White-collar jobs typically demand greater flexibility, autonomous judgment, and decision-making; complete standardization is not possible. One automobile is pretty much like another automobile; when a belt breaks it is replaced, and the individual idiosyncracies of the car (or its driver) matter little to the person who replaces the belt. But any two high school students differ in an infinite number of ways. Both may fail a chemistry examination, but the reasons for their failure and the steps necessary to correct their problems are likely to be different. Third, blue-collar workers tend to be more closely supervised and thus less autonomous than white-collar workers. Individual creativeness, initiative, and problem-solving ability are less valued in the blue-collar ranks, but are at a premium in white-collar jobs.

The point is that blue- and white-collar workers have different on-the-job experiences and are rewarded for possessing and exercising different kinds of skills. This should foster different values in the two classes, or at least different priority rankings of values. Specifically, Kohn hypothesized that white-collar workers are likely to place relatively high value on personal characteristics such as self-direction, creativity, and individualism, while blue-collar workers will place higher priority on values involving conformity to externally imposed standards: obedience, orderliness, and neatness. These things are valued differently by the members of the different classes because the criteria for occupational success differ according to class, and because occupation is such a central and dominant component of one's life that its characteristics lend themselves to ready generalization to other arenas. Consequently, parents act toward their children in ways consistent with these differing value priorities, and both intentionally and unintentionally foster these values in their children.

These hypotheses have been quite strongly supported by a variety of data collected and analyzed by Kohn (1959a, 1959b, 1963, 1969). White-collar parents do tend to value the development of internal standards for control in their children, such as consideration of others, curiosity, self-motivation, and creativity; in addition, they place relatively high value on personal properties such as honesty and happiness or self-satisfaction. Blue-collar parents do not necessarily devalue these traits, but rather rank characteristics representing conformity to externally imposed standards more highly. White-collar parents do not negatively value obedience and conformity; they do, however, regard these traits as less problematic than do blue-collar workers, and thus rank the self-direction characteristics higher. Pearlin, in a replication of Kohn's work in Italy, concludes that ". . . external control is valued throughout the culture, but the middle class also emphasize internal control" (Pearlin 1971:57).

In summary, the characteristics or "personal system properties" which parents value most hightly in their children tend to be those which the parents themselves have found useful or functional in the occupational world. Class differences in values exist because the occupational experiences of the various social classes are different. These experiences differ on three important dimensions: closeness of supervision; whether the work deals with people and ideas or things; and a dimension which might be termed complexity (or nonroutinization) of work (Kohn 1969; Gecas and Nye 1974).[8] Internalized control, self-direction, personal happiness, and consideration for others are likely to be highly valued by people whose work is not closely supervised, who deal with people or ideas rather than objects in their work, and whose jobs require judgment and decision-making skills—in other words, the white-collar workers. Blue-collar workers, whose work tends to be more closely supervised, who deal with physical objects, and whose jobs tend to be routinized, find that conformity to external sources of control leads to the successful accomplishment of one's occupational tasks, and value this conformity highly for themselves and for their children.[9]

Pearlin's (1971) study of family relationships in Turin, Italy was designed in part to determine the cross-national generality and applicability of Kohn's theory of parental values. His work was guided by what we have termed above (Chapter Two; Przeworski and Teune 1970) the "most similar systems" methodology. He was interested in determining the extent to which variation in parental values across different cultural conditions could be attributed to the structural factors identified by Kohn. The ability to make this determination depends upon (1) similarity of structural conditions, and (2) variation in cultural conditions. According to Pearlin,

> With regard to this inquiry, there is reason to believe that the social conditions studied in relationship to the Turinese family also prevail in the United States, for most of these conditions are associated with industrialization and urbanization. Thus, Turin's system of stratification, the range of its occupations, the organization of its occupational settings, the nature of the goals toward which people strive and its opportunity structure are comparable to those of this country. (Pearlin 1971:14)

But cultural conditions differ. Specific differences abound with regard to socialization values and practices. Turinese parents are, for example, much less favorable toward autonomy or independence in children than American parents (1971:41). Cultural differences can be readily observed by comparing univariate distributions on parental values between the two societies. Pearlin compared his sample of parents of fifth-grade children with comparable data collected in the United States by Kohn (1959a); parents were asked to select the three most important characteristics for children from a list of 17 possible choices. There were, of course, some cross-national similarities: parents in both countries, for example, ranked honesty at the top of the list. But certain cultural differences emerged quite clearly: American parents were more likely to value happiness, popularity, and consideration for others; Italian parents were more favorable toward good manners, seriousness, and obedience (Pearlin 1971:53–54). Another way of putting this is that on the cultural level, Italians differ from Americans in many of the same ways that the working class differs from the middle class.

But there is considerable variation on parental values within each society. This intranational variation is much more central to Pearlin's objectives than are the cultural differences. Specifically, he examined the extent to which intranational variation in parental values could be explained, in Italy as well as in the United States, by reference to social class and occupational characteristics. Cultural differences are, in terms of his theoretical and explanatory objectives, residual.[10]

In general, Pearlin found that the theory developed with American data applied equally well to the Italian case. Values relate to social class in a highly similar manner in both societies, with the working classes valuing obedience and conformity most highly and the middle classes giving priority to happiness, self-control, dependability, and consideration (Pearlin 1971:55). Furthermore, Pearlin found (1971:58–68) that the same elements of occupational experience which account for the class-values relationships in the United States (closeness of supervision; working with people and ideas or things; and self-reliance in work) also explain the majority of this relationship in Italy. The effects of these elements are additive; that is, they each make an independent contribution to the explanation, as in the United States.

It is clear, then, that both the parameters of economic systems (the subsistence base) and the location of individual families within these systems are important in determining the traits and characteristics which parents value in their children. Later we will discuss the relationships between these values and actual outcomes of socialization, as mediated by parental behaviors and the influence of peers and others. For the moment, the following generalizations concerning the relationship between economic factors and parental values are appropriate as summary statements.

First: In hunting, gathering, or fishing economies, valued personal system properties consist heavily of traits involving individualism, assertiveness, autonomy, and aggressiveness. These traits are functional for individuals in situations where subsistence depends upon continuous success in the pursuit of resources (especially food) which cannot be accumulated or stored, and where the efforts required for success depend more upon individual capacities than cooperative group efforts.

Second: Personal system properties involving compliance, obedience, and conformity are highly valued under two related sets of circumstances: (a) In relatively undifferentiated economies, primarily pastoralist and secondarily horticultural, where food can be accumulated and where its production depends upon group cooperation and a rudimentary division of labor, it is functional for the group if individuals place higher priority on collective welfare than upon their own immediate self-interests. People must cooperate in both the production and consumption of resources. Therefore compliance and cooperation are highly valued personal traits. (b) In highly differentiated economic systems, those segments of the occupational structure directly involved in the production, maintenance, and distribution of goods and materials are rewarded for following the directions of others, and for cooperating with their co-workers in the operative and technical aspects of their tasks. Here again, compliance, obedience, and conformity are valued personal traits. In both of these situations, autonomous decision-making and individualistic behavior are likely to have negative consequences for group welfare or the collective enterprise; these traits are therefore valued less highly.

Third: In the managerial segments of differentiated economies, certain individualistic kinds of personal properties are once again assigned valuative priority. Here, personal decision-making skills are important for economic success; hence, autonomy, creativity, and self-direction or internal control are emphasized. But since virtually all tasks in this segment of the occupational structure in differentiated societies involve dealing with or managing people, the kinds of skills required do not precisely parallel those in preindustrial societies with low food accumulation. Individuals need to be simultaneously self-directed and cooperative. The conceptual dimension employed by Barry *et al.* (1959) ranging from "compliance" to "assertion" is not strictly appropriate for socialization values in the white-collar segment of industrial societies; highest value is placed upon a combination of certain aspects of these traits. Alex Inkeles (1969:616-617) has argued that socialization is a more complex process in differentiated societies because the social structure is differentiated, because statuses and roles are achieved rather than ascribed, and because of the rapidity of social change. To this we might add that socialization becomes more complex as differentiation increases because the qualities requisite for successful role performance are more heterogeneous, less unidimensional, and more variable across social strata.

Parental values and disciplinary practices

We know, then, that parental values in socialization in differentiated societies vary according to social class, and that this relationship is explained largely in terms of the different criteria for successful job performance between occupational strata. But what consequences follow from variation in parental values? Parents do not automatically produce offspring who are compliant or self-directed simply because they want to. If parental values have effects upon the outcomes of socialization, these effects must be mediated in part by parental behaviors. One dimension of parental behavior which may be relevant here is that of disciplinary practices.

Urie Bronfenbrenner (1958) argued that, in the post-World War II era, middle-class parents in general treat their children in a more permissive fashion than working-class parents. One manifestation of this greater permissiveness is a relatively less frequent use of physical punishment among the middle classes. But this does not mean that middle-class parents punish their children less; they are more likely than the working class to employ love- or affection-oriented disciplinary techniques. That is, a middle-class child is likely to be punished for misbehavior by the temporary withdrawal of parental affection; for the same infraction, a child of the working class would probably be spanked. Bronfenbrenner attributes this difference to the greater likelihood that middle-class parents will be informed concerning the advice and recommendations of "experts" in child-rearing. He documents, by a review of research and advisory literature over a large part of the twentieth century, a parallel between trends in expert advice and the styles of child-rearing prevalent in the middle classes. Middle-class parents had changed from relatively restrictive to relatively permissive in virtual conjunction with a similar change in the advice of experts; working-class changes in these directions occurred as well, but only after a considerable time lag. In other words, middle-class parents get their advice from experts, while working-class parents model their behavior after that of the middle class. This means that changes in working-class styles of parenting come much more slowly than middle-class changes. It also means, though, that if Bronfenbrenner is correct in attributing the causes of class differences in styles of punishment to variation in expert opinion, behavioral differences between classes at any given point in time are likely to be transitory and limited in terms of generalizability and theoretical significance.

Subsequent research on social class differences in the use of physical punishment, in the United States and elsewhere, has shown that working-class parents, especially mothers, are indeed more likely to employ physical punishment than their middle-class counterparts. However, this difference is consistently reported to be small (Kohn 1959a, 1969; Devereux *et al.* 1969; Devereux 1970; Pearlin 1971:103; Gecas and Nye 1974). Furthermore, Gecas and Nye found, for a sample of parents in Washington state, that punishment by withdrawal of affection was not common at any socioeconomic level.

The class differences in styles of punishing posited by Bronfenbrenner do not, then, appear to be either large or enduring. However, it does appear that there are important class differences in two related categories of disciplinary behavior: the use of reason and explanation in directing a child's behavior and the circumstances under which punishment will be employed. Middle-class parents are more likely than working-class parents to use reason and explanation in controlling the behavior of their children, and they appear to be more selective in their use of punishment. Both of these class differences are explicable in terms of the greater value placed on internal control in middle-class socialization.

Kohn argues (1969:104) that, because blue-collar parents value conformity to external control, they are likely to punish children directly for the consequences of behavior. On the other hand, white-collar parents, who are interested in the development of internal control, are prone to take into account not only the child's behavior and its objective consequences, but also the child's motives or intentions. A standard example of this difference has to do with a child spilling his milk. Blue-collar parents are likely to punish the child because the consequences of the act are disruptive and they do not wish the act repeated. White-collar parents are likely to attempt to infer motives: did the child spill his milk in the process of taking a swing at his younger sibling (if so, he should be punished), or in the process of clumsily trying to cut his own meat? If the latter is the case, the intention should be encouraged; spilling the milk would be an unintended and incidental consequence, and should not entail punishment. Gecas and Nye (1974), in their study of parents of third-graders in Washington state, asked parents what they would do in two hypothetical situations: (1) if their child accidentally breaks something they value; and (2) if their child intentionally disobeys them. Although parents in both the middle and working classes were more likely to punish in the latter circumstance than the former, Gecas and Nye found, as predicted, that middle-class parents discriminated between the two cases to a greater extent than working-class parents (1974:747-748).

In his study of Italians, Pearlin (1971:104-121) found that the nature of occupational experiences, particularly involving supervision, is more useful in explaining the use of physical punishment than a simple class distinction. He discovered that the working-class man who is under the close supervision of others, and who has no supervisory responsibilities himself, is quite likely to employ physical punishment, especially in disciplining a son. But frequent physical punishment of sons was also characteristic of one category of middle-class man: those who themselves supervise large numbers of workers. Furthermore, in each class those workers who were directly under the supervisory authority of only one superordinate were more likely than others to punish their children physically. Thus the use of physical punishment by fathers appears to depend more upon their location within their on-the-job authority structure than upon class itself.[11] Occupation is crucial to socialization not only because of the values learned, but also because one acquires particular modes of responding to children's misbehavior from work-related experiences:

> The location of men in the authority system at work and their exposure to power that is both direct and resides in a single superordinate are factors disposing men to employ physical discipline. The structure of constraints regulating the behavior of men at work serves as a basis of what men come to think as *necessary* to manage the misbehavior of their children. By employing with children a style of constraint consistent with that they experience, perhaps fathers are unknowingly training their children for the same kinds of occupational contexts in which they are located. (Pearlin 1971:122)

I would add that the same appears to pertain to parental values: they are learned within a particular occupational context and are largely specific to that context. Thus, although occupations in industrial societies are not inherited, parents socialize their children in such a way as to increase the probability of occupational continuity, at least in categorical terms.

Our discussion so far has focused exclusively on the effects of subsistence and occupational types upon parental values and disciplinary practices. However, the variables we have employed to explain variation in socialization attitudes and behaviors are more abstract than that; they may thus be generalizable beyond the realm of economics. Individual autonomy, self-reliance, closeness of supervision, and the other dimensions of economic/occupational systems we have discussed are concepts which may be applied to other arenas of behavior as well. Comparative researchers have recently realized that Kohn's theory, and others like it, may be extended to certain other systems, particularly the family system. In the next section we deal with this theoretical elaboration and the data upon which it is based.

Socialization and family structure

Two studies conducted in Taiwan by Nancy Olsen (1973, 1974) provide evidence to the effect that Kohn's logic regarding the relationship of parents to the economic structure may be generalizable, and that variation in family structure may have effects on socialization values similar to those of variation in socioeconomic position. Specifically, parents in nuclear families may differ from parents in extended families in the same ways that the middle class differs from the working class in industrial societies.

In the first of these articles, Olsen (1973) conceptualized the grandparental generation of an extended family as "alternative caretakers."[12] She argues, following J. Whiting (1959), that the presence of grandparents (especially grandmothers) within the immediate family structure obviates the need for high levels of independence training in the socialization process. Children do not need to be independent in extended families as they do in nuclear families because the grandmother is present to watch over them when the mother is otherwise occupied. In nuclear families, though, children must learn to fend for themselves; if the mother is not available, there are fewer substitutes for her in the child-care role. Some previous research supports this hypothesis. J. Whiting *et al.* (1966a) found that anxiety over status transitions is greater for children in nuclear families than for those in extended families. This may indicate that independence training is more severe in nuclear families. But not all earlier research is supportive. Murdock and Whiting (1951) report that independence training begins at earlier ages in three-generation families; but Whiting and Child (1953) found no correlation between age at which independence training begins and parental severity in reacting to manifestations of dependency by children.

Olsen hypothesized that if the necessity for independence training does decrease as the number of available alternative caretakers increases, then it should be the case that mothers in nuclear families should value independence in their children to a greater extent than mothers in extended families. This is, in fact, what she found for a sample of 37 mothers in a Taiwanese village. Twenty of these families included a grandmother, 17 did not. Measuring independence training by four items taken, in modified form, from the "Six Cultures Mother Interview" (Whiting *et al.* 1966b), Olsen found that mothers in nuclear families place considerably greater value on independence in their children than do mothers in extended families. Furthermore, within extended families, the greater the number of alternative caretakers available the less likely was the mother to emphasize independence in children. But mothers in extended families which contained more than one mother of young children were more likely to value indpendence, because these mothers must share the services of the grandmother.

> When the mother has the help of one "low-cost" parental surrogate (a grandmother), she is not very likely to emphasize independence training, and when two such surrogates are available (a grandmother and a daughter or great-grandmother), this type of training is even less likely. On the other hand, when sisters-in-law are present, causing a reduction in the amount of caretaking help the grandmother can give to any one mother, the tendency to emphasize self-reliance is increased. (Olsen 1973:516)

This logic does not, however, appear to apply to nuclear families. One might expect that the presence of older siblings in a family would obviate the need for independence training concerning the younger children. Grown daughters especially should be capable of playing the caretaker role, and their presence might then have the same effects on socialization as the presence of a grandmother. But this is not the case according to Olsen's data: the presence of older daughters in nuclear families had no effect on training for self-reliance. Olsen concludes (1973:516–517) that there is something inherent in the distinction between nuclear and extended families which produces the greater emphasis on independence training in the former.

How is all of this related to Kohn's theory relating socialization values to socioeconomic status? It is apparent that in primarily nonindustrial societies such as Taiwan, parents in nuclear families have something in common with middle-class parents in industrial societies: both value independence or self-reliance in children. But there is more to it than this, as Olsen makes explicit in a second (1974) study involving Taiwanese data. If, in societies like Taiwan, nuclear families are similar to the American middle class in terms of the value of self-reliance, then extended families may be similar to the working classes in terms of valuing conformity to external sources of control. There are both theoretical and empirical reasons to expect that this is the case. Olsen draws a parallel between the position of the working-class employee in an industrial system, as described by Kohn, and the position of a wife-mother in an extended family, especially a patrilineal extended family as is common in Taiwan. Both are closely supervised: the employee by his immediate superior, the wife-mother by her mother-in-law. Rewards, in both cases, are contingent upon conforming to the wishes of the superior and following directions. Mothers in extended families should thus value conformity and obedience in their children, whereas those in nuclear families, removed from the direct supervision and authority of their mother-in-law, should emphasize autonomy and self-reliance. Furthermore, following Kohn's logic (1969; Gecas and Nye 1974), if parents in extended families value conformity to external sources of control, they should also be more likely than parents in nuclear families to employ physical punishment.

There is some previous research to buttress these arguments. Cancian (1965), for example, found for a sample of Mexican mothers that those in three-generation families were more demanding of conformity in their children, and more dominating in their interactional style. And Olsen's previous (1973) study of Taiwan, of course, documented the greater value on self-reliance among nuclear family mothers than among those in extended families.

Olsen's sample, in this study, consisted of 107 mothers selected in such a way as to control for social class, family size, and family composition. She found, as predicted, that mothers in three-generation families (whose mothers-in-law were present) were considerably less likely to value self-reliance in children; this conforms to the results of her earlier study. She also found that these same mothers were more likely than those in nuclear families to value conformity and obedience, and more likely to employ physical punishment in dealing with the transgressions of their children.[13] Olsen thus concludes that close supervision of a mother by her co-resident mother-in-law has effects on parental socialization values similar to the effects of close supervision on the job in industrial societies.

There is one complicating factor in Olsen's analysis, which she recognizes and examines. That is, extended families are not only structurally more complex than nuclear families, they also tend to be larger in terms of the sheer number of members.[14] Previous research (Elder 1962; Elder and Bowerman 1963) has demonstrated that parents in larger families establish more rules for children's behavior, and employ more direct forms of punishment.[15] It is possible, then, that some of the effects that Olsen has attributed to variation in family structure are actually due to family size. By instituting sequential controls for family size and family structure, Olsen shows (1974: 1412) that each variable has independent effects on socialization practices. A high value on conformity is positively related to both size and structural complexity. The employment of physical punishment is related only to structural complexity; size has no effect. But the value on self-reliance is primarily a function of family size; autonomy is less valued in larger families.

Olsen concludes that the value of her study lies in the demonstration that Kohn's theory of the antecedents of socialization values and practices is generalizable beyond the occupational realm:

> When custom requires a woman to live together with a mother-in-law who supervises and controls her domestic activities, the woman's daily experiences are very similar to those of the typical working-class man in the United States. In both cases, the opportunity for autonomy and self-direction is absent. This paper presents evidence that the effects of "close supervision" on socialization are similar in the two settings. . . . Taiwanese women who live together with their mothers-in-law value behavioral conformity in their children, and use direct, external forms of discipline in preference to those which appeal to the child's feelings. These results could not be explained by the simple fact of expanded group size, or by the more conservative attitudes of women in extended families. (Olsen 1974:1413)

Not incidentally, we should point out that for the American working classes the effects of these two structural sources of close supervision (occupational and familial) are in all probability overlapping. Working-class nuclear families are more likely than the middle classes to be residentially proximate to their kin, particularly one or the other set of parents (Adams 1968). And the day-to-day involvement of these parents in the lives of their children and their children's families is also extensive compared to the middle classes (Willmott and Young 1960; Komarovsky 1967; Adams 1968).[16] Thus close supervison by a mother or mother-in-law may also be common among working-class mothers in the United States. This should, according to the theory, reinforce the tendency of working-class parents toward emphasizing obedience and conformity in their children.

Further observations regarding the effects of family structure on parental behavior, particularly maternal, come from the study by Minturn and Lambert (1964). They investigated maternal behavior in six cultures: Mexico, India, the Philippines, Okinawa, the Gusii of Africa, and a New England village in the United States. They found that the availability of help in domestic and child-rearing work, generally coming from co-resident relatives, is positively related to maternal consistency in child-rearing. This is perhaps attributable to the presence of others to minimize demands on the mother's time and energy; she is then able to devote these resources to the achivement of her objectives in child-rearing and to conform her behavior to her intentions more consistently.

Minturn and Lambert also discovered that mothers who contribute to family income or productivity differ systematically from those who do not, particularly in terms of responsibility training. Mothers who contribute resources to the family emphasize responsibility in their children more than do others. They are also more severe in punishing insubordination or defiance by children, and less permissive in general than noncontributing mothers. Their greater emphasis on responsibility may be attributable to their more frequent absence from the home and/or the necessity to concern themselves with activities other than child care, while their lower levels of permissiveness and tendency toward greater severity in punishment might be explained in terms of the Kohn-Olsen theory. That is, in the course of their productive activities these women may well be subject to close supervision, and their tasks are likely to be of the routine variety involving work with physical objects rather than people or ideas. This would account for their greater strictness and demand for obedience, even though they place higher value on responsibility in their children.

Socialization and political structure

Olsen also points out (1974:1413) the possibility of generalizing Kohn's theory to the political realm. She notes Stephens' observation that obedience training tends to be more severe in societies with centralized political authority ("kingdoms") than in tribal societies which lack any history of such centralization. Stephens shows (1963:372) that societies with autocratic states, or with an immediate history of autocracy, have "autocratic" family practices: marked intrafamily deference customs, clear cut power relationships, strict sex segregation in productive tasks, and relatively severe socialization practices. These restrictive family customs tend to moderate as the autocratic agrarian state gives way to democratic political organization.[17] Stephens offers no explanation for this relationship except an argument for cultural consistency: the family, in autocratic societies, ". . . looks like a sort of kingdom in microcosm" (1963:355).

But within the context of Kohn's theory, as elaborated by Olsen, this relationship between autocratic political organization and severity of socialization practices takes on additional significance. Parents in such societies may demand greater conformity, obedience, and restriction of spontaneity in their children because these are the traits which they perceive to be instrumental in getting along in the social world. These values guide their own behavior in relating to superiors; they therefore are valued in children as well. Variables such as closeness of supervision and routinization of tasks would undoubtedly have high values in autocratic agrarian states, thus intervening between political structure and parental values just as they mediate the effects of occupational structure on parental values in industrial societies. Empirically, this is consistent with our previous arguments: autocratic states or kingdoms tend to be agrarian, thus possessing high potential for food accumulation (Barry *et al.* 1959), and also typically manifesting extended family systems (see Chapter Five). Both of these features, as we have noted, promote high parental valuation of conformity, compliance, and obedience.[18]

Summary

We have found evidence to the effect that in the socialization process, parents are likely to value traits such as obedience, conformity, and compliance under the following kinds of conditions: (1) in horticultural and pastoral economies, where work is routine and must be accomplished collectively, and where the potential for food accumulation is high; (2) in extended families, where parents are themselves closely supervised by parents or in-laws and where the authority structure is clearly demarcated; (3) in societies with centralized political authority, where once again the economy tends to be horticultural, and workers are likely to be under close supervision; and (4) in the working classes of industrial societies. Under all of these conditions a similar set of variables may be operative to produce this value structure. These variables involve the structure of economic, political, and familial systems. Work tends to be routinized and cooperative; workers are usually closely supervised; individual initiative and creativity are not highly rewarded by the system. Under different conditions (in hunting and gathering economies, in the middle classes of industrial societies, and in nuclear families) individual initiative is at a greater premium. Parents are more likely to desire their children to possess traits such as self-control, independence, and autonomy. Although the theory we have been employing was developed to account for class differences in industrial societies, we have seen that it is potentially applicable to differences in socialization values arising from variation in type of economy and family structure as well.

We will proceed shortly to a discussion of the effects of these different parental values, and associated differences in parental behaviors, upon the personalities and behaviors of children. However, up to this point we have been ignoring a very important axis of differentiation in socialization: sex. It is almost universally the case that parents treat boys differently from girls (although the precise nature of the differences varies considerably), and that fathers relate to their children differently than do mothers. Variation in socialization values and practices according to sex of child and sex of parent forms the subject of our next section.

Sex differences in socialization

Differential socialization of boys and girls

There is little doubt that on both the individual and cultural levels of analysis, males and females systematically evince different kinds of behavioral traits. Research has consistently found girls to be more nurturant, obedient, compliant, responsible, affectionate, and adult-oriented, while boys are known to be more aggressive, achieving, self-reliant, egoistic, explorative, and peer-oriented.[19] There are, of course, many exceptions to these generalizations on the individual level, and even some cultures in which certain typical sex differences are reversed along some dimensions (see particularly Mead 1935; Barry *et al.* 1957; Ember 1973; Whiting and Edwards 1973). However, the patterns described above do characterize the great majority of cultures, including, in general, those of the contemporary United States and other Western nations. The crucial question is not whether these differences exist, but why.

I do not wish to resurrect the perennial nature-nurture controversy here.[20] To the extent that sex differences in behavior and personality are direct consequences of physiological or hormonal differences between the sexes, they are not subject to explanation by social theory. Some authors contend that most sex differences are in fact "innate" (for example, see Spiro 1958:247-248). D'Andrade (1966:191-194) cites evidence to the effect that on many dimensions of behavior, the largest sex differences occur at the youngest ages; these differences moderate as children grow older. This would imply that behavioral differences are not learned, but instead are modified or suppressed by cumulative social experience. Draper (1975) provides some valuable data on this issue in a comparison of two bands of !Kung Bushmen, who live on the edge of the Kalahari Desert in Africa. One group lives in a very lush forest environment; they make their living by foraging, and the land is so productive that they don't have to work at it very hard. Children, in consequence, have virtually no economic roles and are not trained in any particular tasks or skills. The other group consists of sedentary horticulturists; these people work quite a bit harder and children are assigned economic roles early in life. Draper reasons that if sex-linked behavior patterns are inherent in the species, sex differences should appear in both groups; if, on the other hand, they are socially acquired, they should be present in children of the horticultural group and absent, or virtually so, among the foragers. The data, recalcitrant as usual, fail to provide absolute support for either position. But among the foragers, Draper found that girls were more likely to stick close to home and parents than boys of comparable ages, showed a greater preference for adult companionship than boys, and were guarded more closely and corrected more often than boys. Draper concludes that boys and girls may to some extent be "preadapted" for their respective sex roles (1975:613). This reinforces her basic premise that biological and social explanations of behavioral sex differences are complementary rather than contradictory.

It is quite possible, as far as we know currently, that males and females may have inherently different capacities in certain respects.[21] In addition to the data already noted, the general consistency of sex differences across cultures lends credibility to this position. But is would be a major error to emphasize cross-cultural consistencies in sex differences at the expense of variations, which are considerable. In some societies girls and boys are subjected to similar experiences and evince similar behavior patterns. In others, their roles and behaviors differ markedly. While it is probably true that biology influences sex differences, there is no doubt whatsoever that social structure, culture, and learning are extremely important. We will concentrate, for the remainder of this section, on that proportion of the variance in sex-linked behavior patterns which is attributable to social and cultural factors. Although we cannot precisely estimate what proportion of the variance this is, we can be confident that it is both empirically and theoretically significant.

The basic thesis of D'Andrade's (1966) review article on "sex differences and cultural institutions" is that

> . . . the division of labor by sex comes about as a result of generalization from activities directly related to physical sex differences to activities only indirectly related to these differences. (D'Andrade 1966: 178)

A corollary of this proposition is that differences in the training, roles, and consequent behavior of children according to sex are attributable to differences in sex roles as they are defined for adults. There is a considerable amount of research which both documents and specifies this proposition.

We start, once again, with a research report by Barry and his associates (Barry, Bacon, and Child 1957) which involved a coding and analysis of just over one hundred ethnographic reports. Their specific objective was the description and explanation of sex differences along five dimensions of socialization: nurturance, obedience, responsibility, achievement, and self-reliance. Consistent with our generalization above, they found that most cultures trained girls most strongly in the first three of these traits, while the last two were more emphasized in the training of boys. They then rated each culture in their sample as to the extent of overall sex differences in socialization emphases. They found that the extent to which the sexes are differentially socialized is positively related to two factors, one involving economy and the other pertaining to family structure.

According to Barry *et al.* (1957) sex differences in socialization are greatest when the mode of subsistence places a premium on strength and motor skills thought to be characteristic of males. When large animals are either hunted or domesticated, and/or when horticultural activities involve the growing of grain rather than root crops, a certain amount of sheer physical size and strength is required for the successful accomplishment of subsistence activities. These activities are thus typically assigned to males. The division of labor along sexual lines is quite sharp; the economic experiences of boys and girls also tend to be different, with males trained to be achieving and self-reliant, while females are encouraged in the areas of nurturance, responsibility, and obedience.

Second, the researchers found that large sex differences in socialization are most likely to occur in societies with large family groups which cooperate as economic units in productive endeavors. The extent of sex differences was found to be positively correlated both with polygyny and with the presence of extended families.[22] Barry *et al.* reason that in smaller nuclear families, adult members must be relatively flexible in terms of role performance because of the lack of same-sex helpers or substitutes. If "men's work" or "women's work" is defined too rigidly, and if this work becomes temporarily excessive or if one spouse is disabled or otherwise prevented from doing the work, it would not get done. Consequently, men and women in smaller families must be able to substitute for one another in their economic roles; to a greater extent than members of large, more differentiated families, they must be flexible in task performance. This is reflected in socialization practices, such that sex differences are de-emphasized in comparison to the situation in societies with more differentiated family structures.[23] Thus it is clear that sex differences in socialization follow, to a considerable extent, from sex differences in adult role performance. The latter, in turn, depend upon type of economy and upon the composition of relevant economic units, which, in preindustrial societies, tend to be families.

There is also evidence from industrial societies to the effect that the extent to which boys and girls are differentially socialized depends on the degree to which adult sex roles differ, particularly in the occupational sphere. In virtually all industrial systems, males are expected to follow occupational routes to success, while for females occupational roles are typically regarded as secondary to domestic and family roles. We would therefore expect aggression, achievement, and self-reliance to be emphasized more strongly for males, and the more interpersonal skills and traits such as nurturance and responsibility to be more prominent in the socialization of females. In general, this is what has been found. Devereux (1970, 1972) and his associates (Devereux et al. 1969) have systematically compared children in the United States, England,[24] and Germany, and have found that in each society boys are subject to greater achievement demands and punishment for nonachievement than are girls, who receive more protection from parents and more training in assuming domestic responsibility. This has been replicated by Smart and Smart (1973) for New Zealand, although differences were smaller there than in other countries, and by Pearlin (1971) in Italy. Pearlin, in addition, found that the use of physical punishment on boys is positively related to parents' aspirations for their sons' achievement, particularly in the realms of educational and occupational success. Boys and girls are socialized differently because, in part, the roles they are expected to play as adults are different.

We know, from the research cited above, that the extent of sex differentiation in socialization is greater in England and Germany than in the United States (Devereux 1970), and apparently greater in the United States than in New Zealand (Smart and Smart 1973). We also know that parents in Germany, England, and the United States differ systematically in their relations to children. German parents are, in comparison to the others, highly nurturant and protective and tend to punish their children by withdrawal of affection. English parents are high on physical punishment and expressive rejection of children, and comparatively low on nurturance. Americans rank high on achievement demands and consistency, and low on indulgence. Devereux (1970) sums up differences between these nations by saying that compared to Americans, German parents tend toward overprotectiveness and English parents toward authoritarianism.[25] Unfortunately, no systematic attempts have been made to empirically determine why these differences exist. Research has focused on the differential consequences of these parental tendencies for children. We might speculate, based on the theory developed above, that there are systematic differences between Germany and England, on the one hand, and the United States on the other, in terms of adult sex-role definitions, such that the role behaviors of men and women are more differentiated in the former nations than in the United States. This should lead to the more similar socialization of American boys and girls which Devereux and others have documented.

Some support for this possibility is given by Boulding (1972) in a study which employed data from the Human Relations Area Files, governmental statistics, and demographic data from the United Nations on 58 industrializing nations in Asia and Africa. She attempted to determine the antecedents of female enrollment in primary schools. Presumably, the greater the proportion of girls enrolled, the more similar they are to boys on this dimension, and thus the smaller the sex differences in socialization. Boulding found that the strongest predictor of female enrollment was the extent to which adult women, in both traditional culture and the contemporary situation, occupied nondomestic positions, particularly occupational and political. She attaches a "role model" interpretation to this finding, based on the assumption that girls learn from observing examples of role involvement by women that they, too, can occupy these roles and acquire the training for them. It is also plausible to conceive of the presence of women in important occupational and political positions as indicative of properties of the economic and political systems allowing or favoring the utilization of women in these positions. Girls receive formal education because, as adults, they stand a good chance of performing roles for which this education is a prerequisite. But in spite of the fact that female enrollment in primary schools shows a strong positive correlation with gross national product, an indicator of industrialization, Boulding argues (1972:32-33) that industrialization narrows the range of the role opportunities for women in societies where they have traditionally performed important nondomestic roles (see also Ward 1963; Sadie 1967; Wheeler 1967; and Chapter Eight above). Thus industrialization will not necessarily result in changes in sex-linked socialization patterns. This is consistent with our observation that differences between boys and girls in industrial societies are quite similar to those found in preindustrial societies.

The studies by Whiting and Edwards (1973) and Ember (1973) also support this position. Whiting and Edwards report the result of nonparticipant observations of children in six societies (Kenya, the Philippines, Okinawa, India, Mexico, and a New England town in the United States). While they discovered that children do in fact manifest many of the sex differences in behavior attributed to them by the common stereotypes (i.e., boys are more aggressive, girls are more nurturant), they find that these differences are neither as large nor as consistent as the stereotypes imply. More important for our present purposes, they argue that differences in childhood behavior between the sexes are largely attributable to differences in socialization processes. Specifically, girls are assigned more tasks which involve domestic duties and caring for other family members, particularly infants; these tasks call for high rates of interaction with both adults and infants. Boys, on the other hand, are required to engage in activities such as herding large animals which necessitate either solitary work or cooperation with peers. The original tasks, and the patterns of association which arise from them, are held to be the antecedents of behavioral sex differences (see especially Whiting and Edwards 1973:187). The most significant of their findings, at least with respect to the theory we are currently pursuing, is that the cross-cultural consistency of sex differences in behavior may be due to consistency of the adult roles for which male and female children are being prepared. In their words,

> . . . all of the behaviors that are characteristic of males and females seem remarkably malleable under the impact of socialization pressures, *which seems to be remarkably consistent from one society to another.* (Whiting and Edwards 1973:171; italics added)

Ember's (1973) study of sex differences in Kenya adds credence to the proposition that behavioral sex differences are attributed to differential sex-specific task assignment. She took advantage of some unusual demographic conditions which caused many boys to be assigned domestic tasks which were, under normal conditions, the province of girls. She found that those boys who were assigned domestic tasks exhibited more responsibility and less aggressiveness and egoistic dominance than boys who were not assigned such tasks. But boys who performed normatively "feminine" tasks outside the home environment did not show these tendencies.

Whiting and Edwards (1973) found that the extent of behavioral differences between boys and girls, on the cross-cultural level, depends on the extent to which the tasks they are assigned differ:

> In sum, in both the East African societies where "feminine" work is assigned to boys and in Orchard Town, New England, where less "feminine" work is assigned to girls and where there is less difference in the daily routine of boys and girls, the behavior of girls and boys does not show as great differences as in other societies. (Whiting and Edwards 1973:187)

It thus appears that behavioral differences between the sexes may have some basis in physiology. But, as D'Andrade (1966) argues, most behavioral differences result from generalizations from differences directly related to physiology, to differences which are much more remotely connected to sexual dimorphism. Behavioral sex differences between adults at once have their origin in differentiated socialization practices and at the same time are causes of differential sex-specific socialization, in that children are trained to behave in accordance with the roles they are expected to perform as adults. The greater the extent of adult sex-role differences, the more the socialization experiences of girls will differ from those of boys and the more the sexes will differ from one another in terms of modal behavioral characteristics.

Variation in behavioral sex differences may also be linked to an important factor which we have not yet considered: the identities of the primary socializing agent(s). In particular, the extent to which the father is involved in child care and socialization varies considerably across cultures, and this variation may have important consequences in terms of the degree to which boys and girls are socialized differently.

Socialization and socializing agents

In general, mothers are more involved in child-rearing than are fathers (see Devereux *et al.* 1969; Devereux 1970; Pearlin 1971; and Smart and Smart 1973, among many others, for empirical evidence of this difference). However, there is much variation in the extent to which fathers are involved in the socialization process, and this variation may well have important effects on the behavior of children and adolescents. Furthermore, peers may be heavily involved in socialization; this involvement may be, from the point of view of parents and other adults, either intentional or unintentional. The structural identity of those who play a significant role in the socialization process appears to have a great deal to do with the outcomes of socialization.

There has been increasing concern, in recent years, over the American father's involvement, or lack thereof, in the child-rearing and socialization arenas. There is evidence that American fathers play a less prominent role in the rearing of children than do fathers in, for example, Germany (Devereux *et al.* 1962; Rabbie 1965; Lynn 1974), Scandinavia (Britton and Britton 1971; Kandel and Lesser 1972b), India (Sundberg *et al.* 1969), New Zealand (Smart and Smart 1973), and Ghana (McIntire *et al.* 1974). An influential psychoanalytic theory of early sex-role development holds that in infancy, both males and females interact primarily with the mother, and are expected to behave in a passive-dependent fashion which is somewhat consistent with the female sex role, but quite inconsistent with role behaviors which later come to be expected of males. Boys, therefore, must go through a "reorientation period" in early childhood, which involves the rejection of "feminine" identity and associated behaviors and the establishment of a "masculine" self-concept.[26] It appears that this reorientation process for males is considerably facilitated by the presence and consistent availability of a father (Parsons 1954b:304–305; Lynn and Sawrey 1959; Hetherington 1966), and by father-child relationships manifesting high interaction rates, emotional involvement, and affection (Sears 1953; Payne and Mussen 1956; Mussen and Distler 1959). Antisocial behavior on the part of boys (aggression, delinquency or crime, etc.) is often attributed to a failure to adequately make the transition from a feminine to a masculine identity. The male infant learns what constitutes "good behavior" within the context of his relationship with his mother. Later, when he learns that he must reject his feminine identity, he also rejects the norms defining socially acceptable behavior which he learned in this context, and which he then identifies with femininity. Therefore, the stronger the child's early identification with mother, and the less available the father is to the boy during early childhood, the more likely the boy will evince antisocial behaviors. Miller (1958) has argued that this process is particularly likely to produce behavior problems in the lower-class American male because of the father's frequently marginal role in the family. The young boy, rejecting the early feminine identity and the normative guidelines which go with it, has no effective model available to him to facilitate the learning of a socially acceptable masculine role.

This theory has some important cross-cultural implications. Many cultures customarily allow or require mothers and children to associate intimately with one another for a considerable length of time following the child's birth; these customs frequently specify shared mother-child sleeping arrangements. J. Whiting *et al.* (1958) found that societies in which such arrangements are quite prolonged are likely to have significant male "initiation rites," which boys must go through at about the time of puberty. They argue that these rites are necessary in such societies to clearly demarcate and establish the boy's identification with masculine roles and behaviors, and to minimize his problems in attaining a masculine identity.

In a study of the correlates of crime on the cross-cultural level, Bacon *et al.* (1963:292) hypothesize that ". . . crime arises partly as a defense against strong feminine identification." Under the assumption that the continuous presence of a father in the typical family facilitates the young boy's transition to a firm masculine identity, they posit that the frequency of crime in a society varies according to typical family structure. Family structures were ranked on the extent to which the father's presence is continuous. In monogamous nuclear families, the father should be quite consistently present in the household and available to the children. In polygynous societies with mother-child households (that is, "hut polygyny," where each wife and her children have a separate dwelling), the husband-father is only sporadically available to each child. Thus crime should be more frequent in societies with polygynous mother-child families than in those with monogamous nuclear families. Employing family structure as a measure of father's availability and judges' ratings of the frequency of crime from ethnographic reports of 48 preliterate societies, they found marked and significant negative relationships between the presence of the father and both theft and "personal crimes." They also found theft to be positively related to socialization anxiety, and personal crimes positively related to anxiety over independence and prolonged mother-child sleeping arrangements. They conclude:

> . . . the cross-cultural findings indicate that a high frequency of both
> theft and personal crime tends to occur in societies where the typical
> family for the society as a whole creates lack or limitation of oppor-
> tunity for the young boy to form an identification with his father.
> (Bacon *et al.* 1963:299)[27]

Further support for this position is lent by Beatrice Whiting (1965), who found
that factors predisposing to sex identity problems are related to physical violence
(see also Inkeles 1969:622).

Thomas *et al.* (1974:63-72) found, on samples of
adolescents from two cities in the United States, one in Mexico, and one in
Puerto Rico, that extent of adolescent conformity to the wishes of parents is
negatively related to degree of urbanization-industrialization on the cross-societal
level. As we noted in Chapter Two, this finding is difficult to interpret theoretically because of the generality of the independent variable; it is hard to determine what it is about urbanization-industrialization that should produce increased
nonconformity. (This is assuming that the relationship is not spurious.) However,
the theory of Bacon *et al.* (1963) may be relevant here. Part of the association
may be due to the increasing separation of work and home or family which
accompanies urbanization-industrialization, and the consequent removal of the
father from the household and from continuous association with sons. This
would be only a partial explanation, however, since conformity scores showed
essentially the same pattern for daughters as for sons; the theory we are interested in here has implications only for sons. Thomas *et al.* (1974:72-75) find
that in each sample, the strongest predictor of adolescent conformity is parental
support; we shall recur to this below.

Generalizations from cross-cultural data to the level of
individual families must be made with extreme caution. To argue that the studies
reported above demonstrate that individual boys whose opportunity to identify
with their fathers is restricted stand a relatively greater risk of manifesting
antisocial behavior would place us in danger of committing the "ecological
fallacy." However, Walters and Stinnett, in a review of research on parent-child
relations during the 1960s, are led to conclude that ". . . father-absence is
associated with lower masculine identification of male children" (1971:81).
Pedersen (1966) found a significant association between father-absence and
emotional disturbance for males on a sample of young adolescent military dependents, and Siegman (1966) found an association among medical students
between father-absence during early childhood and scores on an antisocial
behavioral scale. While these samples do not lend themselves to great generalizability, the results of these studies conform to those of the cross-cultural
investigations reported above.

John Mogey (1957) has written what is probably the

strongest contemporary statement of the argument (often attributed to the French sociologist Frederick LePlay) that a dominant father figure is a primary source of family stability. He points to historical examples from England, France, and Russia to the effect that legal and/or cultural declines in paternal authority have been followed by increases in family instability, juvenile delinquency, and other forms of "social disorganization."[28] He raises the possibility that decreases over time in paternal authority in the United States and other industrializing nations may have, or may currently be having, similar effects. However, he also argues that the father role may be in a state of transition in terms of its cultural definition, from authoritarian to companionate. This would increase the father's family involvement, create opportunities for the formation of masculine self-concepts for boys, and perhaps forestall the disorganizing effects of the decline in the authoritarian role.[29]

A study which supports Mogey's contention that the father role changes in the companionate direction with modernization was reported by LeVine et al. (1968). They sudied a small sample of 20 Yoruba families in Ibadan, Nigeria. The sample was selected in such a way that 10 of these families were classified as "traditional" and 10 as "modern," according to criteria including area of residence, father's occupation, and education. The authors then investigated differences in father-child relations between the two groups. The "modern" fathers, compared to the "traditional" ones, showed greater warmth in relation to their children and were notably more involved in family affairs, including particularly the making of decisions concerning the children. (Note how this corresponds to Robert Blood's [1967] finding that Japanese love-match husbands exercised decision-making influence in areas such as child care which arranged-marriage husbands left entirely to their wives. See Chapter Eight.) These differences existed in spite of the fact that the occupations of the "modern" fathers were such that they were physically present in the home much less often than were the "traditional" fathers. LeVine et al. conclude that modernization leads to greater paternal concern over the behavior and welfare of children, increased warmth and affection in father-child relations, and an emphasis on autonomy and self-direction rather than obedience and submissiveness in children.[30]

Although the sample in this study was extremely small and not selected in such a way as to be representative of any particular population, the authors point out that their findings are consistent with those of Prothro (1961) in Lebanon, Inkeles (1963) in Russia, and Bronfenbrenner (1963) in the United States. These studies do not, however, investigate the effects of differential paternal socialization involvement on children. The effects of variation in socialization practices and socializing agents on children are discussed in the next section.

Consequences for child behavior

There is a great deal of research on socialization pertaining to the outcomes or consequences of differential socialization experiences for children. We shall be able to cover only a very small fraction of this body of research. Because of this limitation, we will concentrate specifically on areas in which comparative research has proven to be instrumental in the development and testing of theoretical propositions. Some of the most salient work of this type has been done by Devereux, Bronfenbrenner, and their associates (Devereux *et al.* 1962, 1969; Devereux 1970, 1972; Rodgers *et al.* 1968). Their studies involve comparisons among American, English, German, and Russian children, and focus upon the antecedents of the development of internalized control.

Differences among the subject nations in terms of parental behaviors have already been noted. In essence, Germans tend toward overprotectiveness compared to Americans; they are also highly nurturant (Devereux 1970) and slightly more authoritarian (Devereux 1972). The English, however, are the most authoritarian, the most likely to employ physical punishment, and the least nurturant (Devereux *et al.* 1969; Devereux 1970).

In their discussion of differences between English and American patterns of child-rearing, Devereux *et al.* (1969) report the following systematic distinctions:

1. The American family has less parental role differentiation and is more egalitarian than the English family.
2. American children are treated differently from English children in many of the same ways in which girls are treated differently from boys in both cultures.
3. American children are treated differently from English children in many of the same ways in which middle-class children are treated differently from working-class children in both cultures.

They then proceed to hypothesize that American-English differences in child behavior will parallel those between the three sets of categories noted above.

They argue first that children from egalitarian homes with warm, permissive, and relatively undifferentiated parents are more spontaneous, extroverted, sensitive, expressive, and cheerful than those from homes with greater parental role differentiation, but also less emotionally mature, responsible, and persistent, and lower on leadership qualities (see Bronfenbrenner and Devereux 1961; Slater 1961). Studies by Butcher *et al.* (1963) and Barker and Barker (1963) report that American and English children do differ in these same ways, with American children typically approximating the characteristics of children from egalitarian families.

According to studies by Bronfenbrenner (1961a, 1961b) and others, many of which were noted above, girls tend to be more compliant, obedient, conforming, and responsible than boys. Devereux *et al.* (1969:268) hypothesize that this is due to the tendency of parents to use more love-oriented disciplining techniques with girls, and to accord them greater emotional support than boys. Since these differences in parental behavior are also evident in American-English comparisons, they expect American children in general to be more similar in their behaviors to modal patterns for girls, and English children closer to boys. This, in fact, is what they found: American children are more adult-oriented than English children, more likely to conform to rules, and less susceptible to peer pressure toward deviant behavior.[31] Although the expected boy-girl differences did emerge in both samples, the differing cultural patterns were also quite clear.

Devereux *et al.* (1969) then explicate Kohn's logic (1959a, 1959b), discussed above, regarding the differences between middle- and working-class children. They contend that the English style of child-rearing parallels Kohn's description of working class, while Americans tend toward his middle-class model. They focus particularly on the aspect of Kohn's work which indicates that children reared in the working-class style should develop, because of pressures toward obedience and the relative de-emphasis of self-direction, an "externalized conscience"; that is, they are responsive to the presence of an authority figure, an adult, for direction and control. Since English styles of child-rearing closely approximate the working-class model,

> (T)he implication would seem to be that for the English children, control of behavior may depend more heavily upon external authority symbols and constraints than upon an internalized feeling of commitment to some standard of conduct. (Devereux *et al*. 1969:269)

Data reported by Barker and Barker (1963), Anderson *et al.* (1959), and Sarnoff *et al.* (1959) as well as the present study show that English children are in fact more anxious about the exercise of authority, more likely to behave differently when adults are present than when they are absent, and more responsive to peer pressure toward deviant behavior. American children, on the other hand, indicate more internalized standards of behavior.

Devereux carries this line of reasoning considerably further in his report (1972) of the comparison between German and American schoolchildren. He argues that children will be more likely to internalize "adult standards" for behavior when they can personally identify with the representatives of those standards, primarily their parents. Such identification will be facilitated if parents are nonarbitrary and nonauthoritarian. Devereux points out that small but consistent differences in authoritarianism in child-rearing practices have been found between German and American parents, with the former being more authoritarian (Devereux *et al.* 1962; Devereux 1970:100–

101). For children with authoritarian parents, conformity to adult standards depends upon the presence of an authority figure; for those with internalized standards, the presence of an authority figure will make little difference.

To test these hypotheses, Devereux administered a version of the "Dilemmas Test" to samples of sixth-graders (120 in Germany, 174 in Ithaca, New York). The Dilemmas Test (see Bronfenbrenner 1967) consists of a series of hypothical situations in which the subjects are asked to choose a course of behavior where the choice involves a conflict between "adult" values and peer group pressure:

> In one such situation, for example, the peers are proposing to steal some apples from a tree in an unfenced but posted field, and the subject must indicate "what he would really do"—go along with friends and steal some apples too, or take no part in this activity. (Devereux 1972:105)

Responses to these dilemmas are scored according to the degree to which they conform to adult-approved conduct (that is, not stealing the apples). The experimental variable in this study involved the physical presence of an authority figure. In half of the classrooms in each country, the teachers were asked to leave the room; in the other half the teachers stayed in the classrooms, but remained at their desks and were instructed to show no interest in the experiment or in the children's responses.

Devereux hypothesized that the presence of the teacher, a symbol of authority, would cause children to respond in greater accordance with adult values, even though the teacher was not supervising or even observing the experiment. But more importantly, he predicted that the presence of the teacher would have a greater impact on German children than on American children because of the more authoritarian German style of parenting, which would lead to low internalization of standards. This turned out to be the case. Furthermore, in Germany, Devereux found the presence of the teacher to have the most significant effects for boys and for working-class subjects; this is due, he contends, to the more authoritarian upbringing to which males in general, and working-class children in particular, are subjected.[32]

Devereux also included a measure of "guilt-anxiety" in this study, which involves questions about the subject's attitudinal reaction to situations in which he or she had engaged in some adult-disapproved behavior.

> We reasoned that for children who have experienced a high level of authoritarian control at home and at school, guilt-anxiety will be associated with the fear of punishment more than with the thought of misconduct. This line of reasoning led to the prediction that, in the German sample, children would score significantly higher on our measure of guilt-anxiety in the teacher present than in the teacher absent condition,

while in the American sample there would be no difference. (Devereux
1972:109)

This hypothesis was strongly supported, adding further credibility to the proposition that an "internalized conscience" is fostered by nonauthoritarian socialization practices.

Additional evidence for this proposition comes from a
comparison of American and Danish schoolchildren by Kandel and Lesser
(1969, 1972b). In this comparison, American parents turn out to be relatively
more authoritarian; Danes tend more toward democratic and equalitarian
parent-child relations. Kandel and Lesser (1972b) report that, although democratic and equalitarian modes of child-rearing are more common in Denmark
than in the United States, they have similar consequences in each society. They
are associated with high levels of communication, affection, and desire to model
the parent on the part of the adolescent. Furthermore, Kandel and Lesser contend (1969) that Danes, because they are more democratic than Americans in
the socialization process, are more successful in internalizing standards for
conduct in their children. Americans, in comparison, socialize for conformity
to external constraints. American parents have more rules for their children to
follow, and produce conformity by applying the rules. In Denmark, on the other
hand, conformity to parentally desired behavior is more likely to occur in the
absence of specific rules. Danish adolescents feel that they have more independence or freedom of action than their American counterparts. Feelings of
independence, in both countries, are positively related to both democratic
parent-child relations and affection for parents. As a consequence, Danish
adolescents feel more affection toward their parents than do Americans.

However, Kandel and Lesser point out (1972b) that
the relationships between parental authority and the various adolescent behaviors
in their study are not linear. They found, in fact, that in most ways the children
of "permissive" parents (those who allow the child to make virtually all of his
or her own decisions) were least likely of any category to evaluate their parents
positively, to have a "close" relationship with their parents, or to communicate
well with their parents. Democratic parents, in both countries, clearly ranked
highest on these and similar dimensions. They conclude that "(P)arents can
reject their children in two ways, either by controlling them tightly or by
ignoring them" (1972b:79).[33]

Further support for the importance of close parent-
child relations in producing adolescent conformity comes from the study by
Thomas et al. (1974:69-79), who found that parental support is positively
correlated with adolescent conformity to persons in authority (including parents),
but parental control is not (see also Rosen 1964; Maccoby 1968; Aronfreed
1969). These findings emerged for all four of their samples, which included two

from the United States and one each from Puerto Rico and Mexico. In conjunction with the findings by Devereux, Kandel and Lesser, and others, this documents our contention that parental values are not likely to be perfectly realized in the behavior of children. Parents who value conformity are likely to be highly controlling, but this has no clear effect on conformity. They are less likely to be highly supportive; however, parental support evinces a fairly strong and consistent positive association with conformity. The crucial dimension appears to be the development of internal control, which is fostered by supportive parental behaviors but is, according to Devereux and others, inversely related to parental authoritarianism and control. Paradoxically, it may be that parents who value conformity most highly are the ones whose children are least likely to be conforming.

Devereux also reports (1970) that in England, Germany, and the United States strong orientation to peers is associated with both high punitiveness and high permissiveness on the part of parents. Since English parents are comparatively both punitive and permissive, this results in high levels of peer orientation among English children, particularly boys. Devereux also points out (Devereux *et al.* 1969) that high peeer orientation means, to a certain extent, opposition to parental authority.

One consequence of strong peer orientation, in most cultures, is reflected in responses to "adult pressure" and "peer pressure" in the Dilemmas Test, discussed above. A measure of the degree to which children are dependent upon external authority for control is the extent to which their responses to the Dilemmas Test differ between three experimental conditions. Subjects may be told that their responses will be either (1) completely anonymous, (2) shown to their peers, or (3) shown to their parents. There is evidence (Smart and Smart 1973) that children who give the most adult-oriented responses under the condition of anonymity are most likely to change toward peer-oriented responses when they believe their peers will see the results. This may, of course, simply be a function of the limits of the scale: a change away from a relatively extreme position is likely to be in the direction of moderation. The more extreme the initial response, the more "room" there is for the moderation effect to operate. However, it is clear that in most cases, children tend to respond in terms of adult-oriented choices when they believe adults will see their responses, and in terms of behavior which would not be approved by adults when they think peers will see their responses.

There is one striking exception to this, however: the Soviet Union. Bronfenbrenner (1970), in his comparison of Soviet and American patterns of child-rearing, reports that the responses of Russian children to the Dilemmas Test change in the direction of *adult orientation* when they expect their *peers* to see their responses (Bronfenbrenner 1970:78). Bronfenbrenner's explanation for this has two interrelated facets. First, he points to the predominance of affection-related techniques of discipline in the U.S.S.R, such as withdrawal of parental love and approval in cases of misbehavior; this may be due, he feels, to the high frequency of female-headed families following World War II and to the fact that women dominate the school staffs. This, he argues, results in a tendency for children (especially girls) to assume responsibility for their own behavior and that of others. This tendency is greatly magnified by the extensive use which the Soviets make of the peer group in the socialization process. Very early in a child's educational career, he or she is firmly ensconced as a member of a peer group, a subset of the child's class in school, defined and created by the teacher. These groups are pitted against one another in competition involving behaviors reflecting conformity to adult-approved standards. If one individual fails in his or her attempts to emulate the desired adult standards, the group as a whole suffers, and all members of the group are held responsible. This results in great pressure from peers in the direction of conformity with the adult standards, and the peer group is highly effective in this regard. Bronfenbrenner argues (1970:76–81) that this practice produces children (and later adults) who are obedient, conforming, and orderly, but low on creativity and individual initiative. Russian children also place lower priority than children from countries such as England, Switzerland, and the United States on values involving personal honesty and intellectual understanding (Rodgers *et al.* 1968).[34]

One might expect that this mode of socialization would be relatively ineffective in fostering the internalization of behavior standards in children, and that they would consequently depend on the presence of external authority symbols for behavioral guidelines. However, since in the Soviet system peers are clearly symbolic of authority, the child is virtually always subject to such a presence. The high rates of conformity noted by Bronfenbrenner are thus not at all surprising. Furthermore, the child's role as a source of authority with respect to his or her peers in all probability serves to inculcate in the child the normative system which he or she represents.

As a partial summary to this section, Devereux's (1972) conclusions regarding the relationships between styles of parenting, the development of behavior standards, and behavioral outcomes are appropriate. His conclusions are supplemented here with observations gleaned from related research which expand the range of the independent variables.

First, authoritiarian and punitive styles of child-rearing lead to, in Devereux's terms, an "externalized conscience" in children; this is probably true of highly permissive styles of child-rearing as well.

Second, under conditions of temptation to deviate from "adult-approved" standards of behavior, children with externalized consciences will tend to experience high levels of guilt-anxiety only in the presence of an authority figure. Children with internalized consciences will experience high levels of guilt-anxiety regardless of the presence of an authority figure.

Third, guilt-anxiety is positively associated with resistance to temptation toward deviant behavior.

Fourth and finally, children reared in an authoritarian manner are better able to resist temptations to deviate in authority-bounded situations. Children from democratic or egalitarian families show less variability in resistance behavior and are better able to resist temptation than those from authoritarian (or permissive) homes in authority-free situations.

Conclusions

We have seen in this chapter how systemic factors such as mode of subsistence affect univariate distributions on variables such as parental socialization values. Parents tend to value traits in their children which are functional for survival and success in their particular ecological/economic system. In hunting, gathering, or fishing economies, individual initiative, aggressiveness, and self-reliance are valued; in pastoral or horticultural economies, children are encouraged to be conforming and, perhaps most importantly, cooperative, since subsistence depends upon the success of the collective enterprise. The situation is more complex in industrial systems with highly differentiated occupational structures, because different behavioral traits are differentially functional across levels of the occupational structure. Self-reliance and interpersonal skills are valued by the middle classes, while the working classes give higher priority to conformity to external sources of control. In addition, parental values vary systematically according to characteristics of familial and political systems; these patterns are explicable according to the same theory which relates socialization values to the occupational system.

The modest ability we now possess to explain variation in parental values does not mean that we can explain variation in child behavior by direct extrapolation. Parents do not produce valued traits in their children simply because they value them. In fact, it appears that a value priority on conformity may be inversely related to conformity in children, at least under certain circumstances (primarily the absence of an immediate authority figure). But parental values do affect parental behavior in matters such as disciplinary practices, warmth or affection, and style of family decision-making; these behaviors, in turn, have important consequences for the behavior of children and adolescents.

Finally there is the matter of sex differences in socialization. Behavioral differences between the sexes have been implicated in virtually every substantive topic we have discussed in this book. Although some small proportion of sex differences in behavior may be directly attributable to physiological differences, the great majority of the differences are more reasonably explained by the differential positions allocated to men and women in social structures and the consequently different socialization experiences to which the sexes are subjected. Whether this should or should not be the case is, of course, not the prerogative of this book to decide. Social science studies values, their causes and their consequences; it does not and cannot legislate or manipulate them. But the fact of the matter is that sex differences appear in every known culture and social system, and marital, familial, and kinship systems are everywhere based in large part on divisions of labor between the sexes which are consistent with the ways in which male and female sex roles are differentially perceived and defined. Another fact of the matter, however, is that these differences in culturally stipulated sex roles appear to be smaller in differentiated industrial societies than in other kinds of social systems, and the chronological trend appears to be in the direction of further reductions in sex differences. This is demonstrated in many of the studies of socialization and of parent behavior reviewed in this chapter. If, as most social analysts predict, sex differences in behavioral characteristics continue to decrease, the implications for the structure of social systems and their component institutions, particularly the family, will be tremendous.

Notes

1. Even this statement of purpose is a bit too broad. There are certain branches of socialization research and theory which we will explicitly ignore because of space limitations, and because they are relatively peripheral to contemporary sociological theory. Among these are the "national character" studies, which often extrapolate beyond the bounds of their data, and the "culture and personality" school of anthropology. The latter is excluded because its theoretical concerns are more psychoanalytic than sociological, and because there are other good texts which explicate its logic and empirical support better than could be done here (see, for example, Barnouw 1963).

2. See Campbell (1966) and LeVine (1969) for excellent discussions of the influence of natural selection, which LeVine in particular relates directly to socialization. The issue of the extent to which socialization and child-rearing are consciously recognized, rationalized components of adult role definitions is an interesting one. For evidence that child-rearing was not recognized as a concrete responsibility until the nineteenth century in the

United States, see Demos and Demos (1969) in addition to LeVine's more general discussion.

3. See Chapter Five for our discussion of the value of large and differentiated work groups in societies based upon horticulture.

4. However, in a recent unpublished paper, Michael Welch (1976) found support for the Barry *et al.* hypothesis on a sample of 28 preindustrial societies employing a smallest-space analysis. He found that societies with horticultural and/or herding economies emphasize obedience in socialization, while those with a hunting, gathering, or fishing economic base rank high on independence training. His findings differ from those of Barry *et al.* (1959) on one point, however. The earlier authors hypothesized a positive association between food accumulation and an emphasis on nurturance in socialization, but did not find it. Welch's data, however, do indicate the existence of such an association. The different findings may well be attributable to differences in sampling and measurement; at this point, we cannot ascertain with any confidence whether or not nurturance and food accumulation are associated.

5. Another seminal work in this area was Miller and Swanson's (1958) analysis of differential socialization values and behaviors between "entrepreneurial" and "bureaucratic" workers. This study certainly deserves careful attention, but we shall bypass it here because it has spawned less subsequent research than Kohn's work, particularly in the comparative area, and because the empirical bases of their theory are less well documented than those of Kohn's propositions.

6. The following summary of Kohn's work is gleaned selectively from a number of his publications on the subject, including Kohn (1959a, 1963, 1969) and Pearlin and Kohn (1966), as well as secondary accounts contained in Pearlin (1971:51-72) and Gecas and Nye (1974).

7. By this I mean that Kohn analyzes his data and communicates his results in terms of discrete social class comparisons rather than employing socioeconomic status as a continuous variable or set of continuous variables. For analytic purposes, it is clear that much information is lost by categorization. Luther Otto (1975) has made explicit to family sociologists the analytic advantages which follow from treating socioeconomic status as a set of continuous variables, and I am in complete agreement with his position. However, Kohn's logic is very effectively phrased in social class terms. Since this terminology does lend itself to rather efficient communication, I will retain it here, with the caution that some distortion and loss of information is inherent in this conceptualization of the variables.

8. Each of these components of the work situation is related independently to parental values; together, they account for the majority of the covariance between class and values. See Kohn (1969:139-140) and Pearlin (1971:63-70).

9. Of course this does not mean that parents automatically produce children who possess the traits they value. In fact, it is not even certain that there is a correlation between, for example, a parental value on conformity and the trait of conformity in children. The relationship between parental values and outcomes in terms of child behavior is much more complex than this. Parental values do affect the behaviors of children, but not necessarily in a direct linear fashion; parental behaviors must be considered as intervening variables. More of this below.

10. This is a clear example of the difference between sociological (social structural) and anthropological (cultural) explanatory perspectives of which we spoke in Chapter One. Pearlin is obviously a sociologist.

11. See also Pearlin (1971:104-112) for an interesting discussion of relationships between parental aspirations and the use of physical punishment.

12. See Lambert (1971) for an analysis of the effects of parental surrogates in exchange theory terms.

13. Actually the independent variable was operationalized in a slightly more complex fashion than the simple dichotomy between two- and three-generation households. The more complete empirical generalization is that the greater the contact with grandparents, the less likely are mothers to value self-reliance, the higher their value on conformity, and the greater their use of physical punishment.

14. See our distinction in Chapter Five between family size and family complexity.

15. Cross-cultural research has also shown that there is a positive correlation between family size and severity of punishment for aggression. See Minturn and Lambert (1964), J. Whiting et al. (1966a), and LeVine (1969:518-519).

16. On the other hand, for data showing no relationship between occupational status and proximity to or interaction with kin, see Klatzky (1973).

17. J. Whiting and Child (1953), in their cross-cultural survey of socialization practices, found American parents to be above the median in severity on four of their five dimensions (oral, anal, sexual, and aggression training), and at the median on the other (independence training). This would appear to be contrary to Stephens' logic. However, as Stephens (1963:371) points

out, the sample which Whiting and Child utilized contained few kingdoms, and tribal societies (those without centralized political authority) were markedly overrepresented. Stephens argues that modern American child-rearing practices may well be severe and restrictive when compared with those of tribal societies, but would be much less so in comparison with kingdoms.

18. We should also point out here that this logic is consistent with the work of Swanson (1968, 1969, 1974), who related socialization values to kinship structure (see Chapter Six). Swanson contended that socialization in matri-lineal societies tends to be guided by values involving cooperation, confor-mity, and compliance. Swanson regards these socialization values as causally prior to the type of kinship structure; Paige (1974) and others have argued that the causal ordering should be reversed. Although this does not settle the debate, we should note that matriliny tends to occur most frequently among horticultural societies, which have a relatively high potential for food accumulation, are likely to evince extended families, and quite possibly have some kind of centralized political authority. There are thus many reasons to expect parents in matrilineal societies to emphasize conformity and obedience in socialization. The applicability of Kohn's theory, which employs closeness of supervision, routinization of tasks, and the nature of work as intervening variables, makes it appear more useful to conceive of parental values as dependent variables in this set of relations.

19. A few of the studies which document and/or discuss these sex differences are the following: Barry *et al.* (1957); Sears *et al.* (1957); Spiro (1958); Bronfenbrenner (1961a, 1961b); Maccoby (1961); B. Whiting (1963); D'Andrade (1966); Devereux *et al.* (1969); Inkeles (1969); Devereux (1970); Whiting and Whiting (1971); Whiting and Edwards (1973); Thomas *et al.* (1974); and Draper (1975).

20. Perhaps "resurrect" is an unfortunate term here. This debate is alive and well and living in many professional journals. I intend to indicate simply that there is no point in trying to resolve the issue here, since it would occupy more time, space, and other resources than are currently available.

21. For a direct and forceful disagreement with this position, see S. Linton (1970).

22. The former correlation was very slightly stronger than the latter.

23. Romney (1965), in a reanalysis of these data, suggests that the association between family structure and sex differences may explain, in part, the relationship between food accumulation and the emphases on obedience, compliance, etc. reported by Barry *et al.* (1959). He argues that societies

with a high potential for food accumulation are likely to have high frequencies of father-absent families, and the mother thus takes on most or all of the socialization responsibilities. If mothers are more likely than fathers to emphasize compliance, nurturance, and obedience, which seems likely, this should result in a greater manifestation of these traits by children in these cultures. See also D'Andrade (1966:194).

24. See also Beloff and Paton (1970) on England.

25. This contradicts some widely held stereotypes, particularly about Germans. For further debunking of the myth of German authoritarianism, at least with respect to socialization, see Rodgers (1971) and Koomen (1974).

26. For detailed expressions of this theory, see Parsons (1954b), Lynn (1961), and Lidz (1963:39-76). A good introductory discussion of the basic logic is contained in Udry (1974:53-58).

27. Bacon *et al.* (1963) also found a number of other variables to be correlated with crime, most of which we are not considering here because they are not ostensibly related to family phenomena. Unfortunately, their results were reported only as bivariate relationships; the extent to which family structure and identification with father make *independent* contributions to the explanation of crime is not investigated. Therefore, their statement that "... lack of opportunity for the young boy to form a masculine identification is in itself an important *antecedent* of crime" (1963:299; italics added) is not entirely warranted by their analysis.

28. It hardly needs saying that these examples document neither a correlation nor, particularly, a causal relationship.

29. Another of Mogey's hypotheses was that this process would eventuate in a declining divorce rate. The fate of this prediction needs no comment.

30. This latter distinction parallels Kohn's differentiation between the middle and working classes, as discussed above. It is quite probable that in this study, the emphasis on self-direction among "modern" fathers could be due to their occupational characteristics which, in comparison with occupations of the "traditional" fathers, were distinctively middle-class.

31. The measurement procedures employed to index these characteristics will be described below.

32. Sex and class differences in the same direction were found in the United States sample, but these differences were smaller than in Germany and not statistically significant. Devereux argues that, in particular, sex differences in socialization experiences are more pronounced in Germany.

33. See also Elder (1962), Bronfenbrenner (1961b), and Devereux (1970).

Bronfenbrenner and Devereux, in particular, have argued for what they call an "optimal level hypothesis," which is that desirable behavior in children is produced by moderate amounts of control, support, warmth, etc. in the parent-child relationship, and is prevented or discouraged by extreme permissiveness or authoritarianism. While this hypothesis is interesting and has, indirectly, informed my treatment of much of the material in this chapter, I am uncomfortable with it as a scientific proposition because of the unclear meaning of, and possible value judgments contained in, the concept of "desirable" behavior. I prefer to stand on statements to the effect that, for example, the relationship between parental authoritarianism and child's affection for parents is curvilinear.

34. Several other cultures explicitly and intensively involve children in the socialization of other children. In Tahiti, for example, Robert Levy (1968) reports that the responsibility for the control, supervision, and training of the children is diffused throughout the family, particularly its female members. Some of the consequences he perceives are similar to those noted by Bronfenbrenner for the Soviet Union. For instance, Levy argues that since there is no single source of authority for the Tahitian child, the child tends to perceive the normative system as nonmanipulable. This, in combination with the child's own role as a source of authority in the system, promoted conformity and compliance in children. See Ritchie (1956) for similar observations on the Maori, and John Whiting (1960) for a further explication of the theoretical issues involved.

References

Aberle, David F.
  1961   "Matrilineal descent in cross-cultural perspective." Pp. 655-727 in David M. Schneider and E. Kathleen Gough (eds.), *Matrilineal Kinship*. Berkeley: University of California Press.

Ackerman, Charles
  1963   "Affiliations: Structural determinants of differential divorce rates." *American Journal of Sociology* 69 (July):13-20.

Adams, Bern N.
  1968   *Kinship in an Urban Setting*. Chicago: Markham.

  1970   "Isolation, function, and beyond: American kinship in the 1960s." *Journal of Marriage and the Family* 32 (November):575-597.

  1971   *The American Family*. Chicago: Markham.

  1974   "Doing survey research cross-culturally: Some approaches and problems." *Journal of Marriage and the Family* 36 (August):568-573.

Adams, Richard N.
  1960   "An inquiry into the nature of the family." Pp. 30-49 in Gertrude Dole and Robert L. Carneiro (eds.), *Essays in the Science of Culture: In Honor of Leslie A. White*. New York: Thomas Y. Crowell Company.

Adelman, Irma, and Cynthia Taft Morris
  1967   *Society, Politics, and Economic Development.* Baltimore: Johns Hopkins University Press.

Aldous, Joan
  1965   "The consequences of intergenerational continuity." *Journal of Marriage and the Family* 27 (November):462–468.

Aldous, Joan, and Murray A. Straus
  1966   "Social networks and conjugal roles: A test of Bott's hypothesis." *Social Forces* 44 (June):576–580.

Almond, Gabriel A., and Sidney Verba
  1963   *The Civic Culture: Political Attitudes and Democracy in Five Nations.* Princeton, N.J.: Princeton University Press.

Anderson, H.H., G.L. Anderson, I.H. Cohen, and F.A. Nutt
  1959   "Image of teacher by adolescent children in four countries: Germany, Mexico, England, and the United States." *Journal of Social Psychology* 50 (August):47–55.

Anderson, Michael
  1971   *Family Structure in Nineteenth-Century Lancashire.* Cambridge: Cambridge University Press.

  1972   "Standard tabulation procedures for houses, households and other groups of residents, in the enumeration books of the censuses of 1851 to 1891." Pp. 134-145 in E.A. Wrigley (ed.), *Nineteenth-Century Society.* Cambridge: Cambridge University Press.

  1973   "Family, household, and the industrial revolution." Pp. 59–75 in Michael Gordon (ed.), *The American Family in Social-Historical Perspective.* New York: St. Martin's Press.

Anderson, R. Bruce W.
  1967   "On the comparability of meaningful stimuli in cross-cultural research." *Sociometry* 30 (June):124–136.

Andreski, Stanislav
  1964   *The Use of Comparative Sociology.* Berkeley: University of California Press.

Arensberg, Conrad M.
  1955   "American communities." *American Anthropologist* 57 (December): 1143-1162.

  1957   "Discussion of methods of community analysis in the Caribbean by Robert Manners." In *Caribbean Studies: A Symposium.* Mona, Jamaica: Institute of Social and Economic Studies.

Arensberg, Conrad M., and Solomon T. Kimball
  1940   *Family and Community in Ireland.* Cambridge, Mass.: Harvard University Press.

Aronfreed, Justin
  1969   "The concept of internalization." Pp. 263-323 in David Goslin (ed.), *Handbook of Socialization Theory and Research.* Chicago: Rand McNally.

Aronoff, Joel, and William D. Crano
1975   "A re-examination of the cross-cultural principles of task segregation and sex-role differentiation in the family." *American Sociological Review* 40 (February):12-20.

Bachofen, J.
1897   *Das Mutterecht* (second edition). Stuttgart: Krais and Hoffman.

Bacon, Margaret K., Irvin L. Child, and Herbert Barry III
1963   "A cross-cultural study of correlates of crime." *Journal of Abnormal and Social Psychology* 66 (April):291-300.

Bagley, Christopher J.
1969   "Incest Behavior and incest taboo." *Social Problems* 16 (Spring): 505-519.

Bahr, Stephen J.
1972   "Comment on 'The study of family power structure: A review 1960-1969.'" *Journal of Marriage and the Family* 34 (May):239-243.

1973   "The internal consistency of Blood and Wolfe's measure of conjugal power: A research note." *Journal of Marriage and the Family* 35 (May):293-295.

Bales, Robert F., and Philip E. Slater
1955   "Role differentiation in small decision-making groups." Pp. 259-306 in Talcott Parsons and Robert F. Bales (eds.), *Family, Socialization and Interaction Process*. Glencoe, Ill.: The Free Press.

Bardis, Panos D.
1964   "Family forms and variations historically considered." Pp. 403-461 in Harold T. Christensen (ed.), *Handbook of Marriage and the Family*. Chicago: Rand McNally.

Barioux, M.
1948   "Techniques used in France." *Public Opinion Quarterly* 12 (Winter): 715-717.

Barker, R.G., and L.S. Barker
1963   "Social actions in the behavior streams of American and English children." Pp. 127-159 in R.G. Barker (ed.), *The Stream of Behavior*. New York: Appleton-Century-Crofts.

Barnouw, Victor
1963   *Culture and Personality*. Homewood, Ill.: The Dorsey Press, Inc.

Barry, Herbert III, Margaret K. Bacon, and Irvin L. Child
1957   "A cross-cultural survey of some sex differences in socialization." *Journal of Abnormal and Social Psychology* 55 (November):327-332.

Barry, Herbert III, Irvin L. Child, and Margaret K. Bacon
1959   "Relation of child training to subsistence economy." *American Anthropologist* 61 (February):51-63.

Bell, Charles
1928   *The People of Tibet*. New York: Oxford University Press.

Bell, Norman W., and Ezra W. Vogel
  1968   *A Modern Introduction to the Family* (second edition). New York:
          The Free Press.

Bell, Robert R.
  1966   *Premarital Sex in a Changing Society*. Englewood Cliffs, N.J.:
          Prentice-Hall, Inc.

Bell, Robert R., and Jay B. Chaskes
  1970   "Premarital sexual experience among college coeds, 1958 and 1968."
          Journal of Marriage and the Family 32 (February):81-84.

Beloff, H., and X. Paton
  1970   "Bronfenbrenner's moral dilemmas in Britain: Children, their peers
          and their parents." *International Journal of Psychology* 1 (January):
          27-32.

Berkner, Lutz K.
  1973   "The stem family and the developmental cycle of the peasant house-
          hold: An 18th-century Austrian example." Pp. 34-58 in Michael
          Gordon (ed.), *The American Family in Social-Historical Perspective*.
          New York: St. Martin's Press.

Bernard, Jessie
  1964   "The adjustments of married mates." Pp. 675-739 in Harold T.
          Christensen (ed.), *Handbook of Marriage and the Family*. Chicago:
          Rand McNally.

  1968   "The status of women in modern patterns of culture." *Annals of the
          American Academy of Political and Social Science* 375 (January):
          3-14.

  1972   *The Future of Marriage*. New York: World.

Bernard, Jessie, Helen C. Buchanan, and William M. Smith, Jr.
  1959   *Dating, Mating, and Marriage Today*. New York: Arco Publishing Co.

Berndt, Ronald M.
  1965   "Marriage and the family in Northeastern Arnhem Land." Pp. 77-104
          in M.F. Nimkoff (ed.), *Comparative Family Systems*. Boston:
          Houghton Mifflin Company.

Bierstedt, Robert
  1957   *The Social Order*. New York: McGraw-Hill.

  1959   "Nominal and real definitions in sociological theory." Pp. 121-144
          in Llewellyn Gross (ed.), *Symposium on Sociological Theory*. New
          York: Harper and Row.

Blake, Judith
  1961   *Family Structure in Jamaica: The Social Context of Reproduction*.
          New York: The Free Press.

Blood, Robert O., Jr.
  1952   "Romance and premarital intercourse—incompatibles." *Marriage and
          Family Living* 14 (May):105-108.

  1967   *Love Match and Arranged Marriage: A Tokyo-Detroit Comparison*.
          New York: The Free Press.

1969   "Kinship interaction and marital solidarity." *Merrill-Palmer Quarterly* 15 (April):171-184.

Blood, Robert O., Jr., and Reuben Hill
1970   "Comparative analysis of family power structure: Problems of measurement and interpretation." Pp. 525-535 in Reuben Hill and Rene Konig (eds.), *Families in East and West*. Paris: Mouton.

Blood, Robert O., Jr., and Y.J. Takeshita
1964   "Development of cross-cultural equivalence of measure of marital interaction for U.S.A. and Japan." *Transactions of the Fifth World Congress of Sociology* (Vol. 4): 333-344. Louvain: International Sociological Association.

Blood, Robert O., Jr., and Donald M. Wolfe
1960   *Husbands and Wives: The Dynamics of Married Living*. New York: Macmillan.

Blumberg, Rae Lesser, and Robert F. Winch
1972   "Societal complexity and familial complexity: Evidence for the curvilinear hypothesis." *American Journal of Sociology* 77 (March): 898-920.

Boas, Franz
1896   "The limitations of the comparative method in anthropology." *Science* 4: 901-908.

Bogoras, Waldemar
1909   "The Chukchee." *Memoirs of the American Museum of Natural History* 11 (Part 3).

Boserup, Esther
1970   *Women's Role in Economic Development*. London: George Allen and Unwin, Ltd.

Bossen, Laurel
1975   "Women in modernizing societies." *American Ethnologist* 3 (November):587-601.

Bott, Elizabeth
1957   *Family and Social Network*. London: Tavistock Publications.

Boulding, Elise
1972   "Women as role models in industrializing societies: A macro-system model of socialization for civic competence." Pp. 11-34 in Marvin B. Sussman and Betty E. Cogswell (eds.), *Cross-National Family Research*. Leiden, Netherlands: E.J. Brill.

Bowen, E.S.
1954   *Return to Laughter*. London: Victor Gollancz, Ltd.

Briffault, Robert
1931   *The Mothers*. New York: Macmillan.

Britton, Joseph H., and Jean O. Britton
1971   "Children's perceptions of their parents: A comparison of Finnish and American children." *Journal of Marriage and the Family* 33 (February):214-218.

Bronfenbrenner, Urie
1958   "Socialization and social class through time and space." Pp. 400-425 in E.E. Maccoby, T.M. Newcomb, and E.L. Hartley (eds.), *Readings in Social Psychology* (third edition). New York: Holt, Rinehart, and Winston, Inc.

1961a   "Toward a theoretical model for the analysis of parent-child relationships in a social context." Pp. 90-109 in J.C. Glidewell (ed.), *Parental Attitudes and Child Behavior.* Springfield, Ill.: Charles C Thomas Company.

1961b   "Some familial antecedents of responsibility and leadership in adolescents." Pp. 239-272 in L. Petrullo and B.L. Bass (eds.), *Leadership and Interpersonal Behavior.* New York: Holt, Rinehart, and Winston, Inc.

1963   "The changing American child—a speculative analysis." Pp. 347-356 in N.J. Smelser and W.J. Smelser (eds.), *Personality and Social Systems.* New York: John Wiley and Sons.

1967   "Response to pressure from peers versus adults among Soviet and American schoolchildren." *International Journal of Psychology* 2 (April):199-207.

1970   *Two Worlds of Childhood: U.S. and U.S.S.R.* New York: Russell Sage Foundation.

Bronfenbrenner, Urie, and Edward C. Devereux, Jr.
1961   "Family authority and adolescent behavior." *Proceedings of the Sixteenth International Congress of Psychology.* Bonn, Germany.

Brown, Judith K.
1970   "A note on the division of labor by sex." *American Anthropologist* 72 (October):1073-1078.

Buehler, Marilyn H., Andrew J. Weigert, and Darwin L. Thomas
1974   "Correlates of conjugal power: A five-culture analysis of adolsecent perceptions." *Journal of Comparative Family Studies* 5 (Spring): 5-16.

Bumpass, Larry L., and James A. Sweet
1972   "Differentials in marital instability: 1970." *American Sociological Review* 37 (December):754-766.

Burch, Thomas K.
1967   "The size and structure of families: A comparative analysis of census data." *American Sociological Review* 32 (June):347-353.

1970   "Some demographic determinants of average household size: An analytic approach." *Demography* 7 (February):61-69.

Burgess, Ernest W., and L.S. Cottrell
1939   *Predicting Success or Failure in Marriage.* New York: Prentice-Hall, Inc.

Burgess, Ernest W., Harvey J. Locke, and Mary M. Thomes
1963   *The Family: From Institution to Companionship* (third edition). New York: American Book Company.

Burgess, Ernest W., and Paul Wallin
1953   *Engagement and Marriage.* Philadelphia: J.B. Lippincott Company.

Buric, Olivera, and Andjelka Zecevic
1967   "Family authority, marital satisfaction, and the social network in Yugoslavia." *Journal of Marriage and the Family* 29 (May):325-336.

Butcher, H.J., M. Ainsworth, and J.E. Nesbitt
1963   "A comparison of British and American children." *British Journal of Educational Psychology* 33 (No. 3):278-285.

Campbell, Donald T.
1966   "Variation and selective-retention in sociocultural evolution." Pp. 19-49 in H.R. Barringer, G.I. Blankston, and R.W. Mack (eds.), *Social Change in Developing Areas: A Re-Interpretation of Evolutionary Theory*. Cambridge, Mass.: Schenkman.

Cancian, Francesca
1965   "The effect of patrilocal households on nuclear family interaction in Zinacantan." *Estudios de Cultura Maya* 5: 299-315.

Cantril, Hadley
1963   "A study of aspirations." *Scientific American* 208 (February):41-45.

1965   *Patterns of Human Concerns.* New Brunswick, N.J.: Rutgers University Press.

Cantril, Hadley, and Lloyd A. Free
1962   "Hopes and fears for self and country." *American Behavioral Scientist* 6 (Supplement).

Carden, Maren Lockwood
1970   *Oneida: Utopian Community to Modern Corporation.* Baltimore: Johns Hopkins University Press.

Casagrande, Joseph B.
1954   "The ends of translation." *International Journal of American Linguistics* 20 (October):335-340.

Centers, Richard, Bertram H. Raven, and Aroldo Rodrigues
1971   "Conjugal power structure: A re-examination." *American Sociological Review* 36 (April):264-278.

Christensen, Harold T.
1960   "Cultural relativism and premarital sex norms." *American Sociological Review* 25 (February):31-39.

1962   "A cross-cultural comparison of attitudes toward marital infidelity." *International Journal of Comparative Sociology* 3 (September): 124-137.

1963a   "Child spacing analysis via record linkage: New data plus a summing up from earlier reports." *Marriage and Family Living* 25 (August): 272-280.

1963b   "Timing of first pregnancy as a factor in divorce: A cross-cultural analysis." *Eugenics Quarterly* 10 (September):119-130.

1966   "Scandinavian and American sex norms: Some comparisons with sociological implications." *Journal of Social Issues* 22 (April):60-75.

1969   "Normative theory derived from cross-cultural family research." *Journal of Marriage and the Family* 31 (May):209-222.

Christensen, Harold T., and George R. Carpenter
  1962a   "Timing patterns in the development of sexual intimacy." *Marriage and Family Living* 24 (February):30-35.
  1962b   "Value-behavior discrepancies regarding premarital coitus in three Western cultures." *American Sociological Review* 27 (February): 66-74.

Christensen, Harold T., and Christina F. Gregg
  1970   "Changing sex norms in America and Scandinavia." *Journal of Marriage and the Family* 32 (November):616-627.

Chu, Hsien-Jen
  1969   "A note to utilizing Murdock's ethnographic survey material for cross-cultural family research." *Journal of Marriage and the Family* 31 (May):311-314.

Chu, Hsien-Jen, and J. Selwyn Hollingsworth
  1969   "A cross-cultural study of the relationships between family types and social stratification." *Journal of Marriage and the Family* 31 (May):322-327.

Clayton, Richard R.
  1972   "Premarital sexual intercourse: A substantive test of the contingent consistency model." *Journal of Marriage and the Family* 34 (May): 273-281.

Coale, Ansley J., Lloyd A. Fallers, Marion J. Levy, David M. Schneider, and Sylvan S. Thompkins
  1965   *Aspects of the Analysis of Family Structure.* Princeton, N.J.: Princeton University Press.

Cohen, Albert K., and Harold M. Hodges
  1963   "Characteristics of the lower-blue-collar class." *Social Problems* 10 (Spring):303-334.

Conklin, George H.
  1973   "Emerging conjugal role patterns in a joint family system: Correlates of social change in Dharwar, India." *Journal of Marriage and the Family* 35 (November):742-748.

Coppinger, Robert M., and Paul C. Rosenblatt
  1968   "Romantic love and subsistence dependence of spouses." *Southwestern Journal of Anthropology* 24 (Autumn):310-319.

Cowgill, Donald O., and Lowell D. Holmes
  1972   *Aging and Modernization.* New York: Appleton-Century-Crofts.

Cromwell, Ronald E., Ramon Corrales, and Peter M. Torsiello
  1973   "Normative patterns of marital decision-making power and influence in Mexico and the United States: A partial test of resource and ideology theory." *Journal of Comparative Family Studies* 4 (Autumn): 177-196.

Cromwell, Ronald E., and Stephen G. Wieting
  1975   "Multidimensionality of conjugal decision-making indices: Comparative analyses of five samples." *Journal of Comparative Family Studies* 6 (Autumn):139-152.

Cutright, Phillips
1971a "Economic events and illegitimacy in developed countries." *Journal of Comparative Family Studies* 2 (Spring):33-53.

1971b "Income and family events: Marital stability." *Journal of Marriage and the Family* 33 (May):291-306.

D'Andrade, Roy G.
1966 "Sex differences and cultural institutions." Pp. 173-204 in Eleanor E. Maccoby (ed.), *The Development of Sex Differences*. Palo Alto, California: Stanford University Press.

Davenport, William
1959 "Nonunilinear descent and descent groups." *American Anthropologist* 61 (August):557-572.

Davis, Kingsley
1966 "Sexual behavior." Pp. 322-372 in Robert K. Merton and Robert A. Nisbet (eds.), *Contemporary Social Problems*. New York: Harcourt, Brace & World, Inc.

Day, Lincoln H.
1964 "Patterns of divorce in Australia and the United States." *American Sociological Review* 29 (August):509-522.

DeFleur, Melvin L., William V. D'Antonio, and Lois B. DeFleur
1971 *Sociology: Man in Society*. Glenview, Ill.: Scott, Foresman & Company.

Demos, John, and Virginia Demos
1969 "Adolescence in historical perspective." *Journal of Marriage and the Family* 31 (November):632-638.

Devereux, Edward C., Jr.
1970 "Socialization in cross-cultural perspective: Comparative study of England, Germany, and the United States." Pp. 72-106 in Reuben Hill and Rene Konig (eds.), *Families in East and West*. Paris: Mouton.

1972 "Authority and moral development among German and American children: A cross-national pilot experiment." *Journal of Comparative Family Studies* 3 (Spring):99-124.

Devereux, Edward C., Jr., Urie Bronfenbrenner, and Robert R. Rodgers
1969 "Child-rearing in England and the United States: A cross-national comparison." *Journal of Marriage and the Family* 31 (May):257-270.

Devereux, Edward C., Jr., Urie Bronfenbrenner, and G.J. Suci
1962 "Patterns of parent behavior in the United States of America and the Federal Republic of Germany: A cross-national comparison." *International Social Science Journal* 14 (No. 3):488-506.

Dodd, Peter C.
1973 "Family honor and the forces of change in Arab society." *International Journal of Middle East Studies* 4 (January):40-54.

Drake, Michael
1969 *Population and Society in Norway, 1735-1865*. Cambridge: Cambridge University Press.

Draper, Patricia
1975 "Cultural pressure on sex differences." *American Ethnologist* 2 (November):602-616.

Dressler, David, and Donald Carns
1973 *Sociology: The Study of Human Interaction* (second edition). New York: Alfred A. Knopf.

Driver, Harold E.
1961 *Indians of North America.* Chicago: University of Chicago Press.

Driver, Harold E., and W. Massey
1957 "Comparative studies of North American Indians." *Transactions of the American Philosophical Society* 47: 165-456.

Durkheim, Emile
1893 *De la Division du Travail Social.* Paris: Alcan.

1951 *Suicide: A Study in Sociology.* New York: The Free Press.

Duvall, Evelyn
1954 *In-Laws: Pro and Con.* New York: Association Press.

Eisenstadt, S.N.
1961 "Anthropological studies of complex societies." *Current Anthropology* 2 (June):201-222.

Elder, Glen H., Jr.
1962 "Structural variations in the child-rearing relationship." *Sociometry* 25 (November):241-262.

Elder, Glen H., Jr., and Charles E. Bowerman
1963 "Family structure and child-rearing patterns: The effect of family size and sex composition." *American Sociological Review* 28 (December):891-905

Ember, Carol R.
1973 "Feminine task assignment and the social behavior of boys." *Ethos* 1: 424-439.

Ember, Melvin, and Carol R. Ember
1971 "The conditions favoring matrilocal versus patrilocal residence." *American Anthropologist* 73 (June):571-594.

Engels, Friedrich
1962 "On the origin of the family, private property, and the state." In Karl Marx and Friedrich Engels, *Selected Works, Volume II.* Moscow: Foreign Languages Publishing House.

Eshleman, J. Ross
1974 *The Family.* New York: Allyn and Bacon

Etzioni, Amitai, and Frederic L. DuBow
1970 *Comparative Perspectives: Theories and Methods.* Boston: Little, Brown and Company.

Evans-Pritchard, E.E.
1951 *Kinship and Marriage Among the Nuer.* London: Oxford University Press.

1965 "The position of women in primitive societies and our own." Pp. 37-58 in E.E. Evans-Pritchard, *The Position of Women in Primitive Societies and Other Essays in Social Anthropology.* London: Faber and Faber.

Fallers, Lloyd
1957 "Some determinants of marriage stability in Bugosa: A reformulation of Gluckman's hypotheses." *Africa* 27 (No. 2):106-123.

Farber, Bernard
1964 *Family: Organization and Interaction.* San Francisco: Chandler.

1966 "Kinship laterality and the emotionally disturbed child." Pp. 69-78 in Bernard Farber (ed.), *Kinship and Family Organization.* New York: John Wiley & Sons, Inc.

Faris, Robert E. L.
1964 "The discipline of sociology." Pp. 1-35 in R.E.L. Faris (ed.), *Handbook of Modern Sociology.* Chicago: Rand McNally.

Firth, Raymond
1957 *Two Studies of Kinship in London.* London: Athlone Press.

Ford, Clellan S.
1970 "Some primitive societies." Pp. 25-43 in George H. Seward and Robert C. Williamson (eds.), *Sex Roles in Changing Society.* New York: Random House.

Ford, Clellan S., and Frank A. Beach
1951 *Patterns of Sexual Behavior.* New York: Harper & Row.

Forde, Daryll
1964 *Yako Society.* Cambridge: Oxford University Press.

Fortes, Meyer
1959a "Primitive kinship." *Scientific American* 200 (June):147-158.

1959b "Descent, filiation, and affinity: A rejoinder to Dr. Leach, Part I." *Man* 59 (November):193-197.

1959c "Descent, filiation, and affinity: A rejoinder to Dr. Leach, Part II." *Man* 59 (December):206-212.

Fox, Greer Litton
1973 "Another look at the comparative resources model: Assessing the balance of power in Turkish marriages." *Journal of Marriage and the Family* 35 (November):718-730.

1975 "Love match and arranged marriage in a modernizing nation: Mate selection in Ankara, Turkey." *Journal of Marriage and the Family* 37 (February):180-193.

Fox, Robin
1967 *Kinship and Marriage.* Baltimore: Penguin Books.

Freeman, Linton C.
1958 "Marriage without love: Mate-selection in non-Western societies." Pp. 20-39 in Robert F. Winch (ed.), *Mate Selection.* New York: Harper & Row.

Freeman, Linton C., and Robert F. Winch
  1957   "Societal complexity: An empirical test of a typology of societies."
          American Journal of Sociology 62 (March):461–466.

Freese, Lee
  1972   "Cumulative sociological knowledge." *American Sociological Review*
          37 (August):472–482.

Freud, Sigmund
  1922   *Group Psychology and the Analysis of the Ego.* London: Hogarth.

Frey, Frederick W.
  1970   "Cross-cultural survey research in political science." Pp. 175–294
          in Robert T. Holt and John E. Turner (eds.), *The Methodology of
          Comparative Research.* New York: The Free Press.

Friedl, Ernestine
  1967   "The position of women: Appearance and reality." *Anthropological
          Quarterly* 40 (July):97–108.

Furstenberg, Frank F., Jr.
  1966   "Industrialization and the American family: A look backward."
          American Sociological Review 31 (June):326–337.

Garigue, Philip
  1956   "French Canadian kinship and urban life." *American Anthropologist*
          58 (December):1090–1101.

Gecas, Viktor, and F. Ivan Nye
  1974   "Sex and class differences in parent-child interaction: A test of
          Kohn's hypothesis." *Journal of Marriage and the Family* 36 (Novem-
          ber):742–749.

Gibson, Geoffrey
  1972   "Kin family network: Overheralded structure in past conceptualiza-
          tions of family functioning." *Journal of Marriage and the Family*
          34 (February):13–23.

Gillespie, Dair L.
  1971   "Who has the power? The marital struggle." *Journal of Marriage and
          the Family* 33 (August):445–458.

Ginsberg, Yona
  1975   "Joint leisure activities and social networks in two neighborhoods in
          Tel Aviv." *Journal of Marriage and the Family* 27 (August):668–
          676.

Glick, Paul C.
  1957   *American Families.* New York: John Wiley & Sons, Inc.
  1975   "A demographer looks at American families." *Journal of Marriage
          and the Family* 37 (February):15–26.

Gluckman, Max
  1950   "Kinship and marriage among the Lozi of Northern Rhodesia and
          the Zulu of Natal." In A.R. Radcliffe-Brown and Daryll Forde (eds.),
          African Systems of Kinship and Marriage. London: Oxford Univer-
          sity Press.
  1955   "Estrangement in the African family." Pp. 54–80 in Max Gluckman,
          Custom and Conflict in Africa. Oxford: Basil Blackwell.

Goldschmidt, Walter
    1953   "Values and the field of comparative sociology." *American Sociological Review* 18 (June):287-293.
    1959   *Man's Way: A Preface to the Understanding of Human Society*. New York: Holt.

Goode, William J.
    1956   *After Divorce*. New York: The Free Press of Glencoe.
    1959   "The theoretical importance of love." *American Sociological Review* 24 (February):38-47.
    1960   "Illegitimacy in the Caribbean social structure." *American Sociological Review* 25 (February):21-30.
    1962   "Marital satisfaction and instability: A cross-cultural class analysis of divorce rates." *International Social Science Journal* 14 (October): 507-526.
    1963   *World Revolution and Family Patterns*. New York: The Free Press.
    1964   *The Family*. Englewood Cliffs, N.J.: Prentice-Hall, Inc.
    1966a   "Family patterns and human rights." *International Social Science Journal* 23 (No. 1):41-54.
    1966b   "Family disorganization." Pp. 479-552 in Robert K. Merton and Robert A. Nisbet (eds.), *Contemporary Social Problems* (second edition). New York: Harcourt, Brace & World, Inc.
    1971   "Civil and social rights of women." Pp. 21-39 in Cynthia Epstein and William J. Goode (eds.), *The Other Half: Roads to Women's Equality*. Englewood Cliffs, N.J.: Prentice-Hall, Inc.
    1973   "Functionalism: The empty castle." Pp. 64-94 in William J. Goode, *Explorations in Social Theory*. New York: Oxford University Press.

Goodenough, Ward H.
    1956   "Residence rules." *Southwestern Journal of Anthropology* 12 (Spring):22-37.

Goody, Jack R.
    1956   "A comparative approach to incest and adultery." *British Journal of Sociology* 7 (December):286-306.
    1970   "Marriage prestations, inheritance and descent in preindustrial societies." *Journal of Comparative Family Studies* 1 (Autumn): 37-54.

Gordon, Michael
    1973   *The American Family in Social-Historical Perspective*. New York: St. Martin's Press.

Gore, M.S.
    1965   "The traditional Indian family." Pp. 209-231 in M.F. Nimkoff (ed.), *Comparative Family Systems*. Boston: Houghton Mifflin Company.

Gough, E. Kathleen
    1955   "Female initiation rites in the Malabar Coast." *Journal of the Royal Anthropological Institute* 85 (Part 2):45-80.
    1959   "The Nayars and the definition of marriage." *Journal of the Royal Anthropological Institute* 89 (Part 1):23-34.

1961a   "Nayar: Central Kerala." Pp. 298-384 in David Schneider and E. Kathleen Gough (eds.), *Matrilineal Kinship.* Berkeley: University of California Press.

1961b   "Variation in residence." Pp. 545-576 in David Schneider and E. Kathleen Gough (eds.), *Matrilineal Kinship.* Berkeley: University of California Press.

1971   "The origin of the family." *Journal of Marriage and the Family* 33 (November):760-771.

Gouldner, Alvin W., and Helen P. Gouldner
1963   *Modern Sociology: An Introduction to the Study of Human Interaction.* New York: Harcourt, Brace & World, Inc.

Gouldner, Alvin W., and R.A. Peterson
1962   *Notes on Technology and the Moral Order.* Indianapolis, Ind.: Bobbs-Merrill.

Greenfield, Sidney M.
1961   "Industrialization and the family in sociological theory." *American Journal of Sociology* 67 (November):312-322.

1965   "Love and marriage in modern America: A functional analysis." *Sociological Quarterly* 6 (Autumn):361-377.

Habakkuk, H.J.
1955   "Family structure and economic change in nineteenth-century Europe." *Journal of Economic History* 15 (No. 1):1-12.

Hacker, Helen Mayer
1975   "Gender roles from a cross-cultural perspective." Pp. 185-215 in Lucile Duberman, *Gender and Sex in Society.* New York: Praeger.

Hadden, Jeffrey K., and Marie L. Borgatta
1969   *Marriage and the Family.* Itasca, Ill.: F.E. Peacock Publishers, Inc.

Handwerker, W. Penn
1973   "Technology and household configuration in urban Africa: The Bassa of Monrovia." *American Sociological Review* 38 (April):182-197.

Handy, E.S.C.
1903   "The native culture of the Marquesas." Bernice P. Bishop Museum Bulletin No. 9.

Harlow, Harry F.
1958   "The nature of love." *American Psychologist* 13 (December):673-685.

1962   "The heterosexual affection system in monkeys." *American Psychologist* 17 (January):1-9.

Harlow, Harry F., and Margaret K. Harlow
1962   "Social deprivation in monkeys." *Scientific American* 206 (November):1-10.

Harris, C.C.
1969   *The Family: An Introduction.* New York: Praeger.

Heath, Dwight B.
1958 "Sexual division of labor and cross-cultural research." *Social Forces* 37 (October):77-79.

Heer, David M.
1963 "The measurement and basis of family power: An overview." *Journal of Marriage and the Family* 25 (May):133-139.

Hempel, Carl G.
1952 *Fundamentals of Concept Formation in Empirical Science.* Chicago: University of Chicago Press.

1959 "The logic of functional analysis." Pp. 271-307 in Llewellyn Gross (ed.), *Symposium on Sociological Theory.* New York: Harper & Row.

Henry, Jules
1941 *Jungle People.* Richmond, Va.: William Byrd Press.

Herskovits, Melville J.
1965 *Cultural Anthropology.* New York: Alfred A. Knopf.

Hetherington, E. Mavis
1966 "Effects of paternal abuse on sex-typed behavior in Negro and White preadolescent males." *Journal of Personality and Social Psychology* 4 (July):87-91.

Hill, Reuben
1962 "Cross-national family research: Attempts and prospects." *International Social Science Journal* 14 (No. 3):425-451.

Hill, Reuben, and Rene Konig
1970 *Families in East and West.* Paris: Mouton.

Hobhouse, L.T., G.C. Wheeler, and M. Ginsberg
1915 *The Material Culture and Social Institutions of the Simpler Peoples.* London: Chapman Hall, Ltd.

Hockett, Charles F., and Robert Ascher
1964 "The human revolution." *Current Anthropology* 5 (June):135-147.

Hoebel, E. Adamson
1966 *Anthropology: The Study of Man* (third edition). New York: McGraw-Hill.

Holmberg, Allan R.
1950 *Nomads of the Long Bow.* Washington, D.C.: U.S. Government Printing Office.

Holt, Robert T., and John E. Turner
1970 *The Methodology of Comparative Research.* New York: The Free Press.

Holy, Ladislav, and John Blacking
1974 "Explanation through comparison." *Journal of Comparative Family Studies* 4 (Spring):57-60.

Hopkins, T.K., and I. Wallerstein
1967 "The comparative study of national societies." *Social Science Information* 6 (October):25-58.

Humphreys, Alexander J.

1965   "The family in Ireland." Pp. 232-258 in M.F. Nimkoff (ed.), *Comparative Family Systems*. Boston: Houghton Mifflin Company.

1966   *The New Dubliners: Urbanization and the Irish Family*. New York: Fordham University Press.

Hunt, Morton M.

1959   *The Natural History of Love*. New York: Alfred A. Knopf.

Hutchison, Ira W.

1974   "The functional significance of conjugal communication in a transitional society." *Journal of Marriage and the Family* 36 (August): 580-587.

Inkeles, Alex

1963   "Social change and social character: The role of parental mediation." Pp. 357-366 in N.J. Smelser and W.J. Smelser (eds.), *Personality and Social Systems*. New York: John Wiley & Sons, Inc.

1969   "Social structure and socialization." Pp. 615-632 in David A. Goslin (ed.), *Handbook of Socialization Theory and Research*. Chicago: Rand McNally.

Jacobsen, Paul H.

1959   *American Marriage and Divorce*. New York: Rinehart & Company, Inc.

Johnson, Erwin H.

1960   "The stem family and its extensions in modern Japan." Paper presented at the annual meetings of the American Anthropological Association, Minneapolis, Minnesota.

Johnson, H.

1960   *Sociology: A Systematic Introduction*. New York: Harcourt, Brace & World, Inc.

Kaats, Gilbert R., and Keith E. Davis

1970   "The dynamics of sexual behavior of college students." *Journal of Marriage and the Family* 32 (August):390-399.

Kandel, Denise, and Gerald S. Lesser

1969   "Parent-adolescent relationships and adolescent independence in the United States and Denmark." *Journal of Marriage and the Family* 31 (May):348-358.

1972a   "Marital decision-making in American and Danish urban families: A research note." *Journal of Marriage and the Family* 34 (February): 134-138.

1972b   "The internal structure of families in the United States and Denmark." Pp. 70-85 in Marvin B. Sussman and Betty E. Cogswell (eds.), *Cross-National Family Research*. Leiden, Netherlands: E.J. Brill.

Kanin, Eugene J., and Karen R. Davidson

1972   "Some evidence bearing on the aim-inhibition hypothesis of love." *Sociological Quarterly* 13 (Spring):210-217.

Kardiner, Abram
1939   *The Individual and His Society.* New York: Columbia University
Press.

Keesing, Felix M., and Marie M. Keesing
1958   *Elite Communication in Samoa: A Study of Leadership.* Stanford:
Stanford University Press.

Kenkel, William F.
1973   *The Family in Perspective* (third edition). New York: Appleton-
Century-Crofts.

Kephart, William M.
1963   "Experimental family organization: An historico-cultural report on
the Oneida community." *Marriage and Family Living* 25 (August)
261-271.

1970   "The dysfunctional theory of romantic love: A research report."
Journal of Comparative Family Studies 1 (Autumn):26-36.

1972   *The Family, Society, and the Individual.* Boston: Houghton Mifflin
Company.

Kerckhoff, Alan C.
1972   "The structure of the conjugal relationship in industrial society."
Pp. 53-69 in Marvin B. Sussman and Betty E. Cogswell (eds.),
Cross-National Family Research. Leiden, Netherlands: E.J Brill.

Kilpatrick, F.P., and Hadley Cantril
1960   "Self-anchoring scaling, a measure of individuals' unique reality
worlds." *Journal of Individual Psychology* 16 (November):158-
173.

Kinkade, Kathleen
1973   *A Walden Two Experiment.* New York: William Morrow & Company, Inc.

Kinsey, Alfred C., W. Pomeroy, and C. Martin
1948   *Sexual Behavior in the Human Male.* Philadelphia: Saunders.

Kirkendall, Lester A.
1961   *Premarital Intercourse and Interpersonal Relationships.* New York:
Julian Press.

Klatzky, Sheila R.
1973   *Patterns of Contact with Relatives.* Washington, D.C.: American
Sociological Association.

Kluckholn, Clyde
1953   "Universal categories of culture." Pp. 507-523 in A.L. Kroeber
(ed.), *Anthropology Today.* Chicago: University of Chicago Press.

Kobben, Andre J.F.
1968   "The logic of cross-cultural analysis: Why exceptions?" Pp. 17-53
in Stein Rokkan (ed.), *Comparative Research Across Cultures and
Nations.* Paris: Mouton.

Kohn, Melvin L.
  1959a "Social class and parental values." *American Journal of Sociology* 64 (January):337–351.

  1959b "Social class and the experience of parental authority." *American Sociological Review* 24 (June):352–366.

  1963   "Social class and parent-child relationships: An interpretation." *American Journal of Sociology* 68 (January):471–480.

  1969   *Class and Conformity.* Homewood, Ill.: Dorsey Press.

Komarovsky, Mirra
  1967   *Blue-Collar Marriage.* New York: Vintage Books.

Konig, Rene
  1957   "Family and authority: The German father in 1955." *Sociological Review* 5 (July):107–127.

Koomen, Willem
  1974   "A note on the authoritarian German family." *Journal of Marriage and the Family* 36 (August):634–636.

Kunzel, Renate
  1974   "The connection between the family life cycle and divorce rates: An analysis based on European data." *Journal of Marriage and the Family* 36 (May):379–388.

Lambert, William E., J. Havelka, and C. Crosby
  1958   "The influence of language-acquisition contexts on bilingualism." *Journal of Abnormal and Social Psychology* 72 (March):77–82.

Lambert, William W.
  1971   "Cross-cultural backgrounds to personality development and the socialization of aggression." In W.W. Lambert and R. Weisbrod (eds), *Comparative Perspectives on Social Psychology.* Boston: Little, Brown & Company.

Lamouse, Annette
  1969   "Family roles of women: A German example." *Journal of Marriage and the Family* 31 (February):145–152.

Lang, Andrew
  1903   *Social Origins.* London: Longmans, Green and Company.

Lang, Olga
  1946   *Chinese Family and Society.* New Haven, Conn.: Yale University Press.

Lantz, Herman R., Margaret Britton, Raymond L. Schmitt, and Eloise C. Snyder
  1968   "Preindustrial patterns in the colonial family in America: A content analysis of colonial magazines." *American Sociological Review* 33 (June):413–426.

Lantz, Herman R., Jane Keyes, and Martin Schultz
  1975   "The American family in the preindustrial period: From base lines in history to change." *American Sociological Review* 40 (February): 21–36.

Lantz, Herman R., Raymond L. Schmitt, and Richard Herman
  1973   "The preindustrial family in America: A further examination of

early magazines." *American Journal of Sociology* 79 (November): 566-589.

Laslett, Peter
1969   "Size and structure of the household in England over three centuries: Mean household size in England since the 16th century." *Population Studies* 23 (July):199-223.

1972   *Household and Family in Past Time.* Cambridge: Cambridge University Press.

1973   "The comparative history of household and family." Pp. 19-33 in Michael Gordon (ed.), *The American Family in Social-Historical Perspective.* New York: St. Martin's Press.

Lee, Gary R.
1974   "Marriage and anomie: A causal argument." *Journal of Marriage and the Family* 36 (August):523-532.

1975a   "The problem of universals in comparative research: An attempt at clarification." *Journal of Comparative Family Studies* 6 (Spring): 89-100.

1975b   "In defense of normal science: Confessions of a sociological methodolatrist." *Journal for the Scientific Study of Religion* 14 (March): 57-61.

1977   "The effects of social networks on the family." In Wesley R. Burr *et al.* (eds.), *Contemporary Theories About the Family.* New York: The Free Press; forthcoming.

Leik, Robert
1963   "Instrumentality and emotionality in family interaction." *Sociometry* 26 (June):131-145.

Leplae, Claire
1968   "Structure des taches domestique et du pouvoir de decision de la dyade conjugale." Pp. 13-49 in Pierre de Bie (ed.), *La Dyade Conjugale.* Brussels, Belgium: Editions Vie Ouvriere.

Leslie, Gerald R.
1973   *The Family in Social Context* (second edition). New York: Oxford University Press.

Leslie, Gerald R., Richard F. Larsen, and Benjamin L. Gorman
1973   *Order and Change.* New York: Oxford University Press.

LeVine, Robert A.
1965   "Intergenerational tensions and extended family structures in Africa." Pp. 188-204 in Ethel Shanas and Gordon F. Streib (eds.), *Social Structure and the Family: Generational Relations.* Englewood Cliffs, N.J.: Prentice-Hall, Inc.

1969   "Culture, personality, and socialization: An evolutionary view." Pp. 503-541 in David A. Goslin (ed.), *Handbook of Socialization Theory and Research.* Chicago: Rand McNally.

Levine, Robert A., Nancy H. Klein, and Constance F. Owen
1968   "Modernization and father-child relationships." Pp. 558-574 in

Norman W. Bell and Ezra F. Vogel (eds.), *A Modern Introduction to the Family* (second edition). New York: The Free Press.

Levi-Strauss, Claude
1956   "The family." Pp. 261–285 in Harry L. Shapiro (ed.), *Man, Culture, and Society*. New York: Oxford University Press.

Levy, Marion J.
1949   *The Family Revolution in Modern China*. New York: Atheneum.

1955   "Contrasting factors in the modernization of China and Japan." Pp. 496–506 in Simon S. Kuznets, Wilbert E. Moore, and Joseph J. Spengler (eds.), *Economic Growth: Brazil, India, Japan*. Durham, N.C.: Duke University Press.

1965   "Aspects of the analysis of family structure." Pp. 1–64 in Ansley J. Coale *et al.*, *Aspects of the Analysis of Family Structure*. Princeton, N.J.: Princeton University Press.

Levy, Marion J., and Lloyd A. Fallers
1959   "The family: Some comparative considerations." *American Anthropologist* 61 (August):647–651.

Levy, Robert I.
1968   "Child management structure in Tahitian families." Pp. 590–598 in Norman W. Bell and Ezra F. Vogel (eds.), *A Modern Introduction to the Family* (second edition). New York: The Free Press.

Lidz, Theodore
1963   *The Family and Human Adaptation*. New York: International University Press.

Lieberson, Stanley, and Lynn K. Hansen
1974   "National development, mother tongue diversity, and the comparative study of nations." *American Sociological Review* 39 (August): 523–541.

Lindzey, Gardner
1967   "Some remarks concerning incest, the incest taboo, and psychoanalytic theory." *American Psychologist* 22 (December):1051–1059.

Linton, Ralph
1936   *The Study of Man*. New York: Appleton-Century-Crofts.

1939   "Marquesan culture." Pp. 137–196 in Abram Kardiner, *The Individual and His Society*. New York: Columbia University Press.

1959   "The natural history of the family." Pp. 30–52 in Ruth N. Anshen (ed.), *The Family: Its Function and Destiny*. New York: Harper & Row.

Linton, Sally
1970   "Primate studies and sex differences." *Women: A Journal of Liberation* 1 (Summer):43–44.

Lipset, Seymour M., and Stein Rokkan
1967   *Party Systems and Voter Alignments*. New York: The Free Press.

Livingstone, Frank B.
1969   "Genetics, ecology, and the origins of incest and exogamy." *Current Anthropology* 10 (February):45–61.

Lobodzinska, Barbara
  1975   "Love as a factor in marital decisions in contemporary Poland."
         Journal of Comparative Family Studies 6 (Spring):56-73.
Lowie, Robert
  1920   *Primitive Society.* New York: Boni and Liveright.
Luckey, Eleanor B., and Gilbert D. Nass.
  1969   "A comparison of sexual attitudes and behavior in an international
         sample." *Journal of Marriage and the Family* 31 (May):364-379.
Lupri, Eugen
  1969   "Contemporary authority patterns in the West German family: A
         study in cross-national validation." *Journal of Marriage and the
         Family* 31 (February):134-144.
Lynn, David B.
  1961   "Sex differences in identification development." *Sociometry* 24
         (December):372-383.
  1974   *The Father: His Role in Child Development.* Monterey, Calif.:
         Brooks/Cole Publishing Company.
Lynn, David B., and William L. Sawrey
  1959   "The effects of father-absence on Norwegian boys and girls." *Journal
         of Abnormal and Social Psychology* 59 (September):258-262.
Maccoby, Eleanor E.
  1961   "The taking of adult roles in middle childhood." *Journal of Abnor-
         mal and Social Psychology* 63 (November):493-503.
  1968   "The development of moral values and behavior in childhood." Pp.
         227-269 in J.A. Clausen (ed.), *Socialization and Society.* Boston:
         Little, Brown & Company.
Mace, David, and Vera Mace
  1960   *Marriage East and West.* Garden City, N.Y.: Doubleday and Com-
         pany, Inc.
Maine, Henry Sumner
  1885   *Ancient Law* (third edition). New York: Henry Holt, & Company,
         Inc.
Marsh, Robert M.
  1967   *Comparative Sociology.* New York: Harcourt, Brace & World, Inc.
Masters, William H., and Virginia E. Johnson
  1966   *Human Sexual Response.* Boston: Little, Brown and Company.
McEwen, W.J.
  1963   "Forms and problems of validation in social anthropology." *Current
         Anthropology* 4 (April):155-183.
McIntire, Walter G., Gilbert D. Nass, and Albert S. Dreyer
  1974   "Parental role perceptions of Ghanian and American adolescents."
         Journal of Marriage and the Family 36 (February):185-189.
McKinley, Donald G.
  1964   *Social Class and Family Life.* Glencoe, Ill.: The Free Press.
McLennan, J.F.
  1896   *Studies in Ancient History.* New York: Macmillan.

Mead, Margaret
    1935   *Sex and Temperament in Three Primitive Societies.* New York: William Morrow & Company, Inc.

Mencher, Joan P.
    1965   "The Nayars of South Malabar." Pp. 163-191 in M.F. Nimkoff (ed.), *Comparative Family Systems.* Boston: Houghton Mifflin Company.

Merrit, Richard L., and Stein Rokkan
    1966   *Comparing Nations: The Use of Quantitative Data in Cross-National Research.* New Haven: Yale University Press.

Merton, Robert K.
    1968   *Social Theory and Social Structure* (enlarged edition). New York: The Free Press.

Metropolitan Life Insurance Company
    1952   Statistical Bulletin.

Michaelson, Evelyn, and Walter Goldschmidt
    1971   "Female roles and male dominance among peasants." *Southwestern Journal of Anthropology* 27 (Winter):330-352.

Michel, Andree
    1967   "Comparative data concerning the interaction in French and American families." *Journal of Marriage and the Family* 29 (May):337-344.
    1970   "Wife's satisfaction with husband's understanding in Parisian urban families." *Journal of Marriage and the Family* 32 (August):351-359.

Michel, Andree, and Françoise L. Feyrabend
    1969   "Real number of children and conjugal interaction in French urban families: A comparison with American families." *Journal of Marriage and the Family* 31 (May):359-363.

Middleton, Russell
    1962   "Brother-sister and father-daughter marriage in ancient Egypt." *American Sociological Review* 27 (October):603-611.

Miller, Daniel R., and Guy E. Swanson
    1958   *The Changing American Parent: A Study in the Detroit Area.* New York: John Wiley & Sons, Inc.

Miller, Walter B.
    1958   "Lower class culture as a generating milieu of gang delinquency." *Journal of Social Issues* 14 (No. 3):5-19.

Mindel, Charles H.
    1972   "Kinship interaction: Structure and process in divorce." *Journal of Comparative Family Studies* 3 (Autumn):254-264.

Minturn, Leigh, and William Lambert
    1964   *Mothers of Six Cultures: Antecedents of Child-Rearing.* New York: John Wiley & Sons, Inc.

Mitchell, J.C.
    1961   "Social change and the stability of African marriage in Northern

Rhodesia." Pp. 316-329 in Aidan Southall (ed.), *Social Change in Modern Africa*. London: Oxford University Press.

Mitchell, Robert Edward
1965   "Survey materials collected in the developing countries: Sampling, measurement, and interviewing obstacles to intra- and international comparisons." *International Social Science Journal* 17 (No. 4): 665-685.

Mogey, John M.
1957   "A century of declining paternal authority." *Marriage and Family Living* 19 (August):234-239.

1964   "Family and community in urban-industrial societies." Pp. 501-534 in Harold T. Christensen (ed.), *Handbook of Marriage and the Family*. Chicago: Rand McNally.

Monahan, Thomas P.
1955   "Is childlessness related to family stability?" *American Sociological Review* 20 (August):446-456.

Moore, Frank W.
1961   *Readings in Cross-Cultural Methodology*. New Haven, Conn.: HRAF Press.

Morgan, Lewis Henry
1878   *Ancient Society*. New York: Henry Holt & Company, Inc.

Murdock, George Peter
1937   "Correlations of matrilineal and patrilineal institutions." Pp. 445-470 in G.P. Murdock, *Studies in the Science of Society*. New Haven, Conn.: Yale University Press.

1949   *Social Structure*. New York: The Free Press.

1950   "Family stability in non-European cultures." *Annals of the American Academy of Political and Social Science* 272 (November):195-201.

1957   "World ethnographic sample." *American Anthropologist* 59 (August): 664-687.

1967   "Ethnographic atlas: A summary." *Ethnology* 6 (April):109-236.

1968   "Cognatic forms of social organization." Pp. 235-253 in Paul Bohannan and John Middleton (eds.), *Kinship and Social Organization*. Garden City, N.Y.: The Natural History Press.

Murdock, George Peter, and D.R. White
1969   "Standard cross-cultural sample." *Ethnology* 8 (October):329-369.

Murdock, George Peter, and John W.M. Whiting
1951   "Cultural determination of parental attitudes: The relationship between the social structure, particularly family structure, and behavior." In Milton J.E. Senn (ed.), *Problems of Infancy and Childhood*. New York: Josiah Macy, Jr., Foundation.

Murphy, R.F.
1957   "Intergroup hostility and social cohesion." *American Anthropologist* 59 (December):1018-1035.

Mussen, Paul, and Luther Distler
1959 "Masculinity, identification, and father-son relationships." *Journal of Abnormal and Social Psychology* 59 (November):350-356.

Nadel, S.F.
1951 *The Foundations of Social Anthropology.* New York: The Free Press.

Nagel, Ernest
1961 *The Structure of Science: Problems in the Logic of Scientific Explanation.* New York: Harcourt, Brace & World, Inc.

Naroll, Raoul S.
1960 "Controlling data quality." *Series Research in Social Psychology,* Symposia Studies Series (No. 4):7-12.

1961 "Two solutions to Galton's problem." *Philosophy of Science* 28 (January):15-39.

1962 *Data Quality Control.* New York: The Free Press.

1964 "A fifth solution to Galton's problem." *American Anthropologist* 66 (August):863-867.

1968 "Some thoughts on comparative method in cultural anthropology." Pp. 236-277 in Hubert B. Blalock, Jr., and Ann B. Blalock (eds.), *Methodology in Social Research.* New York: McGraw-Hill.

1970 "What have we learned from cross-cultural surveys?" *American Anthropologist* 72 (December):1227-1288.

Naroll, Raoul S., and Roy G. D'Andrade
1963 "Two further solutions to Galton's problem." *American Anthropologist* 65 (October):1053-1067.

Needham, Rodney
1971 *Rethinking Kinship and Marriage.* London: Tavistock.

Nelson, Joel I.
1966 "Clique contacts and family orientations." *American Sociological Review* 31 (October):663-672.

Nimkoff, Meyer F.
1965 *Comparative Family Systems.* Boston: Houghton Mifflin Company.

Nimkoff, Meyer F., and Russell Middleton
1960 "Type of family and type of economy." *American Journal of Sociology* 66 (November):215-225.

Nye, F. Ivan, and Felix M. Berardo
1973 *The Family: Its Structure and Interaction.* New York: Macmillan.

Ogburn, William F.
1922 *Social Change.* New York: Viking Press.

1938 "The changing family." *The Family* 19 (July):139-143.

1955 *Technology and the Changing Family.* Boston: Houghton Mifflin Company.

Ogburn, William F., and Meyer F. Nimkoff
1950 *Sociology.* Boston: Houghton Mifflin Company.

Oliver, Douglas L.
1955 *A Solomon Island Society.* Cambridge, Mass.: Harvard University Press.

Olsen, Marvin E.
1968 *The Process of Social Organization.* New York: Holt, Rinehart & Winston, Inc.

Olsen, Nancy J.
1973 "Family structure and independence training in a Taiwanese village." *Journal of Marriage and the Family* 35 (August):512-519.

1974 "Family structure and socialization patterns in Taiwan." *American Journal of Sociology* 79 (May):1395-1417.

Olson, David H., and Carolyn Rabunsky
1972 "Validity of four measures of conjugal power." *Journal of Marriage and the Family* 34 (May):224-234.

Oppong, Christine
1970 "Conjugal power and resources: An urban African example." *Journal of Marriage and the Family* 32 (November):676-680.

1971 "'Joint' conjugal roles and 'extended' families: A preliminary note on a mode of classifying conjugal family relationships." *Journal of Comparative Family Studies* 2 (Autumn):178-187.

Osmond, Marie W.
1965 "Toward monogamy: A cross-cultural study of correlates of type of marriage." *Social Forces* 44 (September):8-16.

1969 "A cross-cultural analysis of family organization." *Journal of Marriage and the Family* 31 (May):302-310.

Otterbein, Keith F.
1968 "Internal war: A cross-cultural study." *American Anthropologist* 70 (April):277-289.

Otto, Luther B.
1975 "Class and status in family research." *Journal of Marriage and the Family* 37 (May):315-332.

Paige, Jeffrey M.
1974 "Kinship and polity in stateless societies." *American Journal of Sociology* 80 (September):301-320.

Parsons, Talcott
1943 "The kinship system of the contemporary United States." *American Anthropologist* 45 (January):22-38.

1951 *The Social System.* New York: The Free Press.

1954a "The incest taboo in relation to social structure and the socialization of the child." *British Journal of Sociology* 5 (June):101-117.

1954b *Essays in Sociological Theory* (revised edition). Glencoe, Ill.: The Free Press.

1959 "The social structure of the family." Pp. 241-274 in Ruth N. Anshen (ed.), *The Family: Its Function and Destiny.* New York: Harper & Brothers.

Parsons, Talcott, and Robert F. Bales
1955 *Family, Socialization and Interaction Process.* Glencoe, Ill.: The Free Press.

Patai, Raphael
  1959   *Sex and Family in the Bible and the Middle East.* New York: Doubleday & Company, Inc.

  1967   *Women in the Modern World.* New York: The Free Press.

Payne, Donald E., and Paul H. Mussen
  1956   "Parent-child relations and father-identification among adolescent boys." *Journal of Abnormal and Social Psychology* 52 (May):358-362.

Pearlin, Leonard I.
  1971   *Class Context and Family Relations: A Cross-National Study.* Boston: Little, Brown & Company.

Pearlin, Leonard I., and Melvin L. Kohn
  1966   "Social class, occupation, and parental values: A cross-national study." *American Sociological Review* 31 (August):466-479.

Pedersen, Frank A.
  1966   "Relationships between father-absence and emotional disturbance in male military dependents." *Merrill-Palmer Quarterly* 12 (October): 321-331.

Peter, Prince of Greece and Denmark
  1956   "For a new definition of marriage." *Man* 46 (March):48.

  1965   "The Tibetan family system." Pp. 192-208 in M.F. Nimkoff (ed.), *Comparative Family Systems.* Boston: Houghton Mifflin Company.

Petersen, Karen Kay
  1969   "Kin network research: A plea for comparability." *Journal of Marriage and the Family* 31 (May):271-280.

Pineo, Peter C.
  1961   "Disenchantment in the later years of marriage." *Marriage and Family Living* 23 (February):3-11.

Platt, J.
  1969   "Some problems in measuring jointness of conjugal-role relationships." *Sociology* 3 (September):287-298.

Pleck, Elizabeth H.
  1972   "The two-parent household: Black family structure in late nineteenth-century Boston." *Journal of Social History* 6 (Fall):1-31.

Podmore, David, and David Chaney
  1972   "Attitudes towards marriage and the family amongst young people in Hong Kong, and comparisons with the United States and Taiwan." *Journal of Comparative Family Studies* 3 (Autumn):228-238.

Popenoe, David
  1971   *Sociology.* New York: Appleton-Century-Crofts.

Popper, Karl R.
  1968   *The Logic of Scientific Discovery.* New York: Harper Torchbooks.

Prothro, E.T.
  1961   *Child-Rearing in Lebanon.* Cambridge, Mass.: Harvard University Press.

Przeworski, Adam, and Henry Teune
1966-   "Equivalence in cross-national research." *Public Opinion Quarterly*
67   30 (Winter):551-568.
1970   *The Logic of Comparative Social Inquiry.* New York: Wiley-Inter-
science.

Rabbie, J.M.
1965   "A cross-cultural comparison of parent-child relationships in the
United States and West Germany." *British Journal of Social and
Clinical Psychology* 4 (December):298-310.

Radcliffe-Brown, A.R.
1930   "The social organization of Australian tribes." *Oceania,* Monograph
I.

Radcliffe-Brown, A.R., and Daryll Forde
1950   *African Systems of Kinship and Marriage.* New York: Oxford University Press.

Rainwater, Lee
1960   *And the Poor Get Children.* Chicago: Quadrangle Books.
1965   *Family Design.* Chicago: Aldine Publishing Company.
1966a   "Crucible of identity: The Negro lower-class family." *Daedalus* 95
(Winter):172-216.
1966b   "Some aspects of lower-class sexual behavior." *Journal of Social
Issues* 22 (April):96-108.

Rainwater, Lee, Richard P. Coleman, and Gerald Handel
1959   *Workingman's Wife.* New York: Oceana Publications.

Rapoport, Rhona, Robert Rapoport, and Victor Thiessen
1974   "Couple symmetry and enjoyment." *Journal of Marriage and the
Family* 36 (August):588-591.

Reiss, Ira L.
1960   *Premarital Sexual Standards in America.* New York: The Free Press.
1967   *The Social Context of Premarital Sexual Permissiveness.* New York:
Holt, Rinehart & Winston, Inc.
1971   *The Family System in America.* New York: Holt, Rinehart & Winston, Inc.
1972   "Premarital sexuality: Past, present, and future." Pp. 167-189 in
Ira L. Reiss (ed.), *Readings on the Family System.* New York: Holt,
Rinehart & Winston, Inc.

Reynolds, Vernon
1968   "Kinship and the family in monkeys, apes, and man." *Man* 3 (June):
209-233.

Richards, Audrey I.
1950   "Some types of family structure amongst the Central Bantu." Pp.
207-251 in A.R. Radcliffe-Brown and Daryll Forde (eds.), *African
Systems of Kinship and Marriage.* London: Oxford University Press.
1956   *Chisungu: A Girl's Initiation Ceremony Among the Bemba of Northern Rhodesia.* London: Faber.

Riegelhaupt, Joyce
  1967   "Saloio women: An analysis of formal and informal political and economic roles of Portuguese peasant women." *Anthropological Quarterly* 40 (July):109-126.

Ritchie, J.E.
  1956   *Basic Personality in Rakau.* Wellington, Australia: Victoria University of Wellington.

Rivers, W.H.R.
  1906   *The Todas.* New York: Macmillan.

Robertson, Constance Noyes
  1970   *Oneida Community: An Autobiography, 1851-1876.* Syracuse, N.Y.: Syracuse University Press.

Robertson, Ira E., Karl King, and Jack O. Balswick
  1972   "The premarital sexual revolution among college females." *Family Coordinator* 21 (April):189-194.

Rodgers, Robert R.
  1971   "Changes in parental behavior reported by children in West Germany and the United States." *Human Development* 14 (No. 3):208-224.

Rodgers, Robert R., Urie Bronfenbrenner, and Edward C. Devereux, Jr.
  1968   "Standards of social behavior among children in four cultures." *International Journal of Psychology* 3 (No. 1):31-41.

Rodman, Hyman
  1961   "Marital relationships in a Trinidad village." *Marriage and Family Living* 23 (May):166-170.

  1963   "The lower-class value stretch." *Social Forces* 42 (December): 205-215.

  1965a   "Middle-class misconceptions about lower-class families." Pp. 219-230 in Hyman Rodman (ed.), *Marriage, Family, and Society.* New York: Random House.

  1965b   "Talcott Parsons' view of the changing American family." Pp. 262-286 in Hyman Rodman (ed.), *Marriage, Family, and Society.* New York: Random House.

  1966   "Illegitimacy in the Caribbean social structure: A reconsideration." *American Sociological Review* 31 (October):673-683.

  1967   "Marital power in France, Greece, Yugoslavia, and the United States: A cross-national discussion." *Journal of Marriage and the Family* 29 (May):320-325.

  1968   "Controversies about lower-class culture: Delinquency and illegitimacy." *Canadian Review of Sociology and Anthropology* 5 (November):254-262.

  1971   *Lower-Class Families: The Culture of Poverty in Negro Trinidad.* New York: Oxford University Press.

  1972   "Marital power and the theory of resources in cultural context." *Journal of Comparative Family Studies* 3 (Spring):50-69.

Rogers, Susan Carol
  1975   "Female forms of power and the myth of male dominance: A model

of female/male interaction in peasant society." *American Ethnologist* 2 (November):727-756.

Rokkan, Stein
1968 *Comparative Research Across Cultures and Nations.* Paris: Mouton.

Romney, A.K.
1965 "Variations in household structure as determinants of sex-typed behavior." In Frank Beach (ed.), *Sex and Behavior.* New York: John Wiley & Sons, Inc.

Rose, E., and G. Willoughby
1958 "Culture profiles and emphases." *American Journal of Sociology* 63 (March):476-490.

Rose, Jerry D.
1971 *Introduction to Sociology.* Chicago: Rand McNally.

Rosen, Bernard C.
1964 "Family structure and value transmission." *Merrill-Palmer Quarterly* 10 (Spring):59-76.

Rosenblatt, Paul C.
1967 "Marital residence and the functions of romantic love." *Ethnology* 6 (October):471-480.

Rosenblatt, Paul C., and Paul C. Cozby
1972 "Courtship patterns associated with freedom of choice of spouse." *Journal of Marriage and the Family* 34 (November):689-695.

Rosenblatt, Paul C., and David Unangst
1974 "Marriage ceremonies: An exploratory cross-cultural study." *Journal of Comparative Family Studies* 5 (Spring):41-56.

Rossi, Alice
1964 "Equality between the sexes: An immodest proposal." *Daedalus* 93 (Spring):607-652.

Roy, P.K.
1974 "Industrialization and 'fitness' of nuclear family: A case study in India." *Journal of Comparative Family Studies* 5 (Spring):74-86.

Sadie, Jan L.
1967 "Labor supply and employment in less developed countries." *Annals of the American Academy of Political and Social Science* 369 (December):121.

Safilios-Rothschild, Constantina
1967 "A comparison of power structure and marital satisfaction in urban Greek and French families." *Journal of Marriage and the Family* 29 (May):345-352.

1969 "Family sociology or wives' family sociology? A cross-cultural examination of decision-making.' *Journal of Marriage and the Family* 31 (May):290-301.

1970 "The study of family power structure: A review 1960-1969." *Journal of Marriage and the Family* 32 (November):539-552.

1972 "Answer to Stephen J. Bahr's 'Comment on "The study of family power structure: A review 1960-1969." " *Journal of Marriage and the Family* 34 (May):245-246.

Sarnoff, J., F. Lighthall, R. Waite, K. Davidson, and A. Sarason
1959   "A cross-cultural study of anxiety among American and English schoolchildren." *Journal of Educational Psychology* 49 (June): 129-136.

Schachter, S.
1954   "Interpretative and methodological problems of replicated research." *Journal of Social Issues* 10 (No. 4):52-60.

Scheuch, Erwin K.
1967   "Society as context in cross-cultural comparisons." *Social Science Information* 6 (October):7-23.

1968   "The cross-cultural use of sample surveys: Problems of comparability." Pp. 176-209 in Stein Rokkan (ed.), *Comparative Research Across Cultures and Nations.* Paris: Mouton.

Schneider, David M.
1961   "Introduction: The distinctive features of matrilineal descent groups." Pp. 1-29 in David M. Schneider and E. Kathleeen Gough (eds.), *Matrilineal Kinship.* Berkeley: University of California Press.

Schneider, David M., and E. Kathleen Gough
1961   *Matrilineal Kinship.* Berkeley: University of California Press.

Sears, Pauline Snedden
1953   "Child-rearing factors related to playing of sex-typed roles." *American Psychologist* 8 (August):431.

Sears, Robert R.
1961   "Transcultural variables and conceptual equivalence." Pp. 445-455 in Bert Kaplan (ed.), *Studying Personality Cross-Culturally.* Evanston, Ill.: Row, Peterson & Company.

Sears, Robert R., Eleanor E. Maccoby, and Harry Levin
1957   *Patterns of Child Rearing.* Evanston, Ill.: Row, Peterson & Company.

Segre, Sandro
1975   "Family stability, social class and values in traditional and industrial societies." *Journal of Marriage and the Family* 37 (May):431-436.

Shaw, L.A.
1955   "Impressions of family life in a London suburb." *Sociological Review* 3 (December):175-195.

Siegman, Aron Wolfe
1966   "Father absence during early childhood and antisocial behavior." *Journal of Abnormal Psychology* 71 (February):71-74.

Simmons, Leo
1945   *The Role of the Aged in Primitive Society.* New Haven, Conn.: Yale University Press.

Slater, Mariam K.
1959   "Ecological factors in the origin of incest." *American Anthropologist* 61 (December):1042-1059.

Slater, Philip E.
　1961　"Parental role differentiation." *American Journal of Sociology* 67 (November):296-311.

Smart, Russell C., and Mollie S. Smart
　1973　"New Zealand preadolescents' parent-peer orientation and parent perceptions compared with English and American." *Journal of Marriage and the Family* 35 (February):142-148.

Smelser, Neil J.
　1973　"The methodology of comparative analysis." Pp. 42-86 in Donald P. Warwick and Samuel Osherson (eds.), *Comparative Research Methods*. Englewood Cliffs, N.J.: Prentice-Hall, Inc.

Smigel, E.O., and R. Seiden
　1968　"The decline and fall of the double standard." *Annals of the American Academy of Political and Social Science* 376 (March):6-17.

Smith, Harold E.
　1973　"The Thai family: Nuclear or extended." *Journal of Marriage and the Family* 35 (February):136-141.

Smith, Raymond T.
　1956　*The Negro Family in British Guiana: Family Structure and Social Status in the Villages*. London: Routledge and Kegan Paul.

Spanier, Graham B.
　1972　"Romanticism and marital adjustment." *Journal of Marriage and the Family* 34 (August):481-487.

Spencer, Herbert
　1876-　*Principles of Sociology*. London: Williams and Norgate.
　96

Spiro, Melford E.
　1954　"Is the family universal." *American Anthropologist* 56 (October):
　(1968)　839-846. Reprinted with addendum, pp. 68-79 in Norman W. Bell and Ezra F. Vogel (eds.), *A Modern Introduction to the Family* (second edition). New York: The Free Press.

　1956　*Kibbutz: Venture in Utopia*. Cambridge, Mass.: Harvard University Press.

　1958　*Children of the Kibbutz*. Cambridge, Mass.: Harvard University Press.

Sprey, Jetse
　1971-　"On the origin of sex roles." *Sociolological Focus* 5 (Winter): 1-9.
　72

　1972　"Family power structure: A critical comment." *Journal of Marriage and the Family* 34 (May):235-238.

Stephens, William N.
　1963　*The Family in Cross-Cultural Perspective*. New York: Holt, Rinehart & Winston, Inc.

Steward, Julian
　1955　*Theory of Culture Change: The Methodology of Multilinear Evolution*. Urbana, Ill.: University of Illinois Press.

Stinchcombe, Arthur L.
  1968   *Constructing Social Theories.* New York: Harcourt, Brace & World, Inc.

Stolte-Heiskanen, Veronica
  1972   "Contextual analysis and theory construction in cross-cultural family research." *Journal of Comparative Family Studies* 3 (Spring):33-49.

Straus, Murray A.
  1968   "Society as a variable in comparative study of the family by replication and secondary analysis." *Journal of Marriage and the Family* 30 (November):565-570.

  1969   "Phenomenal identity and conceptual equivalence of measurement in cross-national comparative research." *Journal of Marriage and the Family* 31 (May):233-239.

  1970   "Methodology of a laboratory experimental study of families in three societies." Pp. 552-577 in Reuben Hill and Rene Konig (eds.), *Families in East and West.* Paris: Mouton.

Stryker, Sheldon
  1972   "Symbolic interaction theory: A review and some suggestions for comparative family research." *Journal of Comparative Family Studies* 3 (Spring):17-32.

Suchman, E.A.
  1964   "The comparative method in social research." *Rural Sociology* 29 (Summer):123-137.

Sundberg, Norman, Vijay Sharma, Terry Wodtlie, and Pritan Rohila
  1969   "Family cohesiveness and autonomy of adolescents in India and the United States." *Journal of Marriage and the Family* 31 (May):403-407.

Sussman, Marvin B.
  1965   "Relationships of adult children with their parents in the United States." Pp. 62-92 in Ethel Shanas and Gordon F. Streib (eds.), *Social Structure and the Family: Generational Relations.* Englewood Cliffs, N.J.: Prentice-Hall, Inc.

Sussman, Marvin B., and Lee Burchinal
  1962a   "Kin family network: Unheralded structure in current conceptualizations of family functioning." *Marriage and Family Living* 24 (August):231-240.

  1962b   "Parental aid to married children: Implications for family functioning." *Marriage and Family Living* 24 (November):320-332.

Swanson, Guy E.
  1960   *The Birth of the Gods.* Ann Arbor: University of Michigan Press.

  1967   *Religion and Regime: A Sociological Account of the Reformation.* Ann Arbor: University of Michigan Press.

  1968   "To live in concord with society: Two empirical studies of primary relations." Pp. 87-124 in Albert J. Reiss, Jr. (ed.), *Cooley and Sociological Analysis.* Ann Arbor: University of Michigan Press.

1969   *Rules of Descent: Studies in the Sociology of Parentage.* Anthropological Paper No. 39, Museum of Anthropology, University of Michigan.

1974   "Descent and polity: The meaning of Paige's findings." *American Journal of Sociology* 80 (September):321-328.

Sweetser, Dorrian Apple
1964   "Urbanization and the patrilineal transmission of farms in Finland." *Acta Sociologica* 7:215-224.

1968   "Intergenerational ties in Finnish urban families." *American Sociological Review* 33 (April):236-246.

Talmon, Yonina
1964   "Mate selection in collective settlements." *American Sociological Review* 29 (August):491-508.

Teevan, James J., Jr.
1972   "Reference groups and premarital sexual behavior." *Journal of Marriage and the Family* 34 (May):283-291.

Terman, Lewis M.
1938   *Psychological Factors in Marital Happiness.* New York: McGraw-Hill.

Theodorson, George A.
1965   "Romanticism and motivation to marry in the United States, Singapore, Burma, and India." *Social Forces* 44 (September):17-28.

Theodorson, George A., and Achilles G. Theodorson
1969   *A Modern Dictionary of Sociology.* New York: Thomas Y. Crowell & Co.

Thomas, Darwin L., and Andrew J. Weigert
1971   "Socialization and adolescent conformity to significant others: A cross-national analysis." *American Sociological Review* 36 (October):835-847.

1972   "Determining nonequivalent measurement in cross-cultural family research." *Journal of Marriage and the Family* 34 (February):166-177.

Thomas, Darwin L., Viktor Gecas, Andrew J. Weigert, and Elizabeth Rooney
1974   *Family Socialization and the Adolescent.* Lexington, Mass.: D.C. Heath & Company.

Tiger, Lionel
1970   "The possible biological origins of sexual discrimination." *Impact of Science on Society* 20 (January-March):29-44.

Tiger, Lionel, and Robin Fox
1971   *The Imperial Animal.* New York: Holt, Rinehart & Winston, Inc.

Troll, Lillian E.
1971   "The family of later life: A decade review." *Journal of Marriage and the Family* 33 (May):263-290.

Tumin, Melvin M.
1973   *Patterns of Society.* Boston: Little, Brown & Company.

Turk, James L., and Norman W. Bell
1972   "Measuring power in families." *Journal of Marriage and the Family* 34 (May):215-222.

Turner, Christopher
1967   "Conjugal roles and social networks: A re-examination of an hypothesis." *Human Relations* 20 (May):121-130.

Tylor, Edward B.
1889   "On a method of investigating the institutions applied to the laws of marriage and descent." *Journal of the Royal Anthropological Institute* 18:245-269.

Udry, J. Richard
1974   *The Social Context of Marriage* (third edition). Philadelphia: J.B. Lippincott.

Udry, J. Richard, and Mary Hall
1965   "Marital role segregation and social networks in middle-class middle-aged couples." *Journal of Marriage and the Family* 27 (August): 392-395.

Underhill, Ruth M.
1965   "The Papago family." Pp. 147-162 in M.F. Nimkoff (ed.), *Comparative Family Systems.* Boston: Houghton Mifflin Company.

United States Bureau of the Census
1972   "Marital status and living arrangements." *Current Population Reports,* Series P-20, No. 2. Washington, D.C.: U.S. Government Printing Office.

United States Department of Health, Education, and Welfare
1975a   "Summary report: Final mortality statistics, 1973." *Monthly Vital Statistics Reports,* Vol. 23, No. 11, Supplement 2. Rockville, Md.: Public Health Service.

1975b   "Annual summary for the United States, 1974: Births, deaths, marriages, and divorces." *Monthly Vital Statistics Reports,* Vol. 23, No. 13. Rockville, Md.: Public Health Service.

1975c   "Summary report: Final divorce statistics, 1973." *Monthly Vital Statistics Reports,* Vol. 24, No. 4. Rockville, Md.: Public Health Service.

1975d   "Births, marriages, divorces, and deaths for September 1975." *Monthly Vital Statistics Reports,* Vol. 24, No. 9. Rockville, Md.: Public Health Service.

Vallier, Ivan
1971   *Comparative Methods in Sociology: Essays on Trends and Applications.* Berkeley: University of California Press.

van den Berghe, Pierre
1973   *Age and Sex in Human Society: A Biosocial Perspective.* Belmont, Calif.: Wadsworth Publishing Company.

Ven Velzen, H.U.E. Thoden, and W. Van Wetering
1960   "Residence, power groups, and intrasocietal aggression." *International Archives of Ethnography* 49 (No. 2):169-200.

Vener, Arthur M., and Cyrus S. Stewart
  1974   "Adolescent sexual behavior in middle America revisited: 1970-1973." *Journal of Marriage and the Family* 36 (November):728-735.
Vener, Arthur M., Cyrus S. Stewart, and David L. Hager
  1972   "The sexual behavior of adolescents in middle America: Generational and American-British comparisons." *Journal of Marriage and Family* 34 (November):696-705.
Vincent, Clark E.
  1966   "Familia spongia: The adaptive function." *Journal of Marriage and the Family* 28 (February):29-36.
Vogel, Ezra F.
  1963   *Japan's New Middle Class: The Salary Man and His Family in a Tokyo Suburb.* Berkeley: University of California Press.
  1965   "The Japanese family." Pp. 287-300 in M.F. Nimkoff (ed.), *Comparative Family Systems.* Boston: Houghton Mifflin Company.
Wagley, Charles
  1960   "Luso-Brazilian kinship." Unpublished paper, cited by Greenfield (1961).
Wallace, Walter L.
  1969   *Sociological Theory.* Chicago: Aldine Publishing Company.
Waller, Willard
  1938   *The Family: A Dynamic Interpretation.* New York: The Dryden Press, Inc.
Walters, James, and Nick Stinnett
  1971   "Parent-child relationships: A decade review of research." *Journal of Marriage and the Family* 33 (February):70-111.
Ward, Barbara
  1963   *Women in the New Asia.* Paris: UNESCO.
Warwick, Donald P., and Samuel Osherson
  1973   *Comparative Research Methods.* Englewood Cliffs, N.J.: Prentice-Hall, Inc.
Washburn, S.L., and I. DeVore
  1961   "Social behavior of baboons and early man." Pp. 91-105 in S.L. Washburn (ed.), *Social Life of Early Man.* Chicago: Aldine.
Weigert, Andrew J., and Darwin L. Thomas
  1971   "Family as a conditional universal." *Journal of Marriage and the Family* 33 (February):188-194.
Welch, Michael
  1976   "Subsistence economy and socialization practices: Barry, Bacon, and Child revisited." Unpublished paper, Department of Sociology, University of North Carolina, Chapel Hill, N.C.
Westermarck, Edward
  1921   *The History of Human Marriage* (fifth edition). London: Macmillan & Company, Ltd.

Wheeler, Elizabeth H.
1967   "Sub-Saharan Africa." Pp. 325–340 in Raphael Patai (ed.), *Women in the Modern World.* New York: The Free Press.

Whiting, Beatrice B.
1950   "A cross-cultural study of sorcery and social control." Pp. 82–91 in Beatrice Whiting, *Paiute Society.* New York: Viking Fund.

1963   *Six Cultures: Studies of Child Rearing.* New York: John Wiley & Sons, Inc.

1965   "Sex identity conflict and physical violence: A comparative study." *American Anthropologist* 67 (No. 6): Part 2.

Whiting, Beatrice B., and Carolyn P. Edwards
1973   "A cross-cultural study of sex differences in the behavior of children aged three through eleven." *Journal of Social Psychology* 91 (December):171–188.

Whiting, Beatrice B., and John W.M. Whiting
1971   "Task assignment and personality: A consideration of the effect of herding on personality." Pp. 33–44 in W.W. Lambert and R. Weisbrod (eds.), *Comparative Perspectives on Social Psychology.* Boston: Little, Brown and Company.

Whiting, John W.M.
1954   "The cross-cultural method." Pp. 523–531 in Gardner Lindzey (ed.), *Handbook of Social Psychology,* Vol. 1. Reading, Mass.: Addison-Wesley.

1959   "Cultural and sociological influences on development." *Maryland Child Growth and Development Institute* (June 1–5):5–9.

1960   "Resource mediation and learning by identification." Pp. 112–126 in I. Iscoe and H.W. Stevenson (eds.), *Personality Development in Children.* Austin, Texas: University of Texas Press.

1961   "Socialization process and personality." Pp. 355–380 in Francis L. K. Hsu (ed.), *Psychological Anthropology.* Homewood, Ill.: The Dorsey Press.

Whiting, John W.M., and Irving L. Child
1953   *Child Training and Personality: A Cross-Cultural Study.* New Haven, Conn.: Yale University Press.

Whiting, John W.M., E.H. Chasdi, H.F. Antonovsky, and B.C. Ayres
1966a   "The learning of values." Pp. 83–125 in E. Vogt and E. Albert (eds.), *People of Rimrock: A Study of Values in Five Cultures.* Cambridge, Mass.: Harvard University Press.

Whiting, John W.M., Irving L. Child, and William W. Lambert
1966b   *Field Guide for a Study of Socialization.* New York: John Wiley & Sons, Inc.

Whiting, John W.M., R. Kluckhohn, and A. Anthony
1958   "The function of male initiation ceremonies at puberty." Pp. 359–370 in E.E. Maccoby, T. Newcomb, and E.L. Hartley (eds.), *Readings in Social Psychology* (third edition). New York: Holt.

Whorf, Benjamin L.
1952   *Collected Papers on Metalinguistics.* Washington, D.C.: Department of State, Foreign Services Institute.
Willmott, Peter, and Michael Young
1960   *Family and Class in a London Suburb.* London: Routledge and Kegan Paul.
Wilson, Elmo C.
1958   "Problems of survey research in modernizing areas." *Public Opinion Quarterly* 22 (No. 3):230-234.
Wilson, Everett K.
1966   *Sociology: Rules, Roles, and Relationships.* Homewood, Ill.: The Dorsey Press.
Wimberley, Howard
1973   "Conjugal-role organization and social networks in Japan and England." *Journal of Marriage and the Family* 35 (February):125-131.
Winch, Robert F.
1971   *The Modern Family* (third edition). New York: Holt, Rinehart & Winston, Inc.
1972   "Theorizing about the family." *Journal of Comparative Family Studies* 3 (Spring):5-16.
1974   "Some observations on extended familism in the United States." Pp. 147-160 in Robert F. Winch and Graham B. Spanier (eds.), *Selected Studies in Marriage and the Family* (fourth edition). New York: Holt, Rinehart & Winston, Inc.
Winch, Robert F., and Rae Lesser Blumberg
1968   "Societal complexity and familial organization." Pp. 70-92 in Robert F. Winch and Louis W. Goodman (eds.), *Selected Studies in Marriage and the Family* (third edition). New York: Holt, Rinehart & Winston, Inc.
Winch, Robert F., and Scott Greer
1968   "Urbanism, ethnicity, and extended familism." *Journal of Marriage and the Family* 30 (February):40-45.
Winch, Robert F., Scott Greer, and Rae Lesser Blumberg
1967   "Ethnicity and extended familism in an upper-middle-class suburb." *American Sociological Review* 32 (April):265-272.
Winnington, Alan
1957   *Tibet.* London: Lawrence and Wishart, Ltd.
Wonnacott, Ronald J., and Thomas H. Wonnacott
1970   *Econometrics.* New York: John Wiley & Sons, Inc.
Yarrow, Leon J.
1964   "Separation from parents during early childhood." Pp. 89-136 in Martin L. Hoffman and Lois W. Hoffman (eds.), *Review of Child Development Research*, Vol. 1. New York: Russell Sage Foundation.
Yorburg, Betty
1975   "The nuclear and the extended family: An area of conceptual confusion." *Journal of Comparative Family Studies* 6 (Spring):5-14.

Young, Michael
  1954   "Kinship and family in East London." *Man* 54 (September):137–139.

Young, Michael, and Peter Willmott
  1957   *Family and Kinship in East London.* Baltimore: Penguin Books.
  1973   *The Symmetrical Family.* New York: Pantheon Books.

Zelditch, Morris, Jr.
  1955   "Role differentiation in the nuclear family: A comparative study." Pp. 307–352 in Talcott Parsons and Robert F. Bales (eds.), *Family, Socialization and Interaction Process.* Glencoe, Ill: The Free Press.
  1964   "Cross-cultural analyses of family structure." Pp. 462–500 in Harold T. Christensen (ed.), *Handbook of Marriage and the Family.* Chicago: Rand McNally.
  1971   "Intelligible comparisons." Pp. 267–307 in Ivan Vallier (ed.), *Comparative Methods in Sociology: Essays on Trends and Applications.* Berkeley: University of California Press.

Zimmerman, Carle C.
  1947   *Family and Civilization.* New York: Harper & Brothers.
  1956   "The present crisis." Pp. 3–131 in Carle C. Zimmerman and Lucius F. Cervantes (eds.), *Marriage and the Family.* Chicago: Henry Regnery Company.
  1970   "The atomistic family—fact or fiction." *Journal of Comparative Family Studies* 1 (Autumn):5–16.

Zimmerman, Carle C., and Lucius F. Cervantes
  1960   *Successful American Families.* New York: Pageant Publishers.

index of names

index of subjects